The Artful Plan

the art ful plan

Martin Søberg
Anna Hougaard (eds.)

Architectural Drawing Reconfigured

Birkhäuser Basel

Contents

PART TWO

PART THREE

Preface

A few lines on a surface can almost magically evoke a building, a landscape, or a city. Ideas and matter entangle, a new world opens up before our eyes. Maybe it is this simplicity yet richness that make architectural drawing so fascinating, at least from the point of view of an architectural historian and an architect, respectively. Even though we have studied and worked with architectural drawing in and through research and practice for many years, we still can't help but feel tremendously fascinated with the agencies of architectural drawing, its power of generating and capturing ideas, sometimes its sheer beauty or its straightforwardness, the care by which drawings are executed, often testifying to this process in itself, as documents of measures and movements. We hope that others will share our fascination while leafing through the pages of this book, reading its articles and contemplating its many drawings. And that such a process of absorption will spark puzzlement, discoveries, and new lines of thinking. Because those are our aims: to contribute to architectural drawing's development and reconfiguration and to stimulate the thoughts and ideas that reflect on and inspire architectural drawing.

A book usually results from the efforts of many people. This one is not an exception. We are grateful to our contributors, who have allowed us to compile their articles and projects into this volume. It is not our first collaboration with them. They also contributed to the exhibition and conference *Drawing Millions of Plans* at the Royal Danish Academy of Fine Arts, School of Architecture in Copenhagen in November 2017, yet everyone has kindly and enthusiastically updated, extended, and adapted their papers and drawings into the format of this book. It is indeed a great pleasure for us to see them all gathered again on these pages. We would also like to thank our colleague, architect Jacob S. Bang, who took part in the initial phases of our project, and not least to send a deepfelt thank-you to our eminent editor for the publisher, Andreas Müller, who has been an invaluable source of energy and elucidation. Finally, it would not have been possible to produce this book without generous support from the Danish Arts Foundation, the 15. Juni Fonden, and the Royal Danish Academy of Fine Arts, School of Architecture, for which we are equally thankful.

Martin Søberg and Anna Hougaard, February 2020

Introduction: Agencies of the Plan

Martin Søberg and Anna Hougaard

Architectural representation is currently ramifying as analog and digital media interweave and new hybrid media are being invented within our post-digital condition.[1] The orthogonally projected plan drawing has been divested of its role as an organizational, prescriptive, and technical means in processes leading to the construction of buildings. Liberated in this way from its habitual functions, the plan reconfigures into a medium for social, aesthetic, and communicative enquiry, feeding on exchanges between architecture and other artistic and poetic sensibilities and imaginaries. Rather than an instrument of definition and control, we propose to think of the plan as a means—to avoid at this point the instrumentally rational notion of tool—a means of interaction and communication in the process of artfully adjusting towards a new, expanded media situation. This implies that we consider the plan not only in terms of what it represents but also in terms of what it does; its agencies as related to architectural and societal practices.

To ask what the plan is and does and what it allows us to do, as an integral part of architectural culture, is an intricate question that produces multiple answers. We might describe the plan as indexing spatial structures; as an emblematic composition of these structures; or even as diagrammatizing spatial and thereby social relationships, that is, as a means of rendering visible particular biopolitical agendas and power relations. The plan may be appraised for its graphic beauty and disciplined geometries, evidencing a relationship projected between mathematical principles and a configuration of physical matter. What the plan shows, as a horizontal section of a building or part of it, is in reality something invisible. If anything, the plan is an abstraction that may help us generate a mental image of a particular spatial situation. Plans are tremendously good at enhancing an overview of an architectural project or idea, allowing us to synthesize and mend gaps, and bringing together loose ends. The plan is thus diagrammatic, made to communicate relationships, how space is divided, made distinct, scaled, sectioned, and how decisions should be made. Taking our finger for a walk through the drawn plan allows us to project ourselves into its future implementation, a building. It is not just that space and imagination are being activated: Something or someone is being divided; physical matter, bodies, territories. In that regard, plans are not neutral tools, but are deeply connected to symbolic and ethical concerns. Plans are made in order to order,[2] and by expressing particular ideas about ordering they may be viewed as cosmologies or even as invented worlds. Plans can be applied as a technical means of rigid ordering or as a mere suggestion of ambiguous flows. And plans constitute difference; they separate and join, indicate zones and continuities, and allow us to imagine how walls, passages, and openings interact in a building, a landscape, or a city.

This immense variety of agencies suggests that plan drawing is worth considering at length, as this book sets out to do. A great pile of literature on architectural drawing and other related kinds of architectural media exists, yet most of what has been published tends to describe drawing as one node connecting plans, alongside elevations, sections, isometrics, perspectives, etc. The plan was nevertheless once considered of prime importance in comparison with other means of architectural representation. As Le Corbusier famously claimed, the plan was assumed to be able to generate entire architectural schemes.[3] Today, new sorts of generators seem to have conquered a large share of that status and disrupted the hegemony of the plan. When it comes to construction, the plan drawing, particularly in the format of the technical working drawing, is still very important for communicating precise spatial and material conditions, to engineers and construction workers, for instance. Yet the process of producing plan drawings is changing. New media such as building information modeling (BIM) and other forms of computational design, including parametric and virtual or augmented reality tools, push the limits of what it is possible to generate, control, construct, and imagine, in 2D, 3D, or time-based simulation. The plan drawing might still be an important type of architectural representation but is now just one among many types of media for generating, exploring, communicating, and constructing architecture.

As the articles in this book and the projects presented demonstrate, this contemporary expanded field of architectural media repositions the role of the plan drawing within architectural culture, opening it up for reconfiguration and repurposing. *The Artful Plan* presents contemporary explorative drawing projects and topical texts that reflect, unfold, and extend the potentials of the architectural drawing in the post-digital condition, as well as giving attention to the pitfalls of the plan. Material and affective aspects of architectural media are investigated, as are questions of how architecture creates meaningful spatio-temporal relations. Architectural drawing in theory and practice as it emerges in this book is an epistemic practice, a way of exploring and reasoning through graphic, material, and discursive means.[4] All contributors have been involved in some sort of academic work; some of them pursue scholarly research within history and theory, others based on an architectural practice of making and fabricating buildings or other kinds of materialized projects—this latter type of research could be termed artistic or design-based research, or simply a reflected practice.[5] Such research confidently voyages into the fields of film, photography, sculpture, and even literature, with an eye to imagining architecture anew and to exploring the semantic and sensorial ambiguities that art fosters and conventional orthogonal projection marginalizes.

The book provides thoughts about and analysis of architectural representation and media in the post-digital condition, and also visual evidence of contemporary drawing practices that pursue both aesthetic and analytic ends, for instance, through strategies of mapping and diagramming. It is divided into three parts that may be, but do not necessarily have to be, read as a narrative.

The first part, *The Conventional Plan, Its Formation and Reconfiguration*, presents articles and projects that historically, exploratively, and/or critically address the conventions and traditions of the plan drawing. Although these conventions have been subject to change and questioning, they have also been sustained to some degree within architectural culture. Conventional techniques of representation may act as sources of inspiration and starting points for the development of new architectural practices and ideas.

Changes in and criticism of the plan's supposed hegemony is more strongly advanced in the second part, *Point Clouds, Chance Operations, and the Disappearance of the Plan*. The advent of digital media has thoroughly changed how buildings are designed and constructed. Building information modeling (BIM) software, in particular, modifies a conventional notion of architectural representation as an image or index into a datascape. Accordingly, the contributors to this part of the book provocatively ask whether orthogonal drawing is any longer relevant to architectural practice and discourse. New scanning techniques, new ways of generating spatial configurations based on information management and data collection might suggest that the orthogonal, two-dimensional plan drawing has become obsolete. Additionally, more process-oriented practices seem to render superfluous the plan as a means of generating an entire scheme, in Le Corbusier's sense.

The third and final part, *The Plan and the Expanded Field of Architectural Drawing*, demonstrates new kinds of architectural drawing, in which the plan extends and transforms, entangled with new imaginaries and notions of criticality, desire, and communality. This reconfiguration makes the plan drawing as much a means of exploration and unsealing as of fixation. In this expanded, indeed very hybrid, field, of architectural drawing, the floor plan's virtual and material, social, and communicative aspects are artfully reappraised and amplified. The geometric projection of the plan and the indexical grounding of architecture in the plan can be used as a means of representation, applied in order to prescribe separation and control. Yet the plan may just as well be a means to aid liminal transgression, to foster the formation of new social relations, and to question the disciplinary boundaries of architecture. It is towards these ends that the plan reasserts itself within contemporary architectural culture.

1 Gail Peter Borden and Michael Meredith, "Introduction and Material Premise," in *Lineament: Material, Representation and the Physical Figure in Architectural Production*, ed. Borden and Meredith (New York: Routledge, 2017), 1–2; Sam Jacob, "Architecture Enters the Age of Post-digital Drawing," *Metropolis*, http://www.metropolismag.com/architecture/architecture-enters-age-post-digital-drawing/, accessed March 21, 2017.
2 Cf. Klaus-Peter Gast's ground plan analyses in Gast, *Louis I. Kahn: The Idea of Order* (Basel, Berlin and Boston: Birkhäuser, 1998). Ground plan analysis is a core method in formalistically oriented architectural history, for instance, in the work of Rudolf Wittkower and Colin Rowe.
3 Le Corbusier, *Towards an Architecture*, trans. John Goodman (Los Angeles: Getty Publications, 2007), 115–30. Jean-Louis Cohen has discussed what Le Corbusier meant by the term "plan," as well as its historical background; see Cohen, "Introduction," in Le Corbusier, *Towards an Architecture*, 10.
4 Jan Bovelet, "Drawing as Epistemic Practice in Architectural Design," *Footprint: Delft School of Design Journal* 4, no. 2 (2010): 75–84.
5 Anna Katrine Hougaard, Martin Søberg, et al., eds., *Refractions: Artistic Research in Architecture* (Copenhagen: Architectural Publisher B, 2016).

1

The Conventional Plan, Its Formation and Reconfiguration

Martin Søberg and Anna Hougaard

Tracing lines on the ground in preparation for the construction of an edifice has been practiced throughout millennia. Evidence of this exists from as far back as Mesopotamian times, while the oldest preserved written description of architectural drawing stems from Roman times. In the second chapter of the first book of *De Architectura* (*Ten Books on Architecture*), "The Fundamental Principles of Architecture," Vitruvius described three different ways of visualizing an architectural disposition: ground plan (*ichnographia*), elevation (*orthographia*), and perspective (*scenographia*). He also reflects on the way in which such representations should be produced: Only when reflection and invention are at work may the architect hope to be successful. In other words, it implies careful consideration as well as the "discovery of new principles by means of brilliancy and versatility."[1] Of course, the role of a Roman architect should not be confused with our understanding of the role of an architect today: Roman architects were master builders, and drawing was primarily a means to aid construction. A different notion of the architect has dominated since the Renaissance, as someone who primarily produces *representations* of architecture rather than actual buildings: The architect as draftsperson. However, the importance of Vitruvius' books to Renaissance architecture and to architectural culture in the following centuries can hardly be overestimated. The books nourished the formation of a discipline that put drawing, and in particular projective drawing, center stage. Leon Battista Alberti emphasized the difference between the artist and the architect precisely with respect to projective drawing in general and to the plan in particular: "The difference between the drawings of the painter and those of the architect is this: the former takes pains to emphasize the relief of objects in paintings with shading and diminishing lines and angles; the architect rejects shading, but takes his projections from the ground plan."[2]

A profound convention of orthogonal projection—plan, elevation, and section—was established during the Renaissance, with its predecessor in Vitruvius' three forms of disposition. Among these types of drawing, the plan drawing was considered foremost, able to embrace the geometric, organizational, and aesthetic aspects of an architectural project. Famously, the artist *and* architect Raphael described in a letter to Pope Leo X, probably written in 1519, the drawing of the plan, the exterior elevation, and the interior elevation as a conglomerate of orthogonal projective drawing that in total enables a full imaginary impression of the intended spatial configuration to be formed. The beaux-arts schools of architecture, dominating architectural education during the following centuries and far into the 20th century, sustained this tradition of architectural representation.[3] Yet as Robin Evans has argued in his book *The Projective Cast*, while Raphael unites three types of drawing through projection, this is not the only way to understand the plan drawing:

> A plan need not be regarded as a picture; it can just as well be thought of as a set of geometric operations on a flat sheet that can be repeated at a larger scale on a flat plot. (…) *Grundriss, pianta, assiette*, ground plan, and the antiquated English "platform" give reminders of their earthbound origin; so does Raphael's anthropomorphic simile of the plan as footprint (which is not a picture of a man but his trace on the ground).[4]

This aspect of the plan, as a matter of grounding, indicates why the plan drawing has achieved its status as a fundamental tool. While enabling the foundation of a material building, founding a drawing is also a material practice. The choice of materials and tools matters, whether ink wash, red chalk, black chalk, tracing paper, watercolor, or steel pen. Drawing tools matter, as do the supporting surfaces, whether paper, parchment, tracing paper, blueprint, Xerox copying or, more recently, computer screens. The formats of these surfaces contribute to the formation of conventions; indeed, they influence how buildings appear to us.

The Roman plan drawing, as mentioned by Vitruvius, was nevertheless not just a matter of achieving what he terms "the elegance of effect."[5] The task of architecture was, and to some extent still is, to contribute to the ordering of society through various forms of spatial and material configuration. In that regard, the plan discloses certain hegemonies. As Pier Vittorio Aureli stated, "the plan demystifies the naturalization of power relations since it shows how they have always been deliberately constructed by the formation of habit and perception."[6] According to Aureli, plans demonstrate the reification of life so as to authorize the control of it through the manipulation of habits and perception. On a somewhat similar yet profoundly more humorous note, Atelier Bow-Wow has compared the floor plan to sports fields, describing it as something connected to rules, to the control of behavior. This comparison reflects an interest in the plan in terms of agency and performance:

> If we can translate soccer's rules and field as the use and floor plan of architecture respectively, we could say that performance is to soccer what daily activity is to architecture. (…) This perspective might lead us to study the relationship between usage and floor planning, and eventually find a perfect balance between them so that we could build architecture that "echoes" people's behaviors.[7]

Although it might not be completely clear what such a perfect balance would entail, we can still recognize and appreciate the ethical implications of the effort. It is worth noting that Atelier Bow-Wow describes architecture not as an instrument of control, but much more vaguely as an echo of activities. The soccer field does not in itself regulate the way the players move about; this occurs in the interaction between bodies, lines in space, rules, and many other means of communicating and making sense.

Plans and Practices

The establishment of the representational and communicative conventions of which architectural drawings form part is examined by Paul Emmons in his article "Changing Plans: From Footprints as Indexes of Construction to Horizontal Sections." Emmons discusses how plans have been conceived in very different ways, although they may look very similar throughout architectural history. He explores the relationship between plan drawings and buildings, and argues for a deeper connection than the conventional understanding of drawing would have us believe. Since orthogonal projection was recodified by the French École polytechnique around 1800, it has relied heavily on a Euclidean-Cartesian notion of space. The plan is considered to be the result of construction, an imprint of a horizontal section rather than an index, a mark on the ground, of the building to come. Emmons argues that the ancient notion of the plan as an index is profoundly linked with human myths and rituals, and is still latent when drawing a plan today. It allows us to think of the plan not only as a representational sectioning of a building, but as an actual, material indexation on a surface.

Similar links between indexicality and practice are explored in Marian Macken's project *Passage*, an exploration of John Hejduk's *Wall House 2* in the format of an artist's book. Macken reflects on the design process and layered history of the *Wall House 2* by intersecting text and images, embossed onto the pages of the book. The book reflects the indexical nature of the plan drawing, as an evidence of touch. Macken indicates processes of physical engagement, repetition, and semantic sedimentation, which are part of architectural culture. The plan drawings participate in this articulation when documenting, spatializing, perhaps even enchanting Hejduk's architecture. The intimate relationship between architectural imaginaries and material practices is further explored by Poul Ingemann in *My Plans for the Future*. This consists of a selection of sketchbook drawings that Ingemann has documented in a continued endeavor of the floor plan. Although he explores notions of the conventions of the classical in architecture, Ingemann also describes his plans in anthropomorphic terms, i.e., as having particular visual personality features. Their agency is articulated as if the plan possessed a particular character. As daily exercises, these sketches remain in the virtual space of the imaginary, yet, as indicated by Ingemann with reference to his built projects, their latent qualities may eventually crystallize into actual built matter and habitable space.

How does the plan control us or how do we control it? This question is addressed by Athanasiou Geolas in "'Manners of Working': Robin Evans, the Drawing, and a Theory of Practice." Through a close reading of the writings of Robin Evans, Manfredo Tafuri, and Michel Foucault, he examines architectural drawings as part of particular "manners of working," social circumstances and actions in which drawings as artifacts take part. Geolas discusses architectural drawing as a social document which, more than merely transporting ideas from one place to another as a neutral or frozen medium, reflects the architect's manners of behaving in social relations. In this conception, architectural drawing cannot be considered a transparent medium, a representation of architecture. To draw is rather part of a variety of manners by which architects behave and actualize their visions, skills, and influence.

From Plan to Project

In the history of architecture, educational settings have been important frameworks for a particular conservatism as regards the plan drawing, a guarantee for the continuation of tradition. Students have been taught to master conventionalized techniques in particular ways. Yet drawing plans can also be an important analytical tool, for instance, when exploring housing typologies or as part of urban mapping strategies. In this sense, the plan is able to play a more active role in the development of architectural projects, taking on tradition as a reservoir for inventing new types of housing and urban plans. This pedagogic and analytical aspect of the plan drawing includes transformational potential.

Mette Johanne Hübschmann describes an educational project, *Plans of Ideas*, based on a study of Renaissance palaces in Rome. This didactic approach to mapping buildings at similar scale resonates with the Renaissance treatises, which provided catalogs of solutions. Presenting buildings by their plan on the same white paper surface encompasses an idea of sameness, as well as variation. The abstract, diagrammatic character of the plan drawings facilitates the comparison of the drawings. While ignoring location, topology, materiality, and social, cultural, political, and economic conditions, this approach enables formal investigations of spatial configuration. Martin Søberg's article, "Floor Plan Diagrams and the Typology of Difference," addresses a similar question of typology as related to the drawing of floor plan diagrams. It traces different notions of typology within architectural discourse from the Enlightenment to today. While typological studies were initially concerned with deriving natural principles as a basis for architectural practice, Modern Movement architects during the 1920s and '30s applied diagrammatic floor plan analysis in order to advance functionalist programmatic intentions, particularly in the development of new housing typologies. Today, typological studies tend to focus less on the development of universal types, Søberg argues, as attention is shifting towards the possibilities of spatial and semantic variation and the formation of difference.

Architectural education and research are also pivotal topics in Martino Tattara's investigation of "The Project of Mapping: The Design Agency of Drawing City Plans." With urban mapping as a background, contemporary mapping projects by architects are understood as a specific approach of research into spatial conditions within cities. Aldo Rossi's study of Zurich, a project executed by his students over an academic year at the ETH Zurich, offers a case study of such mapping. To Rossi, this extremely detailed map provided a fertile ground for future projects, establishing a kind of precondition for the architectural project *per se*. The project insisted on an aspect of architecture that is not site-specific but site-relational. Beyond representing existing urban conditions, the urban plan, as abstracted as it is, is revealed as a way of creating connections between architectural ideas and an actual place, that is, relations between the imaginary and the real. Turning the prophetic ability of the plan around by looking back in architectural history through plans, Rachel Hurst reanimates the aesthetic and social qualities of historical floor plans in her project *A Million Hours of Plans*. Her considerations suggest a certain fluidity in the plan drawings' conceptualization and use, which has indeed changed several times throughout history. Hurst embraces historical shifts, prompted by different building codes, for instance, with profound implications for the appearance and agency of the architectural plan.

Conventions are far from immobile. Today, almost every available software employs orthogonal and perspectival projection and is able to construct 2D plan drawings, yet digital working methods have turned the floor plan drawing into just one stage in a design process. Conventions may result in a fossilization of architectural practice and a hierarchization of means of architectural representation, yet they may just as well form starting points for an expansion and reterritorialization of architecture. What the emerging new media condition featuring digital tools as a prerequisite implies in terms of ramifications of the representational and a possible disruption of the plan drawing will be further explored in the subsequent parts of this book.

1 Vitruvius, *The Ten Books on Architecture*, trans. Morris Hicky Morgan (New York: Dover Publications, 1960), 14.
2 Leon Battista Alberti, *On the Art of Building in Ten Books*, trans. Joseph Rykwert, Neil Leach, and Robert Tavernor (Cambridge, MA, and London: MIT Press, 1988), 34.
3 James S. Ackerman, "The Conventions and Rhetoric of Architectural Drawing," in *Origins, Imitation, Conventions: Representation in the Visual Arts* (Cambridge, MA, and London: MIT Press, 2002), 293–317.
4 Robin Evans, *The Projective Cast: Architecture and Its Three Geometries* (Cambridge, MA: MIT Press, 1995), 113.
5 Vitruvius, *The Ten Books on Architecture,* 13.
6 Pier Vittorio Aureli, "Life, Abstracted: Notes on the Floor Plan," *e-flux architecture,* https://www.e-flux.com/architecture/representation/159199/life-abstracted-notes-on-the-floor-plan/, accessed July 30, 2019.
7 Atelier Bow-Wow, *Echo of Space, Space of Echo* (Tokyo: INAX, 2009), 56.

Paul Emmons

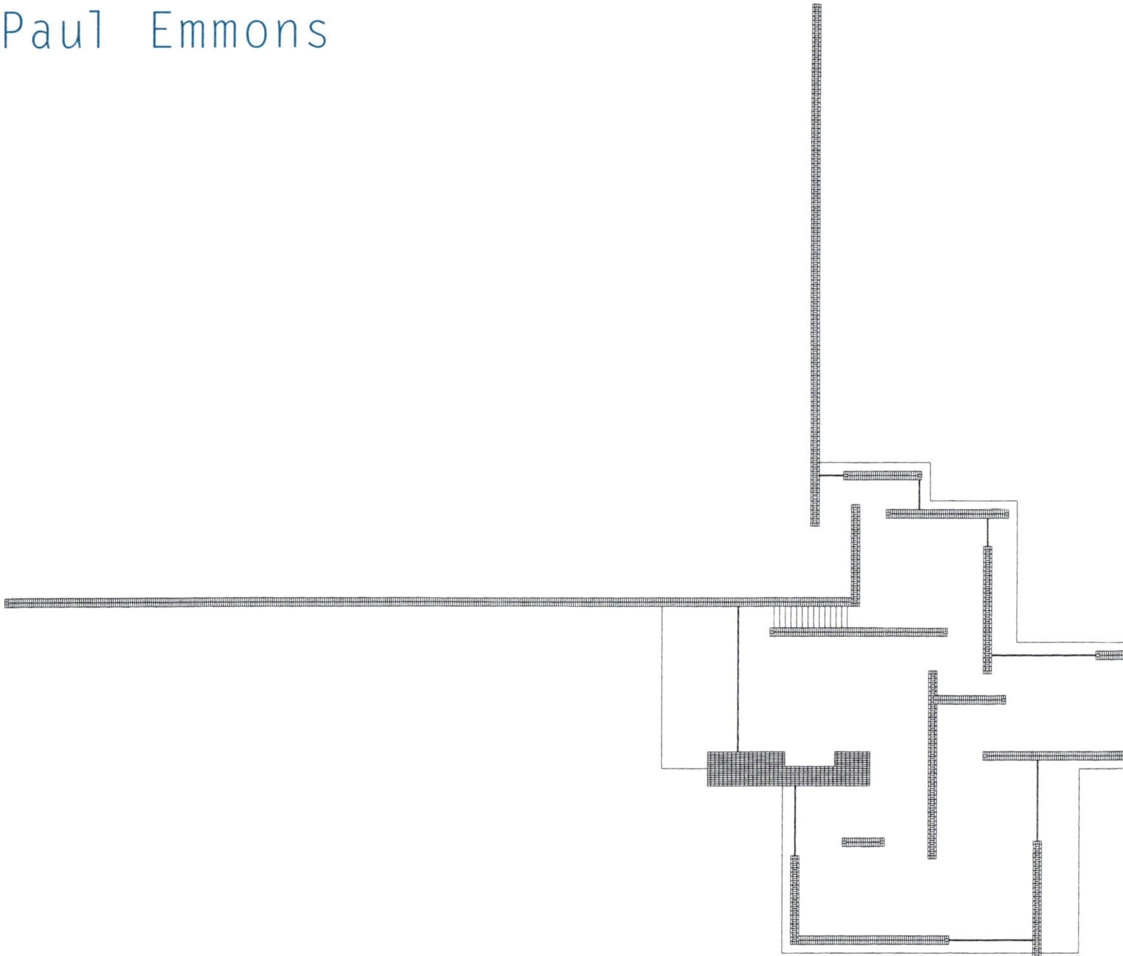

Changing Plans

From Footprints as Indexes of Construction to Horizontal Sections

fig. 1

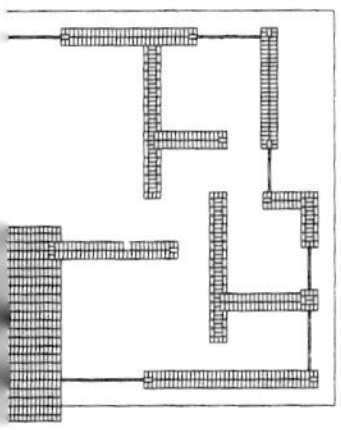

fig. 2

1 Ludwig Mies van der Rohe, *Brick Country House*, plan, 1964. Ink on illustration board, 76.2 × 101.6 cm. New York, Museum of Modern Art.

2 House plan with central courtyard, Ur III period, c. 2000 BCE. Clay tablet. Plan dimensions are recorded in cubits in cuneiform. Berlin, Vorderasiatisches Museum.

Among architectural drawings, the plan is primary. In the ancient world, Vitruvius lists the plan first among architectural drawings, and in modern architecture, Le Corbusier famously asserts in an electrical metaphor that "the plan is the generator."[1] In contemporary practice, the plan gives its name *pars pro toto* to the entire design effort—a set of plans. The primacy of the plan—the floor plan—does not imply that it is necessarily the first step in a design method, but acknowledges the foundational nature of architecture embedded in a particular place on the earth.

Architectural drawings are conceived as conventional representations that have no inherent relationship to building and are assigned their meaning only by common agreement, similar to the human languages, where the Danish word *træ* is no more an essential identification of its object than the Italian word *albero*. However, consider by comparison the two images in figures 1 and 2. The first is the well-known plan for the *Brick Country House* project by Ludwig Mies van der Rohe, originally drawn in 1923 [fig. 1].

fig. 3

The second is an ancient plan for a Babylonian courtyard house [fig. 2]. The two drawings are separated in time by about 4,000 years—by profound changes in human cultures and technologies—and yet we are able to identify both as plans. Although very few people today are able to read the wedge-shaped cuneiform writing on the ancient plan, most are able to comprehend its lines as an architectural plan. This suggests that plans, unlike languages, have more than an arbitrary relation to their meanings; that they are in some way deeply connected to architecture.

The idea that architectural drawings convey information through arbitrary conventions is largely derived from the theory of linguist Ferdinand de Saussure.[2] Focusing exclusively on language, he held words have no meaning in themselves, only in relation to their differences with other words. Philosopher Charles Sanders Peirce, who proposed a broader semiotics of all forms of signs, identified three sorts of signs: icons, indexes, and symbols.[3] Symbols, as in Saussure's definition, are conventional signs such as signs

3 Detail of statue known as *Architect with Plan* showing a plan inscribed on a drawing tablet with tools on the lap of the seated ruler Gudea, c. 2200 BCE. Diorite, 93 × 41 × 61 cm. Paris, Musée du Louvre.

in languages and traffic stop signs that rely on customary agreement for their significance. Icons share an appearance with their objects, such as portrait paintings or photographs. Indexes have a physical relation to their objects, such as a footprint to a foot or smoke to a fire. The contrast in figures 1 and 2 between comprehending cuneiform writing and the house plan demonstrates how architectural plans operate differently from language. By examining an earlier drawing conception, we will see that modern plans derive from indexes of construction.

Perhaps the oldest extant architectural plan was created about 2200 BCE in southern Mesopotamia (in present-day Iraq) [fig. 3]. A sculpture of the steward-king Gudea with a tablet resting on his lap has a plan inscribed upon it.[4] The dedication text on the sculpture explains that it was to live in a temple built by Gudea for the supreme god Ningirsu. The plan probably depicts the actual wall surrounding the sacred precinct of Ningirsu's shrine, resembling the Mesopotamian clay brick architecture of thick walls reinforced with buttresses. This statue shows the prince as the temple's architect; a stylus sits on the right side of the tablet, as if just set down by Gudea after making the drawing. The statue's hands are folded in prayer and an inscription explains that the plan was god-sent to Gudea through a vision.[5] That the plan was given precedence over any other sort of building image indicates its primacy as an inspired description of the temple.[6] Facing the god for eternity, it is a "living statue" that through ritual transformation was animated to manifest the presence of the king. In its lengthy inscription, the statue speaks of how it must be offered food and drink, washed, and dressed with clothing and jewelry.[7] This context demonstrates the plan's importance in combining building information with ritual activity. Beyond Mesopotamia, plans were widely used in ancient Egypt; more than 20 building plans related to construction or surveying survive. Egyptian building rituals record that the temple building itself was given life by ritual animation.[8] Plans are as old as monumental building. They have a profound role that blurs the distinction of planning from building.

Horizontal Section Plans

While the architectural plan is an enduring form of representation that has been in use across more than four millennia, characterizing all these instances simply as plans fuels the erroneous assumption that they are conceived identically. Ideas of plans have changed substantially over time. Today the architectural plan drawing is defined as a "horizontal section."[9] This definition can be found in virtually any handbook on architectural drawing published since early in the 19th century. The plan as a horizontal section was first introduced by Jean-Nicolas-Louis Durand. Durand taught architecture at the École Polytechnique (established in 1794) in Paris and summarized his course in *Précis des leçons d'architecture* (1802–05), which through many later editions and partial translations went on to have an enormous influence on architectural education [fig. 4].[10] Defining the plan as a "building's horizontal arrangement," Durand considered the floor plan as the most important drawing because of its close relation to *utilité,* the functional and economic utility of architecture, and placed it first in the "natural order" of architectural drawings, mechanically directing that "a design should begin with the plan."[11]

Durand's textbook remained in widespread use without significant updates or competitors for over 40 years. Léonce Reynaud, Durand's student and later his successor at the École Polytechnique, wrote explicitly in *Traité d'architecture* (1850–58) that the "plan will be a horizontal section of the building."[12] When architect and theoretician Julien Guadet published an architectural textbook from his lectures at the École des Beaux-Arts some hundred years after Durand, it again largely restates Durand's approach:

fig. 4

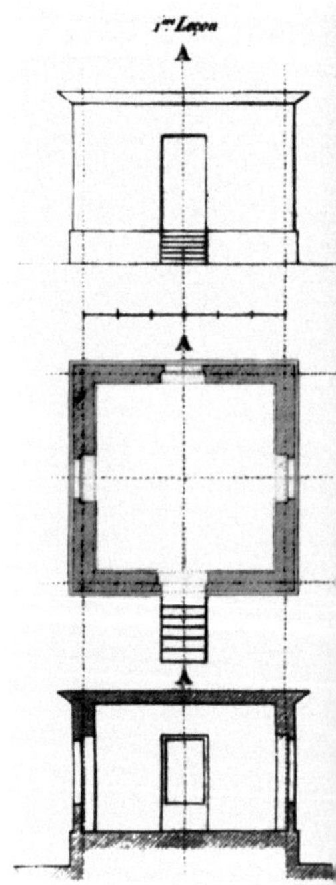

> The plan is a slice or section through a building on a horizontal plane which cuts through the walls, piers, partitions, etc., at a variable height. We assume the plane to be cutting at a convenient height to show all the details of construction, walls, doors and windows, piers, columns or pilasters, chimneys, etc. You can consider the plan as an imprint, taken on a flat surface, when the structure has all reached the same level in the height of a story.[13]

This often-repeated explanation of a horizontal section plan as a print of the partly constructed building reveals its contorted conceptual viewpoint [fig. 5]. Temporally, the plan as an imprint occurs after rather than prior to construction. Physically, the paper surface must face upside down in order to be imprinted so it is inverted from the earth, and finally the entire plan is reversed as a mirror image of the actual construction. While imprinting is invoked to clarify the nature of the horizontal section plan, when critically considered it is actually contradictory.

Durand's approach to architectural drawing derived from the descriptive geometry of mathematician Gaspard Monge, who appointed him to teach architecture in the Polytechnique's department of applied geometry.[14] Monge conceptualized the Cartesian grid of abstract space as the basis of his new graphic science, emphasizing that "space is unlimited; all its parts are exactly alike, not having anything that distinguishes one from another."[15] There is no relation to the human body, nor to the earth, as a defining factor. There is a tendency to extrude building form along the Cartesian spatial axes. Conceiving space as isotropic and undifferentiated by place results in the idea of plan as a horizontal section disconnected from the ground. The

4 Plan, section, elevation. First lesson on the "Elements of Edifices." Jean-Nicolas-Louis Durand, *Partie graphique des cours d'architecture faits à l'École royale polytechnique* (Paris: Firmin Didot, 1821), detail of pl. 1.

fig. 5

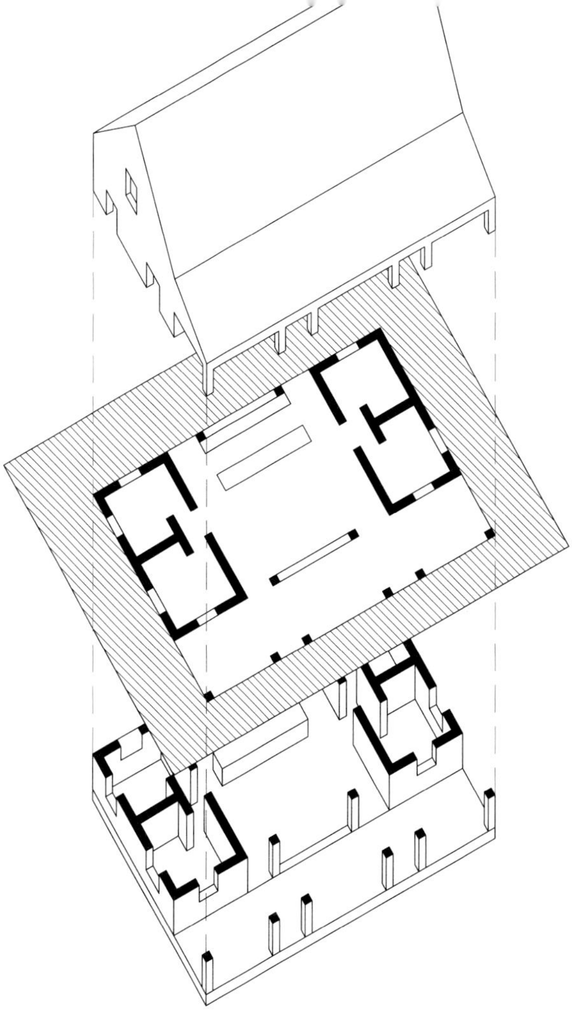

5 Floor plan as a horizontal section, explained as if made from an imprint from construction completed to a continuous height.

horizontal section plan remains uncritically the dominant understanding of plan today among the technical and descriptive drawings in architecture, regardless of the stylistic penchants of architects.[16]

Footprint Plans

Prior to Durand's introduction of the modern conception of horizontal sections, architectural plans were conceived very differently through an embodied approach. More than two millennia ago, Vitruvius recorded the term for the architect's plan drawing as *ichnographia* [fig. 6]. Literally translated, it means "footprint drawing," which he took from Greek (*ichnos*: footstep/track; *graphos*: writing/drawing). In the Renaissance, when modern architectural drawing began as architects first moved away from the construction site with the widespread availability of paper in the West, Vitruvius' text was closely studied to give direction to design. Raphael's letter to Pope Leo X (c. 1519), in which he describes the plan as the first drawing, explains that "just as the space which is occupied by the sole of the foot is the base for the

fig. 6

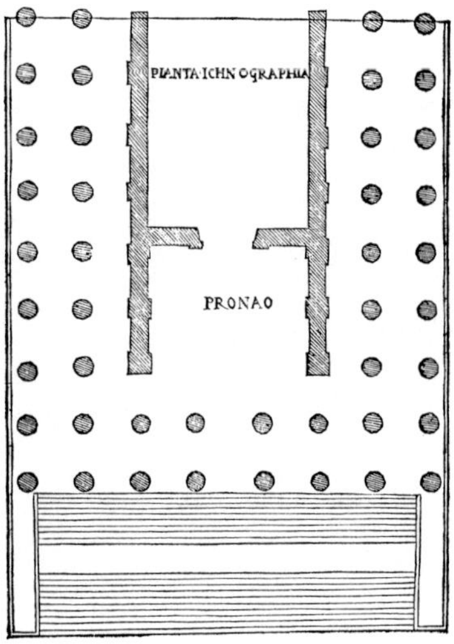

entire body, so the plan is the base for the entire building."[17] The ichnography, or footprint plan, was conceived as an embodied presence, creating a weighty impression upon the earth [fig. 7]. The footprint plan is an expression of the distributed weight of the building pressing downward into the earth.

The close relation between earthen plot and drawn plan suggested by the footprint plan is borne out through practices of inscribing the plan at full scale directly onto its site. The plan appears on site prior to the building, an adumbration of its future presence. The plan has a special relation to the earth that vertical drawings like elevations do not, since the plan can be traced onto the earth prior to construction to foretell the building.

Across history, plans of buildings were meaningfully inscribed onto the earth by stretching cords and driving pegs into the ground.[18] It was a widespread practice to measure out the plan on the ground and draw it with "white earth" including plaster or whitewash. Alberti retells a story of Alexander the Great founding the city of Faro by having its plan laid out with

fig. 7

flour. When birds began to eat the plan, diviners determined it was a propitious sign for the future city.[19] Perhaps the most vivid example of drawing a plan on its site at full size was for the new circular city of Baghdad, begun around 762 CE. The plan was traced upon the ground with lines of ashes and cotton seeds soaked in naphtha. Then the caliph entered and re-entered the cosmological city through each of its four gates facing the cardinal directions and as he reached the very center, the site of his future palace, he ordered that the lines be set on fire in order to enable him to see the three-dimensional form of the city.[20] The full-size plan on site was literally elevated into volume by the flames while inhabited by the patron. Sites were burned to cleanse them physically and spiritually for new construction. The ritualized marking of plans on the earth already begins the inhabitation of the site.

Foundation legends of important structures, often religious, record mundane construction practices that otherwise go unmentioned. Furthermore, the divine signs described in these stories resonate with the role of the plan as a sign of the future building. A common trope of foundation myths is that plans are miraculously outlined by the footprints of a large beast such as a deer, bear or bull, as proof of their divine origin [fig. 8].[21] Their circumambulation describing the plan on the ground parallels the ritual consecration of shrines.[22] Daniele Barbaro's 1567 commentary on Vitruvius, with illustrations by Palladio, explains architectural drawings as "signs" by comparing the mark left by the architect in making a plan to the hoofprint left by the deer; a sign but not the thing itself.[23] The plan is not a simple iconic picture of the future building but a sign of its construction. The footprint plan was conceived in this sense as an indexical sign of building.

The origin legend of the Zurich Fraumünster tells of a stag with flaming antlers leading two sisters to the site of their future convent, when angels stretching a rope in heaven lowered it to the ground to mark the bounds of the future building [fig. 9]. The rope was reportedly preserved in a chest near the high altar until the Reformation.[24] These sorts of practices intertwine the pragmatic with the ritualistic. Stories of divinely drawn plans reflect the actual practices of inscribing full-scale plans on construction sites, such as the pulling of ropes to lay out a building plan.

One divinely directed church plan revealed in a dream was said to be created by an angel drawing with a reed and was recorded in dew on the ground. An 11th-century miniature shows the angel's staff extending from heaven down to earth to draw out the ground plan while the future building is pictured in the distance [fig. 10].[25] The dew, acting as a form of virtual reality, begins to make present an immaterial image, just as architectural drawings are a meeting place between the visible and the invisible.

6 Giacomo Andrea, *Ichnographia*. Published in Vitruvius Pollio, *De Architectura*, ms. cart. (1490–1518), Classe II 176, c. 98r. Ferrara, Biblioteca Comunale Ariostea.

7 The plan as a footprint of the human body. "Architectural drawings are derived from the plan, face, and profile of the human body." Giovanni Biagio Amico, *L'architetto prattico* (Palermo, Dario Flaccovio, 1997), vol. 1, ch. 1, fig. 1. Originally published in 1726.

fig. 8 fig. 9

8 Conversion of St. Eustace seeing a cross between the horns of a stag with chapel plan appearing on the ground. Athanasius Kircher, *Latium, id est, nova et parallela Latii tum veteris tum novi descriptio* (Amsterdam, 1671), 186.

fig. 10

9 Fraumünster. Zurich foundation legend of rope lowered from heaven by angels to outline the church plan on the future building site. From Christoph Silberysen, *Chronicon Helvetiae* (c. 1576), part I, 50. Aarau, Aargauer Kantonsbibliothek, MsWettF 16: 1.

10 Dream of St. Vincent Madelgarius, to found the abbey at Haumont, France, with angel descending to draw its plan in the dew. Artist unknown. From the *Psalter of Cloister of Soignies*, second half of the 11th century, Leipzig, Universitäts-bibliothek, Cod. 774, fol. 28 v.

In this way, sites and plans for important buildings are revealed rather than selected or determined.[26] Divinely imparted or heaven-sent plans take on an air of inevitability that human-made plans do not. The foundation legend of Santa Maria Maggiore in Rome—the *Miracle of the Snow*—relates that in the 4th century, one night during the August heat, the Virgin Mary visited the Pope in a dream asking him to build a church for her where the snow falls. The next morning, upon finding the miraculous snow, Pope Liberius used a hoe to inscribe the plan of the future church into the ground by tracing around the snow.[27] The painter Masolino da Panicale represented the event (c. 1428–32), showing Mary with Christ reaching down out of a heavenly *clipeus,* or ring, to explain divine action in physically casting snow onto earth [fig. 11].[28] While the rest of the image is painted in tempera, the snow is in oil paint, one of the first times it was used south of the Alps, with the pigment applied in bold strokes to create a soft, luminous layer of snow with an otherworldly presence.[29] Inverting the use of white powders to draw a plan's walls, the snow provides a white surface upon which dark walls are drawn by revealing the earth below. In this way, the ritual layouts of plans in the field mentioned before inspired drawing practices. Foundation legends share the importance of downward movement from heaven to earth. The plans are not given directly by the divinity, but are indicated through a transient, subtle materialization that must then be followed by human action. These plans are signs that, like drawing, lack the permanence of masonry walls.

Inscribing the plan onto the earth is a practice that continues in modern construction, still using subtle materialization such as string, spray paint or, more recently, laser lines. In 1928, Frank Lloyd Wright explained that "to plan" is "to foresee" and described plans as the "prophetic soul" of buildings. Wright invoked the idea of the footprint plan, explaining that his plans reveals the nature of the distribution of the weight of the building. A brick pier plan, he argues, concentrates load in few places: "a stone or brick plan is heavy: black in masses, wider in spacing," whereas a wood frame plan has weight more evenly distributed, so that "a wood plan is slender: light in texture, narrower in spacing."[30] These black marks, either concentrated or dispersed, already indicate the nature of what is above the plan. Thus, architects can sagaciously interpret a footprint plan just as hunters identify their prey from its tracks. Like Sherlock Holmes solving a mystery, reading the footprint plan is a practice of abductively interpreting clues for imagining the totality of the building. This material understanding of the plan encourages architects to treat the drawing surface not as merely abstract, empty Cartesian white space, but as material that expresses the divination of the building's footprint.

11 *Miracle of the snow,* foundation of Santa Maria Maggiore, Rome. Masolino, *Pope Liberio Founding the Basilica di S. Maria ad Nives,* c. 1423–28. Tempera and oil on wood, 114 × 76 cm. Naples, Museo di Capodimonte.

fig.11

Vitruvius' brief explanation of *ichnographia* led to disagreement among scholars as to whether it described a scale drawing or a full scale marking directly upon the earthen construction site. Cesare Cesariano, a Milanese architect who studied with Bramante and was the first, in 1521, to publish an illustrated translation and commentary of Vitruvius, interpreted Vitruvius' *ichnographia* as both drawing directly upon the site *and* as scaled architectural plans. Cesariano, as if following the *Miracle of the Snow*, united these two approaches by comparing the architect walking the legs of his compass on white paper to the architect physically pacing out the plan on a snowy site and leaving footprints. Historian Carol Krinsky explains:

> Cesariano's commentary adds to our knowledge of workshop practice in that his definition of *ichnographia* includes the fact that it meant an impression made on the ground or on paper, and a compass, ruler (*regula*), plumbline, level and measures [squares] (*norme*) were used in setting out the plan. He also discussed the practice of laying out the dimensions on the site by using stakes and ropes.[31]

This ambiguity is *ichnographia's* clearest meaning—it cleaves between earthen plot and paper plan. The footprint joins with the geometrical drawing, both of which provide a sign of human occupation.

Plans as Indexes of Construction

When European architects began to leave the construction site in the 15th century to design in the scholar's studio remote from building activity, the techniques for drawing plans on paper were developed from their experience of building practices on site.[32] Architectural drawing instruments originated from construction tools, such as the T-square from carpentry and the triangle or set square from stone cutting. Florentine Antonio Averlino, known as the virtuous architect Filarete, wrote in his 15th-century treatise: "As it is necessary to have a site in order to build and to dig the foundations, so too we will first make the site in which we wish to make our drawing."[33] The leveling of a site to prepare for construction is reflected in the preparation of the paper surface for drawing.[34] Renaissance cotton-fiber paper had an uneven surface that first required flattening by rubbing it with a hare's foot or pumice. Since it was made without sizing agents, early paper held ink better when first dusted with powdered bone, like laying gravel for a foundation, just as Filarete wrote of sites.[35]

The phrase "drawing lines" simultaneously means pulling ropes taut on site and guiding a pencil across paper at the drafting board. These two meanings are so close and their language almost identical, so much so that distinguishing between them can be problematic. Stretched ropes with knotted measures attached to stakes at the building perimeter became "strings of dimension lines" on drawings. Foundation rites related to cutting the earth for building walls are paralleled by drafting practices where stylus-made furrows or "dead lines" incise the paper prior to laying down ink into the grooves.

Returning to C. S. Peirce's consideration of the role of signs in human thought, plan drawings are originally iconic indexes of construction because drawing parallels building. After Durand, plans came to be theorized as conventional symbols and the constructive connection was lost. The Cartesian idea of a horizontal section plan lacking gravity is a disconcerting overturning of the plan as a footprint. Weightlessness is substituted for material presence and human habitation. When architectural drawings are understood to convey information through arbitrary conventions that have no meaning in themselves, they distance designers from their designs. Plans are not merely for conveying previously determined information, and architects not only think with drawings, they also think in them. More than just providing information, drawing a plan is a way of anticipating and imagining that has been in use by architects for as long as there has been monumental building in human culture.

The assumption that architectural drawings convey information through arbitrary conventions that have no meaning in themselves is contradicted by the origins and significance of architectural practices. The value of the intimate relation between drawing and building is that it aids the architect's judgment and imagination when making plans. Paper fixed to a drawing table becomes the building site in the imagination. The architect travels into the design of the imagination as if actually on site. As philosopher Maurice Merleau-Ponty suggests that "my body is the pivot of the world," the drawing is the pivot between the physical body of the drafter and the imaginative body projected into the design.[36] This movement places designers into the future building in such a way that choices are more readily directed toward ethical considerations of human occupation of the environment.

The interrelation between plan drawing practices and mythic foundation rituals that is identified here is usually overlooked in modern times. Philosopher and writer Georges Bataille explains that the greatest modern myth is the absence of myth.[37] Furthermore, cultural rituals are often most embedded in activities that are considered practical, everyday undertakings. The resemblance, writes anthropologist Mary Douglas, between symbolic rites and our pragmatic practices "is sometimes uncannily close."[38] Awareness of the ritual aspects of designing and building can promote deeper engagement. Plan drawing reveals a site that is propitious for building to concretize human dwelling. The cleaving of plot and plan, both joining and separating them, is the chiasm that links the constructions of an architect at a drawing board with those at the building site.

1 Vitruvius, *On architecture*, trans. Frank Granger (Cambridge, MA: Harvard University Press, 1931), 1. II. 2. Le Corbusier, *Toward an Architecture*, trans. John Goodman (Santa Monica, CA: Getty, 2007), 117.
2 James Ackerman, "The Conventions and Rhetoric of Architectural Drawing," in *Conventions of Architectural Drawing: Representation and Misrepresentation*, ed. James Ackerman and Wolfgang Jung (Harvard University: Graduate School of Design, 2000), 9–11.
3 Charles S. Peirce, *Peirce on Signs: Writings on Semiotic by Charles Sanders Peirce*, ed. James Hoopes (Chapel Hill, NC: University of North Carolina Press, 1991); Charles S. Peirce, *Collected Papers of Charles Sanders Peirce*, ed. Charles Hartshorne and Paul Weiss (Cambridge, MA: Harvard University Press, 1931–58).
4 Flemming Johansen, *Statues of Gudea: Ancient and Modern* (Copenhagen: Akademisk Forlag, 1978), 10; Claudia Suter, *Gudea's Temple Building: The Representation of an Early Mesopotamian Ruler in Text and Image* (Groningen: Styx, 2000).
5 Sibylle Edzard and Dietz Otto Edzard, *Gudea and His Dynasty* (Toronto: University of Toronto Press, 1997), Cylinder A, 69 f.
6 Mary Helms, *Craft and the Kingly Ideal: Art, Trade and Power* (Austin, TX: University of Texas Press, 1993), 79.
7 The inscription ends with a curse on anyone who tries to desecrate the sculpture. Irene Winter, "Idols of the King: Royal Images as Recipients of Ritual Action in Ancient Mesopotamia," *Journal of Ritual Studies* 6, no. 1 (Winter 1992), 13–42.
8 The ritual of the *Opening of the Mouth* performed on behalf of the temple was the revivification of the magical power that resided in the Ancestor of the temple. Eve A. E. Reymond, *The Mythical Origin of the Egyptian Temple* (Manchester: Manchester University Press, 1969), 314–15.
9 Frank Ching, *Architectural Graphics* (New York: John Wiley & Sons, 1996), 19.
10 Ulrich Pfammatter, *The Making of the Modern Architect and Engineer: The origins and development of a scientific and industrially oriented education* (Berlin: Birkhäuser, 2000), 62. The 1821 edition of the *Précis* was the first to include the *Partie graphique des cours d'architecture* (Graphic portion of the lectures on architecture) attached at the end. Jean-Nicolas-Louis Durand, *Précis of the Lectures on Architecture*, trans. David Britt (Santa Monica, CA: Getty, 2000), 188; Alberto Pérez-Gómez, *Architecture and the Crisis of Modern Science* (Cambridge, MA: MIT Press, 1983).
11 Durand, *Précis*, 188.
12 Léonce Reynaud, *Traité d'architecture* (Paris: Dunod, 1875); Hilary Bryon, "Building a Modern Vision: Auguste Choisy's Graphic Constructs" (PhD diss., University of Pennsylvania, 2005), 69. Pfammatter, *The Making of the Modern Architect and Engineer*, 67.
13 Julien Guadet, *Éléments et théorie de l'architecture: cours professé à l'École nationale et spéciale des beaux-arts* (Paris: Librarie de la construction moderne, 1906); Paul Stewart, "A Translation from the French of Professor J. Guadet, Entitled *Elements and Theory of Architecture*" (Masters thesis, Virginia Polytechnic Institute, 1937), 48.
14 Robert Jan van Pelt and Caroll William Westfall, *Architectural Principles in the Age of Historicism* (New Haven, CT: Yale University Press, 1991), 146; Pfammatter, *The Making of the Modern Architect and Engineer*, 41.
15 Gaspard Monge (Count de Péluse), *An Elementary Treatise on Descriptive Geometry*, trans. J. F. Heather (London: Weale, 1851), 2.
16 Frank A. Bourne, Hermann Valentin von Holst and Frank Chouteau Brown, *Architectural Drawing and Lettering* (Chicago, IL: American Technical Society, 1920), 10, 13.
17 Carlo Pedretti, "A Letter to Pope Leo X on the Architecture of Ancient Rome," in *A Chronology of Leonardo da Vinci's Architectural Studies after 1500* (Geneva: Droz, 1962), 168; D. Giovanni Amico, *L'Architetto Prattico*, 1726 (Palermo: Dario Flaccovio, 1997).
18 For ancient Egyptian practices, see: Corinna Rossi, *Architecture and Mathematics in Ancient Egypt* (Cambridge, UK: Cambridge University Press, 2004).
19 Leon Battista Alberti, *On the Art of Building in Ten Books*, trans. Joseph Rykwert, Neil Leach, and Robert Taverno (Cambridge, MA: MIT Press, 1988), 101, 381.
20 Al-Tabari, *The History of al-Tabari, Abbasid Authority Affirmed*, Vol. 28, trans. Jane McAuliffe (Albany, NY: State University of New York Press, 1995), 245–46; Nezar AlSayyad, *Cities and Caliphs: On the Genesis of Arab Muslim Urbanism* (New York: Greenwood Press, 1991), 117.
21 Carolyn Carty, "The Role of Medieval Dream Images in Authenticating Ecclesiastical Construction," *Zeitschrift für Kunstgeschichte* 62, no. 1 (1999), 45–90; Amy Remensnyder, *Remembering Kings Past: Monastic Foundation Legends in Medieval Southern France* (Ithaca, NY: Cornell University Press, 1995); Helen Rosenau, *Design and Medieval Architecture* (London: Batsford, 1934), 30–31.

2 These practices also reflect some hurch dedication rites marking the loor in ash and sand. Guillaume Durand, *he Rationale divinorum officiorum f William Durand of Mende: A New ranslation of the Prologue and Book)ne*, trans. Timothy Thibodeau (New ork: Columbia University Press, 2007), 2–67.

3 Daniele Barbaro, commentary in 'itruvius, *I Dieci Libri Dell'Architettura, radotti e Commentati da Daniele Barbaro* [1567] (Milan: Il Polifilo, 1997), :61–70; Margaret D'Evelyn, "Word and nage in Architectural Treatises of the :alian Renaissance" (PhD diss., rinceton University, 1994), 85.

4 Regine Abegg and Christine Barraud Viener, *The Fraumünster in Zurich* Berne: Society for the History of Swiss rt, 2005), 7.

5 This was the dream of St. Vincent Madelgarius for the founding of an abbey t Haumont. Psalter from the Cloister f Soignies (later 11th century) Leipzig, niversitätsbibliothek, Cod. 774, fol. 28 v.

6 Millard Meiss, "The Altered Program f the Santa Maria Maggiore Altarpiece," *Studien zur Toskanischen Kunst; estschrift für Ludwig Heinrich Heydenreich zum 23. März 1963* (1964), 69–90.

7 Margaret Miles, "Santa Maria aggiore's Fifth-Century Mosaics: riumphal Christianity and the Jews," *he Harvard Theological Review* 86, o. 2 (April 1993): 155–75.

8 C. B. Strehlke and M. Tucker, The Santa Maria Maggiore Altarpiece; ew Observations," *Arte Cristiana* 75 987), 105–24. The year of the miracle aries in scholarly publications between 54 and 358 CE.

9 Roberto Bellucci and Cecilia rosinini, "Working Together: Technique Innovation in Masolino's and asaccio's Panel Paintings," in Carl trehlke with Cecilia Frosinini, *The Panel aintings of Masolino and Masaccio: The ole of Technique* (Milan: 5 Continents ditions, 2002), 60.

30 Frank Lloyd Wright, "The Logic of the Plan [January 1928]," in *In the Cause of Architecture* (New York: McGraw Hill, 1975), 154.

31 Carol Krinsky, "Introduction," in Vitruvius, *De Architectura*, trans. Cesare Cesariano (Munich: Wilhelm Fink, 1969), 13.

32 This itinerant, off-site practice was true for both late Gothic and Renaissance architects—suggesting it is less related to styles than to the influence of recently available paper-making technology. Marco Frascari, "A Reflection on Paper and its virtues within the material and invisible factures of architecture," in *From Models to Drawings: Imagination and Representation in Architecture*, ed. Marco Frascari, Jonathan Hale, and Bradley Starkey (London: Routledge, 2007), 23–33.

33 Antonio Averlino, *Filarete's Treatise on Architecture*, trans. John Spencer (New Haven: Yale University Press, 1965), Bk. 23, 177 r.

34 Ibid., 311; David Leatherbarrow, "Leveling the Land," in *Topographical Stories: Studies in Landscape and Architecture* (Philadelphia, PA: University of Pennsylvania Press, 2004), 114–30.

35 Cennino d'Andrea Cennini, *The Craftsman's Handbook 'Il Libro dell' Arte'*, trans. Daniel Thompson, Jr. (New York: Dover, 1954), 6–7.

36 Maurice Merleau-Ponty, *Phenomenology of Perception*, trans. Colin Smith (London: Routledge & Kegan Paul, 1962), 68.

37 Georges Bataille, *The Absence of Myth: Writings on Surrealism*, trans. Michael Richardson (London: Verso, 1994), 48.

38 Mary Douglas, *Purity and Danger: An Analysis of the Concept of Pollution and Taboo* (London: Routledge, 2002), 40, 50.

Marian Macken

Passage

Reading John Hejduk's Wall House 2

fig. 1

1 Marian Macken, *Passage*, 2018; spread 18.

A translucent acrylic Perspex box slides open, split vertically along its middle [fig. 2]. Within sit 20 folded sheets, unbound at the spine. A title reads "Passage"—large font, blind letterpress printed, centered. The next spread repeats this word, printed twice, a certain misalignment becomes apparent, with the addition of "Wall House 2 (Bye House) John Hejduk" with two dates, 1973, 2001, and three addresses—in New York City, Connecticut, and Groningen in the Netherlands.

This artist's book examines representations of architect and theoretician John Hejduk's Wall House 2 (Bye House) from its long history. The house was originally designed in the 1970s for a site in Connecticut, USA, yet it was built in the Netherlands 28 years later, one year after the death of the architect. The project reflects Hejduk's theoretical position regarding temporality; more than this, the aberrant design and construction processes

fig. 2

demonstrate an unusual and extended timeframe. Wall House 2 thus offers a route through architectural temporality and demonstrates the diverse temporal conditions within which architecture operates, is conceived and read.

> *The fifth spread, a large title at the top of the page, "TIME: of making." Underneath sits a quote by Hejduk describing his workspace and its atmosphere. Another page turned, and here, the final documentation plan from 1974 on the site in Connecticut is embossed across the spread. Text intersects the image, running vertically: "of gestation, of drawing, of the drawing, of waiting, of the unbuilt, of construction."*

The discussion of architecture and time typically refers to built architecture: to the life of a particular building and the effect of time upon it. This is demonstrated through a predominance of writing that concentrates on a building's construction, its inhabitation, weathering, and eventual ruin.

2 Marian Macken, *Passage*, 2018. 30 × 30 × 5 cm. Designed, hand-set and hand-printed on an Asbern cylinder proofing press at Wai-te-ata Press, Victoria University of Wellington, New Zealand, on Tiepolo 290 gsm paper, Garamond type, with embossed drawings; etched Perspex covers. Edition of 4.

fig. 3

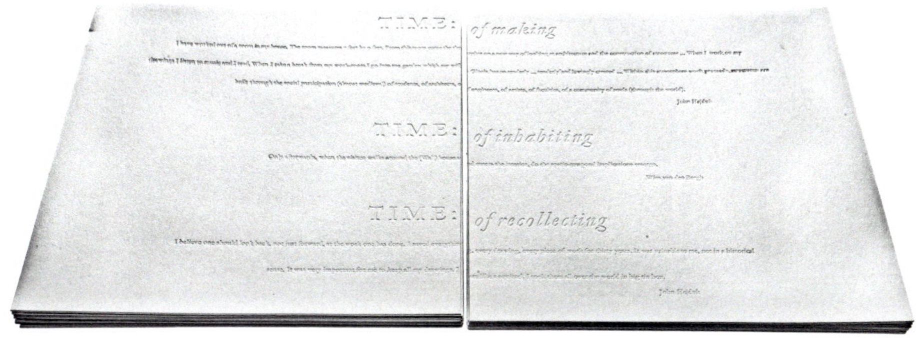

fig. 4

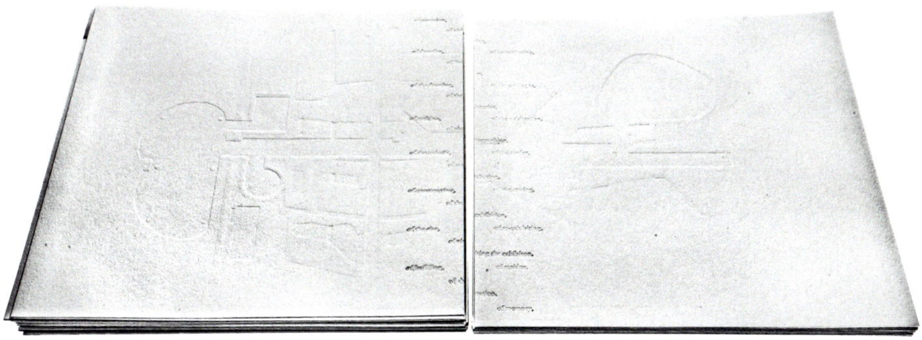

3 Marian Macken, *Passage*, 2018; spread 12.

4 Marian Macken, *Passage*, 2018; spread 14.

But there is a multiplicity, a plurality of "times" that should be included within architecture. These relate to the architectural design process and the life of the building. They alone do not as yet acknowledge the importance of representation in architecture, that "ultimately architecture as a practice is not this thing we're in, but the drawing of it."[1] An appropriate expansion of the temporality of architecture beyond the built work—the space in which we can walk—includes the representation of architecture, its exhibition and archiving, and its dissemination. Proposing an expanded notion of time within and surrounding architecture broadens the context within which architecture exists.

The eighth spread, "TIME: of inhabiting" spans both pages. The page is turned and text intersects with an embossed image from a photograph of the built interior of the house taken in 2007: "of visiting, of living, of the interior, of photographing, of weathering, of the exhibition, of visiting the exhibition, of the

5 Marian Macken, *Passage*, 2018: spread 16, detail.

duration of the exhibition." Another spread opens to show both images superimposed and embossed, with their columns of text clustered about the open spine, doubled.

Embossed images are repeated and superimposed as one leafs through the book [fig.1]; the blind letterpress text is printed using an additive method: each piece of text appears numerous times throughout the book, reprinted over itself [fig.5]. It is as though the time of the house, its gestation, built form, and afterlife are accumulating, with the pages holding their residue.

Examining drawings as artifacts demonstrates the passage of time, by positioning them within different temporal contexts. Just as each document is a product of the time within which it was made, the document may be read in new contexts as time progresses, and be framed *in time*, different from its origins, reflecting when we encounter it. We travel through lineages of representation, entering at different points and recreating sequences ourselves,

fig. 5

through our own interactions. Within this framework, drawings have duration, and the built artifact is framed as a full-scale spatial document within this lineage, rather than an endpoint. Just as the present moment can be simultaneously filled with the past and future, the documents of architecture can simultaneously occupy diverse temporal conditions, becoming intratemporal. The book, as both artifact and exhibition, gathers together documents of architecture and binds them in a way that intersects with various notions of "times" within architecture.

In the twelfth spread, Hejduk writes of his collecting and saving of work, of the importance of looking, not just forward, but back at one's past work, at his drawings as artifacts. This is "TIME: of recollecting [fig. 3]." The next spread shows the embossed image of the iconic model made in 1981, prominently exhibited during both the unbuilt and built phases of the house. Vertical text reads "of

6 *Passage* letterpress type set on Asbern press.

repositioning, of the catalogue, of the publication, of the reader, of re-curating, of re-exhibiting, of residue, of memory." Next, all three images are embossed, their vertical text—some words tripled and doubled in printing—a poem of times [fig. 4].

The pages have a tactility; images and text are felt within the page. The reader participates in a sculptural experience. Books are dependent upon the acts of reading and of handling, and their power lies in their ability to create conducive conditions. Reading suggests an intimacy of engagement—the originator of the book communicates privately with an individual reader—and it is a participatory act: "a book only comes into being when it is read."[2]

ig. 6

"It was meant to heighten the fact that we are continuously going in and out of the past and future, cyclical. We never stop to contemplate the present for we can not; it passes too quickly. In a way, ironically, this house had to do with the 'idea' of the present, the celebration of the two dimensional; it was leading and condensing to a point. It had to do with time."[3] This quote, from Hejduk's book Mask of Medusa, *spans spread 16 [fig. 5].*

Passage highlights the importance of the relationship between the paper, the page, and the drawing, and reinstates the book as a critical practice in architecture, rather than being relegated to the status of cultural artifact. Charles Jencks writes: "architecture stays in one place, while its meaning travels between the covers of books";[4] in this way, the book is cast as a form of spatial practice, exploring new territories for architectural drawing.

Aaron Levy and William Menking, *ur Conversations on the Architecture Discourse* (London: Architectural ssociation, 2012), 167.
Yusuke Minami, "Fukuda Naoyo: *aibun* and Art," in *Artist File 2010: he NACT Annual Show of Contempo- ry Art: 018 Fukuda Naoyo* catalogue okyo: National Art Center, 2010), 6.
John Hejduk, *Mask of Medusa: Works 47 – 1983* (New York: Rizzoli, 1985).
Charles Jencks, "Post-Modernism d the Revenge of the Book," in *This Not Architecture: Media Construc- ons*, ed. Kester Rattenbury (London: outledge, 2002), 176.

Poul Ingemann

My Plans for the Future

fig. 1

My first completed project was a small residential housing project. It was completed in 1988 and was the culmination of a long-term attempt to work seriously in a classical style and therefore had fairly symmetrical floor plans. The plans were mostly cut over the same template, using tripartition and oriented preferably right in the middle. My ambition was to maintain a simple floor plan that would unfold together with a variety of spatialities; vault, long room, short room, two-story room, and so on.

It was a challenge to get the classically oriented plans in place within relatively modest apartment areas. I felt that I had to be faithful to the symmetrical classical plan and not to challenge it significantly. Only the site plan, comprising three buildings, challenged the classical plan's inclination to establish a sort of resting gravity. I more or less intuitively created a sort of rotation and imbalance. Fumbling and investigating, I began to challenge, as well as I could, the classic and sometimes a little too rigid symmetrical plan. My project was harshly classical and stern in the wake of postmodernism's often superficial use of architectural elements and styles.

1-6 Poul Ingemann, sketches, mixed media on paper, 1991-2019.

fig.2

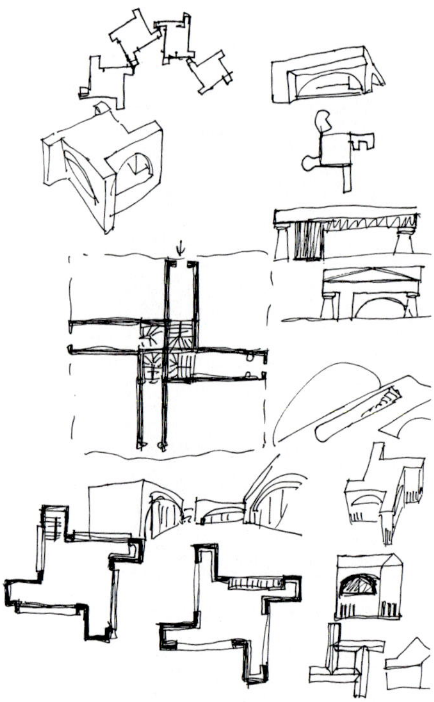

fig.3

fig. 4

ig. 5/6

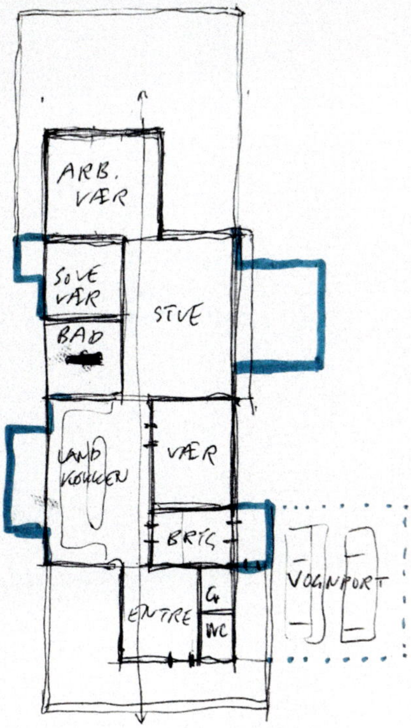

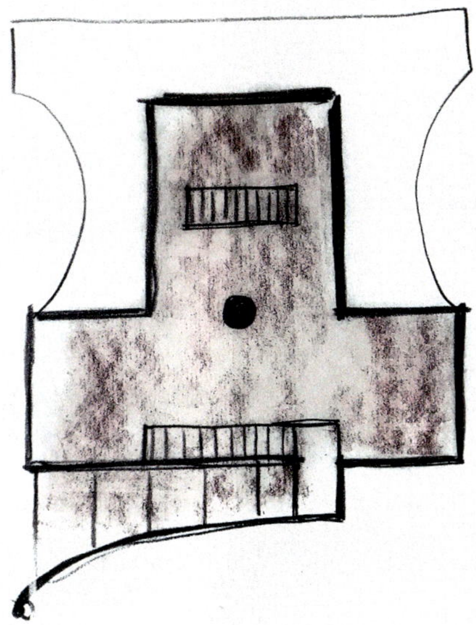

It was then that my sketching of floor plans really took off. Since I am neither excessively intellectual nor academic in my approach to architecture, the discourse I started on the paper had to be silent. The next project was a museum; here I tried to use shifts and interruptions of axes to bring forth some disorder and create a labyrinth effect. The classical plan has become my destiny. My plans always comprise a kind of order, to which I can start to relate as well as I can. Perhaps a duel can be won between the resting plan and the freer one. Perhaps the plan is stupid and naive. Perhaps it is halved, doubled, or decomposing and inquiring.

The floor plans and drawings presented here are mainly taken from my small sketchbooks [fig. 1–6]. I love to draw more or less the same thing over and over again. The plans have almost always been accompanied by spatial sketches. In fact, I usually sketch spatially. I even draw plans three-dimensionally. I draw on a daily basis and consider my floor plans and spatial sketches as exercises just waiting to be converted to a program. These are my plans for the future.

Athanasiou Geolas

"Manner of Working"

Robin Evans, the Drawing, and a Theory of Practice

fig. 1

1 Robert Bénard, *The Art of Writing*, 1763. Engraving, detail. Originally published in *Encyclopédie ou Dictionnaire raisonné des sciences, des arts et des métiers*, vol. 2 (plates), (Paris, 1763).

> Dead things are easier to handle than live ones; they may not be so interesting but they are less troublesome. From the point of view of the architect seeking firmness and stability, the best geometry is surely a dead geometry (…) an inoculation against uncertainty. Yet the architect's attitude to this stabilizing geometry has always been two-faced (…) Its value may be in its deadness, but if it is not kept under control it may revive, like a monster (…) The ideal is of a vital and creative art supported on the dead certain truth of geometry. The very statement is enough to make us think twice. Is the geometry in architecture really so reliable?[1]
>
> — Robin Evans

If not geometry, what about the drawings themselves—are the physical documents of architectural practice reliable? If we see an architectural drawing revive from the state usually assigned to it and begin to move, can we still trust it to faithfully translate architects' (or historians') intentions in the socially contingent expanse between drawing and building?[2] While in this passage Robin Evans writes about geometry, the architect's "two-faced" attitude, both relying upon and questioning the reliability of stabilizing concepts and protocol, is also precisely what is at stake in this analysis of architectural drawings. Taking my cue from this discussion of the lively dead, I will consider a potent phrase from Evans' 1986 essay "Translations from Drawing to Building."[3] Evans claims that each drawing should be understood as "not so much a work of art or a truck for pushing ideas from place to place," but instead as a "locale of subterfuges and evasions."[4] For Evans, architectural history, and the history of drawings in particular, demands an analysis of architects' social engagement, that is, of their *manner of working* with drawings.[5] I will argue for a change in the way practitioners and scholars conceive of architectural drawings—rather than taking them as representations or embodiments of an idea, we might instead think of drawings as artifacts that circulate in the material world, always complicit with existing power structures.[6] As I will show, reframing analysis in this way works within familiar conversations to bring alternative questions to the table.

It seems to be taken for granted that architectural drawings are representations—tools that make something absent (or not yet in existence) appear in the present. Once completed, they tend to be treated as vehicles, transporting ideas from place to place without affecting the content they carry. This position imputes the drawing's deadness and excludes the full-breadth of embodied social circumstance within which architects wield those drawings. Architectural drawings constitute a physical, political context within which various actors engage in power relations. They are the ground on which physical labor is choreographed, economic exchange is scheduled and determined, and legal obligations are measured; but they are also physically within the spaces in which actors negotiate interpersonal relationships as vague as trust, belief, and friendship.[7] Analyzing drawings as a part of embodied social circumstances mandates close attention to the contingencies of the relationships at play around the actual physical documents themselves. Indeed, there may be no need "to interpret" the drawing at all—as if all that matters is the idea hidden within—so much as to account for the social relationships engendered by its form and use.[8] In other words, regardless of what each drawing *is* or what it *says* or to whom it *speaks*, I ask: what must we accept about how the practice of architecture proceeds in order to even enter into a debate about whether, how, or to what effect drawings (and with them architects and their ideas) engage with the world. What do the various forms and uses of architectural drawings themselves already insist upon within the ways in which architects in a particular place and time practice their discipline? Seen this way, drawings, including the hand-drawn plan, are not only pertinent for analysis as a product, as a tool or as an aspiration; but they also allow us to ask in what ways architects interact with a mode of thinking, acting and believing within a given tradition.

I want to raise these questions about architectural drawings by intersecting Robin Evans, Manfredo Tafuri, and Michel Foucault at the phrase "manner of working." This phrase has the quality of an aphorism, and it offers a provocation that allows me to reframe what has been treated as a theory of representation instead as a theory of practice. Anthony Vidler explains that Evans, Tafuri, and Foucault appear in the architectural discourse among a group of scholars in the 1970s and '80s. Collectively, their work addressed issues that arose from beyond the discipline of architecture but became central to distinguishing architectural theory from architectural history.[9] Whatever the historiographical outcome, Evans, Tafuri, and Foucault have been mainstays since this moment of theoretical ferment. Most of us engaged in architectural discourse today have read at least one essay by each author. They are assigned in nearly every semester of architecture school, whether for history, theory, or studio work. While there are many differences in their individual theoretical projects, by reading across them it becomes possible to see architects' engagement with drawings as an embodied practice. Rehearsing Evans' analysis of drawings together with Tafuri's political critiques and Foucault's social construction of bodies does not create a coherent theoretical position, but it does challenge us to consider drawings differently. However overwrought Tafuri and Foucault, and however familiar Evans' essays may be, their intersection at "manner of working" resurrects the hand-drawn plan, investing it with a more visceral energy and insisting once more on the often mysterious link between the visual and the social.

Evans' Aphorism

Evans used the phrase "manner of working" in three distinct texts.[10] Between these uses, Evans lays out the political character of drawing techniques.[11] First, in his 1984 essay on Daniel Libeskind's drawing series *Chamber Works*, Evans intimates the political aspect of this phrase more explicitly than anywhere else. He claims that Libeskind's drawing practice "does not now involve him in the tedious entropy of getting something built, nor in the dubious politics of improving social conditions, nor in the appalling sycophancy of client-sucking, nor in reconstructing his personality to fit his job."[12] Instead, Libeskind focuses on the drawing itself. While it is possible to see this as an argument for disciplinary autonomy or a withdrawal from social and political contingency, I read Evans through his phrase and take this celebration of drawing itself as arguing for the necessity of neither looking at the ends ("something built"; "social conditions") nor the means to those particular ends ("sycophancy"; "personality") of the work of architecture, but rather honing in on ever more present and intimate moments in the engagement with drawings as artifacts.[13]

Evans also employs this phrase in his book *The Projective Cast*. While offering a significant and deep reading of the link between geometry and architecture, Evans somewhat avoids the politics of practice, focusing instead on what some have termed a shift in his research from the social to the formal.[14] Projection, as the title would suggest, was the central theoretical concept in this final book; it constituted the relational zone between geometry and architecture that enabled the design of buildings by making these relations available to perception. In other words, here it was projection that both constituted and filled the gap between drawing and building as a space of translation between the mind and the world.[15] The final pages of Evans' conclusion, titled "The Permeation of Projection," can be referenced as a formalization of his theory of translational, projective space.[16]

The most regularly cited and discussed of these three instances appeared in 1986, when Evans published his essay "Translations from Drawing to Building." Here, he attempted to ascertain the drawing's power as a medium, and to describe how it came to be that drawings, once closely analyzed, posit a seemingly paradoxical reality—they translate architectural ideas via their dissimilarity with the building they attempt to convey. In other words, drawings communicate a building by rigorously remaining distinct from it. This is opposed, for instance, to the case of translating from one language into another, where the goal is for each version to mean precisely the same as the original, and to convey that meaning fluidly. Evoking the etymological roots of the word, Evans speaks of translation as movement where one object moves from here to there, while remaining the same before and after.[17]

This paradoxical, seemingly un-situated, and in Evans' words "peculiar power" of the architectural drawing relies on what he terms the "suspension of critical disbelief."[18] An idea that I think becomes a bit more clear in its positive form—an insistence on un-critical belief—that is to say, an insistence on *faith*—faith in the drawing and its capacities as a medium, faith that the drawing indeed means just what it says, and faith that we can read and understand that meaning. As he later wrote in *The Projective Cast*, "without faith in the genetic message inscribed on paper, there is no architecture."[19] This is the dead certain truth of the architectural drawing when taken as a translation.

However, Evans concludes his 1986 essay by outlining an aspirational model for writing architectural history distinct from that which he later followed. In this context, Evans' phrase "manner of working" appears as part of a new model for analyzing and criticizing architectural drawings within their historical, situated, and transactional circumstances. He writes:

> It would be possible, I think, to write a history of Western architecture that would have little to do with either style or signification, concentrating instead on the manner of working. A large part of this history would be concerned with the gap between drawing and building. In it the drawing would be considered not so much a work of art or a truck for pushing ideas from place to place, but as the locale of subterfuges and evasions that one way or another get round the

> enormous weight of convention that has always been architecture's greatest security and at the same time its greatest liability. This is one of my ambitions.[20]

First and foremost, I should point out that *manners* are not to be confused with *methods*, that is, with a sequence of clearly articulable tasks. Manners are much more embodied.[21] Any claim for how we ought to conceive of, employ, or make drawings, as Evans would likely point out, is at least as moral and political as it is technical. What is it to say that engaging with a drawing is also a practice, a habit or a discipline? What happens to our understanding of practice when we focus on the manner in which these artifacts are used and circulate within the world?

To my knowledge, three eminent scholars of architecture have addressed this phrase explicitly. Each of their analyses set aside the grounded political character of this aphorism passing over the often mundane transactions in the gap between drawing and building.[22] In my reading, Evans calls on us to consider the drawing as neither an end in itself ("a work of art") nor as an instrument of communication ("a truck for pushing ideas"). Instead, we should look to them as a physical location (literally) on, through, and with which conversations take place; as a "locale for subterfuges and evasions" employed to circumvent the conventions that lend architecture both its cultural authority and conservatism. Without such conventions, there can be no subterfuge; it is a condition in which to *both* employ *and* evade authority. With this kind of complicity in mind, I turn toward Manfredo Tafuri.

Tafuri's Graceful Architect

"A vertiginous system of replications, a treacherous conspiracy, a cruel and irreal comedy: the first collective manifestation of humanism in the visual arts assumes disconcerting, even sinister, connotations."[23] So begins Tafuri's final book *Interpreting the Renaissance*, first published in 1993. Apparently, as retribution for failing to attend a dinner party, Filippo Brunelleschi orchestrated "an elaborate ruse." Through a network of friendships in a proto-Kafkaesque "comedy," Brunelleschi convinced a carpenter named Grasso, at work on the dome over Santa Maria del Fiore, that he was, in fact, a man named Matteo Mannini. Brunelleschi informed the local authorities, and since Mannini was guilty of a crime, they imprisoned the carpenter. Only after Grasso's mother confirmed his true identity did they release him.

What is at stake in this story? Tafuri points specifically to "Brunelleschi's cunning and penchant for risky experiment," the quality for which he is so celebrated as an architect.[24] What is this persuasive use of collective action and expectations for which Brunelleschi feels no remorse and for which we praise his capacities as an architect? What is this skill that we might just as easily apply to engineering problems as to interpersonal relationships? With this anecdote, Tafuri exposes his doubts about our *faith* in the architect's (remorseless) cunning. He links the foundational theories of architectural practice, as found in the work of well-known figures in the history of architecture like Brunelleschi and Leon Battista Alberti, with the contemporaneous political practices of well-known political theorists like Niccolò Machiavelli and Baldesar Castiglione. Here we can see, in its full form and contour, the "mentalities informing the 'cosmos of architecture' in the humanist era"—a set of mentalities that Tafuri collapses into Castiglione's term *sprezzatura*.[25] fig. 2 fig. 3

First published in 1528, Castiglione's *Book of the Courtier* has been considered equally a book on courtesy and a book on politics.[26] While there is much to unpack within Tafuri's analysis of Renaissance political theory, I am interested specifically in the correlation Castiglione draws between notions of Beauty and Conduct in the artfulness he expresses with the word *sprezzatura*. He indicates that at its root, artful behavior is founded upon "the concealment of art," and also of skill or training such that whatever act the courtier performs appears as if it were natural, easy, and without significant effort. Castiglione writes: "The courtier has to imbue with grace his movements, his gestures, his way of doing things and in short, his every action"; he must "steer away from affectation at all costs, as if it were a rough and dangerous reef, and (to use perhaps a novel word for it) to practice in all things a certain nonchalance [*sprezzatura*]."[27] Thus it is that *sprezzatura* conceals the cunning work of social (and so political) navigation behind a mask of poised behavior. To put this another way, *sprezzatura* defines an embodied social facility that we might call charm—a way of behaving artfully that wields the borrowed power of conventional norms.

At the same time, however, *sprezzatura* is also a subversion of those same norms. Like charm, but unlike good manners in the Anglo-American tradition, it is a way of behaving that does not preclude upsetting social norms. Hence, Brunelleschi did not behave poorly when he had the carpenter Grasso imprisoned; rather, he artfully and nonchalantly manipulated institutional expectations. Tafuri offers a discussion of language to demonstrate how one can both employ and subvert a social code, arguing that within the concept of *sprezzatura* there also resides a "technique of dissimulation."[28] For Tafuri, Castiglione's book considers language to be a material. We encounter, writes Tafuri, "a threshold separating a conception founded on natural and divine laws from one privileging a functional conception of language." Or, as Castiglione exclaims, "use, more than reason (...) has the power to introduce what is new and erase what is old."[29] This exposes a paradox wherein the meaning of the law is founded upon a principle of transgression—it is no longer natural or

divine *reason* that authorizes it, but rather *the use* of its material presence at a place and time.[30] Tafuri calls this a "*concealed transgression*" that both seeks the authority of the law through all forms of appearance, and also uses this authority through an act of transgression—architectural drawings are no less complicit and no less useful.[31]

Founding this evasive and therefore *graceful* communication upon a constant, transgressive use of language reconnects Tafuri with Evans' account of the architectural drawing—that document necessarily dissimilar to that which it represents. By bringing Castiglione's *sprezzatura* together with Evans' translational paradox, one can begin to see the relevance for architectural practice of what Tafuri refers to as the "connection between art and conduct."[32] Their intersection suggests a history of the practice of architecture that engages a paradox within the conventional and material constraints of our discipline in order to, as Evans writes, "get round the enormous weight of convention."[33]

2 Ercole de' Roberti, *Virgin Enthroned with the Christ Child, St. Anne, St. Elisabeth, St. Augustine and the Blessed Pietro degli Onesti*, 1479–81. Oil on canvas, 323 × 240 cm. Milan, Pinacoteca di Brera.

3 Raphael, *Madonna dell'Impannata* (Madonna of the Cloth Window Covering), 1514. Oil on wood, 158 × 125 cm. Florence, Galleria Palatina, Palazzo Pitti.

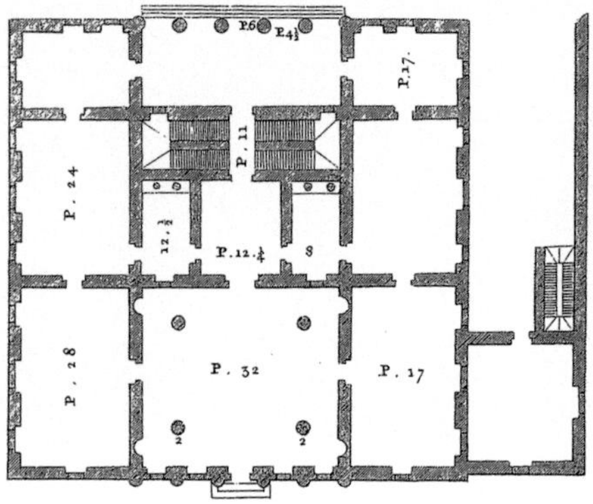

fig. 4

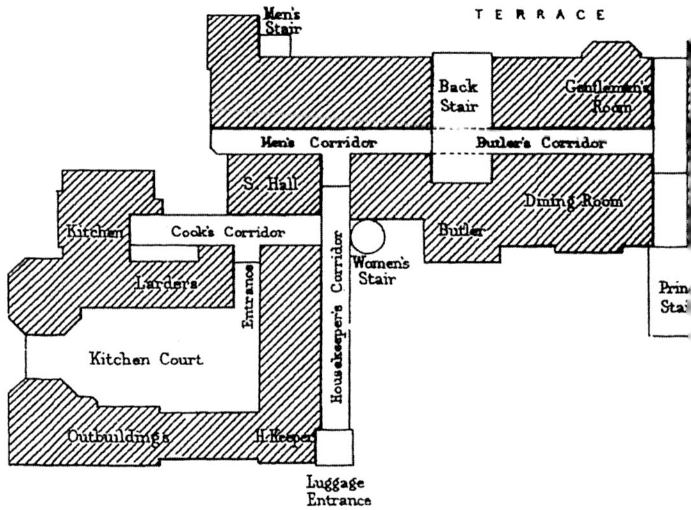

Evans' discussion of the plan drawing in his 1978 essay "Figures, Doors and Passages" exemplifies this graceful subversion well. Constructing a genealogy of the corridor in domestic architecture, he frames his account with two key comparisons that expose a shift in thinking from a 16th-century Italian palazzo to a 19th-century British country residence, which lays the groundwork for new forms of domestic space. Evans initially compares two paintings, one from the 15th century and the other from a 16th-century Italian painter [fig. 2–3].[34] He claims the first exhibits rigorous spatial hierarchies statically reflecting symbolic, social, and political norms of the time, while the second demonstrates dynamic, intertwined bodies receding into a single enveloping space, as if we were witnessing a situation playing out in time. For Evans, this second painting continues to reflect a set of symbolic, social, and political norms, but those of a new mentality wherein bodies exist in embodied rather than abstract spaces. Evans subtly inverts this argument when redeploying it toward a consideration of architectural plans—while in painting bodies become more intertwined, in architectural drawings they

4 Andrea Palladio, *Palazzo Antonini*, Udine, 1556. Published in Andrea Palladio, *The Four Books of Architecture*, 1570.

5 Robert Kerr, *Bearwood*, Hurst, Berkshire, 1864. Published in Kerr, *The Gentleman's House* (London: J. Murray, 1864).

become more stratified [fig. 4–5]. Here Evans identifies a 16th-century plan arrangement in which bodies and spaces necessarily intersect with one another (as in the second painting), and then a 19th-century corridor plan in which bodies have been progressively categorized and distributed (as in the first painting). The corridor processes bodies by limiting potential spatial interactions according to static and symbolic social boundaries.

fig. 5

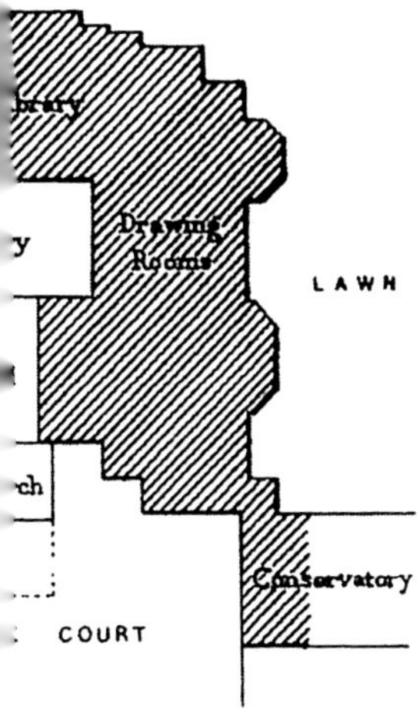

To see what these comparisons have to do with Tafuri's discussion of graceful (possibly sinister) subversions, we can look to Evans' own discussion of Castiglione. In the space opened up between the paradigmatic shifts indicated in the above comparisons, Evans emphasizes the dinner parties and social engagements described in *The Book of the Courtier*, which involved well-known humanist heroes from Brunelleschi and Alberti to Machiavelli. Rather than insisting on the power of the architectural plan to articulate behavior, Evans was struck by the relative insignificance of physical spaces in Castiglione's account of these gatherings, recognizing that they "share a total absorption with the dynamics of human intercourse to the exclusion of all else."[35] Of four such gatherings, in the Ducal Palace of Urbino, Evans writes the following:

> In *The Courtier* a few hyperbolic sentences suffice to eulogize the Urbino Palace, one of the great works of Italian Renaissance architecture, and not one word is said from beginning to end, either directly or indirectly, about the appearance, contents, form or arrangements of the apartments which serve as the setting.[36]

What, then, are we to make of their indifference to architecture? As demonstrated with his two inverted comparisons, Evans sees architectural drawings (and paintings) less as that which produces social relations, and more as modes and conventions of emerging amongst them. Indeed, Evans' comparisons foreground "the dynamics of human intercourse" as no less important and perhaps more useful than the organization of buildings in plan. Ironically it is precisely here that Evans may most agree with Michel Foucault.

Foucault's Art of Writing

Evans' aphorism echoes Michel Foucault's discussion of manners in *Discipline and Punish: The Birth of the Prison*, first published in French in 1975.[37] The popularity of this book in architectural discourse is not surprising given Foucault's influence on humanities scholarship in general since the 1970s, but especially due to the seeming privilege he has afforded the architectural plan. For Foucault, a building is one of many apparatuses that produce modern subjects while allowing for and affecting their behavior. To explain the relationship between an apparatus and a subject, we might consider the images included in the first English language edition, published in 1977, and

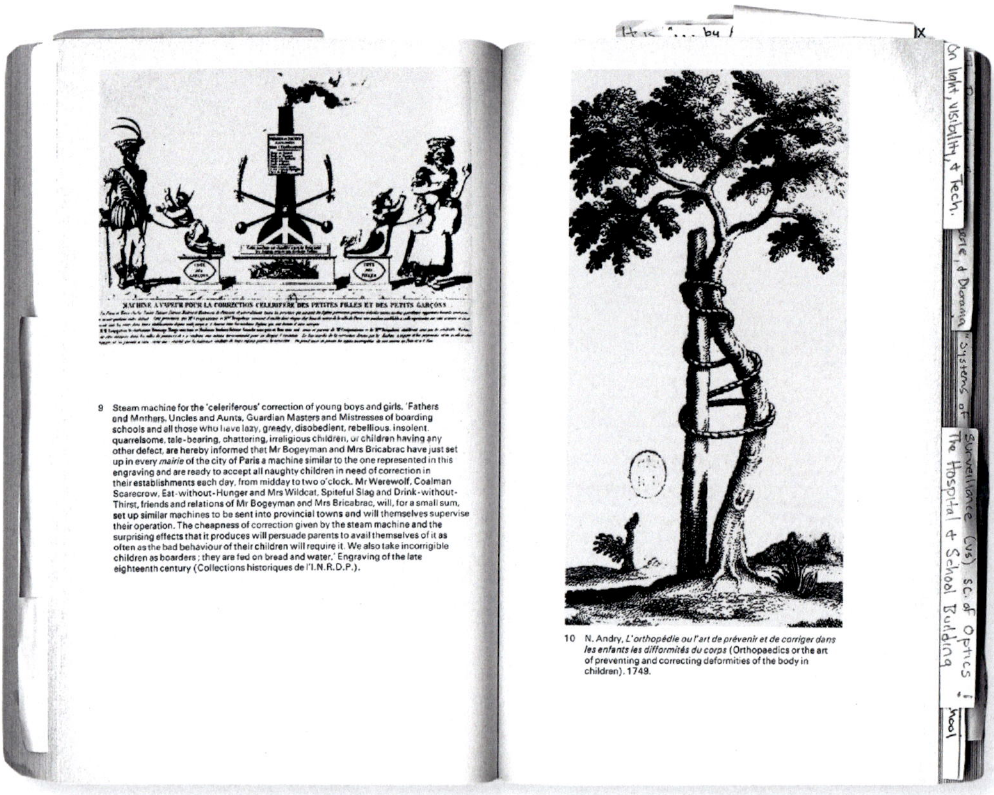

fig. 6

included in each of the subsequent three editions still in circulation today.[38] Many (but by no means all) of these ten figures appear in architecture lectures *ad nauseam* and are likely to do so for some time. Foucault's use of N. Andry's 1749 illustration from *L'orthopédie ou l'art de prévenir et de corriger dans les enfants les difformités du corps* [Orthopedics or the art of preventing and correcting deformities of the body in children] is perhaps the most pointed example of this [fig. 6]. Depicted as well-founded, sturdy, and decidedly "normal," this post seems to straighten a deformed body through a process of binding and detainment. Following this analogy, architectural spaces (such as Jeremy Bentham's *Panopticon*) may be thought capable of refiguring modern subjects [fig. 7]. Strictly speaking, this reading is not incorrect; but it *is* partial. Disciplinary coercion—or the power to affect behavior, subjectivity, and interpersonal relationships—functions through a whole matrix of apparatuses, only one of which is the arrangement of material according to an architectural plan. The more important point to make, as Foucault demon-

6 Book spread showing fig. 9 and 10 from the author's copy of Michel Foucault, *Discipline and Punish: The Birth of the Prison*, trans. Alan Sheridan (New York: Vintage Books, 1979), between pages 169 and 170.

ig. 7

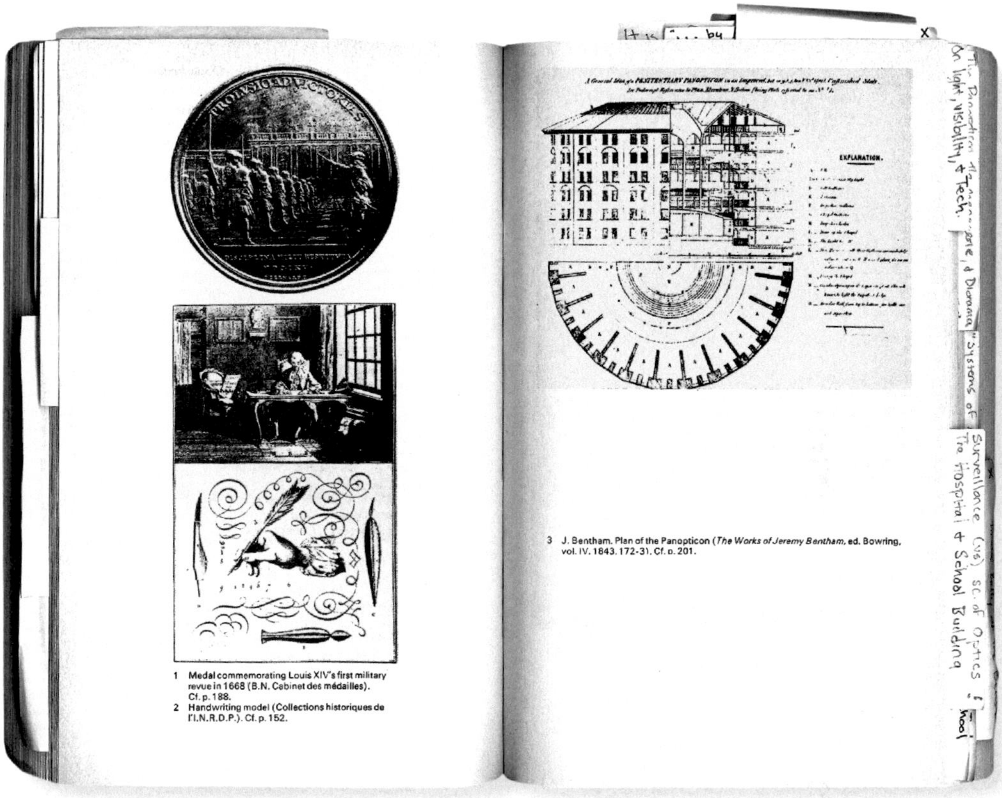

7 Book spread showing fig. 1–3 from the author's copy of Michel Foucault, *Discipline and Punish: The Birth of the Prison*, trans. Alan Sheridan (New York: Vintage Books, 1979), between pages 169 and 170.

strates, is that manners of working and believing are trained into the bodies that experience and perform them.

Prior to his discussion of panopticism, Foucault describes discipline as something perpetrated through a series of "techniques."[39] These techniques easily spread through various disciplinary institutions. It is by their "meticulous, often minute" interventions that they ultimately define what Foucault describes as a "detailed political investment of the body."[40] Each detail of a person's actions, Foucault claims, is important "not so much for the meaning that it conceals within it as for the hold it provides for the power that wishes to seize it," that is (recalling Castiglione), for the *use* each detail provides to that discipline seeking to wield a subject's actions in the name of a belief.[41] Discipline, in other words, is the collection of a set of techniques that regards individuals both as objects and as instruments of its exercise.[42] Although it becomes clearer in his later lectures, Foucault takes these techniques to be as much about changing oneself as affecting others.[43]

Foucault's discussion of this political investment in the body resonates with what Tafuri was referring to with the term *sprezzatura*. In fact, Foucault goes so far as to call these coercive but "apparently innocent" techniques of the body "small acts of cunning."[44] Recalling Brunelleschi and his dinner party diversions, it is important to reframe Foucault's "disciplinary coercion" from its simply negative implications in architectural discourse by understanding that it is not only the *mechanism* (the method) of controlling other people that is at stake, but also the desire to do so and the charismatic performance that makes it possible—after all, Brunelleschi managed to transform Grasso into an entirely different person with no apparent help from the walls of the Ducal Palace of Urbino. Architecture, from this social-theoretical perspective, is the symptom, not the cause. Foucault argues that "discipline" is different from torture and punishment, not because the institutions or the buildings have been redesigned and spatially transformed by new ways of making and thinking about drawings, but because the techniques by which these modes of action and interpersonal violence operate are different.[45]

To tie this back to the interpretation of drawings, Foucault's reading of the Panopticon suggests that when he looked at architectural plans, he did not see spatial organization deployed toward a functionalist agenda (as with the 19th-century domestic corridor plan and Bentham's aspirations); instead, he saw a series of cunning, interpersonal techniques.[46] Take, for instance, the second figure in *Discipline and Punish*, an engraving titled "The Art of Writing" and reproduced from the *Encyclopédie* edited by Denis Diderot and Jean le Rond d'Alembert [fig. 8].[47] This reproduction is an integral, but rarely discussed, figure in Foucault's sequence of illustrations.[48] Good handwriting (like good drawing) is fully habituated [fig. 1, 8]. It presupposes "a whole routine," in Foucault's words, "whose rigorous code invests the body in its entirety, from the points of the feet to the tip of the index finger."[49] Embodied disciplinary facility appears in the articulation of posture and hand position—note, for instance, the peculiar alignment of this person's head, shoulders, elbows, hands, knees, and feet, as indicated by the dotted lines. This is precisely how Foucault refers to this image; it depicts the correctly trained body.

Evans' prior analysis of architectural plans extends the discussion of this illustration a step further. A drawing is not a window *onto* techniques; they are neither *depicted* on the picture plane, nor are they *within* the image. Rather, the techniques Foucault refers to are at work within a social and political situation from which that drawing emerged. Such a position might lead us to ask: how does this artful person conceive of themselves when they write correctly, or what does their poise evince about their potential goals?

fig. 8

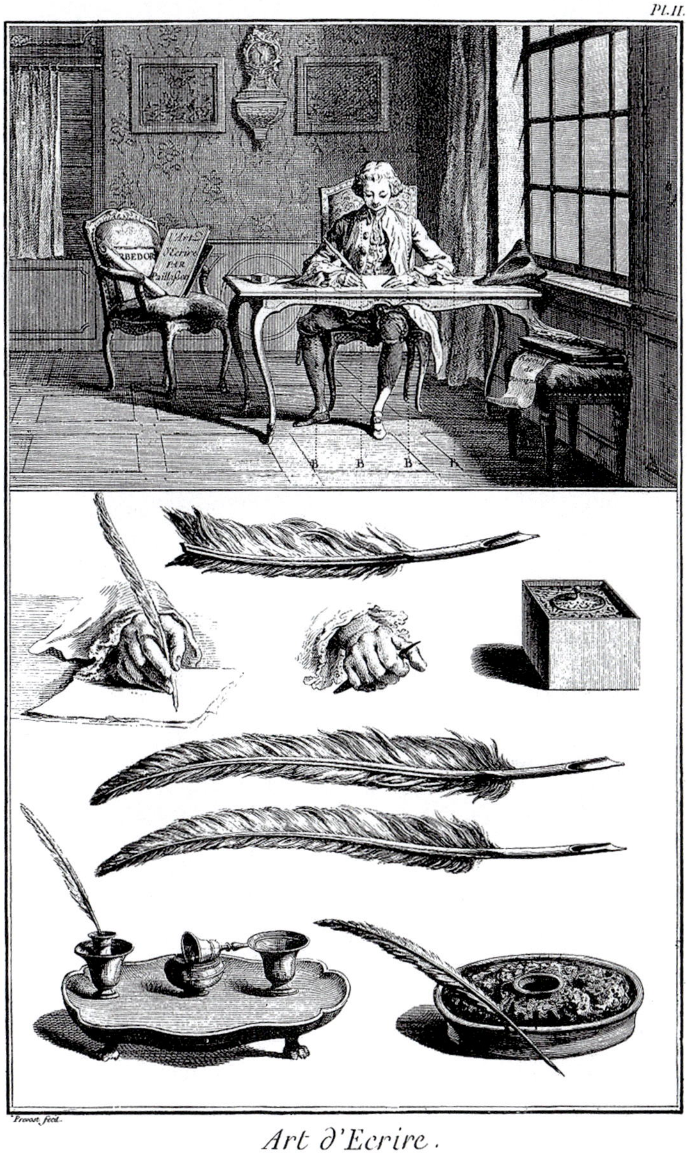

8 Robert Bénard, *The Art of Writing*, 1763. Engraving. Originally published in *Encyclopédie ou Dictionnaire raisonné des sciences, des arts et des métiers*, vol. 2 (plates), (Paris, 1763).

In place of any inquiry into its context, however relevant or important, one might ask instead: what is the *use* of embodying the art of writing in this manner at the particular historical moment of the making of the image? Look at where they are sitting; at *where* the art of writing takes place. Notice what they wear, their hair, the carved table legs, the upholstery patterns, and paintings on the wall behind them. The art of writing is indeed about technique, in the same sense, for instance, as when we refer to *craft*; but it is also at least as much a technique of public self-presentation and self-fashioning.

Then again, the line of thought followed up to this point continues to treat drawings as windows onto a distant social and political world; a world imagined by way of its consideration through these words and in our minds. In order to follow through on the promise of this theory of practice taken from Evans' aphorism, we must insist that drawings are present-tense artifacts lying on the table in front of us. So, what is the actual question? Why did Diderot and d'Alembert commission this engraving and all the others? Why did the "Art of Writing" depict elegantly dressed figures in well-appointed rooms? Foucault would seem to be suggesting that by using this drawing we can understand something of 17th-century France and the transformations of the politics of the body *then* and *there*. But of course, this engraving came to him as a way of making an argument about the politics of the body in the late 1970s within the throes of poststructuralist discourse about the role of power in subject construction. And it comes to me through the browning pages of the book he wrote, useful as it is for writing an article about architectural theory and about how one might interpret a hand-drawn plan at the end of the second decade of the 21st century. In short, however much of a window these drawings might be, they are also always at work right now. They are granted authority and rhetorical potency through the use being made of them. Architects' potentially subversive use of documents constitutes a set of techniques that, like discipline, cultivates others while simultaneously cultivating ourselves; that is, while we conceal our transgressions as graceful movements.

Conclusion

This article has traveled through Evans, Tafuri, and Foucault in order to reveal the potential power of concerning ourselves with the role and use of manners, etiquette, and habituated techniques when we attempt to interpret an architectural drawing. When we add the "Art of Writing" to this potency of the document in constituting *us* as subjects, it raises the question: what do we see in a hand-drawn plan? What are we looking *for* in a drawing, following Evans' aphorism? I have argued that the architectural drawing should be conceived of as a material document at work in the world. As with Tafuri and Foucault, we can understand the drawing as a set of complex social and political conventions that undermine the certainty beneath the projections typically attributed to them. Drawings, in other words, are far more (and far more present) than speculative windows onto some future possibility or long dead past. As with Evans' treatment of geometry in the epigraph to this article, drawings are less a dead certain truth than a prop for artful behavior. A drawing's value may lie in its apparent deadness, but its power comes from the manner in which an architect wields it to achieve some always contingent and always complicit effect.

In the introduction I claimed this article sought to revive drawings and find alternative questions for work yet to come—one final foray through Foucault opens onto those questions. Take the following sentence (and sentiment) that architects are wont to interpret as referring to the special powers of architectural space: "The exercise of discipline presupposes a *mechanism* that coerces by means of observation; an *apparatus* in which the techniques that make it possible to see induce effects of power, and in which, conversely, the means of coercion make those on whom they are applied clearly visible."[50] What if we replace the words "mechanism" and "apparatus" here with the word "drawing" rather than "architecture"? What if we ascribe to drawings, rather than buildings, the affective power to discipline bodies? *To exercise discipline presupposes a drawing that coerces by means of observation*. But how does a drawing observe? Or rather, in what ways does a drawing make a human subject visible? Or, far more importantly, what social processes and relations does an architectural drawing make available? What does the presence of such documents make possible conceptually and materially; historically and practically? Within what particular realities does this paper document exist? What kinds of subjects appear while they hold it in their hands; while they discuss, file or circulate it? In response, this theory of practice has much to offer the interpretation of a paper document like an architectural plan.

Travel to present this paper at Drawing Millions of Plans held by the Royal Danish Academy of Fine Arts, was made possible by the support of the Robert D. MacDougall Memorial Scholarship through the History of Architecture and Urban Development committee in the Department of Architecture at Cornell University. I thank those present and the many conversations that took place in Copenhagen, as well as the helpful comments from the presentation of this work as part of "On the Steps: The Making of Discourse," an event series in the Department of Architecture at Cornell University. Special thanks are due to Medina Lasansky, Salvatore Dellaria, and Sergio Preston who read and commented on drafts of this article as I was preparing it for submission, to Anna Hougaard and Martin Søberg for their generous invitation that inspired this work, and to Andreas Müller and the anonymous reviewer for their comments.

Robin Evans, *The Projective Cast: ›rchitecture and Its Three Geometries* Cambridge, MA, and London: MIT Press, 000), xxvii–xxviii.

For the remainder of this article I will ıake reference only to architects' use of ocuments. However, in each similar ase the same point should be made of istorians, critics, theorists, and anyone lse engaging with architectural rawings.

Robin Evans, "Translations from ›rawing to Building," *AA Files* 12 (1986): –18. All further page numbers from epublication of original essay in Robin vans, *Translations from Drawing to Building and Other Essays* (Cambridge, 1A: MIT Press, 1997), 152–93.

Evans, *Translations from Drawing to Building*, 186.

It is important to note that I am not ooking for or explaining Evans' intended ıeaning of this phrase, although in ertain circumstances he may agree ith my usage. I read Evans closely s a jumping-off point for ongoing ıethodological questions regarding the ıterpretation and use of architectural rawings.

As Bruno Latour pointed out in 1990, ttempts to study the material "bureau-" f bureaucracy offers more insight than n analysis of the abstract concept scribed in the "-cracy," or rule. On ıch material, agonistic encounters and ıe movement of documents organized nder the conceptual term "immutable obile," see Bruno Latour, "Drawing hings Together," in *Representation in cientific Practice*, ed. Michael Lynch nd Steve Woolgar (Cambridge, MA, and ondon: MIT Press, 1990), 19–68. For ome insightful analyses of architectural ocuments in this vein, see the special sue of *ARQ* following up on the urther Reading Required" conference ganized by Tilo Amhoff, Nicholas eech, and Katie Lloyd Thomas, held at e Bartlett School of Architecture, niversity College London in February 011. *arq: Architectural Research uarterly* 16, no. 3 (September 2012).

7 For my particular understanding of a material space see both Henri Lefebvre's classic text and the more recent work of Karen Barad. Henri Lefebvre, *The Production of Space*, trans. Donald Nicholson-Smith (Oxford and Malden, MA: Blackwell Publishers, 2000); Karen Barad, *Meeting the Universe Halfway: Quantum Physics and the Entanglement of Matter and Meaning* (Durham, NC: Duke University Press, 2007).

8 This point is inspired by the ongoing scholarly conversation sparked by Karl Marx's articulation of the concept "commodity fetishism." Karl Marx, "Part 1, Chapter 1, Section 4: The Fetishism of Commodities and the Secret Thereof," in *Capital: Volume 1: A Critique of Political Economy*, trans. Ben Fowkes (London: Penguin Classics in association with New Left Review, 1992), 44–49.

9 For a discussion of Evans' position among others during this moment of architectural discourse reference Anthony Vidler, "*Rethinking Architecture: A Reader in Cultural Theory* and *The Anaesthetics of Architecture* by Neal Leach," review, *Harvard Design Review* 11 (2000), http://www.harvard-designmagazine.org/issues/11/rethinking-architecture-a-reader-in-cultural-theory-and-the-anaesthetics-of-architecture-by-neal-leach (accessed July 22, 2019). Note, however, the relative absence of Evans in the omnipresent anthology: K. Michael Hays, ed., *Architecture Theory since 1968* (Cambridge, MA, and London: MIT Press, 2000).

10 I use "manner of working" to stand in for a variety of phrases that key into the same underlying concept. Robin Evans, "'In Front of Lines That Leave Nothing Behind': Chamber Works," *AA Files* 6 (May 1984): 93 ("a way of drawing"), 96 ("manner of working"; "a way of designing"); Evans, "Translations from Drawing to Building." In *Translations from Drawing to Building*, 186 ("manner of working"); Evans, *The Projective Cast*, 17 ("manner of operation"), 151 ("manner of projection"), 159 ("manner of their creation").

11 The meaning of a drawing "technique" here does not mean "convention" as it is discussed by James S. Ackerman and others. Here, "technique" builds off Marcel Mauss' concept "habitus" referring to an embodied, historical and cultural practice. James S. Ackerman and Wolfgang Jung, eds., *Conventions of Architectural Drawing: Representation and Misrepresentation* (Harvard University: Graduate School of Design, 2000); Marcel Mauss, "Techniques of the Body," trans. Ben Brewster, *Economy and Society* 2, no. 1 (1973): 70–88. Originally presented as a lecture on May 17, 1934.

12 Evans, "In Front of Lines That Leave Nothing Behind," 96.

13 Evans emerged as a scholar and theorist amongst the disambiguation of theory and practice at the Essex School under Dalibor Vesely and Joseph Rykwert (where Evans studied), and the Institute for Architecture and Urban Studies in New York City under Peter Eisenman (see Vidler, "*Rethinking Architecture*"). In Essex, Vesely and Rykwert hitched theory to history, whereas in New York, Eisenman directed theory toward a path of its own. It is thus somewhat ironic that I would be arguing for such a tight link between theory and practice via Robin Evans. This is why I call his phrase an aphorism and set it to work today. For more on the Essex School see Joseph Bedford, "Dalibor Vesely and Joseph Rykwert: University of Essex, Essex, UK, 1968–1978," *Radical Pedagogies*, http://radical-pedagogies.com/search-cases/e10-university-essex/ (accessed July 22, 2019); Helen Thomas, "Invention in the Shadow of History: Joseph Rykwert at the University of Essex," *Journal of Architectural Education* 58, no. 2 (2004): 39–45.

14 As John Bold and Katherine Heron note in their "Acknowledgments" at the outset of *The Projective Cast*, xxi: "Bob's ideas and his expression of them continued to evolve as he sought ways of making still clearer the communication of the highly complex issues and arguments to which his working life as author and teacher had been devoted." Regardless of how his interests may have changed over time, it is certainly clear that Evans' agenda was to develop a theory of architecture grounded directly in a "consideration of architecture." Evans, "Introduction: Composition and Projection," in *The Projective Cast*, xxxvi. For the argument that Evans shifted from the social to the formal see Jianfei Zhu, "Robin Evans in 1978: Between Social Space and Visual Projection," *The Journal of Architecture* 16, no. 2 (April 1, 2011): 267–90. In contrast, I read Evans' use of formalism not as a turn away from the social, but rather as a redefinition of "formal" to include the forms (protocols, manners) of social convention. I take this up alongside Tafuri later in this article.

15 Evans, *The Projective Cast*, xxxi, 355. As discussed later, this notion echoes not so much the "manner of working" Evans sought in 1986, but instead a kind of "vehicle" from the unreal or imagined to the real or literal, the "truck for pushing ideas" he had previously set aside.

16 Ibid., 366–70. For a challenge to Evans' later theory of projection, see Tim Ingold's discussion of "gesture" in his chapter on drawing in Ingold, "Drawing the Line," *Making: Anthropology, Archaeology, Art and Architecture* (London and New York: Routledge, 2013), 125–41.

17 A concept that appears to stand in opposition to (even if in awareness of) the prevailing critical theoretical debates of the 1970s and '80s regarding the social construction of knowledge. Evans seems to be suggesting that an architectural drawing means the same thing regardless of its material situation and in whose hands it appears. However, as I argue, the material and semiotic context of all things and ideas—including architectural drawings—makes a difference to what they mean. On the importance of position and in opposition to universal concepts, consider Evans' claims in conversation with Donna J. Haraway, "Situated Knowledges: The Science Question in Feminism and the Privilege of Partial Perspective," *Feminist Studies* 14, no. 3 (1988): 575–99.

18 Evans, *Translations from Drawing to Building*, 154.

19 The full quote reads: "Without the architect's faith that geometrically defined lines will engender something else more substantial yet discernable through drawing, without faith in the genetic message inscribed on paper, there is no architecture." Evans, *The Projective Cast*, xxvi.

20 Evans, *Translations from Drawing to Building*, 185–86.

21 Here we can refer to Mauss' paradigmatic 1934 lecture and to the work of both Norbert Elias and Pierre Bourdieu in which they discuss conventional bodily techniques as "history turned into nature" (to use Bourdieu's formulation), or their habitus. Mauss, "Techniques of the Body"; Norbert Elias, *The History of Manners* (New York: Pantheon, 1982); Pierre Bourdieu, *Outline of a Theory of Practice*, trans. Richard Nice (Cambridge, UK: Cambridge University Press, 2015), 78.

22 Penelope Dean takes it as a call to follow Banham's 1988 dictum and look to the "how" and not the "what" of architecture. Penelope Dean, "Practice Nouveau," ACSA 97th Annual Conference, The Value of Design (March 26–29, 2009): 307–17; Reyner Banham, "A Black Box," *New Statesman & Society* 3, no. 122 (October 12, 1990): 22–25. Christopher Hight compares Evans' historical examples with his own contemporary examples of digital processes. Christopher Hight, "Manners of Working: Fabricating Representation in Digital Based Design," *The Sage Handbook of Architectural Theory*, ed. C. Geig Crysler, Stephen Cairns, and Hilda Heynen (London: Sage, 2012), 410–29. Both Dean and Hight take "manner of working" to refer to method. Such a focus on design process (the how) is one of the primary ways in which Evans' phrase has been interpreted to date. Likewise, both seem to take the "subterfuge" Evans refers to as a call for novelty, rather than for political engagement. As Hight points out, a conventional relationship between representation and construction is presupposed within discussions of technological advancement. Alternatively, Andrew Benjamin contends that architectural drawings themselves are "that which enables architecture to stage a relation to an outside," that is, one's manner of working (seen here as the act of drawing) exists prior to external relations. Andrew Benjamin, "The Preliminary: Notes on the Force of Drawing," *The Journal of Architecture* 19, no. 4 (July 4, 2014): 470. Benjamin focuses on the "gap" that both Hight and Dean seem to want closed. However, in line with some Feminist poststructuralist critiques of political authority, I disagree with Benjamin's claim that there is a possibility for some *interior* moment between an architect and a drawing prior to an *exterior* relationship; some constitutive pre-political moment from which we might have the power to stage a future relation via the architectural drawing. My point is that any manner of working is always embedded and embodied as part of specific social and material situations. See, for instance, Judith Butler and Joan Wallach Scott, eds., *Feminists Theorize the Political* (London: Routledge, 1992).

23 Manfredo Tafuri, *Interpreting the Renaissance: Princes, Cities, Architects*, trans. Daniel Sherer (New Haven, CT, and London: Yale University Press, 2006), 1.

24 Ibid., 3.

25 Ibid., 3.

26 As a work of political philosophy, it has substantial roots in Cicero and also had a strong influence on later concept of the Gentleman cultivated in England by those who modeled themselves after what they viewed as their Enlightened, Humanist forbears. On the production of the book see George Bull, "Introduction in Baldesar Castiglione, *The Book of the Courtier*, trans. George Bull (London: Penguin Classics, 2003), 10–12. For more on the link between Cicero and gentlemanly behavior see pages 12–17.

27 Baldesar Castiglione, *The Book of the Courtier*, trans. George Bull (London: Penguin Classics, 2003), 65, 67.

28 Tafuri, *Interpreting the Renaissance*,

29 Ibid., 4–5.

) I studied this transition in sovereignty
›ward bureaucracy during the early
ıodern period in a course taught by
hilip Lorenz at Cornell University. For
ıe classic text on this shift refer to
rnst H. Kantorowitz, *The King's Two
odies: A Study in Medieval Political
heology* (Princeton, NJ: Princeton
niversity Press, 1981). See also Michel
oucault and Alessandro Fontana,
*ecurity, Territory, Population: Lectures
t the Collège de France 1977–1978* (New
ork: Picador, 2007); especially Lecture
our given on February 1, 1978.
1 Tafuri, *Interpreting the Renaissance*,
viii, 7. Refer to note 23 above, and
onsider Cornelia Vismann, "Law's
/riting Lesson," *Files: Law and Media
echnology* (Stanford, CA: Stanford
niversity Press, 2008), 1–38.
2 Tafuri, *Interpreting the Renaissance*,

3 In later essays, Evans showed clearly
ıe ways in which architectural drawing
onventions affect social situations,
onceptual understandings, and even
esign capacities. That work exemplifies
ıe ability to analyze the ways in
hich architectural thought progresses
ongside conventions, instruments, and
ocial conditions. Robin Evans, "The
eveloped Surface: An Enquiry into the
rief Life of an Eighteenth-Century
rawing Technique," *9H* 8 (1989): 120–47.
epublished in Evans, *Translations
om Drawing to Building*, 195–231.
evertheless, the implications of words
ke manners, etiquette, and charm
xtend beyond such analyses to include
ehaviors of the body otherwise deemed
arginal, or a mere affectation of little
ote for a theory of architectural
actice.
Originally published as Robin Evans,
igures, Doors, and Passages,"
rchitectural Design 48, no. 4 (April
978): 267–78. All further citations from
obin Evans, "Figures, Doors, and
assages," in *Translations from
rawing to Building*, 54–91. For Evans's
omparative argument see pages 57–62.
vans adapted this comparative
gument from Heinrich Wölfflin,
enaissance and Baroque, trans.
athrin Simon (Ithaca, NY: Cornell
niversity Press, 1966).

35 Evans, "Figures, Doors, and Passages," 67. See Evans, "The Developed Surface" for an even more explicit account of this point, in which Evans does not believe drawings affect conventions themselves so much as emerge with them.

36 Evans, "Figures, Doors, and Passages," 66.

37 Although Evans refers to Foucault only a handful of times in his published materials, he also appears to have read (and at least cited) Foucault's work as it was first published in French rather than waiting for English translations. Robin Evans, *The Fabrication of Virtue: English Prison Architecture 1750–1840* (Cambridge, UK: Cambridge University Press, 1982); Michel Foucault, *Discipline and Punish: The Birth of the Prison*, trans. Alan Sheridan (New York: Vintage Books, 1979).

38 Foucault, *Discipline and Punish*, figures 1–10, no page numbers and appearing between pages 169–70.

39 Ibid., 139.

40 These details can be likened to the kinds of skills learned by artisans. Quoting Marshall de Saxe, Foucault believes that "it is not enough to have a liking for architecture. One must also know stone-cutting." Continuing in his own voice, Foucault evokes Evans' later work: "There is a whole history to be written about such 'stone-cutting'— a history of the utilitarian rationalization of detail in moral accountability and political control," Foucault, *Discipline and Punish*, 139.

41 Ibid., 140.

42 Ibid., 170.

43 Michel Foucault, *The Hermeneutics of the Subject: Lectures at the Collège de France, 1981–1982*, ed. Frédéric Gros, trans. Graham Burchell (New York: Palgrave Macmillan, 2004); Michel Foucault, *The History of Sexuality, Vol. 3: The Care of the Self*, trans. Robert Hurley (New York: Vintage, 1988).

44 Foucault, *Discipline and Punish*, 139.

45 What Foucault means by "techniques" can be fairly well read in the chapter titles of each section in *Discipline and Punish*: distribution, composition, observation, and examination, to name just a few.

46 See Gilles Deleuze's study of Foucault, and in particular his discussion of the plan as a "diagram" for thought. Gilles Deleuze, *Foucault*, trans. Seán Hand (London and New York: Continuum, 2010). For a useful and extended discussion of Foucault's use of visual scenes reference John Rajchman, "Foucault's Art of Seeing," *October* 44 (Spring 1988): 88–117.

47 *The Encyclopedia of Diderot & d'Alembert Collaborative Translation Project*, Ann Arbor: Michigan Publishing, University of Michigan Library, 2010. http://hdl.handle.net/2027/spo.did2222.0001.403 (accessed July 25, 2019). Originally published as "Ecritures," *Encyclopédie ou Dictionnaire raisonné des sciences, des arts et des métiers*, vol. 2 (plates), (Paris, 1763).

48 I was unable to locate or confirm the specific image Foucault uses as his figure 2, which he cites as: "Handwriting Model (Collections historiques de l'I.N.R.D.P.). Cf. p. 152." In its place I have included two plates from the 1763 edition of the *Encyclopédie* each of which are titled "The Art of Writing." Although Foucault's image does not appear to be spliced or otherwise edited, on close inspection of the reproduction, and while it may have appeared in a prior edition of the *Encyclopédie* as he presents it in the 1977 translation, the two plates provided as figure 1 and 8 above may be easily combined to form the single image he used. Indeed, the top half of figure 8 and the bottom half of figure 1 appear identical to the two halves of Foucault's potentially composite image. If for no other reason, including both plates from 1763 underlines the present tense materiality of these illustrations (as discussed further in coming paragraphs) and perhaps suggests a bizarre elision.

49 Foucault, *Discipline and Punish*, 152.

50 Ibid., 170–71, emphasis added.

Mette Johanne Hübschmann

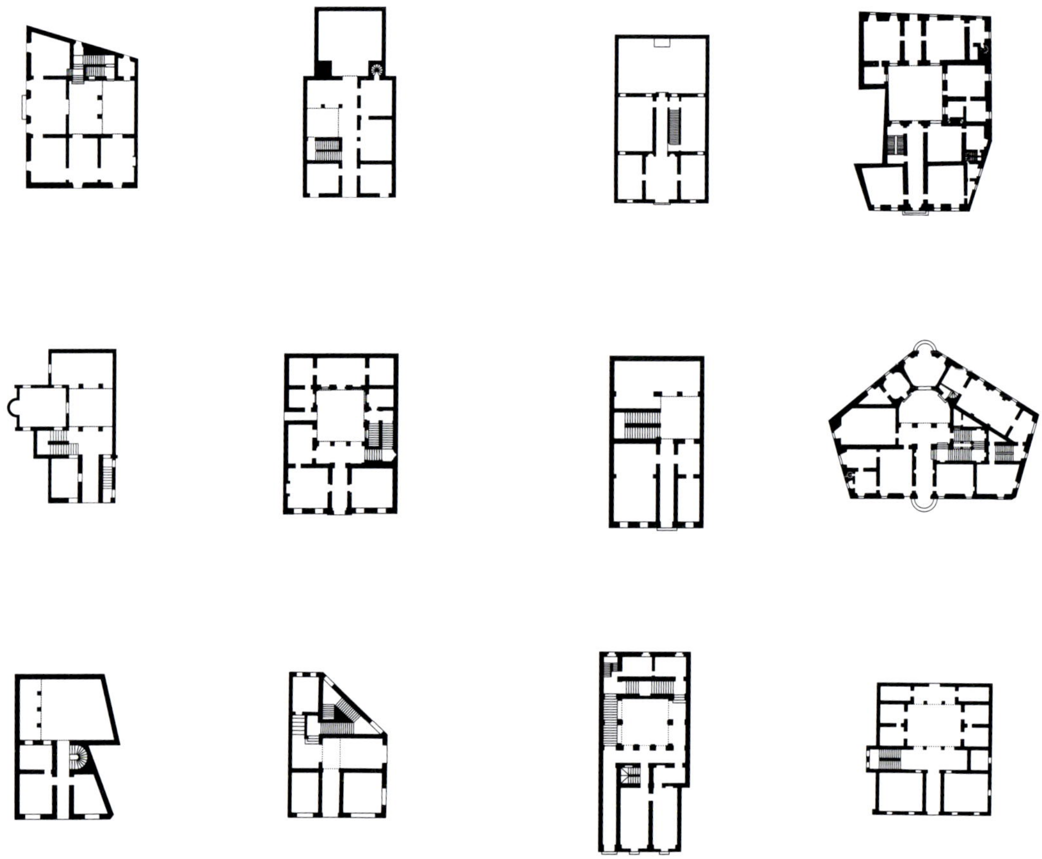

Plans of Ideas

Exploring the Spatial
and Figurative Qualities
of Plans

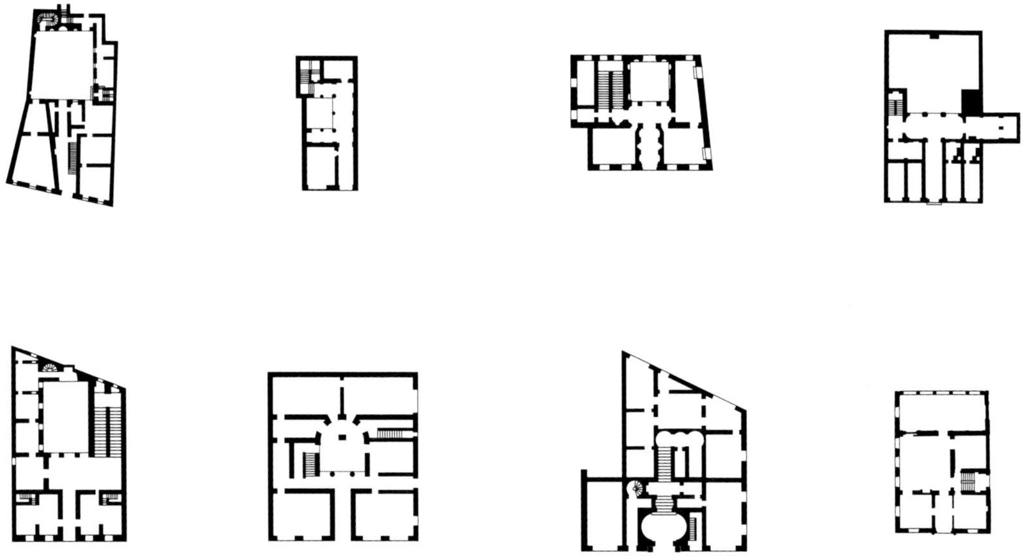

fig. 1

1 The collection of palazzo and palazzetto plans collectively re-drawn by students and edited by teachers from the Kingston School of Art, London, 2016–17.

This project explored domestic plans from the *palazzo* and the *palazzetto* of 16th-century Rome in relation to the specific material configuration of related buildings. The plans and buildings were investigated not so much for their historical or stylistic significance but for their inherent spatial and figurative qualities. The 16th century was a period of great experimentation, invention, and creativity in Italian architecture, and although Renaissance architects took precedent in Antiquity, contemporary societal circumstances and architectural typologies differed extensively from the ancient.

Through a process of analyzing and redrawing palazzo and palazzetto plans, a group of students from the Department of Architecture and Landscape at Kingston School of Art, my colleague Matthew Philips and I investigated the spatial and figurative qualities as well as the fundamental architectural elements found in these plans, such as doors, windows, staircases, and specific room types such as passages, loggias, and courtyards. The plans displayed spaces designed without a specific use in mind. When visiting many of the buildings we understood that, despite their 500 years of age, these buildings were highly adaptable, spatially rich and characterful. The plans of these buildings are flexible in their layout and allow for different routes through a "matrix of connected rooms," as Robin Evans would call it, "clustered together as a whole without corridors thus leaving no clear distinction between routes through the house and inhabited rooms within it."[1] The students were given a number of carefully selected plans to redraw using the same digital drawing style and scale so as to be comparable [fig. 1]. Redrawn in this way, the plan as a figure and the sequence of rooms became more readable, and small differences stood out more clearly.

The redrawn plans are extracted from their context and arranged together side by side, making them parts of a new whole from which emerged an architecture that neither followed a completely ordered classical symmetry nor a loose asymmetrical composition: it showed an architecture that made compromises, being only approximatively symmetrical. A tension showed in buildings that had a strong spatial order but at the same time had to adapt to irregular sites, a tension that can be read as wrestling between the ideal, classical concept and a complex reality. The plans hence seem to represent an ideal architecture, yet one that adapts to and negotiates the found conditions. Notched spaces, fractured edges and chamfered perimeters bear witness to this. These incongruous moments are "exceptional inconsistencies"[2] that distort the otherwise ideally consistent order. We perceived an ambiguity in the spaces that these plans represented, which created a complex spatial construction, despite the persisting simplicity of the plan as a figure. Seen in this way, these plans represent a spatial typology of its own that is real and precise in its language, yet vague and intangible in the principles it follows. Their ambiguity offers a chance for interpretation and rereading.

Redrawing these 16th-century plans in a contemporary manner and representing them spatially through large-scale models enabled us to see them as a reference to our own architecture. Our findings from observing and redrawing led to a series of projects designed through a collective design process employing multiple references. We portrayed the Roman palazzo and palazzetto in drawings and models and then translated these into domestic scale propositions for a constrained site along Via Giulia—a street in Rome laid out by Donato Bramante in 1508.

The palazzetto is a smaller version of the palazzo, adapted to the geometry of its site and engaging with existing structures. What characterizes the palazzetto is its ambition in terms of status, but its small scale. It is a robust, adaptable, idealized typology, adjustable to actual sites.[3] As a way of designing a contemporary palazzetto, the pedagogic strategy was to empha-

fig. 2

size a synthetic and reiterative process, using the 16th-century plans as a source for developing contemporary architecture. Students would reappropriate space through drawing plans, making planometric representations [fig. 2] and building large-scale interior models. They engaged with realistic construction methods and a site in Rome, moving our attention from the abstraction of formal typology to a sense of place [fig. 3–4].

Using 16th-century Roman domestic plans as a reference has led us to see more clearly what constitutes a space in the absence of a predefined function. Age-old topics of spatial sequences, figures, and orders were revitalized and translated into contemporary building techniques and design proposals.

2 Translations of palazzetto plans into spatial propositions for Via Giulia.

fig. 3

fig. 4

1 Robin Evans, "Figures, Doors and Passages," in *Translations from Drawing to Building and Other Essays* (London: Architectural Association, 1997), 90.
2 Robert Venturi, *Complexity and Contradiction in Architecture* (New York: Museum of Modern Art, 1966), 41, 118.
3 Colin Rowe and Leon Satkowski, *Italian Architecture of the 16th Century* (New York: Princeton Architectural Press, 2002), 106–107.

3 Contemporary palazzetto interior, 2016–17, model photograph.

4 Contemporary palazzetto interior, 2016–17, model photograph.

Martin Søberg

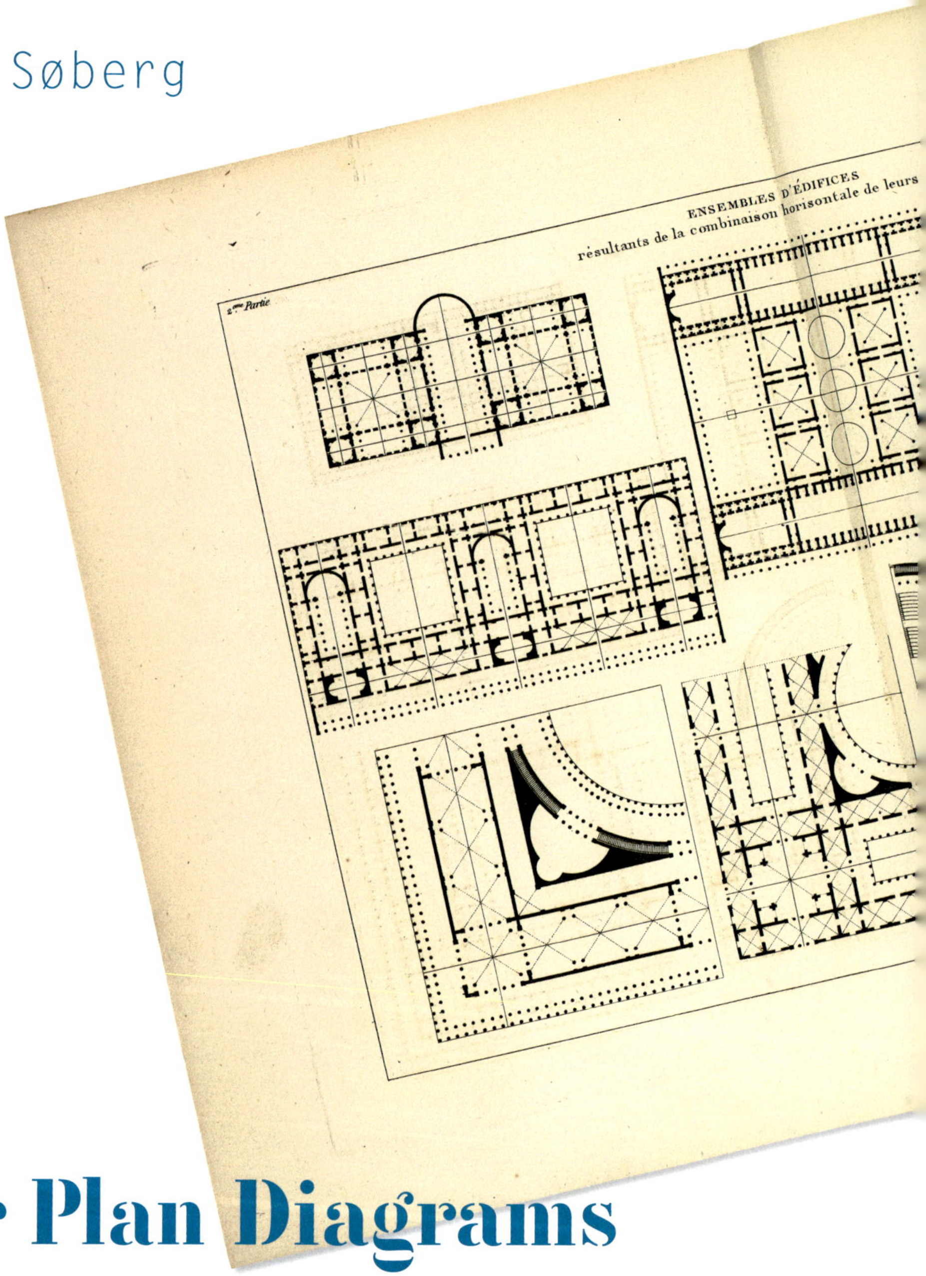

Floor Plan Diagrams and the Typology of Difference

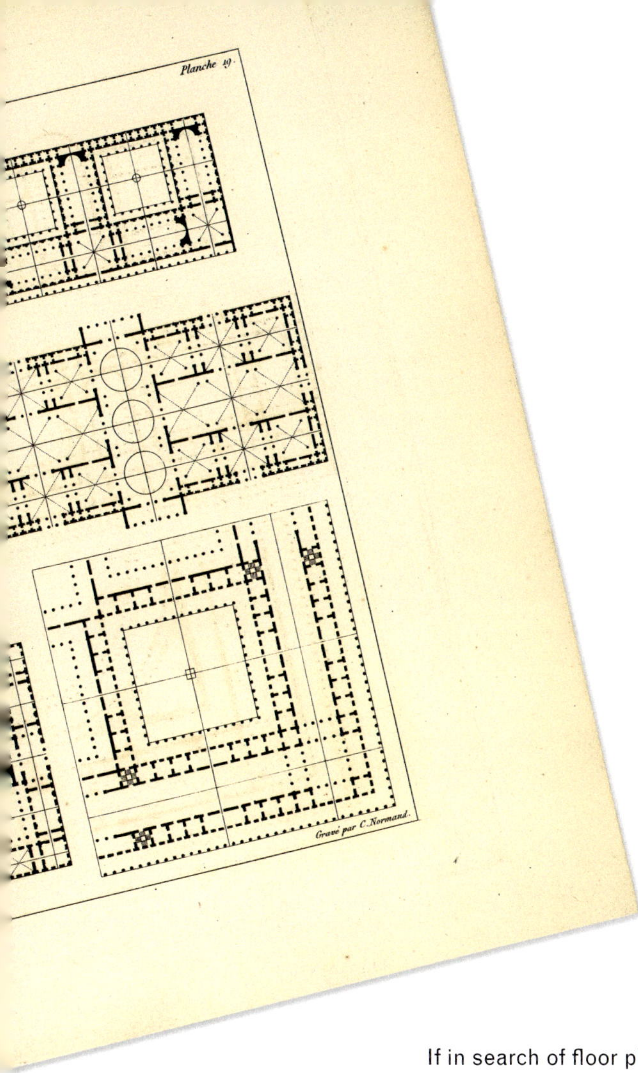

fig. 1

If in search of floor plan drawings, architectural manuals and handbooks provide abundant examples. Publications such as Charles George Ramsey's and Harold Sleeper's *Architectural Graphic Standards* (first edition published in 1932) and Ernst Neufert's *Bauentwurfslehre* (*Architects' Data*, first German edition published in 1936) provide architects with guidelines on how to design in accordance with the dimensions of a normative body, communicated primarily through graphic means and making extensive use of floor plan diagrams.[1] While these publications take an encyclopedic approach, covering a large variety of scales and programs, other publications, including more recent ones, are more specialized and typologically oriented. Housing is a field of architecture in which typological studies based on floor plans are particularly plentiful. The book *Typology+: Innovative Residential Architecture* (2010), for instance, investigates residential typologies in terms of access, interior space, exterior space, and morphology. According to its authors, Peter Ebner, Eva Herrmann, Roman Höllbacher, Markus Kuntscher, and Ulrike

1 Jean-Nicolas-Louis Durand, Ensemble of edifices resulting from the horizontal combination of their parts, 1817. Published in Durand, *Précis des leçons d'architecture données à l'Ecole royale polytechnique*, (Paris: Didot, 1817, Volume II, Plate 19).

Wietzorrek, this book is not intended as a theoretical study but rather "to provide architects with inspiration for their work and with basic research into new developments."[2] Along similar lines, Günter Pfeifer's and Per Brauneck's book *Residential Buildings: A Typology*, a compilation of four previous books published between 2007 and 2009, affords a comprehensive catalogue of contemporary housing floor plans, categorized into four groups: the courtyard house, the row house, the town house, and the freestanding house, each subdivided into further types, such as the garden courtyard house or the patio house.[3] Its back cover states that the "systematic development and evolvement of building types is fundamental to housing design. Whether designing new housing or applying and varying established housing forms at a large scale, a sound understanding of the underlying building types is invaluable."[4]

As the examples and quotations indicate, there is a close connection between architectural typology as a means of analysis and systematization, the use of graphic material, in particular floor plan drawings and diagrams, and the potential of these typologies in their roles as inspiration, generators, and indicators of conventions in architectural design processes. In this article, I investigate various aspects of this connection between typology and floor plans. I suggest that the negotiation between convention and invention—which is present in almost every architectural design—is particularly pertinent when typology is seen as a matter of *difference* rather than *optimization*.

Natural Principles

Typological studies have been part of architectural theorization and teaching at least since the Enlightenment. Changing attitudes towards the capacities and ethos of architecture have influenced how type was understood and to what degree it could form part of architectural analysis and design. The floor plan is the recurrent protagonist in this development, a graphic argument supporting and even visually confirming specific architectural ideas. As Rafael Moneo states in a seminal article on typology in 1978: "To raise the question of typology in architecture is to raise the question of the nature of the architectural work itself. To answer it means, for each generation, a redefinition of the essence of architecture and an explanation of all its attendant problems."[5] According to Moneo, if objects share the same formal structure, they belong to the same type. Yet even though formal structure could easily be understood as simply concerning an abstract geometry, a *Gestalt*, it does also concern social activities associated with particular constructions, a connection which may result in architectural transformations when types are recast and adjusted in order to meet new programmatic demands.[6] He notes: "When a new type emerges—when an architect is able to describe a new set of formal relations which generates a new group of buildings or elements—

then that architect's contribution has reached the level of generality and anonymity that characterizes architecture as a discipline."[7] The implications of this oscillation between convention and invention have differed throughout architectural history. Two years prior to the publication of Moneo's article, Anthony Vidler published an article on typology in which he discusses the changing notion of typology and identifies a renewed interest in the matter, a "third typology."[8] Both articles arguably reflect and promote this contemporary typological pursuit, but they concurrently attempt to nuance, historicize, and criticize it.

According to Vidler, the "first typology," appearing in the mid-18th century, interpreted the notion of type as a question of discerning the abstract nature of the primitive (following Abbé Laugier), while the "second typology," that of the Modern Movement, resembled a technological utopia informed by industrial production processes (following Le Corbusier). As demonstrated by the work of the Neo-rationalists, Aldo Rossi and the brothers Krier during the 1960s and '70s, this second typology was now extended by a typology founded on studies of the traditional city.[9] Vidler argues that this contemporary attitude was based on a purely formal interpretation of the city, emphasizing its continuity primarily with reference to the autonomy of architecture, as a sort of nature in itself: "This concept of the city as the site of a new typology is evidently born of a desire to stress the continuity of form and history against the fragmentation produced by the elemental, institutional, and mechanistic typologies of the recent past."[10]

To systematize and organize human knowledge with the help of human reason was a core endeavor of the Enlightenment, as evident for instance in Denis Diderot's and Jean le Rond d'Alembert's *Encyclopédie* and Carl Linnaeus' division of nature's flora and fauna into classes, orders, and genera. This search for natural principles resonated in architectural theory in the work of Abbé Laugier and others from around the mid-18th century well into the 19th century. While the term "type" was not applied by Jean-Nicolas-Louis Durand, his attempts to discern the elements and compositional rules of architecture were nevertheless founded on typological thinking, even if not in a rigorous way. Durand's attempts to optimize architectural design processes reflect a more general interest in natural processes. There is, according to Antoine Picon, an epistemological connection between the grid of Durand's method of design and contemporary mineralogy and studies of crystallization in which a specific geometric combinatoric approach is demonstrated. Picon identifies in this "the wish to overcome the opposition between the continuity of nature and the discontinuity of the elements that the human being applies as aiding tools."[11] Durand separated the elements of architecture simply in order to suggests a relinking and a return to (a classical notion of) coherence [fig. 1].

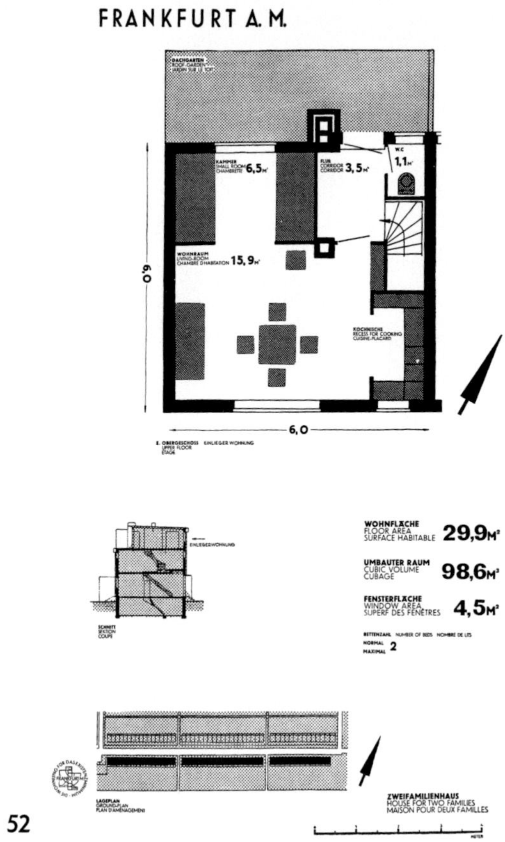

fig. 2

Architectural theorist Antoine Chrysostôme Quatremère de Quincy, a contemporary of Durand, introduced the term "type" to architectural discourse, according to Sylvia Lavin, in order "to transform theoretical speculations about systems inherent in architecture into operative means for making architecture in the modern world."[12] Quatremère understood these systems as something very basic, even primitive. Although likely related to his interest in the origins of architecture, it was through type that new architecture could be developed. Type was, in the words of Lavin, "an operative principle of creation,"[13] but at the same time a hieroglyphical sign of eternal principles. Or, as Vidler states concerning the notion of type in the Enlightenment: "To talk of a building type, then, implied not only its search for original validation, its ultimate restoration to the temple or hut, but also its specific aspect, the form that enabled it to be read as to its purpose at first glance."[14] Type was not only a question of formal structure, but of architectural semantics as well.

Means of Improvement

The typological search for abstract natural principles in architecture during the second half of the 18th century and the first half of the 19th century turned more and more towards the classification of buildings according to function in the course of the 19th century, in a schematic rather than inventive manner. As Rafael Moneo argues, "type was irrevocably flattened. It had become a mere compositional and schematic device."[15] Typological thinking was reinterpreted by the Modern Movement during the 1920s and '30s in an attempt to optimize and rationalize architecture and its production, potentially in order to industrialize it. This "second typology," in Anthony Vidler's term, primarily evolved around questions of mass production of urban housing in response to the interwar period's housing crisis, especially, in Germany, in relation to Neues Bauen and the construction of various *Siedlungen* (settlements) in Frankfurt am Main, Berlin, etc. Floor plans of such housing projects were a particularly valuable tool in the attempt to make construction more efficient and the houses more functional. Based on quasi-scientific methods, floor plans were presented as graphic evidence for comparison and refinement.

An important case of the use of floor plan drawings and diagrams in typological analysis is the method developed by Alexander Klein for the objective evaluation of the quality of designs. Klein presented this graphic method and its criteria in 1927 and the following years in a number of publications.[16] His aim was to support the health condition by facilitating functions and creating less strain on the nerves. The plan was therefore evaluated according to its functionality, aiming for the schematization and standardization of good solutions for mass housing; yet notably, the evaluation also comprised criteria related to the experience of architecture.[17] Similar methods were applied by the CIAM group, although not in as methodologically refined a way as Klein's evaluation. During the CIAM 2 congress in Frankfurt in 1929, on "Die Wohnung für das Existenzminimum" (The minimum subsistence dwelling), an exhibition was presented comprising a total of 207 floor plans, all presented in a graphically uniform way. The floor plans represented minimum units, drawn at a scale of 1:10 and with sections at 1:50, displayed on large boards and organized into categories of one-, two- or multifamily housing [fig. 2]. The theme of the meeting was linked to the satellite suburb schemes developed in the context of an urban extension of the city, "Das Neue Frankfurt" (The new Frankfurt), which included the development of terraced houses with flat roofs and stucco walls. These floor plan schemes, linked to social democratic housing politics, were influenced by Taylorist ideas of standardization and rational production, with the use of precast construction elements and the now famous mass-produced Frankfurt Kitchen.[18] The

2 Floor plan exhibited and published by the CIAM group in connection with its second conference, *Die Wohnung für das Existenzminimum*, in Frankfurt am Main, 1929. Published in Internationaler Kongress für Neues Bauen und Städtisches Hochbauamt in Frankfurt am Main, ed., *Die Wohnung für das Existenzminimum* (Frankfurt am Main: Englert and Schlosser, 1930), 52.

majority of the plans were of German projects, including many from Frankfurt, but several other European cities as well. Yet, as Eric Mumford has noted, the exact location was not provided, neither were the buildings represented in their entirety, whether in plan or perspective, although ground plans of entire buildings were occasionally presented as a sort of figure-ground diagram. It would allow visitors to compare plan solutions regardless of the visual appearance of the individual projects.[19]

In quantitative terms, Ernst Neufert's *Bauentwurfslehre* (*Architects' Data*) was one of the most comprehensive publications of architectural typologies and standardizations of the period. It included 271 plates with 3,600 drawings and proclaimed on its cover to be dedicated "dem Menschen als Mass und Ziel" (to man as measure and aim). According to Gernot Weckherlin, this manual showed "the whole universe of modern man and his modern life (...) In fact it is a strange and at times quite curious collection of domestic requisites, loosely classified by the logic of building 'types' from table size (apartment houses) to runways (airports)."[20] Likewise, Wolfgang Voigt has pointed to the almost cartoon-like quality of the illustrations of everyday activities, "a population of faceless people, who in hundreds of snapshots are pursuing work or rest with an indefatigable sense of reason, makes the books a surrealistic panorama of modern life."[21] The book was based on Neufert's experience with teaching "rapid design" at the Staatliche Bauhochschule Weimar (Weimar State University for Building) from 1926 to 1930. This method had been developed on the basis of a collection of standard or "typical" designs, organized in card-index boxes. It was intended to be more closely related to the building industry than traditional studio teaching. Neufert intended to promote the ideas of the rationalization and standardization of the building industry that had been expressed by his former teacher and employer Walter Gropius.[22] As such, the *Bauentwurfslehre* must be viewed as a contribution to optimization through graphic means and the application of types.

fig. 3

3 Floor plans from Kay Fisker's analysis of residential buildings in Copenhagen, published in 1936. Published in Kay Fisker, "Københavnske boligtyper fra 1914 til 1936," *Arkitekten* 6–7 (1936): 34.

Other German architects published manuals and handbooks of architectural design as well. In 1932, Otto Völckers published the *Wohnbaufibel* (Residential Building Introduction), a book intended for beginners in architectural design.[23] It categorized design into various topics, from hygiene to *Baukunst* (the art of building). Völckers explained house building through various visual material and in particular through floor plan drawings, some of them diagrammatically schematized and mostly without reference to the visual experience of the interior. Concerning norm and type, he states that "creating types means: To refer back to as few ideal models as possible the form and assemblage of functional objects."[24] And further on: "Floor plan

To trapper, beliggende i modsat lejlighedsskel. *1 : 200 og 1 : 500*

a-f: trapperne beliggende i samme side, g-i modsat side

III 34

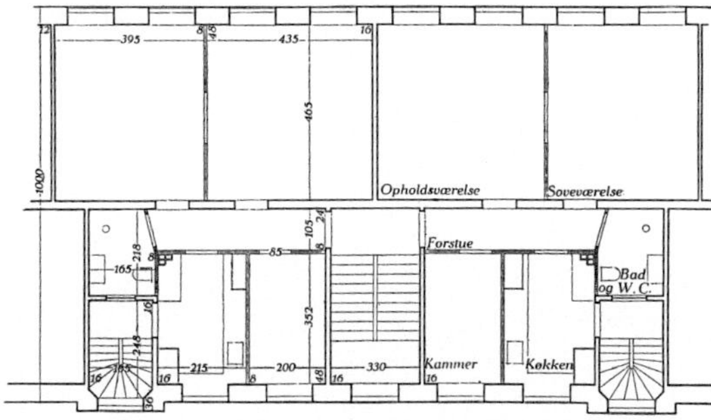

a
1 *Beliggenhed: Amager Boulevard - Amager Fælledvej*
2 *Bygherre: Andelsboligselskabet „Møllegaarden"*
3 *Arkitekt: Povl Baumann*
4 *Opførelsesaar: 1922*
5 *Bebyggelsesmaade: lukket karré*
6 *Værelsesantal: 2 værelser og kammer*
7 *Bruttoareal: 80 m²*
8 *Etageantal: 6 etager*
9 *Sanitære installationer: bad og w.c. fælles, indirekte belysning*
10 *Altansystem: ingen*
11 *Trappesystem: 2 trætrapper*
12 *Trappens beliggenhed: eensidige*
13 *Trappens orientering: øst*
14 *Opholdsstuens orientering: vest*
15 *Antal lejligheder pr. trappe: 2*
16 *Bemærkninger: Statsboligfondstype af indhold som IV, men med varient trappeplacering. Vanskelig at opdele med brandgavle. Een køkkentrappe til hvrr lejlighed*

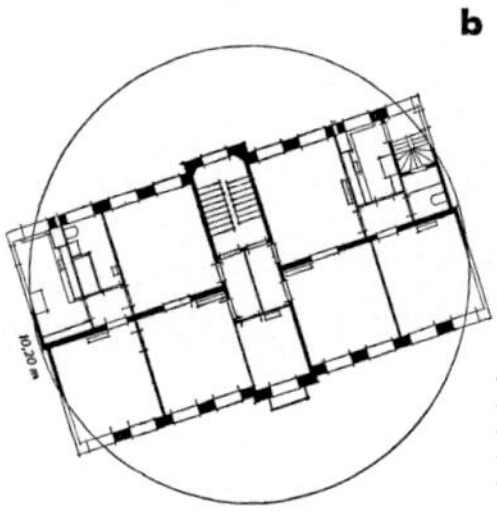

b
1 *Beliggenhed: Strandboulevard, Classensgade, Livjægergade, Arendalsgade*
2 *Bygherre: „Københavns alm. Boligselskab"*
3 *Arkitekt: Carl Petersen, O. Falkentorp, Peter Nielsen, Povl Baumann*
4 *Opførelsesaar: 1924*
5 *Bebyggelsesmaade: halvlukket karré*
6 *Værelsesantal: 3 værelser og 3 værelser og kammer*
7 *Bruttoareal: 91 og 108 m²*
8 *Etageantal: 5 etager*
9 *Sanitære installationer: bad med kar og w.c. indirekte belysning og bad med kar, w.c. og haandvask, direkte belysning*
10 *Altansystem: nogle lejligheder een lille altan*
11 *Trappesystem: 2 trætrapper*
12 *Trappens beliggenhed: eensidige*
13 *Trappens orientering: nordvendt*
14 *Opholdsstuens orientering: nord- og sydvendt*
15 *Antal lejligheder pr. trappe: 2*
16 *Bemærkninger: ingen*

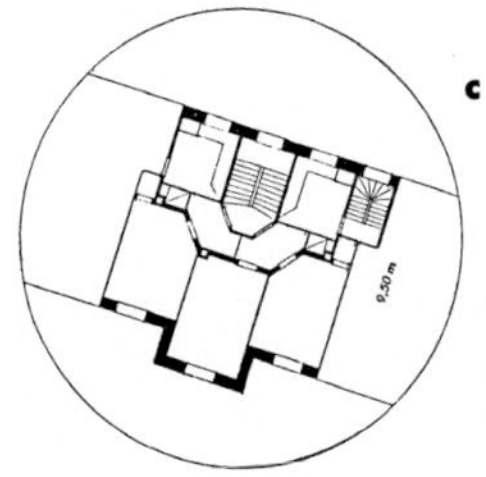

c
1 *Beliggenhed: Genforeningsplads*
2 *Bygherre: Landmandsbankens Byggeselskab*
3 *Arkitekt: N. Rosenkjær og T. H. Hjejle*
4 *Opførelsesaar: 1920*
5 *Bebyggelsesmaade: lukket karré*
6 *Værelsesantal: 1 og 2 værelser*
7 *Bruttoareal: 42 og 63 m²*
8 *Etageantal: 3 etager*
9 *Sanitære installationer: w.c. indirekte belysning*
10 *Altansystem: ingen*
11 *Trappesystem: 2 trætrapper*
12 *Trappens beliggenhed: eensidig*
13 *Trappens orientering: nord*
14 *Opholdsstuens orientering: syd*
15 *Antal lejligheder pr. trappe: 2*
16 *Bemærkninger: ingen*

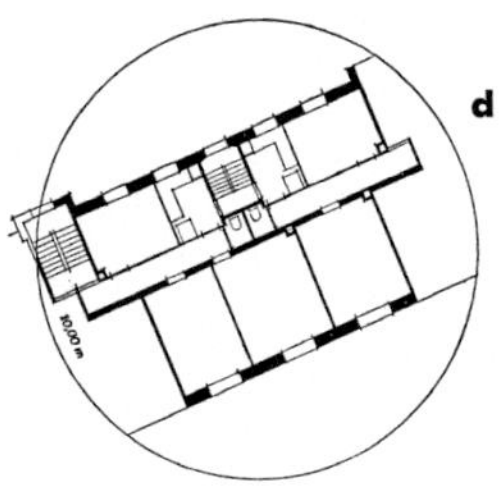

d
1 *Beliggenhed: Strandvejen*
2 *Bygherre: Arbejdernes Andelsboligforening*
3 *Arkitekt: Frederik Wagner*
4 *Opførelsesaar: 1923*
5 *Bebyggelsesmaade: aaben og lukket karré*
6 *Værelsesantal: 2 og 3 værelser og kammer*
7 *Bruttoareal: 58 og 78 m²*
8 *Etageantal: 5 etager*
9 *Sanitære installationer: w.c. indirekte belysning*
10 *Altansystem: ingen*
11 *Trappesystem: 2 trætrapper*
12 *Trappens beliggenhed: eensidige*
13 *Trappens orientering: nord*
14 *Opholdsstuens orientering: syd*
15 *Antal lejligheder pr. trappe: 2*
16 *Bemærkninger: ingen*

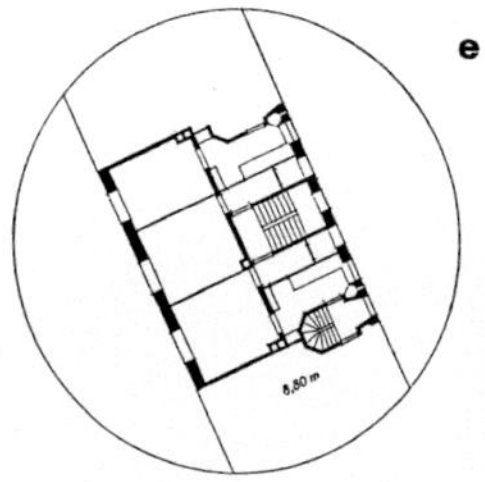

e
1 *Beliggenhed: Sjællands-, Refsnæs-, Fensmark- og Nøddebogade*
2 *Bygherre: Københavns kommune*
3 *Arkitekt: Stadsarkitekt Poul Holsøe*
4 *Opførelsesaar: 1927*
5 *Bebyggelsesmaade: halvlukket karré*
6 *Værelseantal: 1 og 2 Værelser*
7 *Bruttoareal: 39 og 52 m²*
8 *Etageantal: 5 etager*
9 *Sanitære installationer: w.c. direkte belysning*
10 *Altansystem: ingen*
11 *Trappesystem: 2 trætrapper*
12 *Trappens beliggenhed: eensidige*
13 *Trappens orientering: nordøst sydvest*
14 *Opholdsstuens orientering: nordvest-sydøst*
15 *Antal lejligheder pr. trappe: 2*
16 *Bemærkninger: ingen*

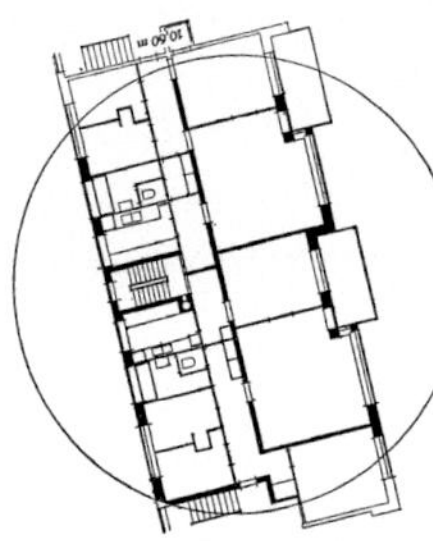

f
1 *Beliggenhed: Godthaabsvej*
2 *Bygherre: akts. „Godthaabsvænge"*
3 *Arkitekt: Hans Hansen og Alvar Lauritzen*
4 *Opførelsesaar: 1934—35*
5 *Bebyggelsesmaade: stokkebebyggelse*
6 *Værelsesantal: 3 værelser eller 2 værelser og 2 kamre, 4 værelser eller 3 værelser og 2 kamre*
7 *Bruttoareal: 95—110 m²*
8 *Etageantal: 4 etager*
9 *Sanitære installationer: bad og w.c. adskilt, bad direkte belysning.*
10 *Altansystem: altan til een side*
11 *Trappesystem: 2 trætrapper*
12 *Trappens beliggenhed: eensidige*
13 *Trappens orientering: øst*
14 *Opholdsstuens orientering: vest*
15 *Antal lejligheder pr. trappe: 2*
16 *Bemærkninger: spise- og opholdsstuernes størrelse kan varieres. Skillerum mellem kamre kan fjernes og kamrene ændres til et soveværelse.*

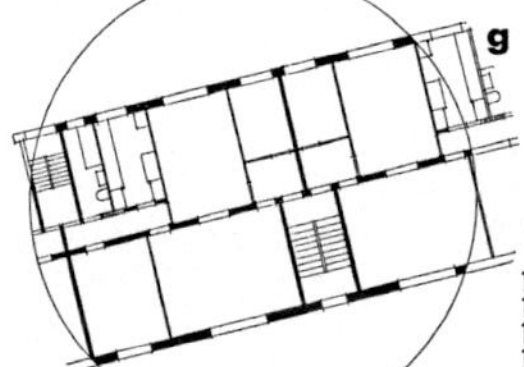

g
1 *Beliggenhed: Rosenørnsallé*
2 *Bygherre: akts. af 1. juli 1929*
3 *Arkitekt: A. Skjøt-Pedersen*
4 *Opførelsesaar: 1930*
5 *Bebyggelsesmaade: karrébebyggelse*
6 *Værelsesantal: 5 værelser og kammer*
7 *Bruttoareal: 180 m²*
8 *Etageantal: 6 etager*
9 *Sanitære installationer: bad og w.c.*
10 *Altansystem: ingen*
11 *Trappesystem: 2 trætrapper*
12 *Trappens beliggenhed: forskudt*
13 *Trappens orientering: syd*
14 *Opholdsstuens orientering: syd*
15 *Antal lejligheder pr. trappe: 2*
16 *Bemærkninger: ingen*

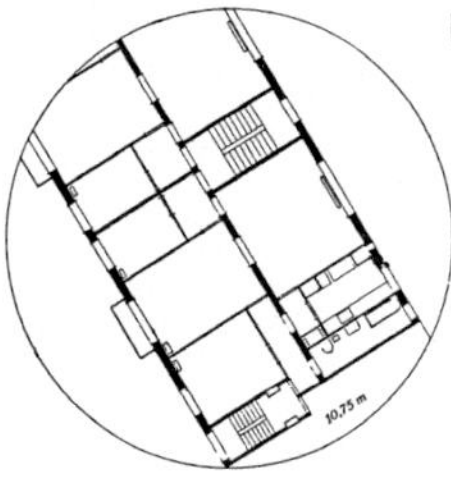

h
1 *Beliggenhed: Gentofte torv*
2 *Bygherre: privat*
3 *Arkitekt: Hilda Rømer og P. Nyboe-Pedersen*
4 *Opførelsesaar: 1932*
5 *Bebyggelsesmaade: halvlukket karré*
6 *Værelsesantal: 3 værelser og 1 kammer*
7 *Bruttoareal: 120 m²*
8 *Etageantal: 5 etager*
9 *Sanitære installationer: bad og w.c. fælles, direkte belysning*
10 *Altansystem: 1 altan*
11 *Trappesystem: 2 trætrapper*
12 *Trappens beliggenhed: forskudt*
13 *Trappens orientering: nordøst*
14 *Opholdsstuens orientering: nordøst*
15 *Antal lejligheder pr. trappe: 2*
16 *Bemærkninger: ingen*

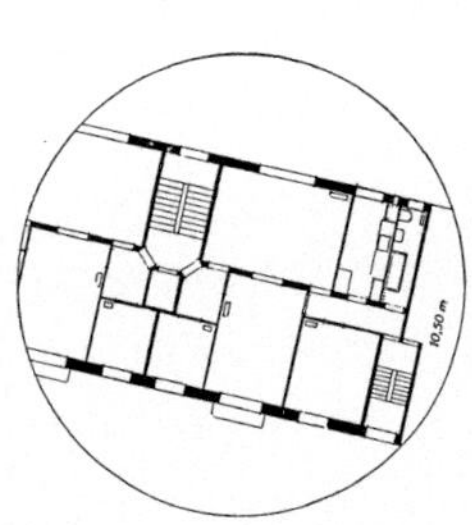

i
1 *Beliggenhed: Kastelsvej*
2 *Bygherre: Københavns alm. Boligselskab*
3 *Arkitekt: Ivar Bentsen og Peter Nielsen*
4 *Opførelsesaar: 1928*
5 *Bebyggelsesmaade: halvlukket karré*
6 *Værelsesantal: 3 værelser og 1 kammer*
7 *Bruttoareal: 125 m²*
8 *Etageareal: 6 etager*
9 *Sanitære installationer: bad og w.c. fælles, direkte belysning*
10 *Altansystem: 1 altan*
11 *Trappesystem: 2 trætrapper*
12 *Trappens beliggenhed: forskudt*
13 *Trappens orien ering: nord*
14 *Opholdsstuens orientering: nord*
15 *Antal lejligheder pr. trappe: 2*
16 *Bemærkninger: ingen*

Tegnet af B. Waagepetersen

types always only have conditioned meaning. But when a solution is termed a 'type' then it must (...) at a minimum not be too limited in terms of place and time so as to be generally useful. Economically, the type only has real significance when it is implemented simultaneously in one or more places in a large number."[25] To Völckers, as to many of his contemporaries, the problem of housing was the most important task of the architect. His book was not meant to provide a formula for the correct construction of housing, but to give examples: "It is not a book of recipes; it will show certain ways, yet not drag anyone along."[26] In 1941, Völckers published the more extensive book, *Das Grundrisswerk* (The Plan Drawing Book), which comprised 1,400 floor plans of built projects, ranging from housing to hospitals and schools, etc.[27] In the introduction, Völckers explains the importance of the floor plan, which is not simply something abstract and a starting point for the building in three dimensions, but is also the best way to understand the use of the building as an organism: "A residential building, a workshop, a department store, or any other building can only be assessed as regards its use value as based on the floor plan."[28] He recognized the importance of Neufert's *Bauentwurfslehre* yet argued that *Das Grundrisswerk* was a sort of supplement or companion to this.

The typological work of Klein, Neufert, and Völckers was important not only in a German context but internationally as well. In Denmark, for instance, the architect Kay Fisker explicitly referred to the work of Klein, to the *Wohnbaufibel* and to the *Bauentwurfslehre* in a survey published in 1936 of housing types built in Copenhagen between 1914 and 1936 [fig. 3].[29] Fisker's survey had been conducted with his students at the Royal Danish Academy's School of Architecture as a critical assessment of the possible compositions and distributions of floor plans and as a basis for further development of modern housing. He insisted that it was not a catalogue of standardized prototypes to be copied directly; not a pattern book. Moreover, this typology was conceived as a basis for transformation and invention. Types that only a decade ago had been preferred now seemed unsuitable to contemporary demands, Fisker noted, thereby indicating a process of gradual adjustment and refinement. Fisker also referred to a survey published in 1926 by architect Steen Eiler Rasmussen [fig. 4]. In this survey, Rasmussen had assessed 10 years of housing construction in Copenhagen. He presented a number of theoretical investigations, schematic plans that were not meant to serve as models for future buildings. As he stated: "We can investigate theoretically possible apartment plans following current demands."[30] In order to do so, he presented a number of plan drawings, all with a building depth of 10 m for reasons of comparability. "*We explicitly note that these drawings are not*

4 No. 1 – 4 of Steen Eiler Rasmussen's theoretical floor plan diagrams. Published in Steen Eiler Rasmussen, "Ti Aars Boligbyggeri i København," *Architekten* 9 – 10 (1926): 89.

1. *2 Værelser + 2 Værelser m. Kammer. Arealer: 2 V. 57,9 m²; 2 V.K. 68,1 m². Velegnet til Kakkelovnsopvarmning.*

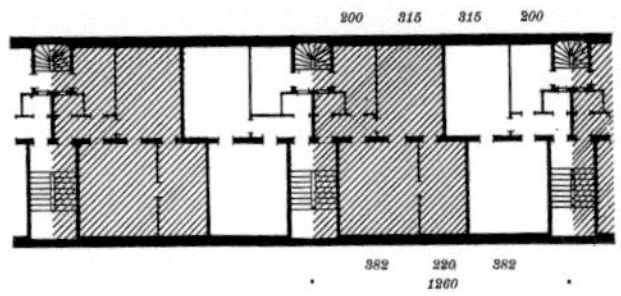

2. *2 Værelser + 2 Værelser m. Kammer. Arealer: 2 V. 57 m²; 2 V. K. 69 m². Egnet til Kakkelovnsopvarmning.*

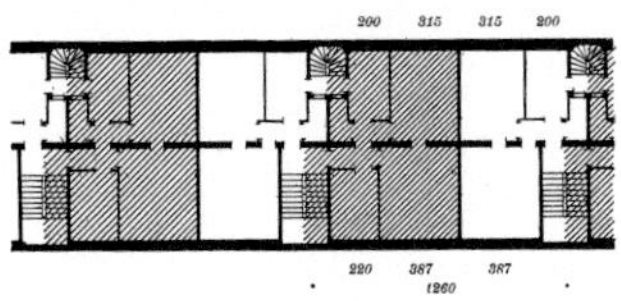

fig. 4

3. *2 Værelser m. Kammer. Arealer: 69,2 m². Velegnet til Kakkelovnsopvarmning.*

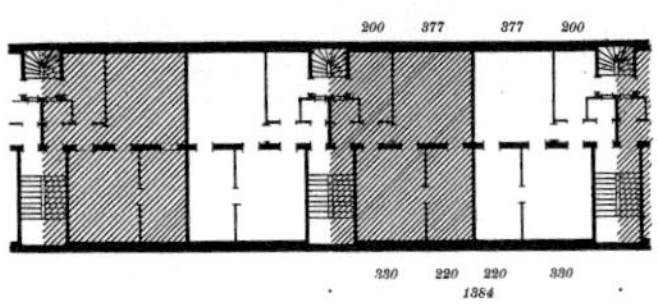

4. *2 Værelser m. Kammer. Arealer: 73,9 m². Egnet til Kakkelovnsopvarmning.*

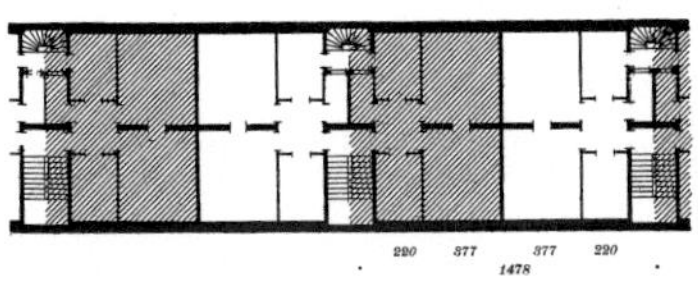

models, but simply a collection of possible apartments of 2 rooms, 2 rooms and a chamber, 3 rooms and 3 rooms and a chamber."[31] The plan diagrams allowed Rasmussen to make comparisons, and he further emphasized where and how these models had actually been realized in built housing projects. In his 1936 survey, Fisker emphasized in retrospect that even though Rasmussen's plans were theoretical, they had nevertheless contributed, "through the methodical analysis of plan options," to a clarification of plan forms during the following years.[32] This referred to the conflation of formal analysis and development as well as to the importance of the plan drawing or diagram in typological processes.

From Type to Norm

Not all Modern Movement protagonists were as interested in types as those mentioned in the previous section. In his article on typology, Rafael Moneo claims that the idea of type was in fact rejected by certain theoreticians of the Modern Movement. In Mies' architecture, type is irrelevant, architecture is fundamentally conceived as an endeavor in the manipulation of space, with little regard to program in the typological sense. The continuous spatiality in Mies' mature work accommodates whatever program is required without essential adjustments to the basic *parti*. This, however, was in conflict with another key agenda of the Modern Movement, argues Moneo, the industrialization of architecture, the promise of prefabrication, the prototypical rather than the typical.[33] As Moneo states: "The singularity of the architectural object which in the 19th century had permitted adaptability to site and flexibility for use within the framework of a structure was violently denied by the new architecture, committed to architecture as mass production."[34] With functionalism, the idea of type as providing a connection with the past was overrun and replaced by a different understanding of the fundamentals: "The type seemed to lose both the abstract and obscure characterization of Quatremère and the frozen description of the academics. Housing types appeared flexible, able to be adapted to the exigencies of both site and program. For Klein, the type, far from being an imposition of history, became a working instrument."[35] This is the notion of typology described by Anthony Vidler as "second typology." In this functionalist perspective, type could lead to standardization, with the aim of producing architecture more quickly and more cheaply, for the benefit of the victims of the housing crisis of that time.

Yet this notion of standardization also had other implications. Nader Vossoughian has pointed out different ways of perceiving a connection between type and standard in architecture, depending on the focus on mechanization, typification, or normalization. This last, argues Vossoughian, should be understood, following Michel Foucault, in the French sense of the term, by which "*normalization*" also translates as "standardization." Normalization and standardization conflated in certain bodypolitics in which they form part of the description of technical devices and their modes of operation.[36] As Vossoughian states:

> In broader terms, standardization must itself be understood as a process that transforms the subject and not just the object. Standardization participates in shaping our thoughts and not just our things. Over the course of the twentieth century, it increased the designer's dependency on handbooks and manuals, which centralized and homogenized the production of architectural knowledge.[37]

5 James Stirling, Michael Wilford and Associates, *Wissenschaftszentrum*, Berlin, site plan, 1979–87. Colored pencil on reprographic copy, 29.6 × 21 cm. Montréal, James Stirling/Michael Wilford fonds. Collection Centre Canadien d'Architecture/Canadian Centre for Architecture.

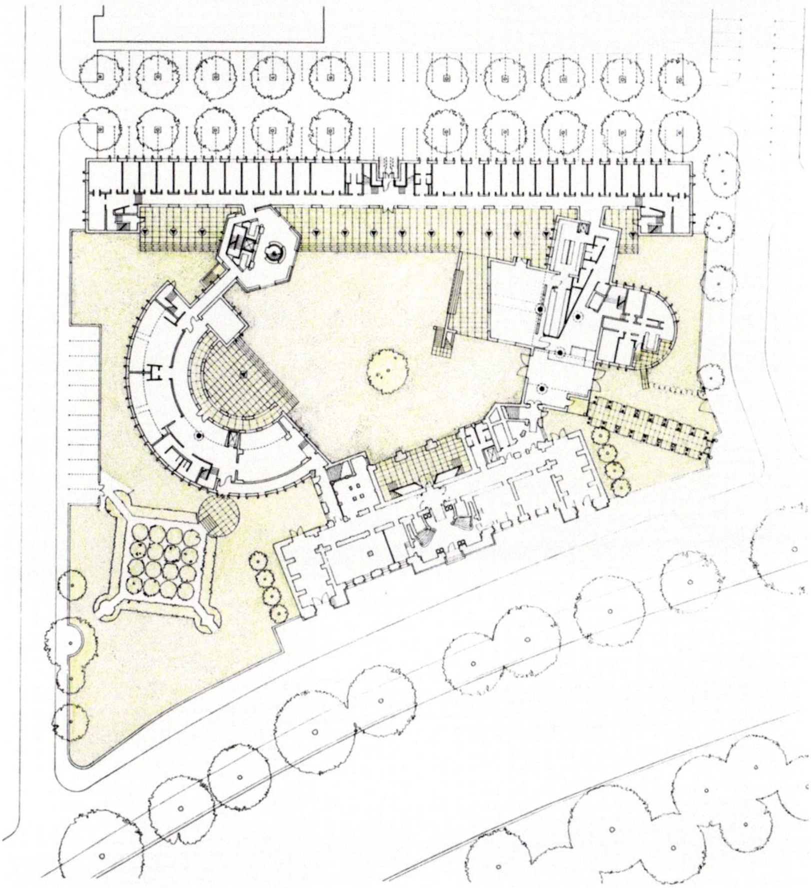

fig.5

After World War II, standardization was subject to criticism in the architectural discourse, yet surveys like Neufert's still influenced building norms and thus had a tremendous impact on the building industry in Western Europe. As Gernot Weckherlin states concerning the situation in Germany, "with totalitarian control of building production during the war, standards and norms became more and more legally binding regulations for architects and building contractors alike."[38] As also suggested by Vossoughian, type could become an instrument of standardization and thereby of control and homogenization, even if this had not been part of the vision of the Modern Movement architects.

This resonates with Robin Evans' critique of Alexander Klein's diagrams in his essay "Figures, Doors and Passages," published in 1978. Evans saw in these diagrams a particular bodypolitics and logic, "the logic now buried in the regulations, codes, design methods and rules-of-thumb which account for the day-to-day of contemporary housing."[39] As Christoph

Lueder has recently demonstrated, this is a somewhat unjust critique of Klein, who never himself proposed that his diagrams were intended to show the way to a "frictionless living," as Evans claimed. Klein did not attempt to separate people, Lueder points out, but to separate activities; his diagrams were received in many different ways, "as scientific instruments, as choreographic notation, as emblems of ideology, and as catalysts for thought."[40] As Lueder states: "While Taylorist conceptions of efficiency usually pertain to performance of physical tasks, Klein's graphical method places equal, even heightened, emphasis on regulating and purifying spatial perception. (...) Klein transposed Taylorist axioms from their origin in scientific management to the realms of perception and aesthetics."[41]

The rational, quasi-scientific approach to floor plans in typological investigations and the hope for more efficient and liberating housing designs may have been the ideal for many Modern Movement architects such as Klein, the CIAM group, Neufert, Völckers, Rasmussen, and Fisker. Nevertheless, such an endeavor lent itself easily also to standardization, which soon thereafter would demonstrate both its social and aesthetic inadequacies. It was this oppressive instrumentalization of their analytical and diagrammatic work and its potentials for optimization and homogenization, which was the real object of criticism during the 1970s, whether in the theoretical work of Moneo, Vidler, and Evans, in the designs of the Neo-rationalists, Rossi and the brothers Krier, or even during the 1980s, in the designs of Postmodernists such as James Stirling [fig. 5].

Typological Difference

The notion of typology gained increasing interest during the 1970s, as witnessed by the articles published by Anthony Vidler and Rafael Moneo. Influenced by semiotics and structuralism, typological searches were directed both at the communicative visibility of architecture and the deep structures of the historical city. While Vidler sees this "third typology" as a purely formal endeavor, stressing the autonomy of architecture, Moneo identifies a new kind of relationality in this particular notion of typology:

> The architectural object can no longer be considered as a single, isolated event because it is bounded by the world that surrounds it as well as by its history. It extends its life to other objects by virtue of its specific architectural condition, thereby establishing a chain of related events in which it is possible to find common formal structures.[42]

Historical layering could be exactly such a case of relations, as Aldo Rossi's work demonstrates. But relationality also discloses questions of difference, recalling contemporary investigations by poststructuralist philosophers such as Gilles Deleuze and Jacques Derrida. Following Deleuze, this would imply a critique of representation and identity, that is, the idea that a particular form could be repeated without alteration.[43] There was a painful revelation—seen from a Modern Movement perspective—that repetition understood as a mere copying is futile, but also an acknowledgment of the liberating potentials of the inherent differentiation. This relationality also indicates a stronger emphasis on the diagrammatic aspects of typology, its dependency on architectural media, including the floor plan drawing.

Today, this relational aspect seems to have grown even stronger. While digital modeling tools may epitomize a new paradigm in architectural representation, recent years have also witnessed what appears to be the increasing interest of certain architects in traditional techniques of line drawing, in particular of floor plans, but also of isometrics and hybrid forms that merge section and perspective. The reductive and abstract quality of the floor plan seems to fit well with analytical methods of comparability, particularly when it comes to comparing different solutions to specific problems and programs such as housing. Analytical work by architectural practices has resulted in a number of theoretical and investigatory publications, sometimes derived from studio teaching.[44] As a result of the teaching at the ETH Zurich, Emanuel Christ and Christoph Gantenbein have published several books on typology and the contemporary city [fig. 6]. As they state in *Typology: Paris, Delhi, São Paulo, Athens*:

> Most of the buildings that constitute the modern city are standard solutions. And they often appear at first glance to be uninteresting or even downright boring. But the typical architecture of the modern city is just that. And however tempting it may be for us architects to focus on the beautiful, ideal object, the perfect exception, we actually do consider the architectonic norm, the typical case, to be more important—and often also more intriguing in design terms.[45]

Mapping and schematizing floor plans for easy comparison forms the basis of a didactic approach that is not purely analytical, but also prescriptive. The empirical material is assembled not in order to be copied or with standardization in mind, but to form part of processes of examination and versioning in what may be described as a critical typology. This kind of typology, emphasizing the formal autonomy of architecture, nevertheless also considers architecture to be in a constant dialogue with whatever projects a society or individual may have or aspire to. Christ and Gantenbein define type as follows:

> We understand the term type to mean first and foremost the spatial organising principle that defines a building. The type is a direct consequence of the often precarious circumstances under which an architectural project unfolds in an urban context. (...) A successful urban type correlates the complex urban reality in its entirety. (...) Urban types, one might say, are the quintessence of a city's architecture.[46]

fig. 6

On the one hand, Christ and Gantenbein thereby align with the "third typology" of the 1970s, in a search for deep urban structure. On the other hand, the "elemental, institutional, and mechanistic typologies" which Anthony Vidler identified as resulting in fragmentation now seem to have become history themselves, a new kind of urban tissue for architects to explore. This points to an alternative reading of typology, not as formal structure but as a matter of *structuring* and—since this process is in constant formation, fluctuating between affirmation and variance—as a matter of *difference.*

At this point, we need to think of typological floor plan diagrams less as representations and more as diagrams in the sense of instruments for thinking. This potential has historical precedents. In this light, Klein's diagrams appear less as instruments of reasoning and control and more as catalysts or even choreographic notations. As Vidler has pointed out, architectural drawing is in itself "coded": "the diagram has held a privileged place in the development of modern architecture as at once responding to the aesthetics of rationalism and the authority of functionalism."[47] Durand's method of systematizing architecture according to material resources and an economy of time can be understood as "diagrammatic." Vidler traces the importance of the diagram in modern architecture and importantly notes the connection of architectural analysis and invention by pointing, for instance, to the friendship between Le Corbusier and the formally oriented art historian Henri Focillon, and to the Neoclassicist interest in linearity and its theorization following Johann Joachim Winckelmann.[48] Formalist art history contributed to "the diagramming of space and structure," argues Vidler, for instance through the work of Paul Frankl and A. E. Brinckmann around World War I and, during the immediate post-World War II years, in the analytical work of Rudolf Wittkower and Colin Rowe, diagrammatizing the work of Palladio and Le Corbusier, respectively.[49]

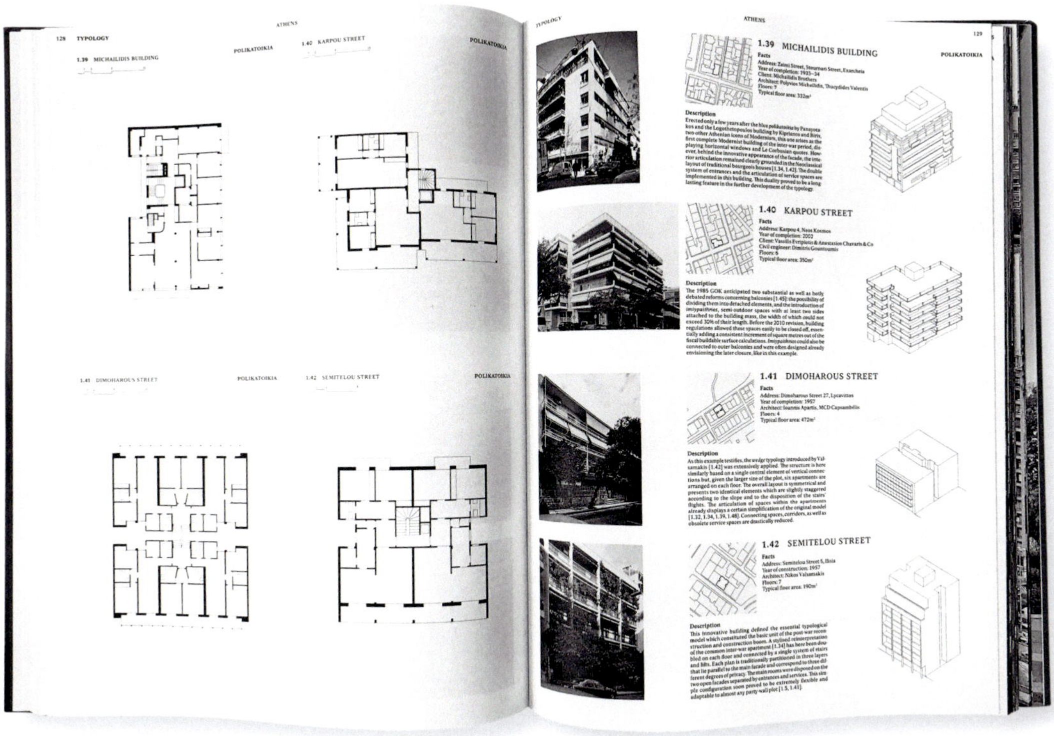

Spread from Emanuel Christ, Victoria Easton, Christoph Gantenbein, and Cloé Gattigo, eds., *Typology: Paris, Delhi, São Paulo, Athens* (Zurich: Park Books, 2015), 128–29.

Today, floor plans can take on the role of diagrammatic evidence of types in formation, of typological difference. The type has a double nature, argue Christ and Gantenbein; it represents an optimization of particular urban conditions, tested through hundreds of instances, yet it is concurrently instable, in flux: "The type represents the optimal solution as well as the (provisional) result of an on-going process. Since it is never more than an interim state of an evolution, it is instable."[50] As they note, type becomes type only by quantity, that is, when the singular building enters into a relationship with the city. Type is not autonomous, neither is it a mere reflection of a particular social condition. A process of subtle adaptation occurs, whether conditioned by changing functions, technologies, regulations, etc. Herein lies a fourth reading of the concept of an architectural typology: neither as a search for architecture's foundations in biological terms, a schematic functionalism, nor an autonomous, introspective formal pursuit, but as a diagrammatic apparatus for both spatial and social differentiation.

1 Charles George Ramsey and Harold Sleeper, *Architectural Graphic Standards for Architects, Engineers, Decorators, Builders and Draftsmen* (New York: J. Wiley & Sons, 1932); Ernst Neufert, *Bauentwurfslehre: Handbuch für den Baufachmann, Bauherrn, Lehrenden und Lernenden* (Berlin: [s.n.], 1936).

2 Peter Ebner, Eva Herrmann, Roman Höllbacher, Markus Kuntscher, and Ulrike Wietzorrek, "In the Residential Building: Type, Style, Model. An Introduction," in *Typology+, Innovative residential architecture* (Basel: Birkhäuser, 2010), 17.

3 Günter Pfeifer and Per Brauneck, *Residential Buildings: A Typology* (Basel: Birkhäuser, 2015), 30–31.

4 Ibid., back cover.

5 Rafael Moneo, "On Typology," *Oppositions* 13 (Summer 1978): 23.

6 Ibid., 24.

7 Ibid., 28.

8 Anthony Vidler, "The Third Typology," in *Oppositions Reader*, ed. K. Michael Hays (New York: Princeton University Press, 1998), 13–16, originally published in *Oppositions* 7 (Winter 1976): 1–4.

9 Ibid., 13.

10 Ibid., 14.

11 Antoine Picon, "Jean-Nicolas-Louis Durand," *Arch+* 233 (2018): 37. My translation.

12 Sylvia Lavin, *Quatremère de Quincy and the Invention of a Modern Language of Architecture* (Cambridge, MA, and London: MIT Press, 1992) 86.

13 Ibid., 88.

14 Anthony Vidler, "The Idea of Type: The Transformation of the Academic Ideal, 1750–1830," in *Oppositions Reader*, ed. K. Michael Hays (New York: Princeton University Press, 1998), 443, originally published in *Oppositions* 8 (1977),: 94–115.

15 Moneo, "On Typology," 32.

16 Alexander Klein, "Versuch eines graphischen Verfahrens zur Bewertung von Kleinwohnungsgrundrissen," *Wasmuths Monatshefter für Baukunst* 11, no. 7 (1927): 296–98.

17 Christoph Lueder, "Evaluator, Choreographer, Ideologue, Catalyst: The Disparate Reception Histories of Alexander Klein's Graphical Method," *The Journal of the Society of Architectural Historians* 76, no. 1 (March 2017): 82–106.

18 Eric Mumford, *The CIAM Discourse on Urbanism, 1928–1960* (Cambridge, MA and London: MIT Press, 2000), 29–30.

19 Ibid., 41–42. The exhibition toured Europe after the Congress and the talks presented at the Congress were published along with the plans in the first CIAM book: Internationale Kongress für Neues Bauen und Städtisches Hochbauamt in Frankfurt am Main, ed., *Die Wohnung für das Existenzminimum* (Frankfurt am Main: Englert and Schlosser, 1930).

20 Gernot Weckherlin, "Ernst Neufert's Architect's Data: Anxiety, Creativity and Authorial Abdication," in *Architecture and Authorship*, ed. Tim Anstey, Katja Grillner, and Rolf Gullström-Hughes (London: Black Dog Publishing, 2007), 153.

21 Wolfgang Voigt, "'Triumph der Gleichform und des Zusammenpassens': Ernst Neufert und die Normung in der Architektur," in *Bauhaus-Moderne in Nationalsozialismus: Zwischen Anbiederung und Verfolgung*, ed. Winfred Nerdinger and Bauhaus-Archiv, Berlin (Munich: Prestel, 1993), 182. My translation: "eine Population gesichtsloser Menschen, die sich in Hunderten von Momentaufnahmen mit unerschütterlicher Vernunft an die Arbeit macht oder zur Ruhe begibt, macht das Buch zum surrealistischen Panorama modernen Lebens."

22 Weckherlin, "Ernst Neufert's Architects' Data," 151.

23 Otto Völckers, *Wohnbaufibel—für Anfänger und solche, die glauben es nicht mehr zu sein* (Stuttgart: Julius Hoffmann Verlag, 1932).

24 Ibid., 100. My translation, "Typen schaffen heist: Form und Zusammenbau von Zweckgebilden auf möglichst wenige Vorbilder von Bestform zurückzuführen."

25 Ibid., 100. My translation: "Grundrisstypen haben immer nur bedingte Bedeutung. Wenn man aber eine Lösung als 'Typ' bezeichnet, so muss sie (...) immerhin in nicht zu engen örtlichen und zeitlichen Grenzen allgemein brauchbar sein. Wirtschaftlich hat der Typ nur dann tatsächliche Bedeutung, wenn er gleichzeitig an einer oder mehreren Stellen in größerer Anzahl ausgeführt wird."

26 Ibid., 3. My translation, "Es will kein Rezeptbuch sein; es will Wege zeigen, aber es will niemand des Wegs tragen."

27 Otto Völckers, *Das Grundrisswerk* (Stuttgart: Julius Hoffmann Verlag, 1941).

28 Ibid., 8. My translation, "Ein Wohnhaus, eine Werkstätte, ein Kaufhaus ode jedes andere Bauwerk kann hinsichtlich seines Gebrauchszwecks nur vom Grundriss her beurteilt werden."

29 Kay Fisker, "Københavnske boligtype fra 1914 til 1936," *Arkitekten* 6–7 (1936).

30 Steen Eiler Rasmussen, "Ti Aars Boligbyggeri i København," *Arkitekten* 9–10 (1926): 86. My translation, "Man ka rent theoretisk undersøge, hvilke Muligheder der er for Lejlighedsplaner efter de nu gængse Krav."

31 Ibid., 86. My translation, "*Det maa udtrykkeligt bemærkes, at disse Tegninger ikke er Forbilleder*, men kun er en Samling af alle mulige Lejligheder med 2 Værelser, 2 Værelser og Kammer, Værelser og 3 Værelser og Kammer.

32 Fisker, "Københavnske boligtyper," 113.

33 Moneo, "On Typology," 32–33.

34 Ibid., 33.

35 Ibid., 35.

36 Nader Vossoughian, "Standardizatior Reconsidered: *Normierung* in and after Ernst Neufert's *Bauentwurfslehre* (1936)," *Grey Room* 54 (2014): 35.

37 Ibid., 49.

3 Weckherlin, "Ernst Neufert's rchitects' Data," 154.

9 Robin Evans, "Figures, Doors and assages," in *Translations from Drawing*) *Building and Other Essays* (London: rchitectural Association, 1997), 85–86.

0 Lueder, "Evaluator, Choreographer, 'eologue, Catalyst," 82, 88.

Ibid., 89.

2 Moneo, "On Typology," 40.

3 Gilles Deleuze, *Difference and epetition*, trans. Paul Patton (London nd New York: Columbia University ress, 1994).

Emanuel Christ, Victoria Easton, and hristoph Gantenbein, eds., *Typology: 'ong Kong, Rome, New York, Buenos ires* (Zurich: Park Books, 2012); manuel Christ, Victoria Easton, hristoph Gantenbein, and Cloé Gattigo, ds., *Typology: Paris, Delhi, São Paulo, thens* (Zurich: Park Books, 2015). or similar, contemporary typological vestigations, see for instance the ublications by the Laboratory for the vestigation of Form at the EPFL, ausanne, and their series of publica-ons, *Architecture Without Content.* ee also Martin Fröhlich, Anja Fröhlich, ago P. Borges, and Sebastian F. Lippok, ds., *Plans and Images: An Archive of rojects on Typology in Architecture 013–2018* (Zurich: Park Books, 2019), nd Dogma, *The Room of One's Own: he Architecture of the (Private) Room* Ailan: Black Square, 2017). The project esented by Mette Johanne Hübsch-ann in this book is yet another example this sort of typology.

Emanuel Christ and Christoph antenbein, "Modern Cities," in *ypology: Paris, Delhi, São Paulo, thens*, ed. Emanuel Christ, Victoria aston, Christoph Gantenbein, and Cloé attigo (Zurich: Park Books, 2015), 3.

Ibid., 4.

Anthony Vidler, "Diagrams of agrams: Architectural Abstraction d Modern Representation," *Rep-sentations* 72 (Autumn, 2000): 9.

Ibid., 8–9, 12.

Ibid., 14–16.

Christ and Gantenbein, "Modern ties," 5.

Martino Tattara

The Project of Mapping

The Design Agency of Drawing City Plans

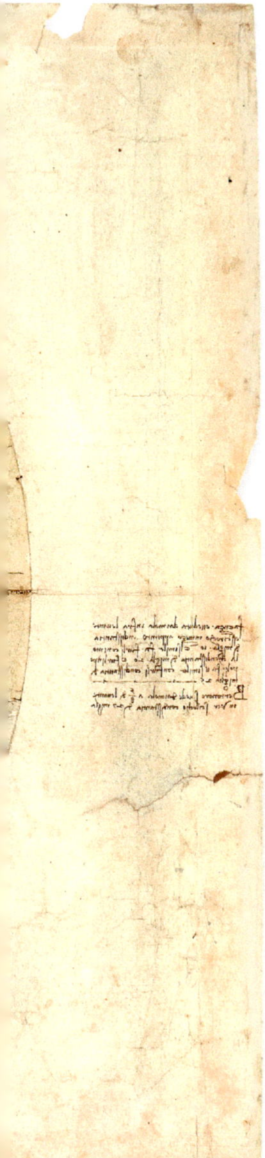

fig. 1

During recent decades, doing research in architecture has become a common undertaking. In research work, architects have proved to be particularly adapted at observing and representing existing spatial conditions—from buildings to larger territories—by deploying traditional design tools in order to produce spatial knowledge. This practice, broadly known as "mapping," has been criticized as a futile exercise in a time when architecture seems increasingly to withdraw from the possibility of engaging with the large-scale project of the city. While urban research has never been as thriving as it is today, both architecture and urban planning have revealed an incapacity to participate effectively in the project of the city. Whereas "mapping" today relies on sophisticated representation tools enhanced by the possibility of managing and controlling large amounts of data, the origin of such activity dates back to the tradition of drawing plans of cities, when architects were often both designers and cartographers. The former overlapping of these two professions is indicative of the fact that plan drawings of existing cities, in many instances,

1 Leonardo da Vinci, *A Map of Imola*, 1502. Black chalk, stylus lines, pen and ink, colored washes, 44 × 60.2 cm. London, Royal Collection Trust.

go beyond the field of representation and contain an implicit projective dimension, thereby overcoming the divide between the practices of mapping and design.

The production of plans of existing cities comprises a process of abstraction based on specific choices concerning the ways in which the complexity of the urban condition is simplified and reduced into the two-dimensional space of paper. These choices concern the selection of the elements that are reproduced in plan, the establishment of hierarchies among them, their omission or simplification, as well as the specific representation techniques through which the drawing is constructed, such as the use of colors or the specific system of notation to represent objects. All this is far from neutral and a simple application of drawing conventions; on the contrary, each plan of cities is always a project in itself, responding to the specific agency behind the making of a plan of a city.

fig. 2 fig. 3

My attempt is to draft a first possible index of large-scale plan drawings of cities through the exploration of selected cases, from the Roman *Forma Urbis Romae* to Sangallo's plan of Pisa, from the famous Nolli map of Rome to Aldo Rossi's plan of Zurich; cases that, despite their differences, allow us to discuss the potential, meaning, and impact of these drawings beyond the scope of representation. Discussing the ambivalence of these drawings, it is interesting to start by considering the meaning of the term "plan" and its etymology, since the word obviously describes both the making of a drawing of any object by projection onto a horizontal plane, and also the act of planning.[1] This is similar to the Italian word for drawing—*disegno*—where the mental process of creation and its material expression overlap. The etymological root of *plan*, recognized in the Proto-Indo-European term "pele-," indicates something "flat" as well as the action of "spreading,"[2] thus clearly displaying the potential transformation of any urban formation. The production of a plan of a city was in many cases motivated by the need, desire, or intention to intervene in the city's structure, whether through concrete physical transformation (e. g., the construction of fortifications or the addition of a building) or through administration (e. g., for fiscal purposes).

The *Forma Urbis Romae*: Defining the Value of Things

Although it was during the Renaissance that the plan of the city was first developed, largely as a visual record of measured spaces,[3] some exceptional plan drawings date back to Roman times. The territory of the early Roman Empire was widely marked by the work of land surveyors (the *agrimensores*) and several written testimonies suggest that at that time plans of Rome already existed. The *Forma Urbis Romae* [fig. 2–4], a large engraved marble plan of the city, created during the reign of Emperor Septimius Severus and

2 Fragment of the *Forma Urbis Romae* (detail of Porticus Aemilias), between 203 and 208 AD. Incision on marble, approx. 183 × 145 cm. Rome, Museo della Civiltà Romana.

3 Fragment of the *Forma Urbis Romae* (detail of the Aedis Iunonis), between 203 and 208 AD. Incision on marble, 21 × 24 cm. Rome, Museo della Civiltà Romana.

fig. 4

4 Fragment of the *Forma Urbis Romae*, between 203 and 208 AD. Incision on marble, 52 × 77 cm. Rome, Museo della Civiltà Romana.

completed between 203 and 208 CE, is certainly the most exceptional city plan both in terms of size (about 235 m^2) and the many surviving fragments. The average drawing scale is 1:240/50, but important buildings are represented at a larger scale. The plan is a remarkable attempt to use conventional notations for all details, from columns to staircases, from trees to bases of statues. Walls are mostly drawn as single lines—the engravings depict almost every ground floor room in the city—yet on some important buildings (temples, aqueducts, the pilasters of the Porticus Aemilia, the structure of the Septizodium, and a few other monuments[4]) lines are drawn double, representing in these cases the real solid thickness of brick walls or columns. In addition, the space between the double lines was slightly recessed and colored in red, standing out boldly amidst the thin single-line pattern of the walls of other buildings, making these architectural elements emerge from the entire representation.[5] Contrary to the representation of each and every architectural component of the city, the plan omits all natural features—the river Tiber is surprisingly absent—and any administrative notations, indicating that what is significant in the city of Rome is what humans have built.[6]

The specific role of such a plan is not certain and has been widely debated among scholars. The most commonly accepted explanation interprets the plan as serving a utilitarian purpose in support of the office of the urban prefect or facilitating the work of *vigiles*—the municipal police, who also acted as a fire service.[7] Yet, engraving a cadastral plan in marble does not seem a reasonable thing to do, since such a property register would quickly be out of date and difficult to update with new transactions.[8] The plan also reveals many ambiguities in notations (e.g., in the meanings of the single line) and it is full of inaccuracies, which, together with the difficulty in accessing and literally looking at a document of that size, corroborate the idea that the *Forma Urbis* was in fact probably not designed with a utilitarian purpose in mind.

Other scholars have interpreted the plan differently, as part of a propaganda campaign to celebrate the extensive works of urban renovation undertaken by the emperor.[9] This hypothesis is reinforced by the observation of previous plans of the city, such as the one by Vespasianus and displayed in Rome in the Forum of Peace, and the one by Augustus that was the outcome of an earlier survey of the city.[10] All three emperors, Vespasian, Augustus, and Severus, gained power after a period of major upheaval and turmoil. Each of them was able to restore order, confidence, and prosperity, and, according to historian Liba Taub, they "instituted important reforms and initiated extensive building programs."[11] Their plans of Rome were therefore public records of their achievements, symbols of their reforms at the service of their political promotion, but also attempts to visually portray the regained sense of order.

And yet the *Forma Urbis* is different from all the other maps in its extensive representation of the city's "private space"—in the sense of spaces of dwellings, commercial buildings such as shops and warehouses, minor neighborhood baths, and other urban facilities. The precise and extensive representation of the "interior" organization of this private space, all indicated by single lines, has to do with the fact that Romans viewed the separation between public and private differently than we do. A great many aspects of Roman public life occurred within privately owned spaces. The *domus* was not just the space of private family life, but was primarily the space where business and social activities were performed by the head of the family and other members.

The main tool to distinguish public and private spaces was the juridical concept of property as addressed in the Roman law. The distinction between private and public was not based on economic or planning purposes, but was related to the concept of use, and therefore dictated by function. In Roman law, sacred and public buildings were excluded from commerce since they, according to historian Yan Thomas, were "inalienable and not-appropriable."[12] Precisely to define the juridical nature of things as commodities and therefore as assessable, available, and appropriable things, it was necessary for a part of these things to be excluded from the area of appropriation and exchange, and therefore destined to the gods or the city.[13] Thomas clearly explains how the Romans operated a separation between things that could be the object of commercial exchange and those that were part of the state's patrimony and therefore considered unavailable.[14] The *res publica* comprised all those lands, constructions, and infrastructures that served for public use and that were available to be freely used and accessed. Differently, other things that did not have a public use, although belonging to public authorities, could be sold by the state. Sacred and public things, to be excluded from the possibility of being sold or bought, needed to be clearly identified, either through a process of dedication to a god of a portion of ground, or through the precise demarcation of their limits, through for example the deployment of *cippi* and the careful work of the land surveyors. These sacred things were meant to remain unavailable even if they were destroyed by an earthquake. As Thomas argues, other things such as matter would become patrimonial through the encounter with its first "owner," as for a craftsman forging a product out of simple matter through the work of his hands. In order to exchange such things on the market, values needed to be defined so that the thing subject to the exchange would be represented by the value itself. It is interesting to note how for Romans the term *pecunia* simultaneously identifies money, the value of a thing, and the thing itself: the thing and its price were two concepts perfectly adhering to each other, to the point that "the value represented

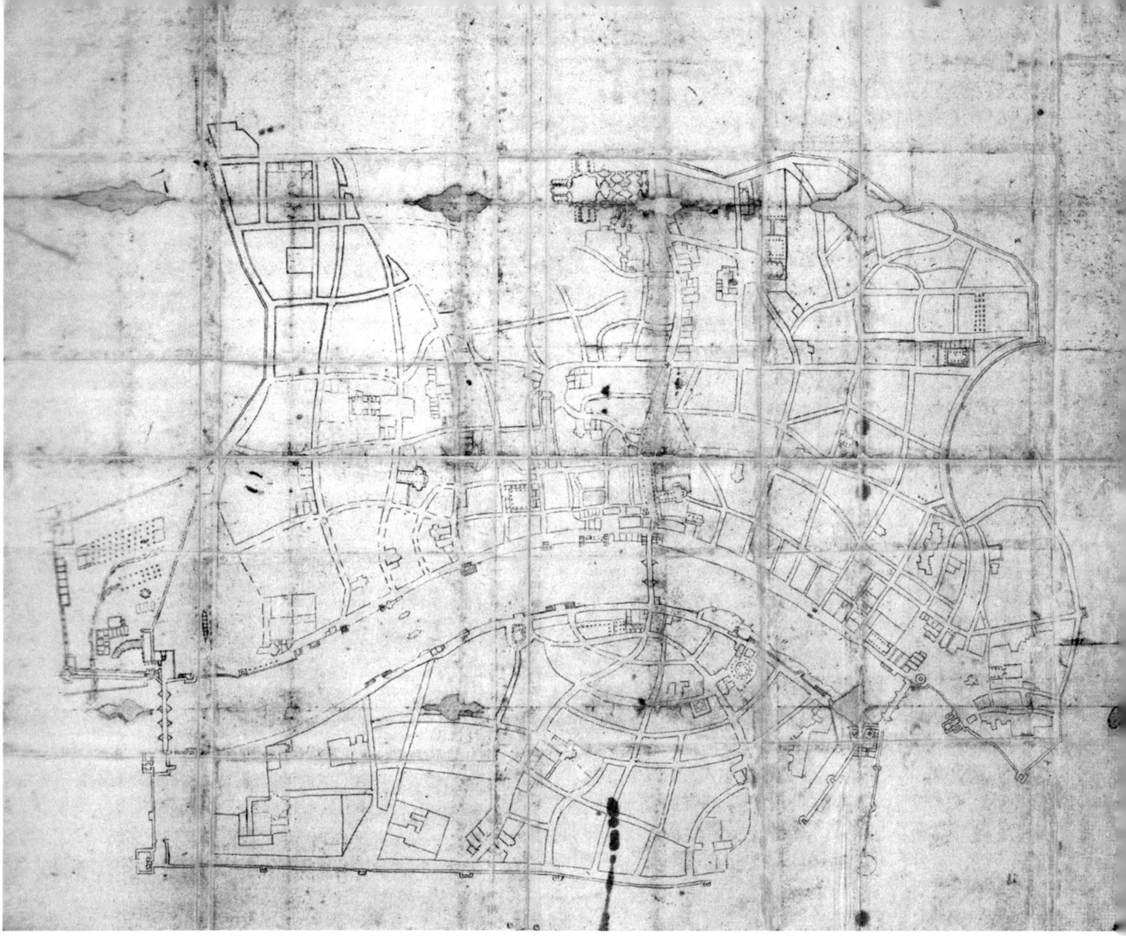

the identity of the thing."[15] It was perhaps for this reason that the *Forma Urbis Romae* gives account of both public and private buildings in great detail. While public and sacred buildings were drawn by representing the real thickness of walls and structures, private buildings such as private houses were carefully detailed in their internal configuration through the representation with single lines of wall partitions, in an unprecedented effort to make things geometrically representable and therefore measurable and commensurable in terms of their value.

The Plans of Imola and Pisa: From Surveying to Urban Reform

Vitruvius defined the three main techniques of architectural representation as *ichnographia*, *orthographia,* and *scenographia*: the plan, the elevation, and the three-dimensional view, respectively. While the last two corresponded to the physical appearance of architecture, the first was the abstract drawing of an invisible dimension—that yet allowed for the value of things to be determined.

If medieval representations of cities were mostly ideal and conventional, those of the Renaissance responded to a new demand for topographic information. Following the Vitruvian recommendations for the drawing and the design of buildings in threefold form, representations of cities were now developed mostly through plans, elevations, and linear perspective.[16] While the latter were originally favored—and perhaps the most extraordinary document of that sort is the bird's-eye view of Venice published by the painter and printmaker Jacopo de Barberi in 1500—this technique was slowly superseded by abstract plan drawings. The original purpose of these plans is in many instances still ambiguous and debated.[17] Many historians have thought that the architects of the time were often asked to act as cartographers and produce plans of cities through their expertise of geometry, mathematical principles, and drawing techniques. Urban plans produced at the beginning of the 16th century may nevertheless be understood as spatial representations for testing design ideas, testifying to the rising ambition of architects to participate in reforming cities through architecture.[18]

fig. 5

Perhaps the first "real" plan of a city, Leonardo da Vinci's famous drawing of Imola (1502) [fig. 1], can be recognized as the city plan where the shift towards the degree of abstract thought required, according to architectural historian James Ackerman, to "visualize a settlement built on uneven terrain,"[19] is fully achieved. The surveying, geometrical, and representational techniques inherent in the plan have been largely explored: Leonardo's plan of Imola is probably the first fully orthogonal plan of a Renaissance city and the first fully geometrical, structured representation of a city.[20] Less attention has been given to the purpose of this drawing. Generally, scholars suggest a link between the plan and the commission that Leonardo received in 1502 from the duke Cesare Borgia to rethink the fortification systems of several towns in the territories surrounding Cesena, at the time dramatically marked by violent conflicts.[21] This is probably true for several other maps that Leonardo developed in those years, including those for the cities of Urbino and Cesena, in which the plan representations focus exclusively on the fortifications, omitting the urban fabric contained by the city walls. Yet it is clear that the plan of Imola is an exception, since it portrays not only the fortifications but also the urban blocks, the road structure, and the surrounding agricultural landscape. If the plan had been destined for the use of Cesare Borgia, it would have been logical for Leonardo to write the accompanying captions from left to right instead of in his idiosyncratic mirror writing.[22] Also, had the plan been the outcome of his surveying activity, it would be inconceivable why it does not represent the actual situation of the fortress, but rather a proposal to change it, and why the Via Emilia, which crosses straight through the city, is here represented as a more undulating road than it really was.[23]

5 Giuliano da Sangallo, *Pisa Unfinished*, 1512–13. Drawing on parchment, 135 × 166.5 cm. Florence, Gabinetto dei Disegni e delle Stampe degli Uffizi.

fig. 6

Although it cannot be excluded that Cesare Borgia knew or even possessed the map, this was most likely a private document that Leonardo prepared for himself. The plan is the result of what at the time was an ongoing exercise in plan representation of both cities and landscape, as manifest also by a series of large-scale maps of Tuscany,[24] in which Leonardo depicts landscape features in plan in a realistic manner for the first time. All these drawings show the emergence of a new type of representation and of efforts to refine it, as if the three-dimensional *scenographia* were no longer a working tool sufficient to formulate ideas about the architecture of the city.

The unfinished plan of Pisa, executed between 1512 and 1513[25] and attributed to Giuliano da Sangallo [fig. 5], is a simple line drawing, depicting the street pattern of the city, with a few notable buildings in higher planimetric detail. The plan supports the interpretation that Sangallo regarded the city as a spatial, architectural object to be drawn with an orthogonal outline, but it also reveals how for architects of the era, "the borders between surveying,

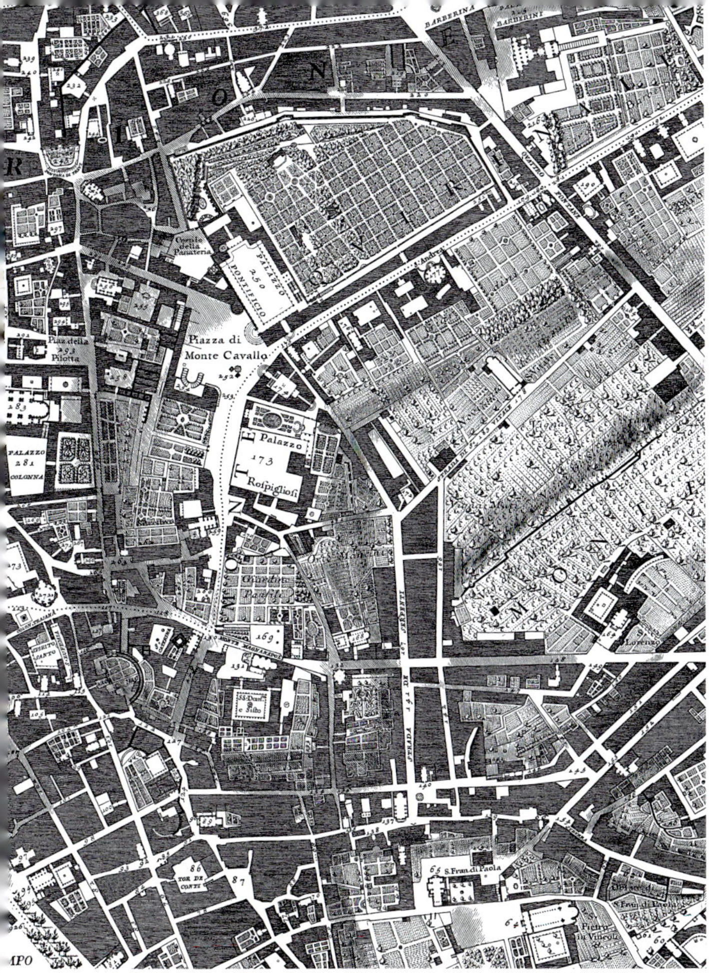

6 Giovanni Battista Nolli, *Nuova Pianta di Roma*, 1748. Etching, 171.6 × 205.5 cm (12 sheets, each: 42.6 × 67.7 cm).

interpreting, and designing were blurred,"[26] as architectural historian Lucia Nuti puts it. Often compared with Leonardo's drawing of Imola, the plan of Pisa has been mostly overlooked because it was considered to be an unfinished sketch. On the contrary, what is crucial to Sangallo's drawing is not the survey of the topographic information of the city. The plan is obviously characterized by a set of divergences and distortions. Parts such as monuments drafted in higher detail reveal several omissions, variability in scale, and the addition of urban parts and architectural elements that did not exist at the time in Pisa.[27] These interventions were by no means the result of the architect's architectural arbitrariness, but responded to the desire to adhere to the Albertian and Vitruvian ideas on architecture, and are in line with the social and political climate in the city at the moment when the drawing was created.[28]

With the plan of Pisa, Sangallo seems to test the possible renewal of the city through selected architectural and urban interventions. Pisa was going through a period of urban and economic decay, its medieval structures were in poor condition, the riverbanks had largely collapsed, and several parts of the city had been transformed into swamps. The plan of Pisa may be understood as a sort of program for urban reform, communicated through the drawing in plan of strategic urban interventions to be developed over a long period of time. In the plan, the peripheral areas inside the city walls, at that time devoid of structures, were transformed into new neighborhoods through a proposed sequence of roads and small squares. Along the river banks, Sangallo proposes the clearing of all utilitarian structures that were affecting the image of the city. In the medieval urban fabric, Sangallo focuses specifically on those churches that were the most distant from the architectural principles of Alberti and Brunelleschi, such as Santa Caterina, San Francesco, and Santo Sepolcro.[29] In the plan representation of the church of Santa Cristina located at the river Arno, the church is transformed in its architectural configuration through a circular portico added to the existing structure, and the entire urban configuration is modified by rotating the church by 90°, so that it offers its main elevation to the river. Far from freewheeling fantasies, Sangallo selected the objects of his urban project carefully, deciding to operate on those architectures that were already affected by reform and transformation, building on previous and ongoing interventions of renovation. His proposals need to be read within the political ambition of the *signoria* of Florence, which at the time extended its control over Pisa, to change the current condition of the city not only by militarily controlling it but also by offering it new perspectives.

If Sangallo's unfinished plan of Pisa is a drawing in between a survey and the expression of an ambition for a large urban reform, it surprisingly brings to mind one of the best-known plans of a city, often considered the blueprint of contemporary "mapping," Giovanni Battista Nolli's 1748 plan of Rome [fig. 6]. This document, which has been thoroughly analyzed in both its making[30] and its meaning in relation to the changing political conditions of the city in the 18th century, clearly reveals a subtle agency of plan representation.[31] It delineates the residential fabric and provides detailed and precise plans for a number of selected elements such as churches, theaters, palace atria, and courtyards, drawn as *poché* within the built mass. Many have recognized in Nolli's plan the differentiation between public (accessible) and private spaces, yet according to Pier Vittorio Aureli, it instead introduces a separation "between architectural space and urban space,"[32] in that the "blacked sections indicate parts of the city that were adaptable to change and reform, while the architectural poché indicates parts that were more fixed."[33] The Nolli plan was therefore a useful tool at a time when the city, rather than adding new monuments, witnessed a shift towards larger urban reforms. The residential and commercial spaces, devoid of clear planimetric notation and represented as abstract line patterns, are thereby represented as governed by non-representable logics, denoting the potential adaptability and transformability of these spaces conceived as being beyond the confines of architecture.

Aldo Rossi's Plan of Zurich: The Pedagogy of the Architectural Plan

Since Nolli, the production of plans of cities has become more and more the work of specialized cartographers. It would only be in recent years, with the rise of the paradigm of urban research, that architects started mapping the city again and representing it, among other representation techniques, through plan drawings.

One of the first architects who again became particularly interested in urban analysis and research was Aldo Rossi, especially during his first years of work as a university professor in the late 1960s. The main outcomes of Aldo Rossi's early teaching activities are a series of texts, research reports, publications, and large-scale plan drawings of cities; and not the students' architectural and urban proposals. In addition to the plans of Pavia, Padua, and Milan, the most relevant and best known is probably the plan of Zurich, the "Survey 1:1000 of the ground floor inside the perimeter of the Baroque walls" of 1973 [fig. 7].[34] This "Rossi Plan," a large-scale drawing of the historical core of the city, is drawn in a peculiar way. The representation omits any detail of the open space, which is left completely white, and focuses exclusively on the architectural features of the urban fabric by carefully surveying and representing without any differentiation the city's monuments and the ordinary residential buildings. The city appears as a constellation of dense urban blocks, appearing as large architectural islands navigating freely on the white space of the paper. Within each block, buildings are drawn similarly, as if a vast horizontal cross section at ground floor level had been traced through the entire city inside the walls. Differently from the ancient *Forma Urbis Romae*, walls are not drawn as single lines, but are represented taking full account of their original thickness. The resulting image portrays the city in its architectural consistency made of walls, stairs, windows, and columns, with all sectioned parts hatched in black.

The plan was produced collectively by half of Rossi's students at the ETH Zurich, who were occupied with this drawing for the entire semester—and beyond—through surveying, extensive archival work in the city cadaster and redrawing. The other half of the student group focused, more traditionally, on developing an architectural proposal without, most of the time, attracting the interest of the professor. It may have been difficult for the first half to participate in a "design semester" without producing an architectural project.

fig. 7

7 Aldo Rossi and collaborators, *Map of Zurich*, Survey 1:1000 of the ground floor inside the perimeter of the Baroque walls, 1973. Drawing on paper, 167 × 138 cm.

Yet for Rossi the plan was a fundamental "project" tool, not in offering design solutions, but in designating a learning field within which students, sooner or later, would be able to locate their design work as part of a progressive evolution of urban history. While the large plan of the city gives a precise account of typologies, urban morphology, and urban events as inexorably fixed in time, the drawing was accompanied by an extensive research report in which primary elements, residential typologies, and the various historical steps of the city evolution were carefully presented in chronological order. Rossi's plan is the tangible manifestation of his core interest as a teacher, namely the search for a definition of a possible "scientific" approach to the teaching of architectural design. For Rossi, this search was identified with the relationship between architecture and urban analysis.

In this respect, this large urban plan is perhaps the most striking outcome, and perhaps the symbol, of Rossi's (early) pedagogical project. After working as an assistant to Carlo Aymonino in Venice (1963–66), Rossi taught at the Politecnico di Milano (1968–71) and the ETH Zurich (1972–75), where he held a visiting professorship following his dismissal from the Italian university for his perceived abuse of experimentation. Influenced by the transformation in the school organization following the students' protests of 1963[35] and breaking with conventional academic hierarchies, Rossi's early teaching activity was based on the idea of the classroom as the space in which professor, assistants, and students actively and jointly develop a common line of research. The ambition to define a school of *tendenza* (a term that would later be reduced to the connotation of a school with a distinct architectural language) aimed in Rossi's understanding for a school based on the "dialectic exchange between students and teachers," working towards the definition of a "field of application and scientific research tools based on primarily formal parameters."[36]

Another pillar of Rossi's pedagogical project was also bridging the theoretical space of the classroom with the practical space of design, revealing them as complementary and irreducible aspects of a common and single approach. In contrast to the professional character of education in the 1950s in Italy, the idea of assigning research tasks to students, by sharing with them vast bibliographies that crossed disciplinary borders (with texts from art, literature, philosophy, cinema, sociology, urban geography, and politics) and, above all, by building up a theoretical ground through lectures, seminars, and the discussions of relevant cases, certainly represented a small revolution in the university. Architecture was to be contaminated with other disciplines, and this was essential to see and tackle architectural "problems" as *real* ones. By looking at the many didactic documents of those years, teaching was recognized as a complex set of activities. Among them, tutoring was perhaps the least important one: in Zurich, students were particularly surprised when Rossi insisted on giving theoretical lectures on a weekly basis. Within this pedagogical experimentation and the interest towards the crossing of disciplinary boundaries, the making of what appears as essentially architectural plans at the scale of (a part of) the city was seen as necessary, for one thing, to explore and solidify those conceptual categories that were central to Aldo Rossi's thought, such as the *singularity of the urban event* and the *city of parts,* and for another, to define potential tools and research outputs that were considered appropriate for the definition of an architecturally scientific approach to the city. By offering a detailed representation of the city's typological dimension in these plans, Rossi aimed to provide his students with the critical understanding of repetition, variation, and evolution of the urban form. By focusing on the study of the type through spatial research rather than on design proposals, Rossi conceived his pedagogical role as a provider of design tools through which it would have been possible to understand the city as a whole. Although his interest in teaching rapidly dissipated parallel to the increase in his professional commissions—in 1990 he even questioned the necessity of a school of architecture[37]—the pedagogic ethos of those early years remains visible in these large collective drawings such as the plan of Zurich.

Conclusion

Large-scale plan drawings of cities are a specific type of map, the meaning of which resides at the intersection between representation and projection, interpreting and designing. While maps generally serve as the basis for registering topographic data and communicating the results of research, thus becoming "devices of information transmission involving the basic rules of communication,"[38] the architectural map or the large-scale plan drawing of the city exemplifies an inherent projective potential. For one thing, architectural plans have the capacity to synthesize and represent, on the limited space of the sheet of paper, sets of otherwise ungraspable, complex information. For another, the focus and the representation techniques cannot be anything if not the result of a project. In the case of the most extraordinary Roman city plan, the *Forma Urbis Romae,* its purpose has been largely debated. Yet the document, through a specific system of notation, not only conveys clearly the spatial organization of the city and the differentiation between public monuments and private properties, but also puts forward also a clear political representation of the power of collective citizenship over the individual one. During the Renaissance, the rise of plans must be seen as being about "concrete concerns about property and identity emerging from political economic transformation of the period."[39] Yet the improvement of surveying skills is for architects also the first possibility to embrace a scale not yet known, the possibility of inserting their design into the vast horizontal field of the city. Lastly, although Rossi's plans were the result of research activities on the city and did not have a design finality, they were essential tools for training young architects in the science of urban design. The exploration of a few key plans of cities supports the understanding that drawing large plans goes far beyond Alberti's demand for a graphic representation of the whole city, and proves to be a fruitful tool in the hands of architects to "design" the city.

The *Oxford English Dictionary* defines ›lan" as a "drawing, sketch, or diagram any object made by projection on a ›rizontal plane" and more generally as ›n organized (and usually detailed) oposal according to which something to be done." *Oxford English Dictionary nline*, s.v. "plan," https://www.oed.com ccessed 14 October 2019).

Online Etymology Dictionary, s.v. ›lan," https://www.etymonline.com/ arch?q=plan (accessed July 29, 2019).

Hillary Ballon and David Friedman, 'ortraying the City in Early Modern ırope: Measurement, Representation d Planning," in *The History of artography, Vol. III*, ed. John Brian arley and David Woodward (Chicago, : University of Chicago Press, 1987), 0–704.

David West Reynolds, "Forma Ur- s Romae: The Severan Marble Plan and e Urban Form of Ancient Rome" (PhD ss., University of Michigan, 1996), 72.

Ibid., 126.

Ibid., 73.

Oswald. A. W. Dilke, "Roman rge-Scale Mapping in the Early npire," in *The History of Cartography, l. I*, ed. John Brian Harley and David oodward (Chicago: University of Chica- Press, 1987), 227. See also Paul Dean dshead Harvey, *The History of pographical Maps* (London: Thames d Hudson, 1980), 128.

James C. Anderson, *The Historical pography of the Imperial Fora*, llection Latomus (Brussels: Latomus, 84), 105.

These works include repairs to the ntheon, the Porticus Octaviae, the mplum Pacis, the Temple of Vaspasian, me arches of the Aqua Claudia ueduct, the restoration of the river ıbankments, the construction of baths, d of a new wing, the Domus Severiana, the Imperial Palace on the Palatine. ynolds, "Forma Urbis Romae," 114.

Liba Taub, "The Historical Function of Forma Urbis Romae," *Imago ındi* 45, no. 1 (1993): 12.

Ibid., 15.

12 Yan Thomas, "Le droit romain hors la religion," *Annales. Histoire, Sciences Sociales* 6 (2002): 1433–34.

13 Ibid., 1432.

14 Ibid., 1432–33.

15 Ibid., 1450–53.

16 Ballon and Friedman, "Portraying the City in Early Modern Europe," 688–89.

17 Ibid., 680–87.

18 Marco Folin, "Introduzione. Piante di città nell'Italia di antico regime: uno strumento di conoscenza analitico-operativa," in *Rappresentare la città: topografie urbane nell'Italia di antico regime*, ed. Marco Folin (Reggio Emilia: Diabasis, 2010), 15–16.

19 James S. Ackerman, *Origins, Imitation, Conventions: Representation in the Visual Arts* (Cambridge, MA: MIT Press, 2002), 154–55.

20 Robert Zwijnenberg, *The Writings and Drawings of Leonardo da Vinci* (New York: Cambridge University Press, 1999), 107.

21 Imola is about 50 km away from Cesena. See David Friedman, "La Pianta di Imola di Leonardo. 1502," in *Rappresentare la città: topografie urbane nell'Italia di antico regime*, ed. Marco Folin (Reggio Emilia: Diabasis, 2010), 124.

22 Zwijnenberg, *The Writings and Drawings of Leonardo da Vinci*, 108; Friedman, "La Pianta di Imola di Leonardo," 124.

23 Carlo Pedretti, *Leonardo Architect* (New York: Rizzoli, 1985), 154–74.

24 Such as the map of the Chiana valley, the map of the Pontine marshes and the map of Western marshes. See Branko Pucekovi , "Leonardo da Vinci and His Contributions to Cartography," *Kartografija I Geoinformacije* 12, no. 20 (2013): 34–52.

25 Giovanni Santucci dates the plan not much after 1509. It is debated among historians whether the plan of Sangallo is a copy of an older and then lost plan of the city drawn probably between 1474 and 1495. On this see Giovanni Santucci, "Giuliano da Sangallo e il disegno della città. La pianta di Pisa 7950 A della Galleria degli Uffizi," in *Giuliano da Sangallo*, ed. Amedeo Belluzzi, Caroline Elam, and Francesco Paolo Fiore (Milano: Officina libraria, 2012), 261–62; and Lucia Nuti, "Surveying, Interpreting, and Designing: The Multiple Essence of a Sixteenth-Century Drawing," *Journal of the Society of Architectural Historians* 75, no. 1 (2016): 5–10.

26 Nuti, "Surveying, Interpreting, and Designing," 20.

27 Ibid., 12–13.

28 Santucci, "Giuliano da Sangallo e il disegno della città," 267–70.

29 Ibid., 267–70.

30 Mario Bevilacqua, "Gian Battista Nolli, *Nuova Pianta di Roma* (1748)," *Rappresentare la città: topografie urbane nell'Italia di antico regime*, ed. Marco Folin (Reggio Emilia: Diabasis, 2010), 373–85.

31 Pier Vittorio Aureli, *The Possibility of an Absolute Architecture* (Cambridge, MA, and London: MIT Press, 2011), 85–140.

32 Ibid., 108–109.

33 Ibid., 109.

34 Chair Aldo Rossi with Sandro Cantoni, Bruno Keller, Orlando Pampuri, Riccardo Serena, Antonio Pisoni, Ivano Martini, Fabio Reinhart, and Bruno Reichlin, *Rilievo 1:1000 del piano terreno entro il perimetro delle mura barocche* (Zurich: ETH/GTA, 1973).

35 Fiorella Vanini, *La rivoluzione culturale. La Facoltà di Architettura del Politecnico di Milano 1963–1974* (Milan: Associazione GRU, 2009).

36 Aldo Rossi, *L'analisi urbana e la progettazione architettonica. Contributi al dibattito e al lavoro di gruppo nell'anno accademico 1968–69* (Milan: Clup, 1970), 11.

37 Aldo Rossi, "Ma ha ancora senso la facoltà di architettura?" *Corriere della Sera*, October 18, 1990.

38 Jan Broek, *Geography: Its Scope and Spirit* (Columbus, OH: Charles E. Merrill, 1965), 64.

39 John Pickles, *A History of Space: Cartographic Reason, Mapping and the Geo-Coded World* (London: Routledge, 2004), 99.

Rachel Hurst

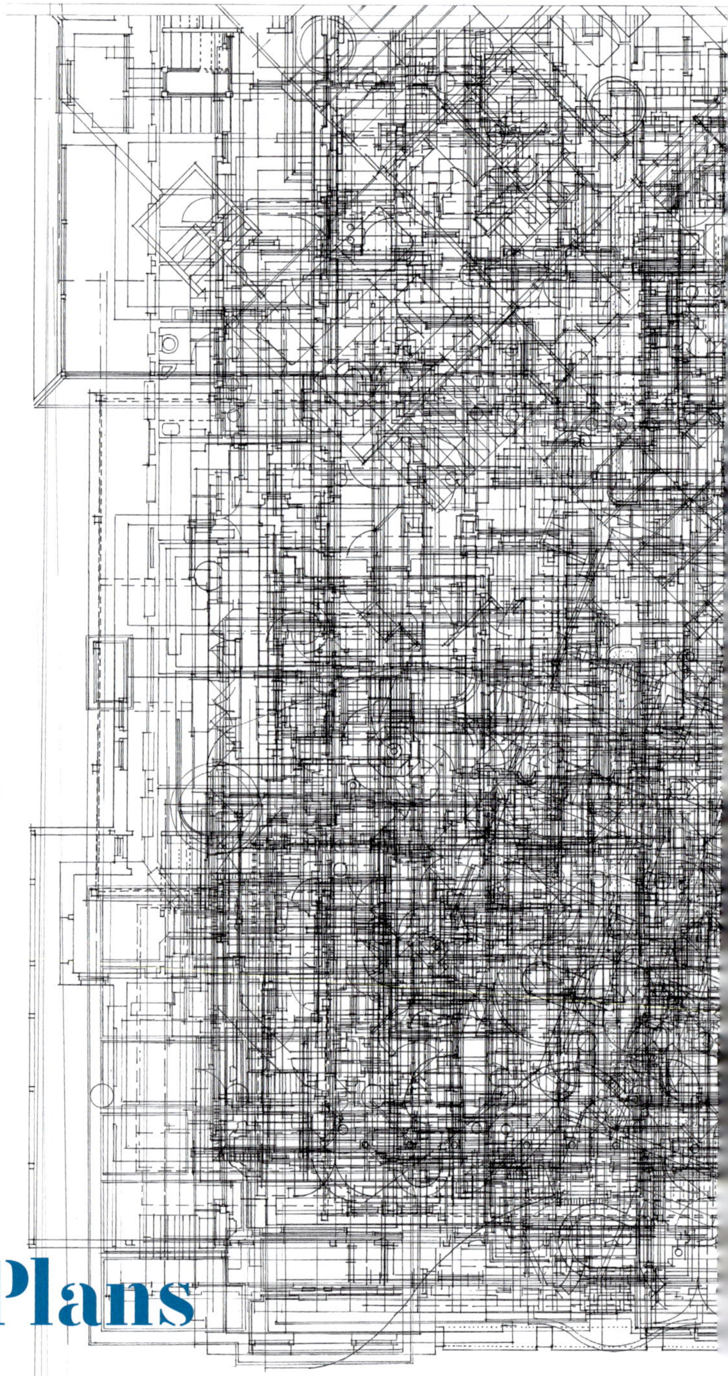

fig.1

A Million Hours of Plans

Exploiting Time and Transparency

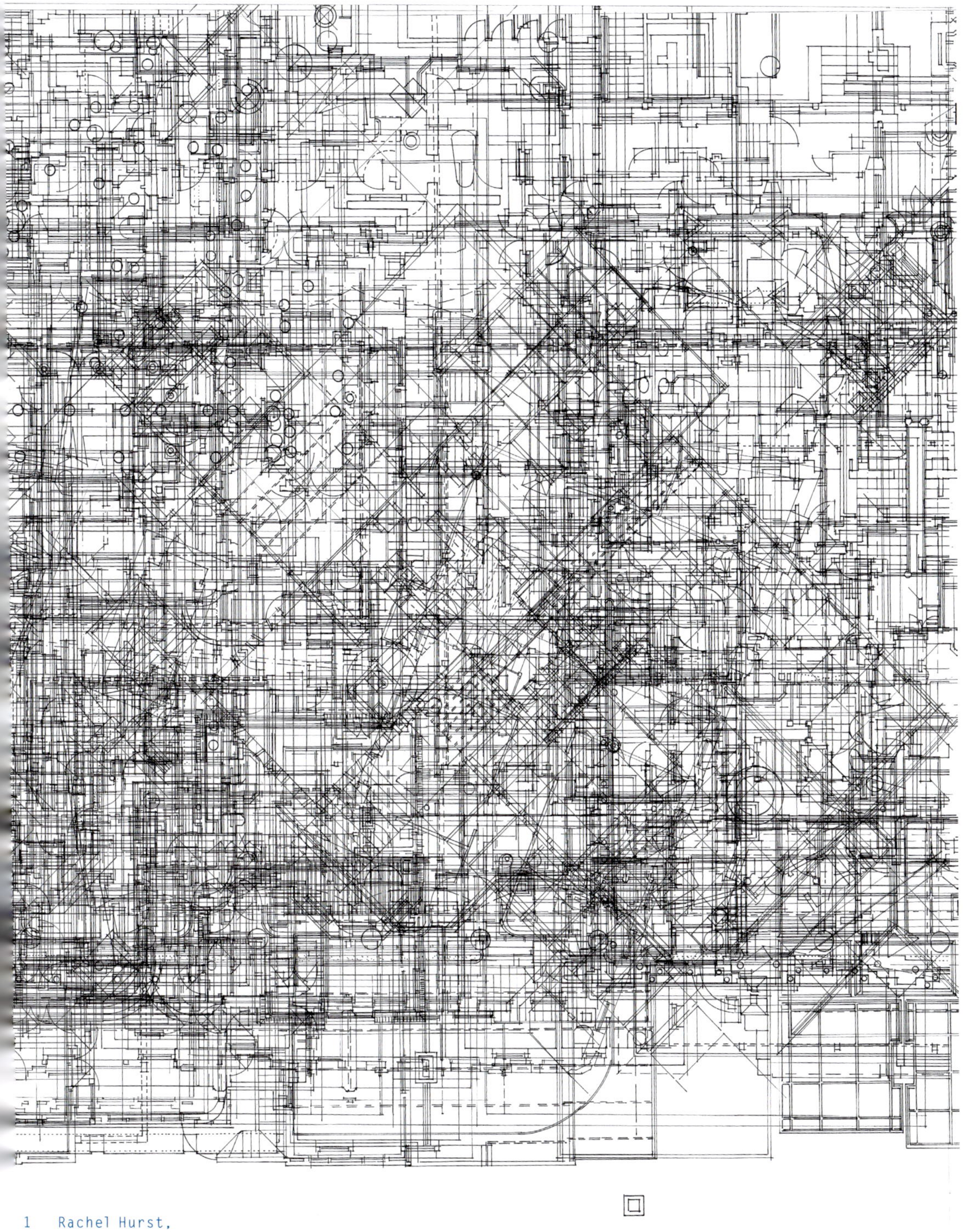

1 Rachel Hurst, *million hours_3 layer drawing*, 2017. Ink on polyester film, 59.4 × 42 cm. The project explores the plans of 30 buildings through superimposed retracings.

Architectural plans are autopsies of unborn buildings, slicing through the material and spatial envelope to reveal views and conjunctions never intended to be seen simultaneously [fig. 1, 6–8]. Marco Frascari writes of the dissecting knife of the pen,[1] and like surgeons, we choose the line of cut to expose the vital innards of the design, the areas most requiring attention. In doing so, each plan becomes a digest of the critical characteristics of a scheme.

Our representational media have evolved in support of the plan's forensic capacity. The transparent tissue of trace or the invisible ether of digital layers allow us to superimpose multiple orthographic drawings to assemble the volumetric whole of the architectural body. In this simulated X-ray vision it is possible to sense the three-dimensionality, if not tactility of the architecture.

What if this diagnostic drawing tool used to cross-section the physical corpus of architecture could also be exploited to cross-section time? The works here—three pairs of ink drawings and oil paintings—are propelled by this possibility, and by the title of the conference and exhibition, *Drawing Millions of Plans,* where they were presented.[2] The intention of this project was to synthesize a nominal 1,000,000 hours from the history of existing plans into a hybrid compilation, creating a kind of graphic DNA, and decode what was embedded there.

In the first stage, 30 plan drawings were chosen from the Architecture Museum at the School of Art, Architecture & Design of the University of South Australia, to cover 1,000,000 hours—114 years, 56 days, and 16 hours. Selected at approximately regular intervals in time, they were put in chronological order and retraced into three single drawings, each containing 10 superimposed plans [fig. 2].

In this way, each of the three drawings spans a defined era: *Drawing 1: 1878–1923*, *Drawing 2: 1924–1945*, and *Drawing 3: 1946–1992*. These groupings were adjusted to obtain a balanced spread from the archive and take account of contemporary events affecting the local industry. For example, in 1923, the South Australian Building Act required that plans be included in any proposal submitted for council approval, resulting in a plethora of plan documentation. The second time span responds to "between the wars" economic conditions, while the final group responds to the influx of Modernist ideas into Australia after the war. Examples were chosen on the basis of drawing quality and consistency of scale,[3] and to represent prevalent typologies (civic, residential, commercial, and later industrial) [fig. 3–5]. The three resulting drawings employ a deliberately non-hierarchical mode of reproduction, using only one pen thickness on polyester film and each aligning consistently at the bottom left hand corner, regardless of the layout of the originals [fig. 1, 6–8].

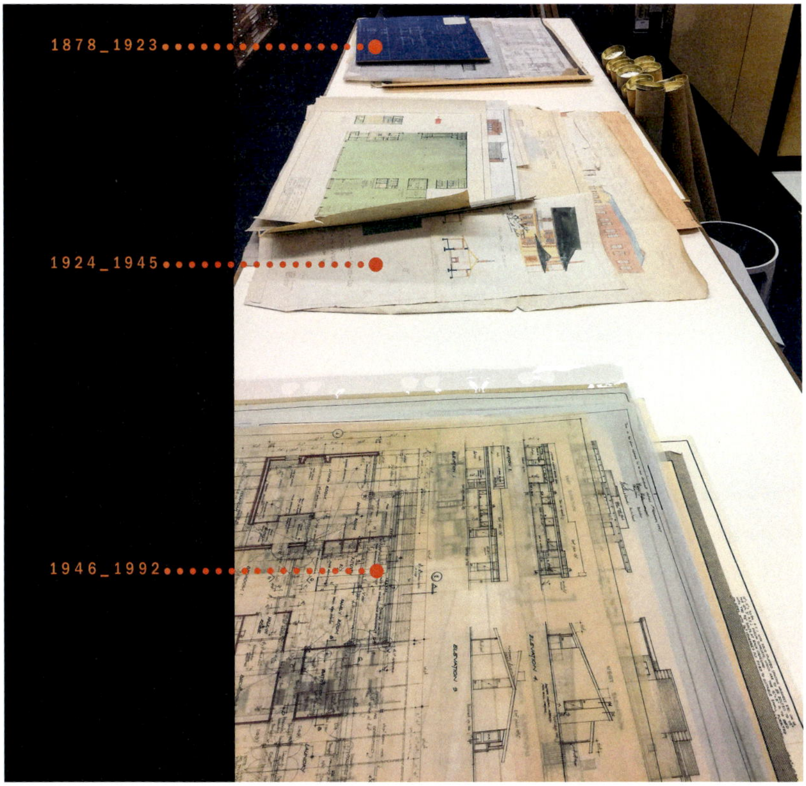

fig. 2

In the second stage, sections of the compilations were magnified in scale [fig. 9] and reinterpreted through oil paintings [fig. 10–12]. The paintings challenge the unambiguous linearity of traditional architectural representation by deploying color, and tonal and textural techniques derived from Cubist phenomenal transparency. The color palette was derived from the fundamental media of architectural representation: yellow trace; white paper; grey graphite; pale green drawing board covers, and was refined using Le Corbusier's color system *Les Couleurs Polychromie Architecturales*, in synergy with the predominantly 20th-century source material.[4] Each painting is accented with a color distinctive to its core collection [fig. 13–15].

Although the resulting drawings initially read as an impenetrable maze, like odd heritage versions of Daniel Libeskind's *Micromegas* drawings,[5] their tracing sets up an embodied communication with the original drafters and reveals nuanced aspects of the making of each drawing included. The accretion of habits inherent in the original drawings condenses through their

2 Drawings were selected as a representative cross section of the collection of the Architecture Museum University of South Australia (AM UniSA).

superimposition. This procedure manifests unifying features across the times, as well as illustrating distinctive characteristics and concerns of the architectural and construction industry in each era. The paintings distil the essence of these findings in a revelatory process.

The drawings exhibit markedly different compositional dispositions: *Drawing 1* shows verticality aligning strongly in two main axes, with a flurry of idiosyncrasy around the same general "entry area" [fig. 16]. The horizontal prevails in *Drawing 2* [fig. 17]. *Drawing 3* is dominated by the diagonal [fig. 18]. These individual dynamics inform each of the paintings. In them the substance of the architectural observations is emphasized through color and figure-ground distinctions. For example, *Painting 1* [fig. 10] shows the pronounced weight of building elements and there is extravagant detail at significant thresholds. Meticulous care in the drafting implies craft in building: tiny variations (with few supporting larger-scale details) assume an informed and skilled workforce able to interpret from minimal description.

If *Drawing 2* shows brisker, less precise linework, with crossed lines suggesting drawings operating on site as direct documentation used to check measure, *Painting 2* foregrounds cavity construction with careful delineation of how it turns corners, as befits a recent constructional advance [fig. 11]. Apart from more diverse geometries, *Drawing 3* and *Painting 3* [fig. 12] demonstrate an overall reductionist hand. There is less architectural substance generally in them, and drafting is now less accurate, with more legends and annotation, and standardized approaches to walls, windows, and insertions.

The paintings are keyed to connect, reinforcing the continuum of architectural activity as one long sequence [fig. 19]. Reading across this suite there is ubiquitous respect for the bottom left-hand corner, the fundamental position for each plan in a set of drawings. There is less consensus in the location of north points though, which orient expediently to suit the layout of the sheets and geometries of schemes, rather than following the convention to point toward the top of the sheet. Across the times, plans were increasingly drawn on transparent ground, a trajectory that continues into the virtual "no ground" of the computer screen.

A Million Hours of Plans retells history through an accumulation of drawing surfaces. Retracing these artifacts inevitably yields insights into their content, but also reinhabits their facture in a way that catalyzes a greater appreciation of ostensibly archaic forms and processes. As a contemporary form of conservation, the project is a recalibration away from the significant edifice towards the "debris" of ordinary drawings, finding value in the amalgamation of fragmentary, modest material for the investigation and reevaluation of threatened architectural processes. But there is a deliberate balance

3 William McMinn, *Mitchell Building*, 1878. The earliest plan used in the project is a university chancellery from the late 19th century. AM UniSA Collection S104/8/6.

4 Kaberry & Chard, *Thebarton Council Chambers*, 1927. The examples from 1923–45 include Art Deco civic projects. AM UniSA Collection S249/10.

5 Robin Boyd, *Walkely House*, 1955. The group from 1946–92 shows the postwar influence of Modernism on contemporary Australian architecture. AM UniSA Walkley Collection S300/15/9.

fig. 3

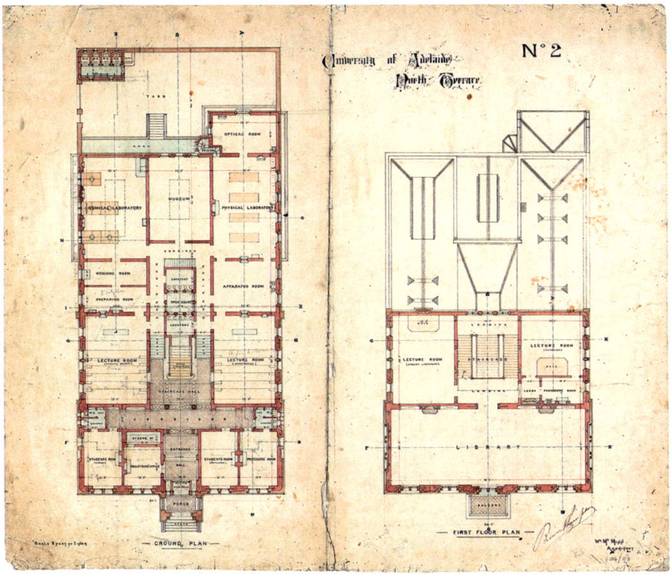

fig. 4

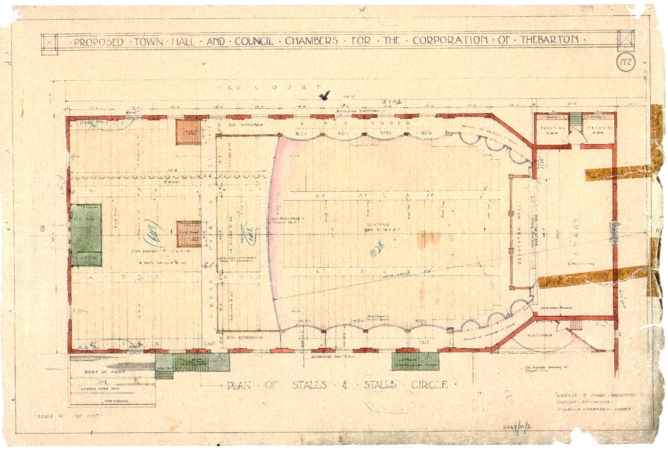

fig. 5

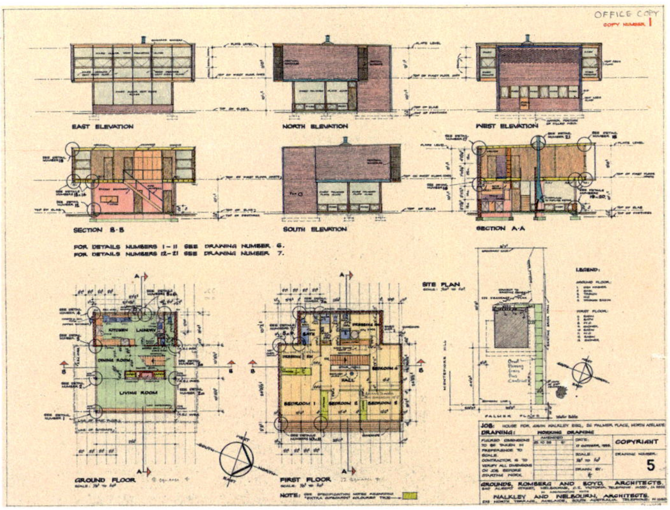

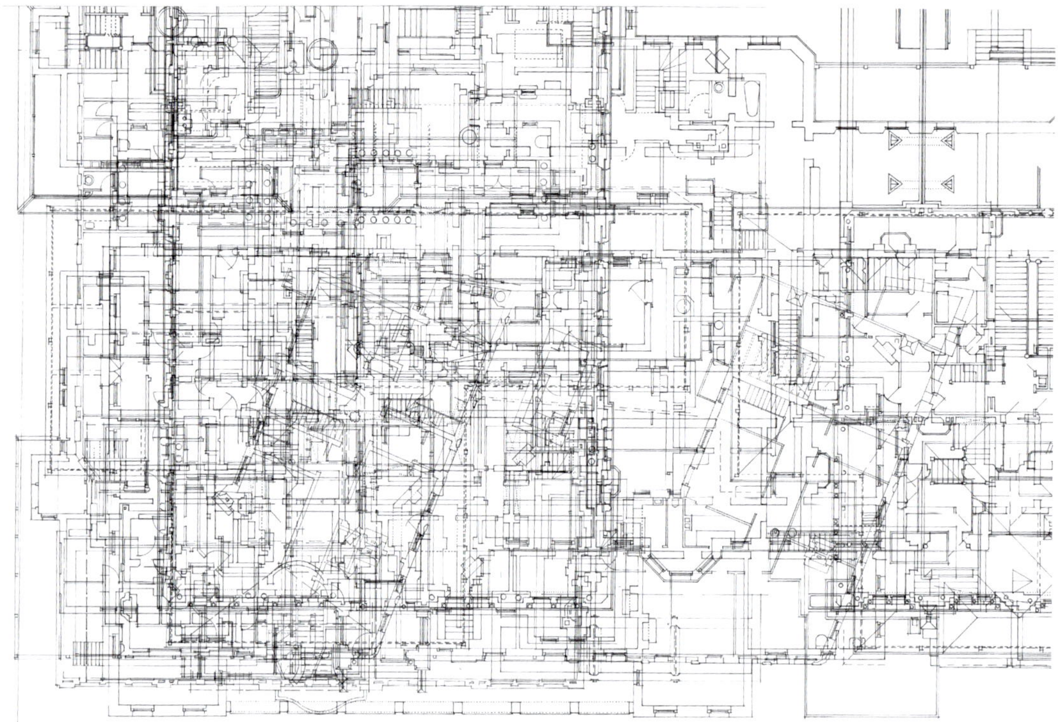

fig. 6

6 Rachel Hurst, *millio[n] hours_Drawing 1: 1878 - 1923*, 2017. Ink on polyester film, 59.4 × 42 cm. The project explores the plans of thirty buildings through superimposed retracings.

7 Rachel Hurst, *millio[n] hours_Drawing 2: 1924 - 1945*, 2017. Ink on polyester film, 59.4 × 42 cm.

8 Rachel Hurst, *millio[n] hours_Drawing 3: 1946 - 1992*, 2017. Ink on polyester film, 59.4 × 42 cm.

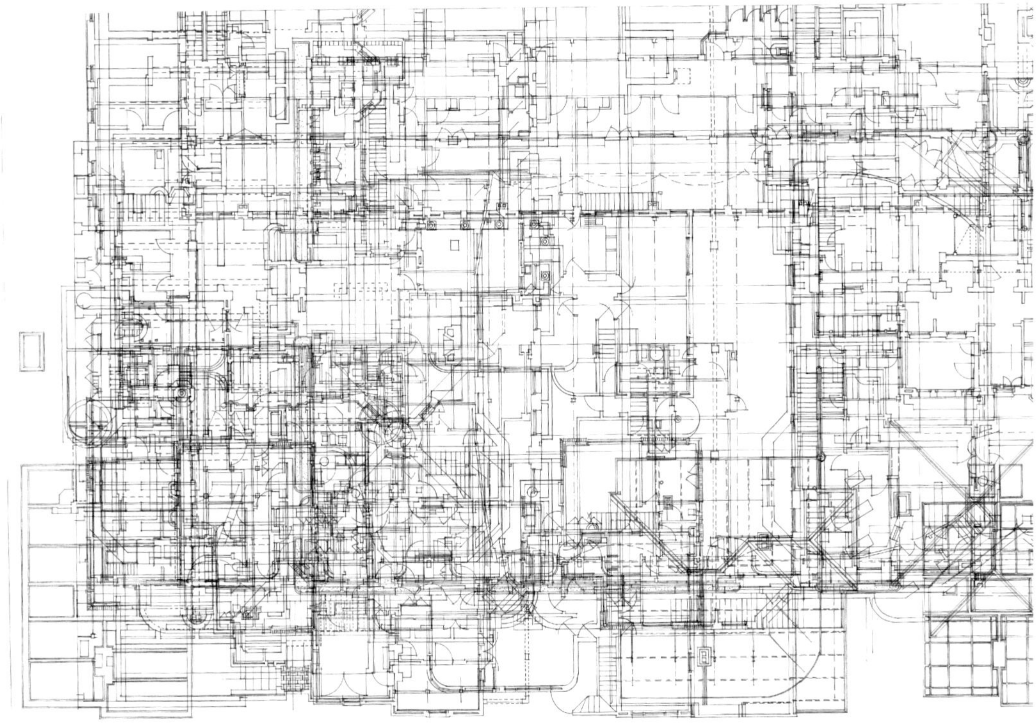

fig. 7

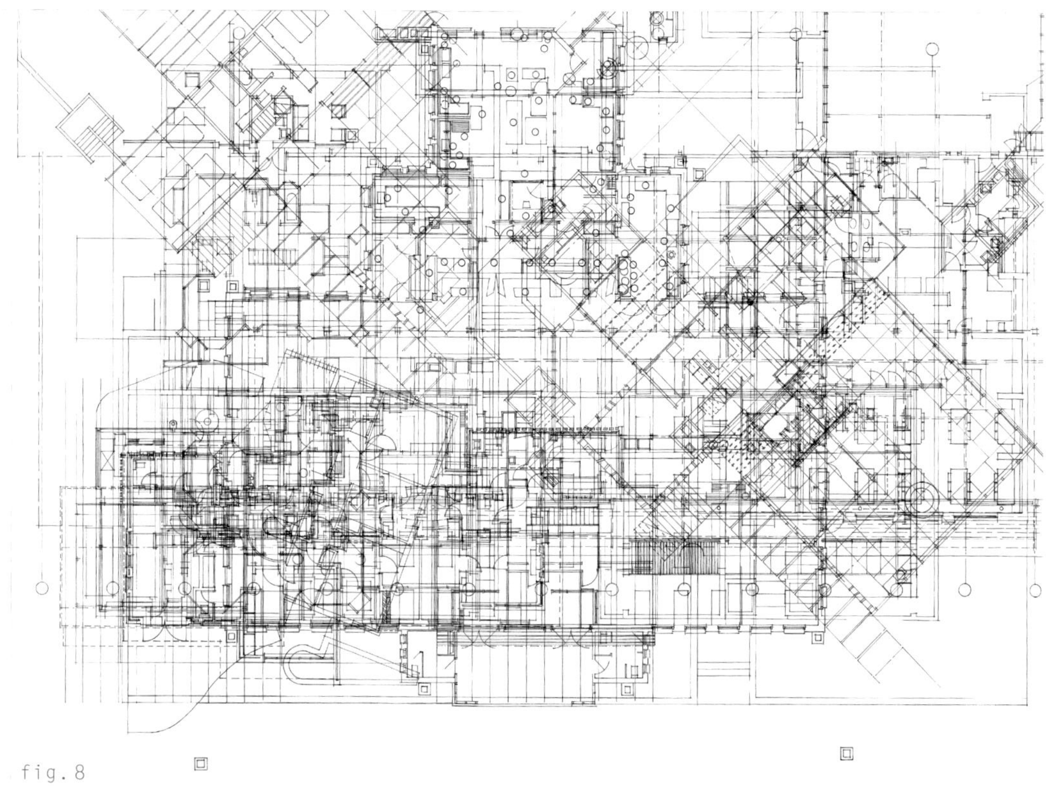

fig. 8

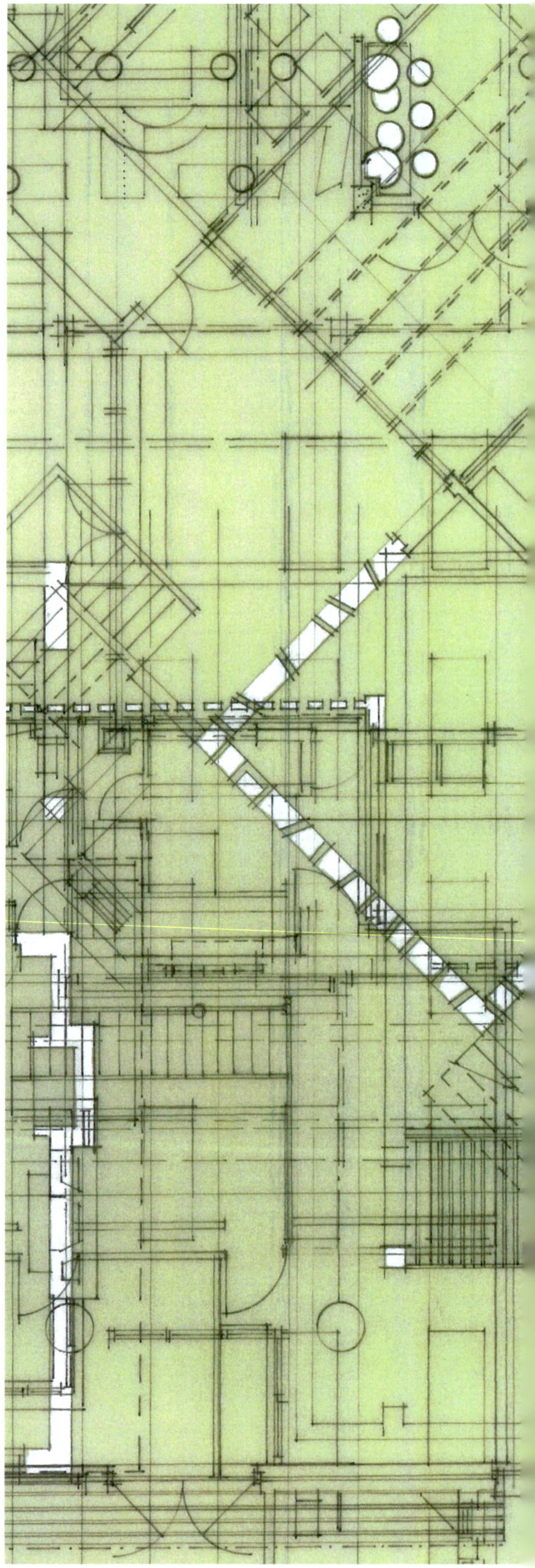

fig. 9

9 During the tracing process recurrent characteristics in individual plans were observed, and recorded as a single salient motif for each. These were isolated as opaque forms against a background of yellow trace, and magnified in scale.

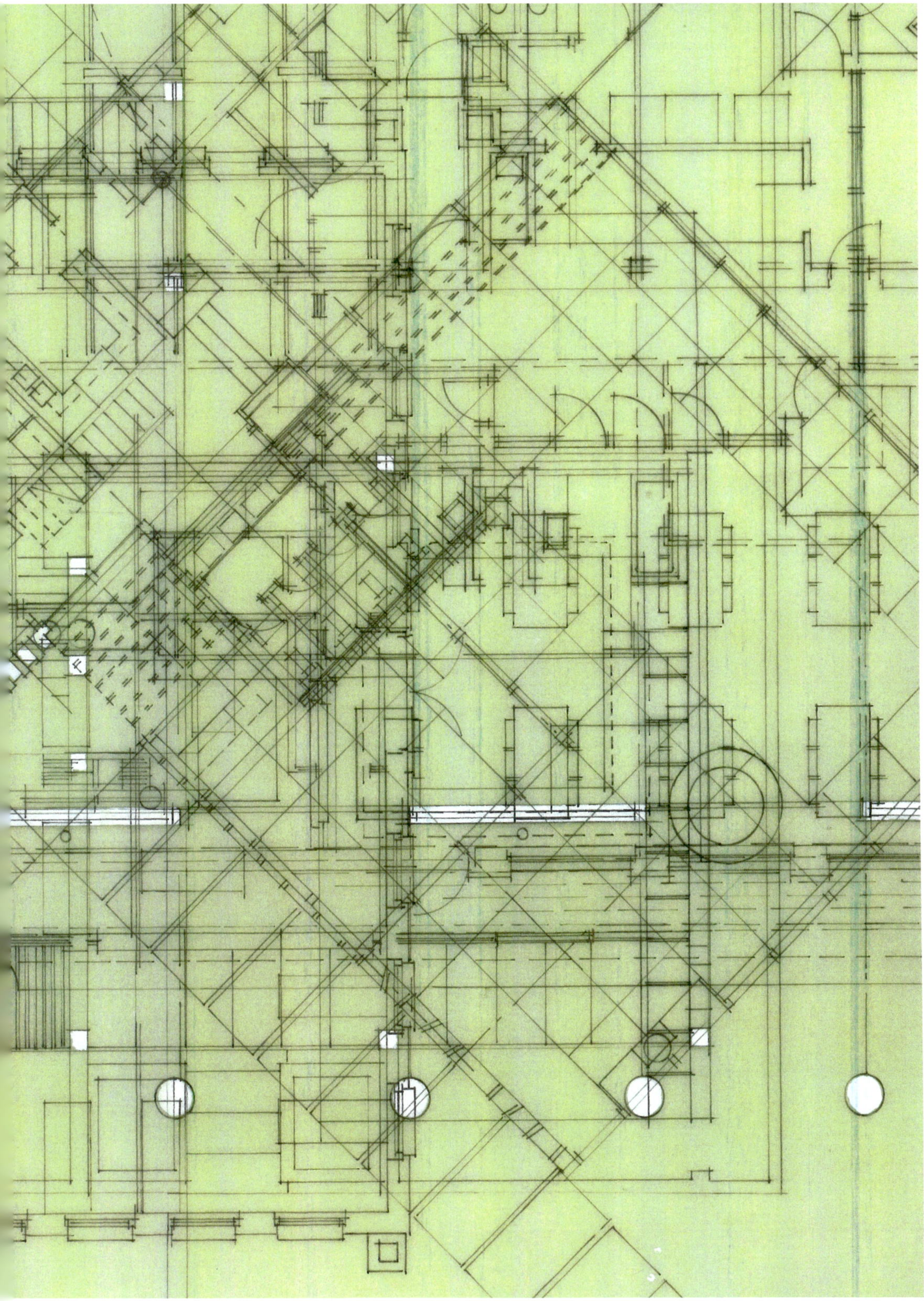

fig. 10-12

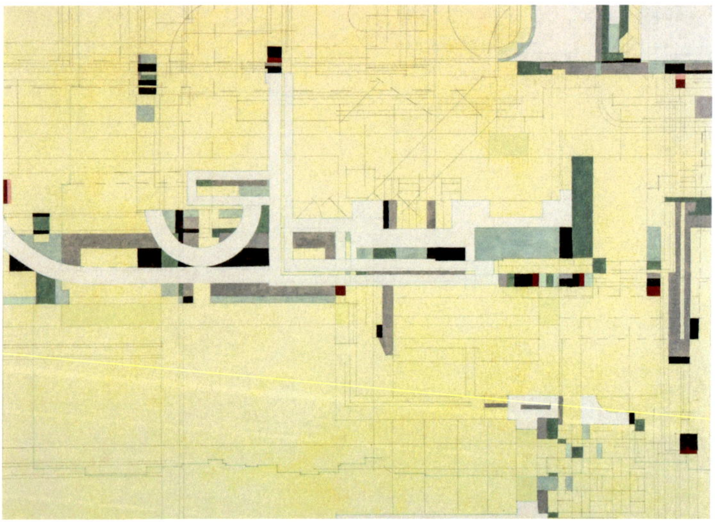

10 Rachel Hurst, *million hours_Painting 1: 1878 - 1923*, 2017. The paintings use Cubist techniques to highlight comparable processes of simultaneous viewing in architectural representation, such as the section and axonometric. Oil, graphite, and colored lead on paper, 59.4 × 42 cm.

11 Rachel Hurst, *million hours_Painting 2: 1924 - 1945*, 2017. Oil, graphite and colored lead on paper, 59.4 × 42 cm.

12 Rachel Hurst, *million hours_Painting 3: 1946 - 1992*, 2017. Oil, graphite, and colored lead on paper, 59.4 × 42 cm.

between preserving the skills of drawing and using them synergistically as an active research tool and generative art form.

This offers a potent pedagogical tactic: rather than admiring nostalgic measured drawings, reconfigured archival data is mined for experimental spatial explorations and creative propulsion. To this end, the methodologies of *Million Hours* are being trialed as part of both design studio and practice-based research courses in undergraduate and postgraduate architecture programs.

The rapid paradigm shift to digitized representation is eroding the craft base of analog skills and knowledge as if it were raining "acid ink." The *Million Hours* project echoes Mark Wigley's tactic "of looking at something that seems to be fading or gone and incubating new life within it."[6] Indeed, *Million Hours* presents the legacy, and future, of analog skills optimistically. Using contemporary expanded drawing practices as a critical framework, we can illuminate design processes and foment creative architectural conversations with the past.

Marco Frascari, *Eleven Exercises in* *·e Art of Architectural Drawing: Slow* *·od for the Architect's Imagination* ondon and New York: Routledge, 2011), 7.
Drawing Millions of Plans, The Royal anish Academy of Fine Arts, Schools of chitecture, Design and Conservation ADK), November 1–3, 2017. Curators: na Hougaard, Martin Søberg, and cob S. Bang, "Programme + stracts," 5, https://kadk.dk/ awing-millions-of-plans (accessed arch 13, 2019).

3 The majority of drawings were 1/8th inch to 1 foot scale, or post 1971, its equivalent metric scale of 1:100.

4 *poLyChro® Les Couleurs® Le Corbusier* Edition 2. Produced by KEIMFARBEN.

5 Daniel Libeskind, *Micromegas: The Architecture of End Space*, 1979, see "Micromegas," Studio Libeskind, https://libeskind.com/work/micromegas/ (accessed March 13, 2019).

6 Mark Wigley, "Introduction," in Rem Koolhaas, *Preservation is Overtaking Us*, ed. Jordan Carver (New York: Columbia University GSAPP, 2014), 7.

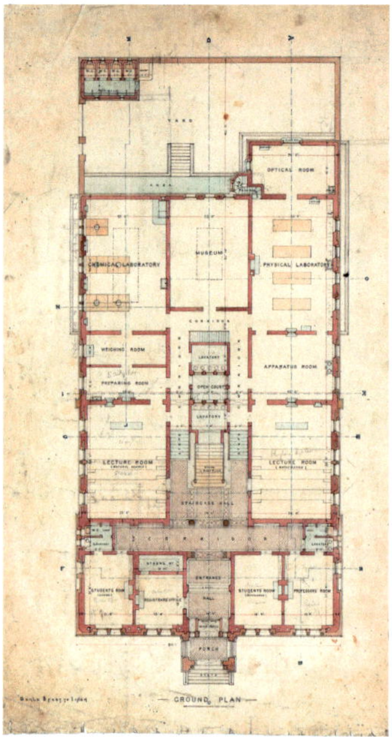

fig. 13

13 *Painting 1* (detail) on right derives its accent color from late-19th-century watercolor renderings. Mitchell Building: AM UniSA Collection S104/8/6.

14 Painting 2 (detail) on right uses the red of color-coded brickwork in early 20th-century documentation. Russell & Yelland, *Kalimna Chambers*, 1927. Russell and Yelland collection, S98AM UniSA Collection.

15 Painting 3 (detail) on right references the increased use of reprographic blueprints in the latter half of the 20th century. E. Gruenberg, Allen Grove Residence, c. 1947. Hurren, Langman and James collection, S247/129, AM UniSA Collection.

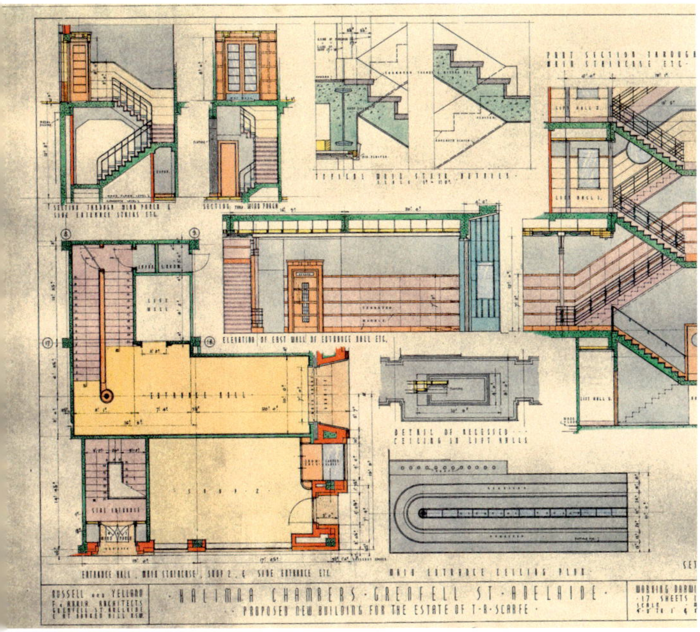
KALIMNA CHAMBERS · GRENFELL ST · ADELAIDE ·
· PROPOSED NEW BUILDING FOR THE ESTATE OF T·R·SCARFE ·
RUSSELL and YELLAND
ENTRANCE HALL
DETAIL OF RECESSED CEILING IN LIFT HALLS
MAIN ENTRANCE CEILING PLAN
ELEVATION OF EAST WALL OF ENTRANCE HALL ETC.

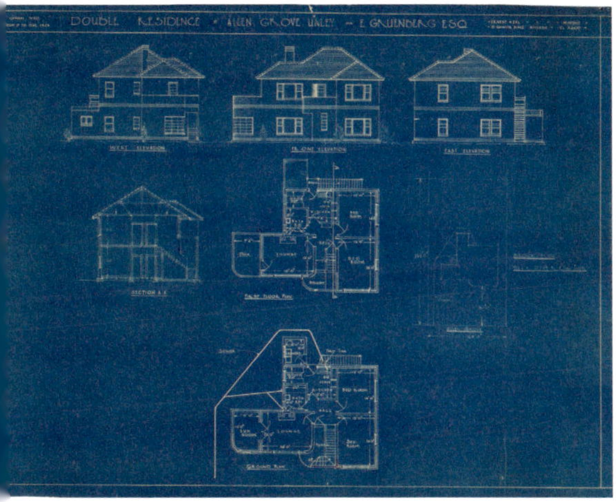
DOUBLE RESIDENCE

ig. 14-15

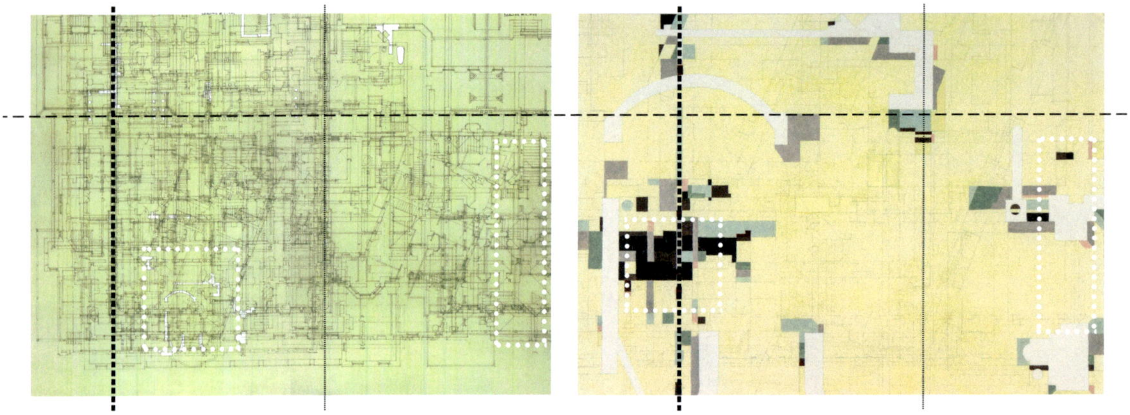

fig. 16

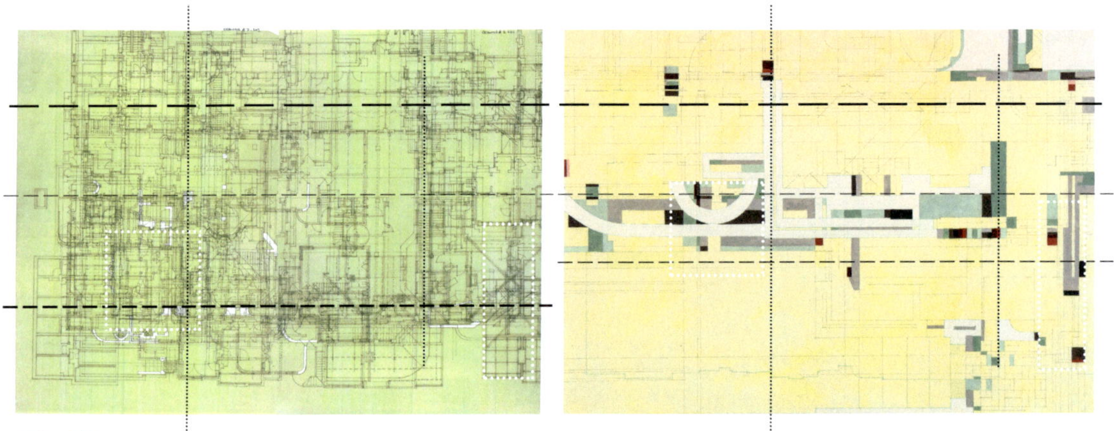

fig. 17

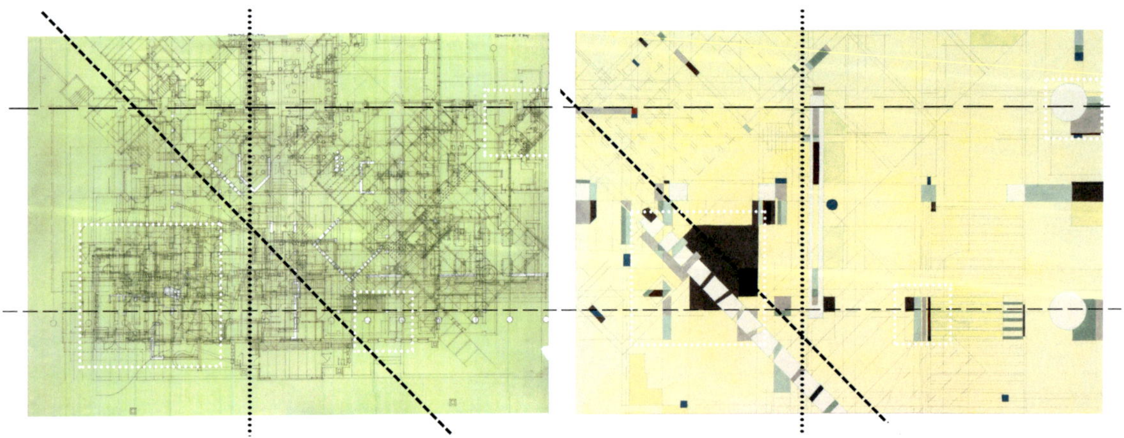

fig. 18

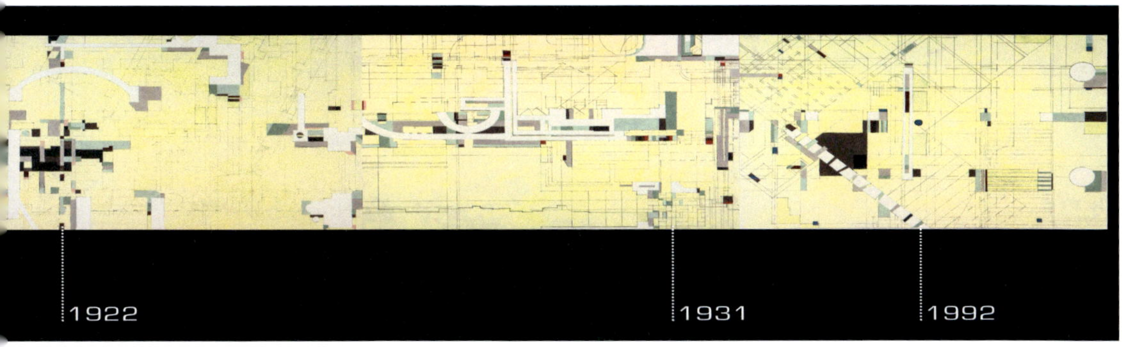

g. 19

16 A comparison of *Drawing 1* and *Painting 1* showing the correlation of compositional characteristics, and significant elements of substantial load bearing elements, the fireplace, and extravagant threshold detail.

17 *Painting 2* responds to the pervasive horizontality of *Drawing 2*, and highlights repeated figures of controlled curvature. Basket-works and hatching emerge as indicators of increased interest in land-scaping around the building.

18 *Drawing 3* and *Painting 3* draw attention to the exploration of diagonal geometries, minimization of structure and increased use of discrete, allied elements such as grids and columns.

19 Assembled chrono-logically, the three paintings make it possible to read the character and development of the architecture.

2

Point Clouds, Chance Operations, and the Disappearance of the Plan

Martin Søberg and Anna Hougaard

A new post-digital condition challenges the dominance of conventional orthogonal projection and modifies the conventional use of the plan drawing. Customized digital design software and digital production and materialization, where architects acquire programming skills and knowledge of digital craftmanship, make up a progressive research field, combining technical know-how with aesthetic sensibility.[1] Moreover, building information modeling (BIM) software combines conventional building and drawing techniques and standards with the possibilities of communicating architectural information digitally. BIM allows architectural teams to work together on one digital model and to integrate collaboration with other groups such as engineers or technical subcontractors, supported by the digital enhancement of conventional architectural communication. As opposed to analog drawing or CAD software, BIM also allows for economic simulations of management, construction costs as well as rentability, and maintenance over the whole lifespan of a building. Conventions are reformed, yet unforeseen side effects also occur, for example, when BIM simulation becomes so strong that the built environments look like a digital simulation.[2] Flexibility and process orientation are also encompassed by BIM's algorithmic constitution, making it effectively a model of information before being a model of space. BIM thus shifts the process of architectural design from a mode of 2D representation to an iterative mode of continuously updated 3D simulation defined by parametrically related data.

This part of the book addresses how new design tools might eventually eradicate the plan from architectural practice, but also how this eradication can be a matter of choice of design methods and ideological convictions that are not necessarily related to digitalization. One threat to the plan's relevance lies in the way in which new, primarily digital design tools imply an alternative notion of space based on the factors of time and extensive amounts of information. It also affects the fundamental issue of how architectural representation is connected with physical matter. Do increased amounts of information allow a frictionless transition from algorithmic design to actual construction, as Mario Carpo has argued?[3] Or is the process of translation from drawing to building still as messy as Robin Evans famously demonstrated? Evans pointed out that things change in translation—information might be lost or added—because projective geometry as the medium of translation is not a stable condition but is itself changeable and ambiguous.[4] Along similar lines, Edward Robbins has demonstrated that a positive constituent of the drawing convention is that it makes a non-limiting condition possible, allowing architects to communicate with peers and other parties involved in design and construction processes. Drawing forms part of a "social act,"[5] in which ideas are transported from representation to sites of construction—but not without a possible loss of information and the risk of misunderstanding. Although information is much more plentiful in contemporary digital design processes, and digital code should ensure correct translation, changes and losses still occur.

Another threat to the plan lies in the entanglement of methods of design with questions of ideology and biopolitics. Beaux-arts tradition and the notion of the plan as generator resulted in a disciplinary quest for compositional inventiveness, staging the architect as a powerful inventor, the artist-genius. This approach has been challenged both by the notion of more democratic, inclusive design processes and through an interest in generic, even anonymous, architecture without any compositional qualities—a typical plan. In 1969, Reyner Banham, Paul Barker,

Peter Hall, and Cedric Price published their ideas about an architectural "non-plan."[6] It conceived of an urban situation with no planning regulations at all, but freedom for everyone to settle according to their own preferences (so as to prevent architects from forcing their aesthetic preferences upon "the people"). In his 1993 essay on the "Typical Plan" in American corporate architecture, Rem Koolhaas stated: "The notion of the typical plan is therapeutic; it is the End of Architectural History, which is nothing but the hysterical fetishization of the atypical plan. Typical Plan is a segment of an unacknowledged utopia, the promise of a post-architectural future."[7] The typical plan in this understanding is based on the rectangle; it does not require anything, but just lets its inhabitants be. And by means of air-conditioning it allows the plan to free itself of the exterior. "It is the stamp of modernity itself,"[8] Koolhaas proclaimed, "an environment that demanded nothing and gave everything was suddenly seen as an infernal machine for stripping identity."[9]

While both the "non-plan" and the "typical plan" are positioned as alternatives, they still retain the idea that plans are biopolitical means, influencing and influenced by people's behaviors. A response to this programmatic potential of the plan might be to reduce its powers by focusing instead on participatory, process-oriented design. Alejandra Celedón has argued that plans might prevent social and economic exploitation: "An absence of plans is ultimately an absence of limits, an undefined and ambiguous field that becomes the perfect site for economic speculation and individual profit. In such a domain the plan offers the possibility of resistance, countering the ways cities have grown and developed."[10] Celedón conceives of plans as necessary tools of regulation that guard the common good, even while their limits are continuously renegotiable. As these examples suggest, plans are ideologically entangled because the plan or the lack of one forms part of architectural manners and practices that differ in scope and intent. Different media enable different agencies.[11]

Digital Media Space

In the atrticle "Drawing (on) the Context" Bernadette Devilat and Felipe Lanuza document and reflect on their process of designing a detached single-family house in Talagante, Chile. Their design process was conventional in the sense that they registered the site and subsequently designed, visualized, and constructed the house. Rather than employing conventional orthogonal plan drawings of the site in this process, they employed a 3D scan of the site, comprising an abundance of information. This allowed the architects to maneuver in a site representation of unprecedented detail. In order to obtain building permits and communicate with local constructors they nevertheless had to produce conventional orthogonal plans. Their narrative testifies to an entanglement between conventional means of architectural representation and the arrival of new media. It also demonstrates how architectural drawing, as a social, communicative document, might have to transmute throughout the different phases of design and construction. Different means of architectural representation possess different agencies, hence the "cloud aesthetics" of 3D scanning—transparency, richness of detail, recording of atmospheric values, light, shadow, color—enables the creation of specific architectural imaginaries.

In a quite different type of design process, Maya Lahmy explores the aesthetic and epistemic potential of 3D cloud scanning in her project *Survey < > Creation.* She focuses on the scanner's point cloud and the visualization of it rather than on the room it records. The project opens up a medial space of fruitful ambiguity, led by an aesthetics cultivated on the basis of the scan. This open-ended, artistically charged approach anticipates a new spatial condition to come, a preoccupation with media space. Lahmy's preoccupation with digital media space is shared by Natalie P. Koerner in her article "Beyond Millions of Plans: A Geometry of Clouds." Koerner probes right into the heart of our digital age by describing a process-oriented, ever-changing space saturated with digital information. "Digital space" is ubiquitous and fluent, overlayering physical surroundings with information that eventually affects human lives. This topological condition destabilizes the prevalent Euclidean-Cartesian understanding of space, which formed the basis for orthogonal projection. In this fluctuating media space, traditional architectural elements such as walls are redefined as thresholds rather than limits, yet architects still seem to lack the right means of representation to grasp these new spatial possibilities.

From Projection to Operation

Since the 1960s, architectural discourse has increasingly questioned the use of orthogonal projection and plan drawings as a means of ordering. This particularly includes plans as biopolitical tools, applied in order to manage people's bodies and actions. In his article, "Plans for a Plentiful Future," Fredrik Torisson examines an urban plan and a housing project in Sweden, both designed to facilitate growth by using generic plan layouts. Such generic plans provide structure rather than form, like the gridiron plan. Rather than a spatial composition, a figure, these plans constitute what Stan Allen has termed a field condition.[12] At the scale of a single house, as one of Torisson's cases demonstrates, decks or slabs would intentionally be left vacant for future occupation and expansion. This "growth paradigm" is situated in the plan, Torisson argues, but might have various implications. On the one hand, freedom of expansion is affiliated with notions of individual freedom, but on the other, it might also offer itself to capitalist adaptation and the pursuit of unlimited economic growth.

Anna Hougaard's project *Real Berlin* zooms in on how plans are being used in combination with renderings to sell and market real estate. Highly detailed photorealistic renderings are powerful ways to market architecture, hidden as the backdrop of design objects and consumer goods. Advertising desired lifestyles, the renderings address buyers' emotions, and in tandem with apartment plans, they communicate the sense of a good investment. This media tandem frames the plan in an economic practice that also has ideological implications and consequences for urban development. Olivia Valentine displays another aspect of growth as related to a loose sort of planning procedure. In the project *Metropoliz Future Forest*, plan patterns from floor tiles found in central Rome were projected 1:1 onto a terrain vague at the outskirts of Rome. The endeavor of this projective procedure was not to facilitate a growing mass of buildings, but to support the further greening of the terrain by vaguely indicating a plan structure. The patterns were used to break the ground open—giving back space through plan drawing rather than converting it to building ground.

The final two articles in this part of the book unapologetically eradicate the orthogonal, projected plan drawing from contemporary architectural practice in favor of operational, time-based design procedures. In his project *Raw Plans*, Robin Schaeverbeke enquires: Who dares to build without the assurance of plans? This question emerges through a house building process that Schaeverbeke carried out using on-site improvisation instead of predefined plans. In a process recalling pre-Renaissance construction, Schaeverbeke used sketches to steer the process on site, in conversation with the constructors. This open, dialogical process allowed for the development and acceptance of unplanned, unforeseen solutions. A comparable design approach is pursued in Sean Griffiths' article "Architecture without Plans: Design Strategies based on Chance Operations." Griffiths argues that life should generate architecture, not the other way around. In a critique of the dominance of visual media in contemporary society—also reflected in the use of plan drawings—Griffiths applies chance operations to the architectural design process, a formalized sort of randomness inspired by composer John Cage. This method was developed to encompass a critique of the limited projective distance from life within the conventional plan drawing. It presupposes the aspiration of working without plan drawings and without thinking of the plan as a stable material condition. Griffiths' strategy follows an ideal that seeks to bring the creation of architecture closer to life as opposed to what a conventional plan drawing does, that is, to occupy a site rather than allowing people to inhabit it. This extreme lack of clearly expressed purpose thoroughly questions contemporary society's striving for optimization. It suggests that abolishing plans might be a way to generate an architecture that prioritizes sound, smell, materiality, and life.

1 Cf. Skylar Tibbits, ed., *Active Matter* (Cambridge, MA: MIT Press, 2017); Achim Menges, ed., *AD Material Computation* 82, no. 2 (March/April 2012).
2 Cf. David Ross Scheer, *The Death of Drawing* (New York and Abingdon: Routledge, 2014); Anh-Linh Ngo, Alexandra Nehmer, Philip Oswalt, Jan Bovelet, and Kilian Enders, eds., "Norm-Architektur – von Durand zu BIM," *Arch+,* 233 (2018).
3 Mario Carpo, *The Alphabet and the Algorithm* (Cambridge, MA, and London: MIT Press, 2011).
4 Robin Evans, "Translations from Drawing to Building," in *Translations from Drawing to Building and Other Essays* (London: Architectural Association, 1997), 153–93.
5 Edward Robbins, *Why Architects Draw* (Cambridge, MA, and London: MIT Press, 1994), 19, 47.
6 Reyner Banham, Paul Barker, Peter Hall, and Cedric Price, "Non-Plan: An Experiment in Freedom," *New Society* 13, no. 338 (1969): 435–43.
7 Rem Koolhaas, "Typical Plan," in Office for Metropolitan Architecture, Rem Koolhaas and Bruce Mau, *S, M, L, XL,* ed. Jennifer Sigler and Hans Werlemann (New York: Monacelli Press, 1997), 336.
8 Ibid., 339.
9 Ibid., 346.
10 Alejandra Celedón, "Footprints," *ARQ* 93 (2016): 74.
11 This is underlined by Steffen Riegas and Michael Drobnik from the Design Technologies Department at Herzog & de Meuron. They argue that BIM does not render other media superfluous, and directly state that "for us, the plan is not dying" (editors' translation). Anh-Linh Ngo, et al., "Komplexitätsmanagement: Steffen Riegas und Michael Drobnik vom Design Technologies Department bei Herzog & de Meuron im Gespräch mit Anh-Linh Ngo und Alexandra Nehmer," *Arch+* 233 (2018), 81.
12 Stan Allen, "Field Conditions," in *Points + Lines: Diagrams and Projects for the City* (New York: Princeton Architectural Press, 1999), 217–43.

Bernadette Devilat
and Felipe Lanuza

fig.1

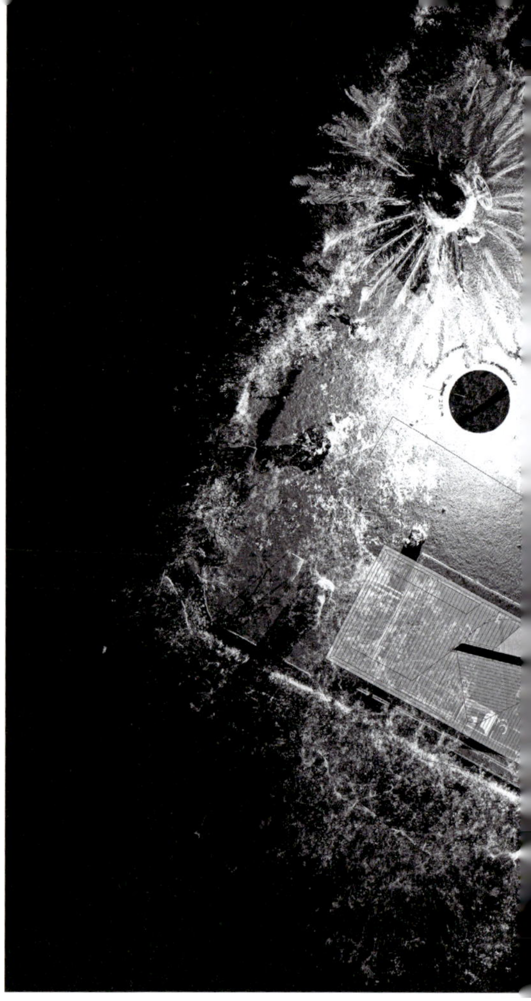

Drawing (on) the Context

Scanning, Designing, Building

1 Bernadette Devilat and Felipe Lanuza, *3D Scan House*, Talagante, 2017. First floor plan. Render of the 3D laser scan data with the 3D design; edited, 2017. 40 × 60 cm.

Drawing the existing site is inherent in any architectural design that seeks to fully engage with its context. For this, 3D laser scanning technology—also known as *lidar*—is an exceptional tool. It provides accurate and comprehensive survey information through a measurable three-dimensional digital model of the reality obtainable in a short period. From capturing the data on-site to postprocessing, we understand this process as a drawing method.

Would the fact of conveying such high amount of information affect the way architects design and draw? To reflect on the impact of this technology from our professional experience, we look at the project of a house near Santiago, Chile, which we designed from London within a 3D laser scan record of the site. The precision of the method informed a remote yet detailed design, where vegetation and other existing elements were closely incorporated in the project.

3D Laser Scanning as Drawing

3D laser scanning is, currently, one of the most accurate methods for surveying the built environment since it collects measurements using a 360° laser beam.[1] The final product of a 3D laser survey is usually an ensemble of several scans, which capture an area from different locations in a three-dimensional point cloud, with a precision of millimeters. The record can be used to generate images, technical drawings, and videos, among other applications in architecture as in many fields, such as archaeology, heritage preservation, forensics, and fabrication.

This survey tool establishes an unprecedented platform for encounter and exploration between the virtual and the real. It enables new modes of architectural practice by offering a way of drawing based on millions of points extracted directly from the environment, triggering different design possibilities that can be translated into built form. One such new possibility is expressed by Bob Sheil when he says: "The tangible has caught up with the intangible, and possibilities that were entirely speculative in non-physical domains just a few years ago are now being materialized and built."[2]

We consider 3D laser scanning as a twofold form of drawing. First, the laser beam that *draws* measurements and color information *from* the reality and translates them into a virtual geometry of measured points with a specific position in space. Second, the creation of images following the data collection on-site where the digital model is edited, dissected, and curated to draw the desired views.

fig. 2

The first process of drawing on-site resembles photography, as light is involved when capturing the reality. Photography is an imprint of light on a sensor, which is subsequently revealed through a chemical or digital process. We can regard photography as the "drawing of light," since the Greek root of the word refers to light (*photo*) and writing or drawing (*graphos*).[3] This etymological definition, although referring solely to "writing," is at the basis of Jean Baudrillard's discussion of photography as an immaterial, illusory presence of reality to question how photographs bring us closer to while distancing us from the world.[4] While the notion of photography as writing of light addresses photographic images from the perspective of semiotics, the less explored etymological root of drawing of light indicates the creative potential of the media to reimagine reality through images that can be framed, obtained, composed, and even manipulated in particular ways, later to be interpreted as texts.[5]

In a way technically more comprehensive and complex than photography, 3D laser scanning captures the environment using light.[6] The word "laser" is "an acronym for Light Amplification by the Stimulated Emission of Radiation."[7] Similarly, lidar means Light Detection And Ranging. Rather than

fig. 3

2 Aerial view of the site with the previous wooden construction. Bernadette Devilat, render of the 3D laser scan data, 2013. 84 × 52 cm.

3 Image of old plan superimposed on the 3D laser scan plan. Bernadette Devilat and Felipe Lanuza, linear plan based on printed architectural drawings over render of the 3D laser scan data, 2019. 19 × 25 cm.

passively capturing the given light and then revealing it—as in photography—3D laser scanning first produces the light with which it captures and measures the distance when impacting on adjacent surfaces, a principle that is known as time-of-flight. Light is intentionally produced *and* captured, in a process repeated multiple times using the reflection of a rotating mirror. The shift occurring from photography to 3D laser scanning is therefore the shift from "drawing of light" to "drawing with light"; the latter being a highly controlled and complex process of projecting light on surfaces to generate a digital model that contains the geometry and spatial properties of the reality.[8]

However, 3D laser scanning captures the reality not only in the form of a point cloud through the repetitive action of projecting a laser beam. Following this process, it captures the given light in a traditional way using an embedded photographic camera, thereby adding the corresponding color information to each of the points that constitute the cloud. Photographs of the type taken by the 3D laser scanner are not meant to be revealed as images,

as they are distributed in millions of points, each of them receiving an RGB value. While two different sources of light are potentially at play here, we will refer only to the first capture with laser light, since we did not capture the color information in this project, due to time constraints. The secondary photographic capture is not essential to this technology and can be left as a subject for further discussion.

In 2013, during a short visit in Chile, we were commissioned to design a guesthouse for a family on a rural plot in Talagante, near Santiago, to be used as a weekend retreat. An old wooden construction used as storage space was to be replaced by a two-story building. We had visited the site before and had some general photographs, as we had developed a project for the refurbishments of the main house a couple of years before. Yet now, as we were to leave the country the next day, we thought of an alternative method of surveying the site since there was not enough time for a traditional architectural survey based on photographs and hand measure-

fig. 4

4 Section of the site after digitally removing the previous construction to start the design. Bernadette Devilat, render of the 3D laser scan data, 2013. 30 × 63.7 cm.

ments. We used 3D laser scanning instead, obtaining all relevant information within only 30 minutes on-site. All physical features and every detail became available to be retrieved at any time without the need for another visit. This allowed us to design this house long-distance from London, where we were based during the whole process.[9]

The particularity here, as we will see, is that we used the 3D laser data not just to draw technical images but also to create an architectural design tailored to the specificity of the context within the three-dimensionality of the record. This means precisely adjusting and responding to the conditions, elements, and details of a captured site, e.g., vegetation, preexisting structures, vistas, and so forth [fig. 2].

Drawing from the Point Cloud

Being the on-site laser record, the first process of *drawing from* the context, the second resembles the conventional production of graphic material, using the site information. Traditionally, technical drawings such as scaled plans, sections, and elevations rely on the dimensions taken on-site, in a process of translating those measurements into the material or digital media of architectural representations. This implies a series of drawing conventions on technical aspects that are part of our discipline, as a specific way of looking at and interpreting the reality. By dissecting the 3D model with virtual means, technical drawings can be obtained directly, without the need to translate the measurements, as the point cloud already contains this information.

In this way, we obtained plans, sections, and elevations, which allowed us to assess the architectural drawings of the construction to be replaced and the site plan provided by the clients. Significant gaps and differences between these and the as-built constructions became evident by superimposing the drawings provided with the 3D point cloud plans and sections [fig. 3]. It also became clear that these documents represented the site in an oversimplified manner.

In a conventional survey, if relevant elements of the site are not included in the initial context drawing or site plan, they may never become part of the design unless the site is revisited for a reassessment. By using 3D laser scan data, in contrast, the physical context was always at hand in its entirety. The process of abstraction, traditionally performed by a selection of the reality represented—inherent in architectural drawing as a way of observing—could now be done later, since the captured data included nearly everything visible.[10]

In this way, the nature of our critical assessment of the context information shifted from drawing what seemed relevant to emphasizing features of the reality while designing. To draw became to withdraw: erasing or hiding unnecessary information so as to focus on what was relevant by way of editing and manipulating the 3D laser scan model and its visualizations. We kept the elements we wanted to preserve and digitally removed the wooden construction to be replaced by the new design. Although not even strictly required for design, generating drawings from the 3D point cloud became a way of understanding the site. In this way we created new representations where the vegetation and trees became an important feature [fig. 4].

In the visualizations we used a black background contrasting with the point cloud. In the process of drawing from the 3D laser scan data, light becomes manifest as an element inherent in the nature of the information captured. Things not reached by the laser beam would not appear in the digital model, known as "occluded areas." Most evidently, these parts are the circles that indicate where the tripod and scanner were placed, or surfaces behind objects that, even after several scans, remained unreachable to the laser beam, e. g., the interior of walls. Also, as the scanner emits light to capture the data up to 120 m according to the model used, there is a higher density of

fig. 5

5 Orthogonal top view of the design over the 3D laser scanning as surveyed. The black circles indicate the position of the scanner. Bernadette Devilat and Felipe Lanuza, render of the 3D laser scan data with the 3D design, 2017. 38.8 × 38.8 cm.

points captured closer to the scanner. When rendering the images, this phenomenon conveys the impression that the scanner is a source of light, which is particularly visible on the plan [fig. 5].

This process of reflective drawing consists of both choosing a position and an angle from which to capture a view on the 3D scanned data—as if it were a photograph—and of hiding information in order to visualize the desired image. These actions of selection, although they do not add anything to the data, are not neutral but full of intentionality, as can be any other mode of drawing or representing a given site. And yet drawing as an authored action starts even earlier, with the capture on-site. An absolute capture is not an option, as there will always be occluded areas. In theory, with an infinite number of scans, any room or space can be covered in its entirety, but with time as a constraint, the surveyor has a limited number of scans with which to capture a site. Thus, by selecting what to record and the resolution of the recording, she or he defines what is not

going to be incorporated. The decisions on the number and locations in space of the scans are the first defining aspect of the authorship in this laser drawing process. According to Manuel de Solà-Morales and Josep Parcerisa, "to draw is to select, to select is to interpret, to interpret is to propose."[11] In this case, the selection does not correspond only with the editing of the model but also, to a significant degree, with the capture of the data on-site.

Drawing on the Point Cloud

The last distinctive action in this particular process of drawing corresponds with the incorporation of the new project. The context information obtained with the scanner became a 3D canvas for an architectural design. Our design process was done directly on the 3D model as if we were digitally building on the real site. The proposal was inserted, with precise measurements, directly into the digital point cloud using Rhinoceros software [fig. 6].[12] The intervention was placed, scaled, and drawn on the digital site.

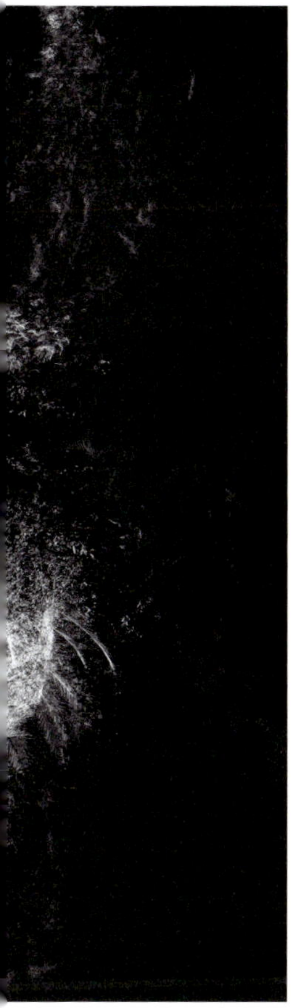

fig. 6

fig. 7

Aerial view of the design placed within the 3D laser point cloud. Bernadette Devilat and Felipe Lanuza, render of the 3D laser scan data with the 3D design, 2017. 30 × 60 cm.

Felipe Lanuza, handmade sketches of design alternatives, 2014. Pencil and pen on paper, 22 × 25 cm.

Nonetheless, for us, the importance of free sketching to define our first ideas was something that the complexity of the 3D laser scan model of the context could not replace. So the first explorative lines were drawn by hand, sometimes on to-scale prints drawn from the point cloud. Our design developed as a back-and-forth process between these two realms of representation [fig. 7].

In contrast to the traditional way of drawing both context and proposal "with the same hand" or the same graphic language, the new project is different in terms of representation. While the reality is rendered as a point cloud from the 3D data, the design is a newly created 3D digital model made of lines and surfaces that asserts this condition by being represented as such, or else as conventional 2D drawings.

2D drawings extracted from the point cloud were useful also for communication purposes. For example, comparing the heights of the old construction and the new design was made easier in this way for the clients,

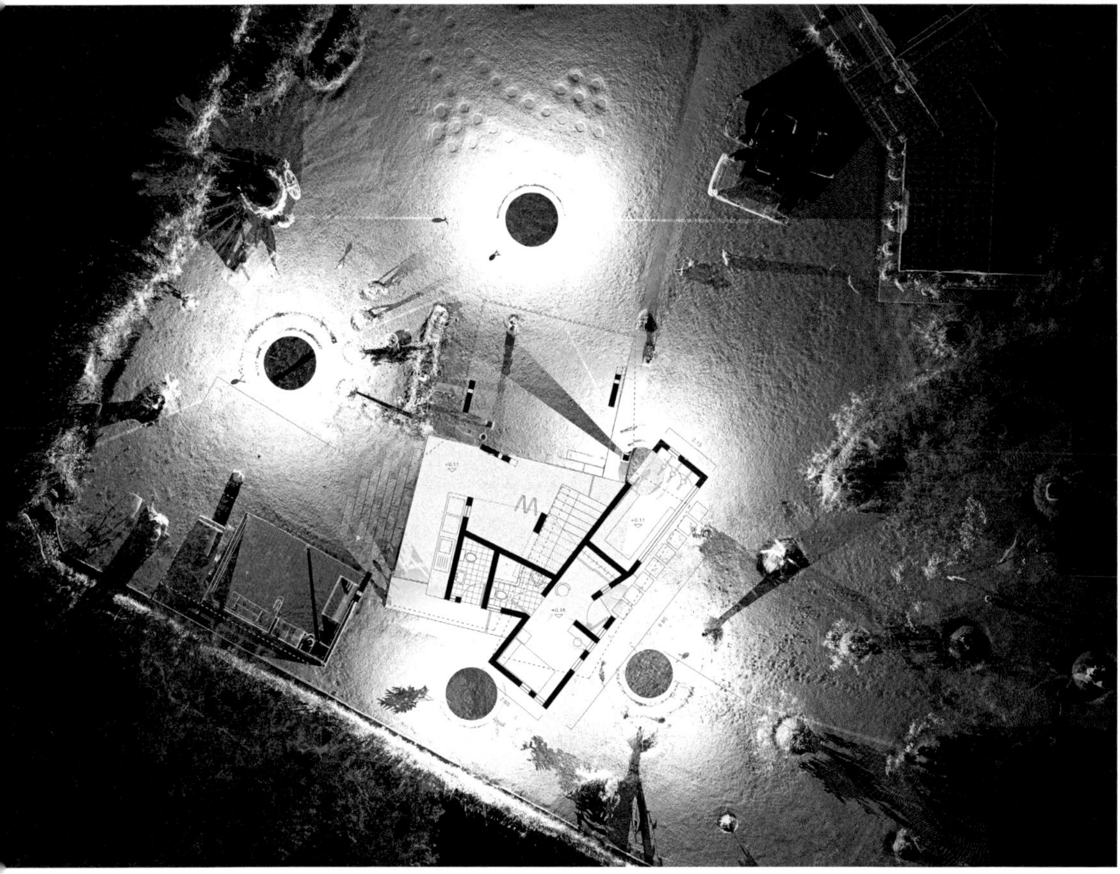

who recognized the existing elements. We used the point cloud showing the context both with and without the old construction to demonstrate and assess how the new house would fit on the site. We also used images obtained from the 3D modeled design within the context to sketch some views as work-in-progress updates for the clients, in which the existing vegetation was key to their spatial understanding.[13] In the same spirit, we also created plans [fig. 1, 8] and a section [fig. 9] of the design and its context. Although designing within a 3D laser scan point cloud does not require drawing two-dimensional representations, they helped us understand the project with its form and functionality by establishing commonly used architectural views, especially the plan. The 3D model was constantly updated accordingly, and further used to 3D print a maquette of the house for us to get a physical grasp of its geometry and proportions [fig. 10].

fig. 8

8 Ground floor plan. Bernadette Devilat and Felipe Lanuza, render of the 3D laser scan data with the 3D design; edited, 2017. 40 × 60 cm.

These 2D renderings and the maquette were ways to visualize or, as suggested by Mario Carpo, "a way to *visit* an actual model—each visit being

ig. 9

ig. 10

9 Section. Bernadette Devilat and Felipe Lanuza, render of the 3D laser scan data with the 3D design; edited, 2017. 30 × 60 cm.

10 3D prints of the design. Photographs by Bernadette Devilat, 2017. 20.7 × 118 cm.

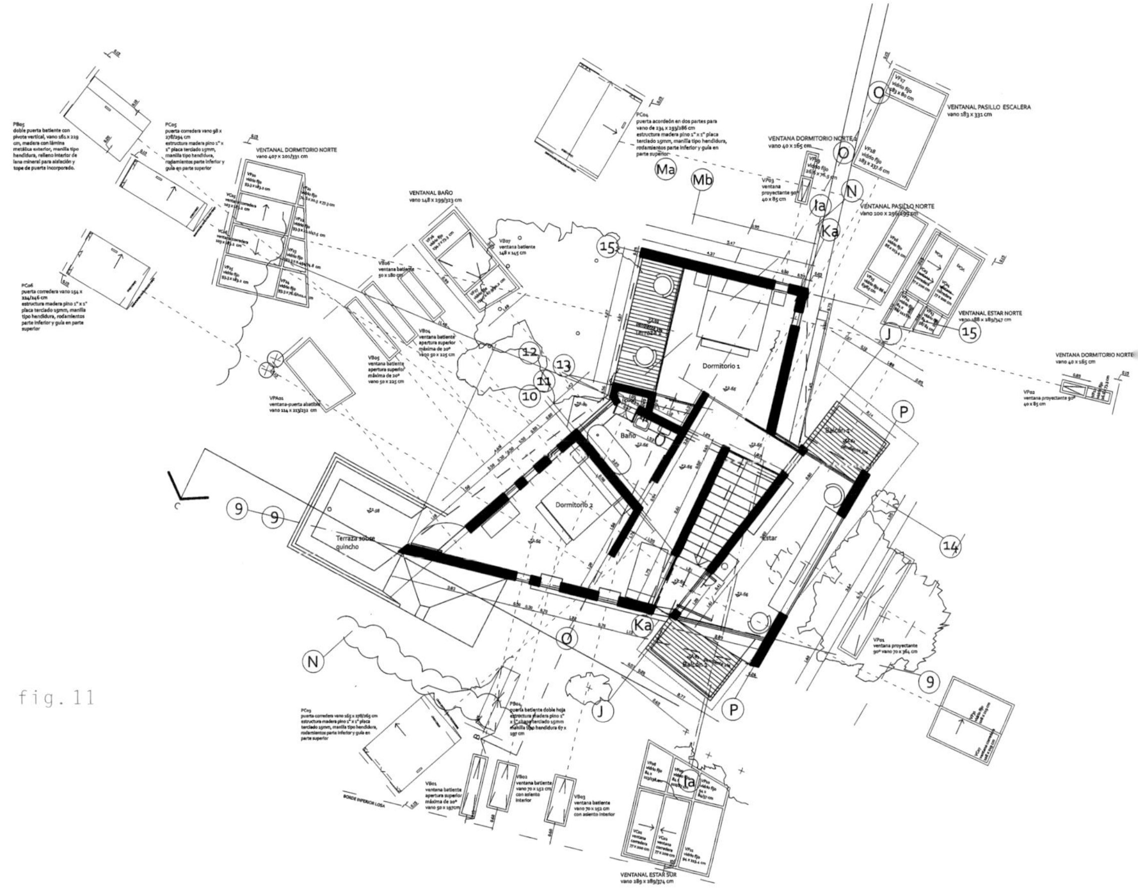

fig. 11

different, based on contingent requirements and intentions. The only stable part, and the keystone and kernel of the whole system, is the 3-D model itself."[14] A model that, in this case, blended the information drawn from the reality—as a point cloud—and the design crafted within it.

Drawing for Construction (and Beyond)

As a fourth stage in the drawing process, we had to elaborate a conventional set of 2D drawings for building permission purposes and construction. This meant translating the design into technical representations for authorities and contractors, where lines were predominant and the point cloud was removed [fig. 11]. The task of drawing, or redrawing in this case, was here to represent the architectural design by moving from one medium to another, from the 3D model to the usual 2D CAD drawings, adding another design iteration where opportunities to refine the project emerged.

This ended up being the final version of the design, with minor adjustments and also incorporating the necessary detailing and annotations

fig. 12

11 First floor plan with the details of doors and windows for construction. Bernadette Devilat and Felipe Lanuza, CAD drawing, 2015. 42 × 59.4 cm.

12 View of the built house from the back part of the site. Photo by Bernadette Devilat, 2017.

for getting the house built. It was a time-consuming task that evidenced a gap in the production line leading from design to construction. This could probably have been done more effectively using Building Information Modeling (BIM) methods, which can be incorporated into point-cloud data. However, we could not find a contractor who would build directly from the 3D model information. The house was finally built [fig. 12] using a complete set of linear drawings.

An important issue that emerges here is the shift from drawing to building. Our distance from the construction site determined that smaller decisions about several details we designed, or existing elements we incorporated thanks to the 3D laser scan, were either not realized or they changed along the way. And like many other construction processes, the house was not built accurately to the drawings, leading to gaps and deviations in addition to a few changes in the project during construction. The design became dynamic to the extent that its existence on the real site became different from its existence in the 3D digital model and the drawings. A scan of the finished

fig. 13

house, which we did in December 2017, offers the possibility to measure and observe these differences, the analysis and imagery of which are left for further study.

The built architecture is not necessarily the end of the architectural project, which we further developed exploring different aspects of drawing and communication. The plans and sections embedded in the point cloud [fig. 8–9, 14] posed new challenges in terms of representation. Regarding legibility, the point cloud is not consistent with the line drawings required for the construction, as they convey information of different nature. In order to better represent how the project engages with the context, the challenge was to achieve a coherent visual language to link the 3D laser scan data with the traditional mode of architectural drawing.

We explored different ways of using white and grey to represent solid cut elements in the plans and the section, yet always leaving shades of grey for projected lines and surfaces to match the appearance of the point-cloud

13 Comparison between model and construction site. Overlay of vista taken from the 3D point cloud and a photograph of the construction taken from the same vantage point. Composite image, 2017. 30 × 20 cm.

14 Elevation. Bernadette Devilat and Felipe Lanuza, render of the 3D laser scan data with the 3D design, edited, 2018. 38.8 × 67.7 cm.

context. We eventually decided to use the same color—black in this case—for walls, structural elements, and the background. This way of representing the design was chosen to be coherent with the future imaging from the 3D laser scanning of the built work, in which the internal matter of walls, roofs, and partitions remained outside the reach of the laser beam.

Beyond aspects of representation, the point cloud offers further possibilities to relate to the reality and other forms to represent it. Just as the metric condition of the point cloud allows the placing of previous drawings to check their accuracy, photographs can also be placed and even "measured" through comparisons with the same view [fig. 13]. In this way, the three-dimensionality of the reality captured by the laser becomes a platform for combining conventional drawings with other media, while potentially giving new dimensions to previous records. Understanding each record as information of a particular moment in time—before, during, and after interventions are built—the point cloud can unify different layers of information in one single three-dimensional data set.[15]

fig. 14

Here it becomes clear that the 3D record stands as an entity in its own right, which establishes a certain distance from what it captures. This allows us to understand the 3D scan point cloud of our site not only as a basis for design but also as a virtual presence of the reality that evidences the distance between the project, as representation of un-built architecture, and its actual construction.[16]

Conclusion

We regard our architectural practice as an opportunity for research, speculating on the possibilities of 3D laser scanning as a mode of understanding and representing the reality [fig. 14]. This project has given us the chance to go back and forth between the design and the experience of built architecture.[17]

Here, we have attempted to understand the relation between 3D laser scanning and drawing in four different yet interrelated ways: The laser light as a form of *drawing from* the context; rendering and visualizing such information by obtaining 2D, 3D, and moving images from the point cloud; using the 3D point cloud as a virtual platform in which to *draw within* to create a new design; and how translating the design into traditional representations ended up being the most effective means of communicating with available contractors since lidar technology had not yet reached that sphere in Chile.

In that regard, the possibilities of the technology go beyond what we have shown in this article. For example, the 3D laser record offers the possibility of extracting literally millions of plans and representations from the reality, a process that can even be automated. By slicing the 3D every millimeter, new plans can be created, different yet similar—iterations of one another.

To handle and give sense to an otherwise sheer accumulation of information, the process of drawing implies making a selection—a curatorial task needed to make effective use of a comprehensive survey technology by navigating through large amounts of data. The selection leads to interpretation and proposal, recalling de Solà-Morales and Parcerisa, to show how drawing, in different ways, remained a meaningful and necessary act throughout our architectural design process. In particular, the drawing of the architectural plans contextualized and made sense of the 3D data to define how the different spaces would be used and how the surroundings of the house would feature in day-to-day activities, bringing the point-cloud context to life.

Therefore, from our understanding of 3D laser scanning as drawing *with* (a laser) light and *from* the reality in the on-site capture, we propose an unconventional drawing process that goes beyond the mechanical measurement of a given site but is a spatial engagement with the reality that defines how the further stages of drawing will follow. This means that carefully selecting what to record is as much part of the drawing process as the act itself. Furthermore, this drawing *with* light implies a greater engagement and control over the captured reality—a possibility to revisit the record virtually, to put it in Carpo's terminology, while the drawing *of* light captured in a photograph is almost impenetrable and is restricted to a single vantage point and framing. Traditional drawing also portraits a point of view to be determined—a plan, a section, a detail, a vista—whereas the 3D point cloud stands as a versatile entity from which new pieces of information can be drawn in the future.

Different techniques of drawing entail particular modes of approaching reality. In the hybrid experience we exposed here we intended to integrate new tools with our previously acquired skills and procedures, to understand, create, and communicate architecture. Perhaps resonating with how photography helped to push painting to different levels as a mode of representing and reimagining reality, we believe that architectural drawing's greatest potential is to seek new creative horizons beyond as well as within what 3D laser scanning—or any other technology—can convey.

Bernadette Devilat, "Recording of eritage Buildings: From Measured rawing to 3D Laser Scanning," in *rawing Futures: Speculations in ontemporary Drawing for Art and rchitecture*, ed. Laura Allen and Luke . Pearson (London: UCL Press, 2016), 36–40, also available at http:// scovery.ucl.ac.uk/1527533/1/ rawing-Futures.pdf (accessed July 22,)19).

Bob Sheil, "Introduction—High efinition: Zero Tolerance in Design and roduction," in *High Definition: Zero olerance in Design and Production*, pecial issue of *Architectural Design*, d. Bob Sheil (London: Wiley, 2014), 10.

Svetlana Alpers, *The Art of Describ- g: Dutch Art in the Seventeenth entury* (Chicago, IL: University of hicago Press, 1983), 136.

Jean Baudrillard, "Photography, Or the riting of Light," trans. Francois Debrix, d. Arthur Kroker and Marilouise Kroker, *Theory*, www.ctheory.net/articles. spx?id=126 (accessed July 22, 2019).

For a more detailed discussion on notography as the drawing of light e: Felipe Lanuza, "Absence through ayering: From Experiencing Urban eftovers to Reimagining Sites" (PhD ss., Bartlett School of Architecture, niversity College London, 2017), 70–72.

The discussion of the cultural impact images of the reality obtained through) laser scanning technology, in the ght of—or compared with—photogra- ny, seems highly relevant to us yet it scapes the scope of this work, which more focused on drawing.

7 William F. Price and J. Uren, *Laser Surveying* (London: Van Nostrand Reinhold International, 1989), 1.

8 Using recently developed software, 3D models and metric information of the reality can be obtained by combining several photographs of a site. This can be regarded as a realm between photography and 3D laser scanning.

9 For more information on this project, see: Bernadette Devilat and Felipe Lanuza, "3D Scan House," *InForma*, Hybrid Realities—*Realidades Híbridas* 11 (Autumn 2018): 110–14.

10 As with any other tool, 3D laser scanning has possibilities as well as limitations. Here we only focus on 3D laser scanning in comparison with conventional architectural drawing applied to design. For example, as the scanner captures surfaces only, data could be missing from its misplacement and inaccessible areas on-site, and also computation issues due to the large amount of points captured. These aspects can be resolved by planning, and by using the latest software and hardware. In addition, sounds, as well as olfactory and tactile dimensions of the reality, cannot be reproduced (although suggested) using this recording method. Nonetheless, they can be integrated in a virtual reality experience combining records of different nature of a given site with a 3D laser scan record.

11 Manuel de Solà-Morales and Josep Parcerisa, "La forma d'un país," *Quaderns d'Arquitectura i Urbanisme* número extra 1 (1981): 4. Translation from Spanish to English by the authors.

12 A video exploring the design inserted on the 3D laser scan point-cloud site is available on our website, DLA Scan / Devilat Lanuza Architectural Studio, https://devilat-lanuza.com/project-5 (accessed October 1, 2019).

13 The new house consisted of a ground floor with storage and services to support the existing barbecue shed, and a first floor comprising bedrooms, a bathroom, and a common area. We designed terraces and openings to the surrounding vegetation, enhancing its relation with the context and protecting privacy when required.

14 Mario Carpo, *The Second Digital Turn: Design Beyond Intelligence* (Cambridge, MA, and London: MIT Press, 2017), 124.

15 This idea of representing layers of time in buildings is especially relevant in contexts of constant change and intervention such as architectural heritage at risk of earthquakes, further explored in: Bernadette Devilat, "Re-Construction and Record: Exploring Alternatives for Heritage Areas after Earthquakes in Chile" (PhD diss., Bartlett School of Architecture, University College London, 2018).

16 The virtual presence of reality in images produced through 3D scanning technology may inform further discussions engaging with Baudrillard's account of photography.

17 Acknowledgments: This house was built in Talagante, Chile, with the constant on-site supervision and help of María Fernanda Vargas. Thanks also to the clients, Isabel Riquelme and César Oyarzo, for their patience and support.

Maya Lahmy

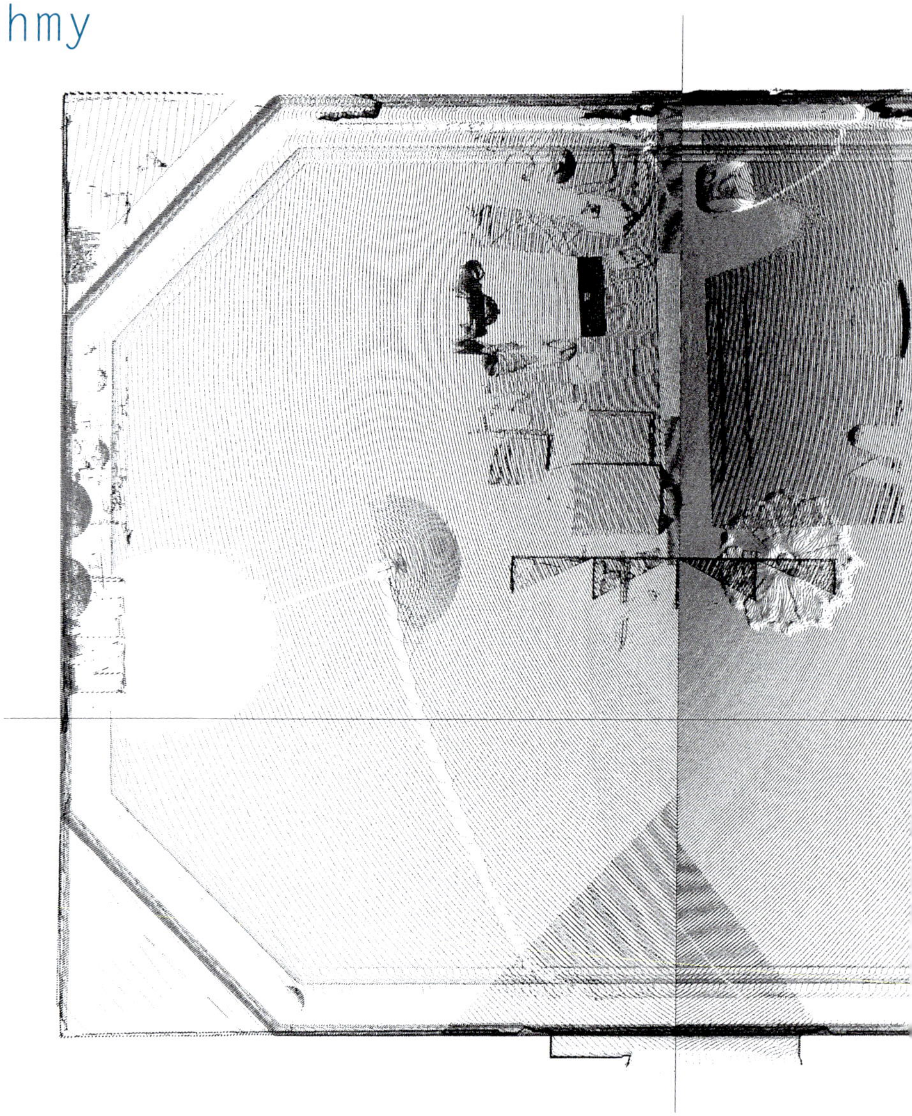

Survey < > Creation

The Illustrative Scan and
the Explorative Drawing

fig. 1

1 Plan of hidden or lost parts.

The project *Survey < > Creation* proposes that point clouds from laser scans of an existing space can be transformed into explorative drawings. Laser scanning was initiated as a site registration of my 20 m^2 office in Aarhus, Denmark, with the intention of subsequently probing into the survey scans and exploring the potential of understanding the space, its occupation, and 3D scanning, in terms of drawing techniques. The scanning positioned the information of the space into point clouds,[1] which were subsequently engaged as drawings. The 3D scans were recorded from two positions that show in the point clouds as two circular formations. The scans from position one [fig. 2, 6] and position two [fig. 3, 6] were combined into a point cloud that depicts the office and myself at my desk [fig. 1–7]. I then scanned people standing or passing through the office at different paces [fig. 8, book cover].

Imperfections appear as strange results, for example the threads of points swaying from the doorway or points floating from the windows [fig. 4–5]. Such strange moments were an inspiration to perform a sort of

fig. 2

fig. 3

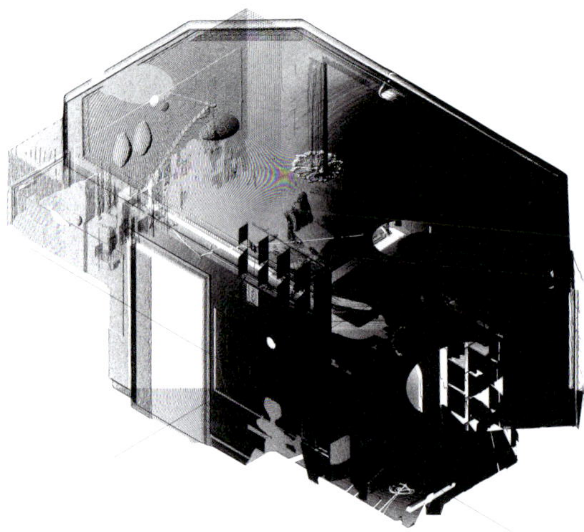

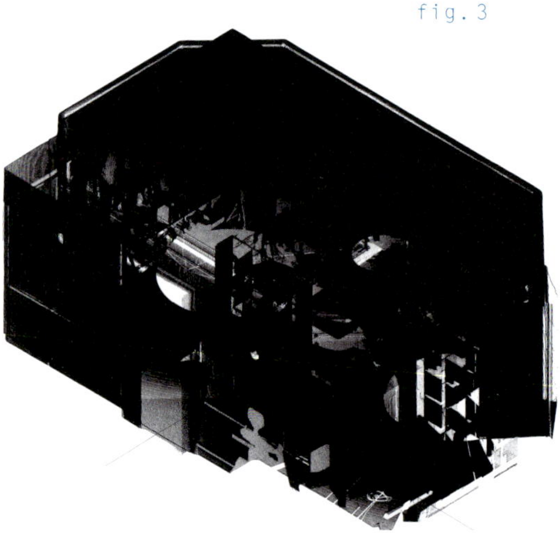

fig. 4

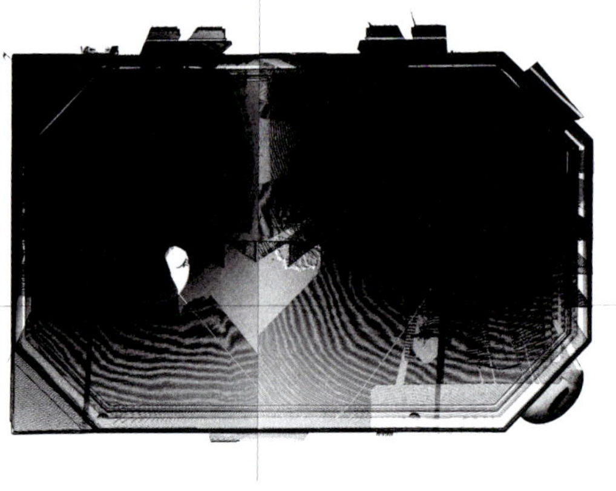

fig. 5

2 Maya Lahmy, *Survey <> Creation*, 2015, digital laser scan, Aarhus. Point cloud recorded from position one.

3 Point cloud recorded from position two.

4 The resulting point clouds from the scan positions one and two were combined into a single point cloud.

5 A plan showing points that drift away from the periphery.

fig. 6

dissection of the point clouds to enable views into the recorded space and look for other surprising details [fig. 6]. The sectioned point clouds were then combined into various configurations [fig. 7]. The composition of parts creates a moiré effect, which appears to fan out from the intense black domains of the plan drawing [fig. 5]. In the axonometric drawings, elements were lost in the shadow of other elements and shadows appear as deformed spatial elements. Most parts of the drawings are recognizable as an interior space; however, the deformed elements destabilize recognition and create an unsettling site condition [fig. 8 and book cover].

Similar to a camera's exposure time, the scanner has a recording time, which enabled the ephemeral event of movement through space to be captured. The resulting point clouds represent people in movement through the office, without rendering an exact geometric representation of a person [fig. book cover]. The section lines form striated elements in an interpretation of the point clouds that unexpectedly causes the moving persons and the surrounding space to merge into one entity. Strange veil-like characters emerging in the drawings undermine the geometric representation of movements and initiate ways to imagine spatial elements [fig. 8 and book cover].

Exploring the exact metric quantification of the existing space through explorative drawings allowed me to imagine and suggest new spatial elements. The project engaged a kind of "creation drawing," which allowed for the development of elements that were new yet affiliated with the existing world. The 3D scanning sparked a surprising reciprocity between the two types of drawings, the survey drawing of the existing and the creation drawing for the anticipated world.

6 The 3D scans were recorded from the two positions that can be seen as two circular formations on the floor of the office. The scanner detected objects that were visible from the two chosen positions but surfaces not in direct line of vision were not recorded.

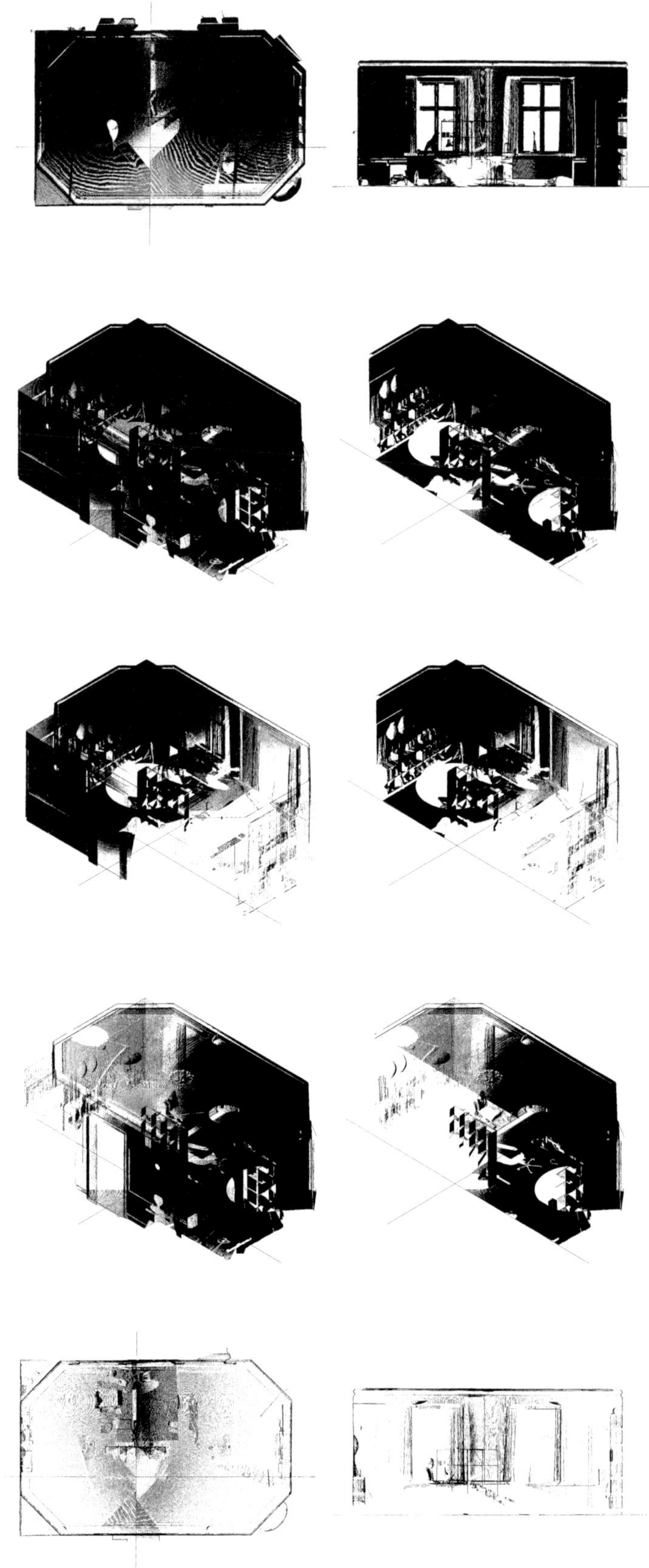

fig.7

7 The section lines were perpendicular to the walls, and they were set to cross at the most trafficked area of the room, which was the entry and exit passage for colleagues from neighboring offices.

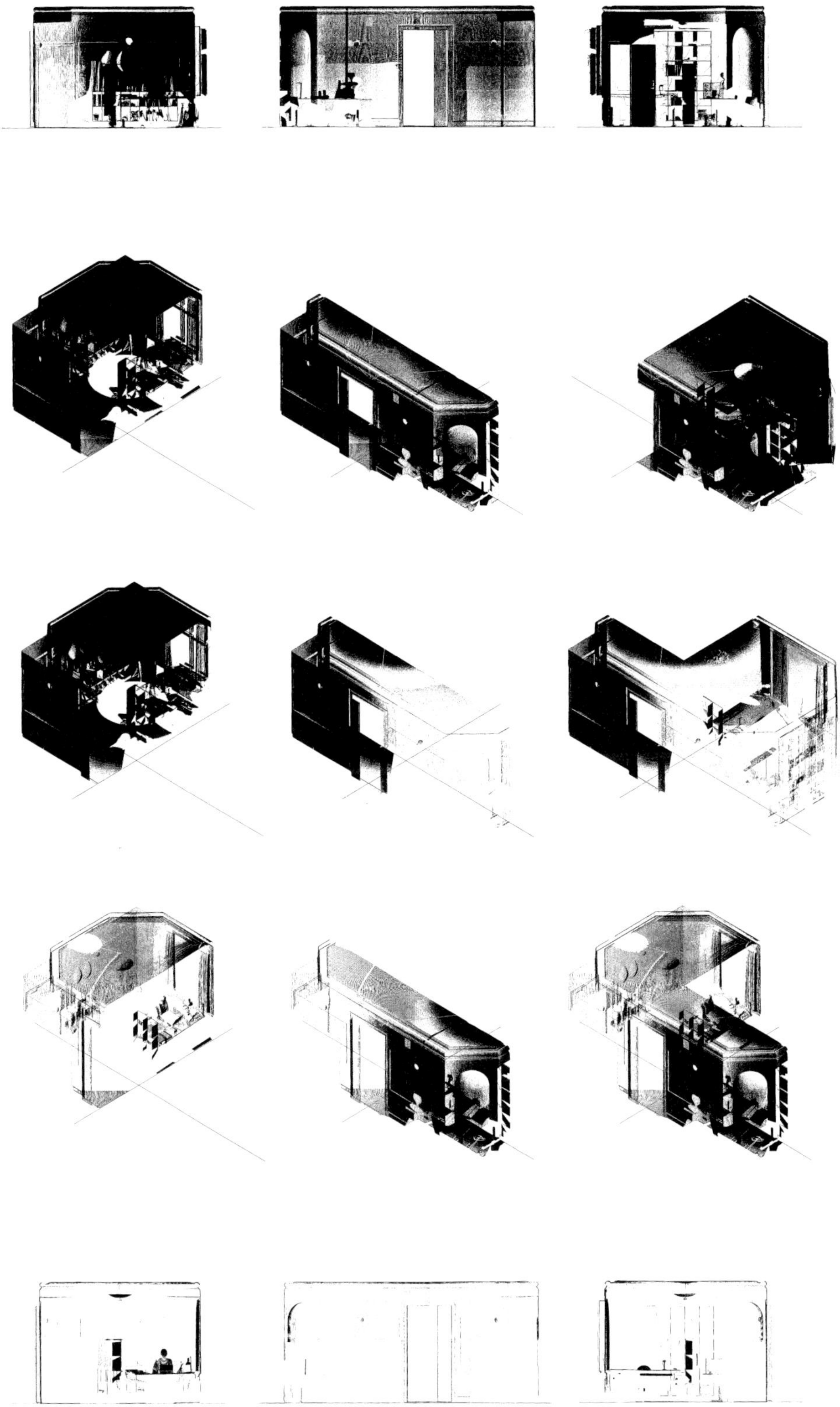

fig.8

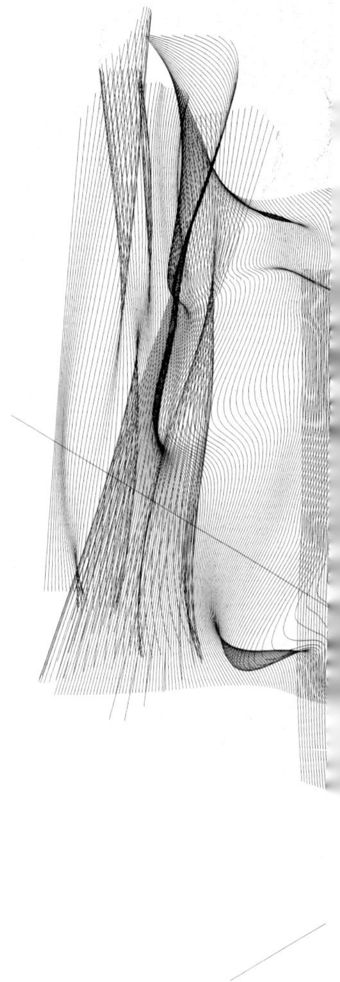

As the cybernetician Ranulph Glanville argues, there is a significant difference in the design process between both physical and digital models *of* an existing condition and the model *for* an anticipated condition. Glanville establishes the differentiating distinction as "models (and knowledge) of (what is) and for (action)."[2] Glanville explains that the distinction between *of* and *for* correlates with the distinction between illustrative and explorative process, respectively.[3]

Glanville's distinction between the illustrative and the explorative process is the source of inspiration for the *Survey < > Creation* drawings presented here; however, not as separate positions. For example, deliberate manipulation of the scanning process produced voids or deformed parts in the resulting point cloud, and the voids became places to develop and imagine elements in the drawing. In this way, scanning created an opportunity for engaging the illustrative survey into the explorative drawing. The illustrative and the explorative drawing processes coexisted; exemplifying that the

8 Point clouds that represented movements were translated into 3D surfaces, and section lines were drawn vertically along the curvature of the 3D surfaces.

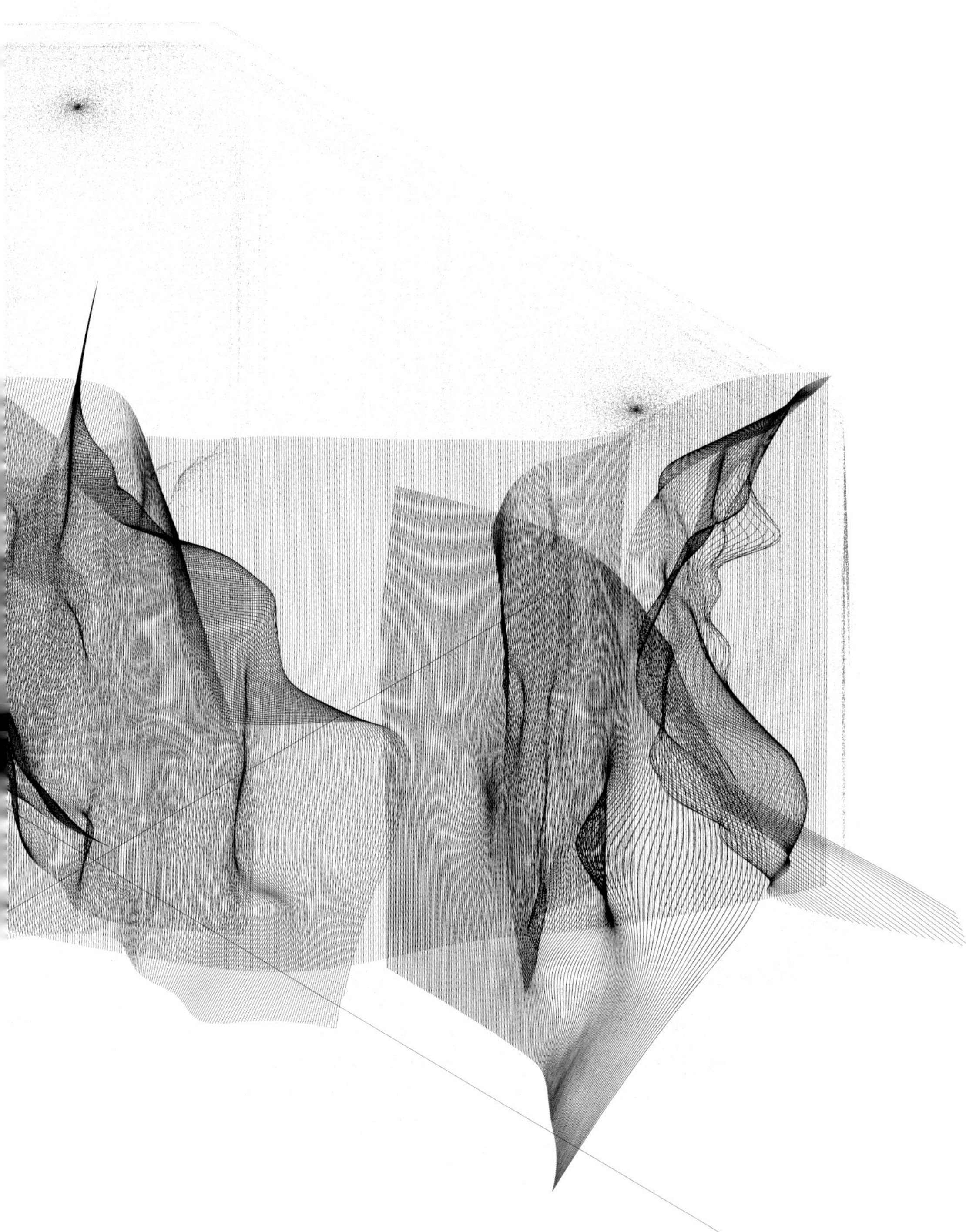

transfers between the explorative and the illustrative can take place within the digital drawing as a gradual change on a spectrum between the two positions.

The scanning process was a way to select data for digital drawings. The resulting drawings possess spatial characteristics: they became a new site to explore the unexpected imperfections that emerged from the scanning procedure. The imperfections, deformations, and voids were generated by manipulation of the scanning process, resulting from deliberate movements of what was scanned or from "insufficient" data selection. Consequently, uncontrolled spatial compositions were formed in the drawings that destabilized the connection to what was scanned. Instead of "correcting" the imperfections, these became the source of further investigations and developments of the drawings. For instance, the digital scanning procedure enabled registration of movement as a fluid entity that engaged spatially through motion. The intersecting warped surfaces that occurred in the drawing flowed together to form a substance hardly recognizable as movements of human figures; they emerge as unexpected stills of veil-like formations in motion.

In my project, the scanner is an example of an optical device that indeed opts for metric control yet also works as a vehicle for artistic expression. Similar to photographic techniques, laser scanning enables interpretation of what is observed. In this vein, Alberto Pérez-Gómez and Louise Pelletier argue that technologies have been used in architecture as projection tools—not to reduce observations of the world, but to enable abstractions in order to discover something that is both recognizable and original. The concern is how to prevent valuable, immeasurable aspects of the architect's creative design process from being lost in translation as it were, and how to enable abstraction for the sake of discovery.[4] As one option, Pérez-Gómez and Pelletier cautiously argue for "deliberately embracing chance and computer 'errors.'"[5] For the project *Survey < > Creation*, embracing chance and errors deliberately meant engaging the misinterpretations, deformation, and errors that destabilize the known conditions, trigger alternative understandings of the scanned, and inspire the invention of elements in the gaps between the metrically controlled parts.

The FARO focus 3D laser scanner sed for this project is a professional easuring device, created for land urvey and "as built" visualization and egistration. The laser scanner, which as operated through the controlled teering of a laser rangefinder, was ositioned on a tripod, and measured ne distance between the head of the otating laser scanner and the urrounding space by sending and eceiving the reflection of a laser beam a rotation. The output data from the aser scanning of the office were nported as point clouds into Rhino 3D.

Ranulph Glanville claims to owe his omplementary distinction between odels of and models for to Gerard de eeuw. Ranulph Glanville, "Intention and e User," in *Persistent Modelling: xtending the Role of Architectural epresentation*, ed. Phil Ayres (Abingdon nd New York: Routledge, 2012), 41–50.

3 Glanville explains: "Illustration demonstrates, even documents, and does not imply question or answer: it just is." "Exploration," by contrast, "is uncertain, questioning to better understand and act." Of course, the intention pursued with a model might change, or a model made to illustrate might become useful for exploration and vice versa. What is more, it applies to both distinctions that the designer or user can initiate a transfer of intention between illustrative/of and explorative/for. But still, with emphasis on computer models at his time of writing, 2012, Glanville states: "The computer modelling tools made for designers rarely, if ever, generate models for. Their intention is not to allow, let alone promote, exploration or modification: they report as well as they can what, under certain circumstances, will be." He continues: "Computer models often exclude the central (conversational) act of design." Glanville, "Intention and the User," 44, 46.

4 In their seminal book *Architectural Representation and the Perspective Hinge*, Alberto Pérez-Gómez and Louise Pelletier debate that computer graphic applications reduced to visual experience diminish the engagement of the diverse human experience fundamental to architecture. Consequently, the digital visual technology would cut away the immeasurable aspects of the architect's sketching process. In contrast, Pérez-Gómez and Pelletier also reflect on the *fascination* of optical devices as a poetic response to the at times reductive persuasiveness of logical arguments and supporting evidence. The optical devices that are referred to are the photographic camera and the stereoscope. Alberto Pérez-Gómez and Louise Pelletier, *Architectural Representation and the Perspective Hinge* (Cambridge, MA, and London: MIT Press, 1997), 2–87.

5 Ibid., 382. For the computer "error" Pérez-Gómez and Pelletier refer to an article by Heinrich Schnoedt, "Cultural Parametrics," in: *Reality and Virtual Reality: Mission—Method—Madness: ACADIA Conference Proceedings* (Los Angeles, CA: University of California, 1991), 223–34.

Natalie P. Koerner

fig. 1

Beyond Millions of Plans

A Geometry of Clouds

1 Diller+Scofidio, *Blur Building*, 2002. Conceptual rendering.

Clouds are bodies "without surface," in the words of Leonardo da Vinci.[1] As such, they are not typically related to either geometrical plan drawings or architecture, unless they float like a dreamy anecdote through what still establishes one of architecture's origin stories: Filippo Brunelleschi's perspectival peeping onto the Florence Baptistery, which is now understood as a turning point in architectural representation. It established linear perspective as an indispensable tool for navigating architectural design and depiction. However, this geometrical method has a fundamental inadequacy: its inability to depict bodies without a static outline, such as clouds, which are subject to a continuous morphological update.[2] Clouds and the concept of bodies without surfaces resonate with the representational challenges faced in the digital production of architecture. Below, I will explore the fading role of the line and the rise of points in digital representation methods such as point clouds.

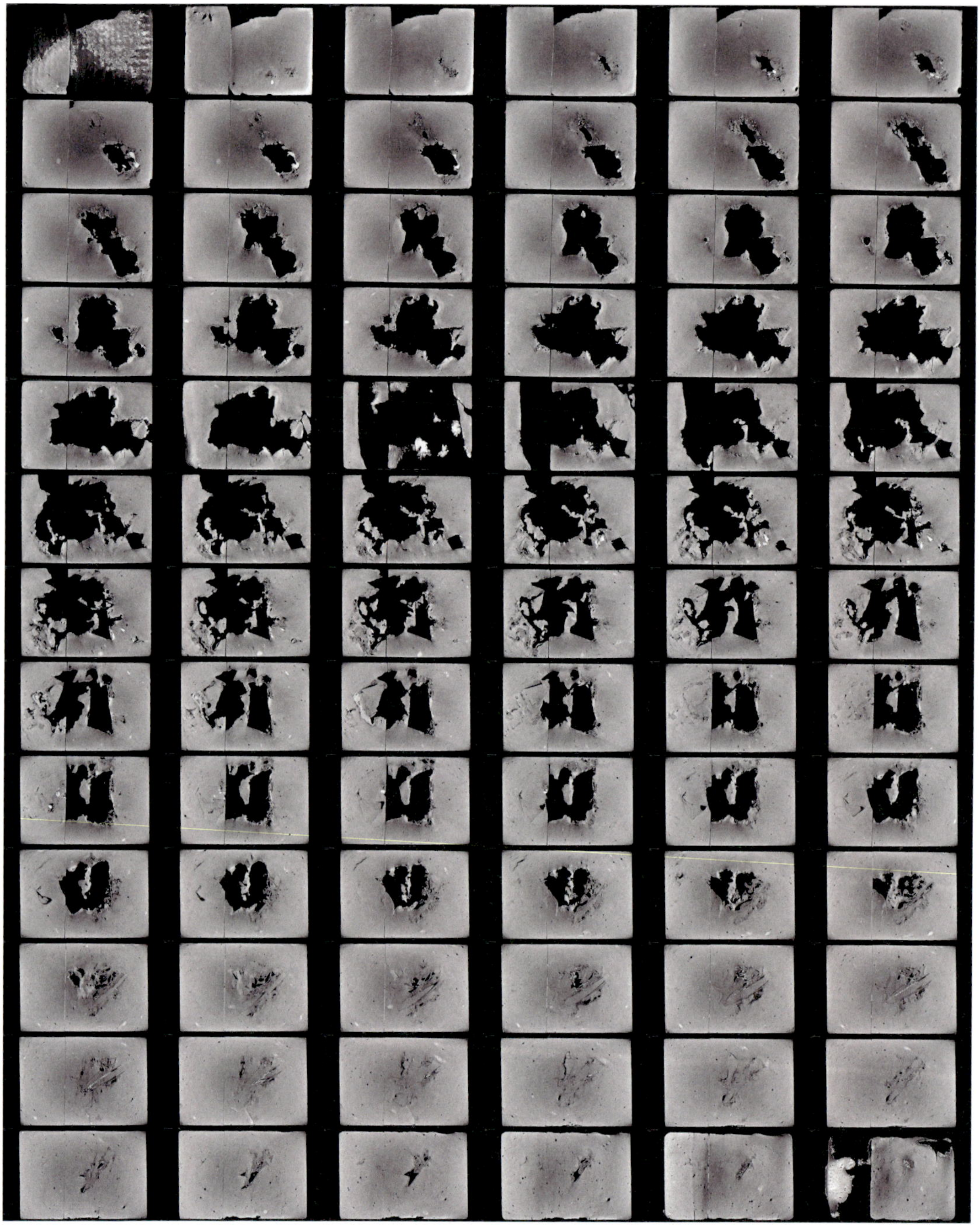

2 Christian Kerez, *Incidental Space*, Venice, 2016. Section images of point cloud data from CT scan (digital tomographic scan) of the initial model by Stefan Hörber, MessX AG.

In architectural drawings, lines demarcate enclosures—the surfaces of physical objects —for example of walls. Lines represent the places where the body will meet resistance, once the drawing has been translated into a building. Lines in their definitive nature—which only varies in thickness or, for dotted lines, in the ratio between line segment and spacing—are well suited for depicting borders but inadequate for depicting indefinite thresholds. The threshold is, in contemporary understandings of space,[3] becoming increasingly nonlinear: it wavers, it thickens, it densifies, and it thins out, it is negotiable. Beatriz Colomina sums up this tendency when she writes that "the status of the wall has changed."[4] While "the way we think about architecture is always organized by the way we think about boundaries,"[5] these borders are no longer "a matter of walls dividing inside from outside, public from private, and so on."[6] In Colomina's understanding, media are the root of this redefinition of the boundaries that delineate space, as they create shifting boundaries of acoustic and visual realms.[7] In resonance with the changing status of the wall and boundary, digital representation practices are transforming the role of the line. For example, the object-based drawing program Autodesk Revit is a building information modeling software that uses 3D building and structural components. Rather than requiring the drafter to draw sections through three-dimensional objects using lines, the program provides volumetric objects. Digital surveyor tools such as lidar technologies have also affected the line. 3D scanners generate point clouds by emitting a rotating beam of laser light and documenting those places where the laser light was reflected off the surrounding objects as points. Whereas in conventional CAD drawing programs (such as archicad, rhino, or vectorworks) a line consists of two mouse clicks (points), the line has become increasingly integrated into objects (Revit) or left out altogether (point cloud). This article turns to two projects that in their articulation of what one might call cloud-space help us explore the notion of threshold, of bodies without surface, in architecture and its representation. By drawing on Diller + Scofidio's *Blur Building* (2002) [fig. 1] and Christian Kerez's 2016 Venice Biennale project *Incidental Space* [fig. 2], I aim to show that the shift from lines to points in architectural representation echoes the reevaluation of the threshold as well.

fig. 2

The Grid and the Cloud

Examining clouds in contemporary architecture benefits from an historical excursion to their representation in Brunelleschi's already mentioned perspectival apparatus. According to oral history first transcribed by mathematician and architect Antonio Manetti in the 1480s, Brunelleschi's device enabled the accurate and life-like representation of architecture's static geometry against an animated background—the sky and its ever-changing clouds. Brunelleschi's constellation consisted of two planes, two points, an architectural object, and a viewer with two arms and one eye. The first plane is a roughly 30 cm^2 panel [fig. 3] featuring Brunelleschi's perspectival drawing of the octagonal Battistero di San Giovanni (Florence Baptistery). The second surface is a mirror facing that painted surface. Instead of coloring in the sky with paint, he covered it with silver, so that the surface would reflect the sky as it is at the time of observation. He painted the scenery from the main entrance of the adjacent Santa Maria del Fiore (the *Duomo*). This specific location in the central portal of the cathedral[8] at eye level, is the first point, the point of origin and of observation. The second point constitutes the drawing's vanishing point, located opposite the viewer, on the portal of the temple of San Giovanni. The two points overlap in a peephole in the panel, precisely where the *second point* is located in the depiction. The hole and the two points thus align when the viewer of the apparatus is correctly positioned in the Duomo, facing the vanishing point. With one hand the viewer holds the panel close to his face, his eye at the peep hole, while his second hand is stretched out at arm's length, holding the mirror. The viewer can move the mirror in and out of view and the perceived image would remain the same: the baptistery in linear perspective, with a sky full of animated clouds above it. From personal experience, Manetti confirms: "With the aforementioned elements of the burnished silver, the piazza, the viewpoint, etc., the spectator felt he saw the actual scene when he looked at the painting."[9] The "burnished silver" embeds the momentary and ever-changing in the representation: the weather, the clouds, the time of day. These mobile, temporal agents are reflected in the mirrored sky of Brunelleschi's apparatus. The depiction is therefore constantly actualized or updated, connecting the representation with a continuous present.

fig. 3

The viewing machine that helped to establish linear perspective, "a system of creating an illusion of depth on a flat surface,"[10] thus relied on the incorporation of the temporal parameter. The clouds in the perspectival apparatus are temporal entities—not of a *linear* temporality of continued progression, as might fit the perspectival method; neither of the cyclical temporality associated with the daily rhythms apparent in the sky; instead, clouds embody a temporality of phasing: Periods of varying densities of visible vapor. Drawing on the philosopher Maurice Merleau-Ponty's description of time, the clouds, as temporal embodiments, create a situating milieu for the viewer in Brunelleschi's perspectival experience: "Time (...) is a milieu to which one can only gain access and that one can only understand by occupying a situation within it."[11] Brunelleschi must have felt that the representation of the baptistery appeared more truthful, more real, with an accurate depiction of the sky. And as this continuously changes, he integrated a continuously updating

3 Reprinted from Samuel Y. Edgerton, *The Mirror, the Window, and the Telescope: How Renaissance Linear Perspective Changed Our Vision of the Universe* (Ithaca and London: Cornell University Press, 2009).

reflection, rather than a fixed representation in his painting. The viewer's gaze, the nebulous embodiments of time and the horizon line all merge on the planes of Brunelleschi's experiment in architectural representation.

As in later drawing aid machinery that incorporated an orientation device for the painter's eyes to ensure the fixity of the vantage point, Brunelleschi's perspectival illusion only worked as long as the viewer remained immobile.[12] In his experiment, the viewing point and the vanishing point merge on the central axis of the representation. The exchangeable static viewer, the fixed gaze, and the immobile building are thus distinguished from the sky, which functions as the ever-actualized present. The sky, as perceived in the mirror surface of Brunelleschi's drawing, is a site of change, featuring "the *καιρὸς* (*kairos*) of weather, rain, hail, thunder and lightning, temperature, and clouds."[13] Media historian John Durham Peters reminds us that the sky has a long history of being understood as temporal medium of duality: "For millennia the sky has presented two faces to humanity: constants and variables, the regular motions of the heavenly bodies and the unpredictable events of the atmosphere."[14] Astronomy and meteorology then each deal with one of the two drastically differing types of heavenly bodies: those with a surface, such as planets, on a cyclical trajectory across the universe, and those without a clear outline and without a fully comprehensible path, the clouds. Each category comes with its own temporal mode, as it traverses space with different degrees of visibility for the human eye. While celestial cartography has mapped the sun, moon, planets, and stars since Antiquity, Brunelleschi's double sky mirror found an unprecedented way of integrating the more elusive and fast-paced variables of the sky into his static drawing observed from a specified position.

Point Cloud and Blur

In the meantime, digital representation has liberated the architectural illustration from the confinements of a static vantage point. The viewer of an architectural representation can move around the virtual building by rotating, panning, and zooming on the representational interface. Further alienating linear perspective, the digital point clouds produced in 3D surveying create a geometrical alternative to the spatiality of lines oriented towards a vanishing point. Point clouds, like the hazy reflections in Brunelleschi's apparatus, defy representation as a momentary cut through space—i. e., in plan or section. Instead, as I will show, they require rethinking the architectural diction in terms of densities, fields, fluctuations.[15]

Point clouds—much like their H_2O counterparts—manifest in near-infinite variety. Static or portable 3D laser scanners gather roughly half a million points per second. Each point represents a place where the light emanating from the rotating laser head was reflected. Digital point clouds composed of laser scans are so dense that, when seen on a screen, they create the illusion of a solid 3D model of surveyed buildings and landscapes.[16] Point clouds capture much more detail—points in space—than analog surveys that measure the distance between select points, which can then be connected by lines and extruded as surfaces in 3D software.

A point cloud documents *everything* that reflects light and is within the range and thickness of a laser beam. The digital points can be thought of as analogous to the aerosols in meteorological clouds onto which water droplets condense. In fact, it would even be possible to generate a point cloud of a cloud, as long as the beam's diameter is in a range of 1–100 microns (the size of aerosols). In the point cloud, space—definitive, tangible space—withdraws into accuracy beyond the realm of human perception. The spectacular accuracy of point clouds results in cloud-specific spatial characteristics. As can be experienced in virtual reality, this point spatiality is somewhat autonomous of the surveyed space. Zooming in on a particular area in the point model results in zooming through surfaces and their bodies. The point cloud representation includes adjacencies, gaps, and near-overlays of point densities that reveal a spatiality of loose dispersal entirely different from the 3D model of a building or landscape experienced as surfaces. As points are scaleless, there is no absolute scale suggested or required to read a point cloud. Similarly, there is no absolute place to which a point cloud is bound. Depending on the scanning method, the cloud is either embedded in the GPS system—and therefore relative in position to the 24 satellites of the GPS constellation—or the various scans that constitute the cloud are oriented around a random point marked by the surveyor in each scan. Unlike a chosen vanishing point, this point of reference does not affect the experience of the point cloud representation.

An archeological study begun in 2013 at the University of California, San Diego, allows us to compare a drawing of a building, such as Brunelleschi's, and its point cloud. Students of the Cultural Heritage Engineering Initiative (CHEI) used lidar technology, ultra-high-resolution photography and thermal imaging techniques to create a dense point cloud model of the baptistery. A flythrough video of the point cloud shows the building in uncanny detail: joints between the façade cladding, chipped off and weathered frieze details—everything is documented "down to the millimeter." The video conveys a sense of constant motion. Viewers see the building from angles (and camera angle widths) that are impossible when physically visiting the building. We are zooming through Lorenzo Ghiberti's closed *Gates of Paradise*, we fly up to the mosaic-covered cupola and find a hidden walkway of ladders accessing the roof structure. Dropping back down, we traverse through the building's mosaic marble pavement, through and below the foundations, to see yet-unexcavated ruins modeled using ground-penetrating radar.[17] As an adverse consequence of this wondrous excursion, the sense of the baptistery's harmonious proportions is lost. For example, the "camera" zooms out at the end of the flythrough, higher and higher above the building, its roof suddenly seems strangely large—something that is never visible from the intended eye-level height, which Brunelleschi's depiction heeded. The impression of enduring gravity known to those who have visited the building is also not quite transmitted in the flythrough which guides us repeatedly through closed doors, walls, roofs, and floors. The visualization of molecule-like rendered bubbles (points with a volume) that make way for the mass-penetrating zoom does not convey the impression of lasting materiality. In its digital cloud rendition, the baptistery is a body without surface.

And yet our senses are geared to perceive architecture in terms of surfaces. Sight is limited to the surface of perceived bodies, hearing relies on enclosures to mirror sound waves, touch does not penetrate beyond skin, and even smell and taste are mostly limited to surfaces. The literal cloud of Diller + Scofidio's 2002 *Blur Building* gives insight into how architecture can, however, navigate the spatiality of the threshold and approximate the surfacelessness suggested by the point cloud scan of the baptistery. The *Blur Building* is the closest architecture has gotten to a model of a cloud. Conceived for the Swiss EXPO in 2002, this temporary structure was constructed on Lake Neuchâtel, where it was reached via a bridge. The pavilion was composed of an infrastructural network of 35,000 nozzles that transformed lake water into mist. The resulting artificial cloud enveloped the walkways and blurred the lake views, complying with the architects' goal to disrupt this stereotypical backdrop of tourist photos. Their reaction to increasingly mainstream high-definition reproduction and simulation technologies was to subvert clean (surface) outlines by literally blurring or clouding them.[18]

Seen from the shore or the bridge, the cloud also hid the infrastructure that supported and generated the cloud. The architects were adamant about creating "a landscape/media project that is architecture-free."[19] On a napkin, they noted the elements of *nothingness* that were to characterize the project: "scaleless, formless, massless, colorless, dimensionless, weightless, odorless, centerless, featureless, depthless, meaningless, spaceless, timeless, surfaceless, white-out, white noise."[20] The resulting cloud creates an interesting dichotomy with the tradition of Minimalist architecture. To some extent this article rethinks similar issues as art historian Rosalind Krauss' 1994 article on Mies van der Rohe titled "The Grid, the /Cloud/, and the Detail." Her article draws analogies between the "revisionary readings" of the Minimalist architect Mies and Minimalist painter Agnes Martin, both dedicated to the grid as an aesthetic device. Drawing on philosopher Hubert Damisch's notion of the semiotic marker /cloud/, which represents, in his reading of Brunelleschi's mirror sky, a reminder of the limitations of linear perspective, she explores /cloud/ as a sign to which no meaning can be ascribed. She also revisits the implications of Minimalism, which "was read as lodging meaning in the surface of objects."[21] (Architectural) clouds as bodies without surface then pose a fascinating conceptual problem, which incorporates the envisioned characteristics on Diller + Scofidio's napkin: if the surface is a site of meaning and /cloud/ is a connotation-free zone, then does the surfaceless blur constitute a double stripping of meaning?

As in Brunelleschi's case, there is an obvious representation gap between Diller + Scofidio's plan drawings of the project and the more atmospheric visualizations (collages) and actual experience, as the plan drawings mostly focus on the infrastructure of nozzles and pipes. The actual cloud is visible only in sketches, collages, photographs, and videos. The photographs reveal that the cloud took on a variety of forms, depending on the direction and strength of the prevailing winds. Video footage shot from the beginning of the footpaths shows the expanded threshold of the blur. It approximates the permeable spatiality suggested by the 3D scan of the baptistery and its seemingly porous walls. On the left bridge, people clad in raincoats disappear from view as they fade into the cloud of the *Blur Building*. On the right, they gradually reemerge into sight on their way back to the shore. The cloud wafts and wavers, at times eating further into the bridges, at times receding. In their twofold existence as excessively accurate visualizations and nebulous evasiveness, clouds, be they digital, artificial, or meteorological, defy the Cartesian logic of binaries: most notably, they have no clear interior or exterior, no beginning or end. Rather than being inside the cloud, visitors were surrounded by its displacing "white out" and "white noise"[22] effects. Due to the cloud's vaporous state, visitors to the *Blur Building* contributed to the ever-changing nature of its outlines. Their (warmer) bodies introduced a larger surface for the water droplets of the cloud to condense onto, thus affecting the cloud's thresholds. As a "body without surface," the *Blur Building* withdrew from touch.

Incidental Space

Just as the cloud could not really be *touched*, it could not be accurately drawn or fully anticipated, despite prototypes and tests. The architects relied on technical line drawings to plan the construction, as the project was realized before 3D scanning technology was used in architecture. I will now turn to a project that pushes the limits of the plan using digital modeling techniques to incorporate the unpredictability and unmappability that I have shown to pertain to clouds. Its representation strategy, juxtaposed with that of the *Blur Building*, reveals how architectural drawing tools have been adjusted to enable the planning of more indefinite threshold spaces than those generated by line drawings. For the 2016 Venice Biennale, Christian Kerez created a solid "cavernous cloud"[23] called *Incidental Space*. The structure was modeled on an "incidental" accumulation of sugar and dust, cast in plaster, scaled up, and reproduced using a complex chain of digital and physical translations and inversions.

Kerez and his students at the ETH Zurich cast found materials and garbage in plaster (resulting in 300 different models). *Model #180* was chosen as a random form that did not resemble anything else—a kind of reverse approach to cloud watching, where since da Vinci an important aspect has been to discover forms in the generic mass. Rather than designing, Kerez calls this process "breeding space." No plans were drawn as, hypothetically, more than "a million plans" would have been necessary to generate an unrecognizable form that could not be associated with other typologies, systems of meaning or trigger immediate architectural associations. The model could thus be understood as a kind of /cloud/ as understood by Krauss.

Next, an also near-infinite number of plans and sections would have been necessary to convey this complex form into construction plans. Instead, the architects scanned the first negative cast with two different techniques: a CT scan and optical scans. The lower-resolution CT scan of the entire object served as a digital structure onto which the high-resolution optical scans (approx. 50 fragments) were stitched. Surface reconstruction converted the dense point cloud into meshes or surface models. The translation of a point cloud into a digital body can be problematic. In the triangulation process of the initial scan of the cast of the 15 × 10 × 30 cm object, there were 3,000,000 glitches and error messages because of three types of conflicts: self-intersecting surfaces, non-manifold surfaces and holes. These are mathematically describable surfaces that are physically impossible and cannot be translated into mass. To reproduce the cloud as accurately as possible, 2,500 individual formwork elements were built using 3D modeling, CNC milling, and 3D printing. Finally, the approx. 250 self-supporting glass fiber reinforced concrete panels, 2 cm thick on average, were cast.

In Venice, *Incidental Space* was exhibited together with large black and white photographs of the digital and handcrafted models and renderings used—along with models explored in virtual reality—during the design process. Renderings and photographs of the project are barely distinguishable. Since the project's production relied on comprehensive spatial models rather than plan drawings of flat sections, it had little use for 2D plans. The sculpture could be entered and looked into via two holes and was best experienced by physically exploring it. Many visitors commented on the fact that it seemed to be more spacious on the inside than expected—harking back to the problem of scale in cloud space. *Incidental Space* creates the spatial disorientation also explored by the *Blur Building*. The sculpture's folds, cavities, crevices, openings, and homogenous surface create a threshold space that challenges the representational ability of the line in architectural drawings. Like the *Blur Building*, it seems to pay tribute to the inconceivable detail (accuracy) and complexity of clouds, which it harnesses by relying heavily on digital point clouds and renderings in its conception. Exploring *Incidental Space* or the *Blur Building* is akin to the digital flythrough described earlier. Their spatialities reveal themselves best through animated exploration, rather than from a fixed vantage point, such as that of Brunelleschi's drawing. An elevation of a cloud-like threshold space reveals little of relevance, while the baptistery exemplifies an architecture of geometrical proportions that is best depicted from a static vantage point.

Kerez's *Incidental Space* stages, accesses, replicates, and scales otherwise inaccessible spaces: you could physically enter the folds and cavities of a little clump of sugar and dust. Similarly, the point cloud as a tool allows architects to mediate between pure information *points* and bodies. I argue that this kind of spatial cloud tool already permeated medieval, religious theatricality. During the Quattrocento, a stage device called "cloud machinery"— later known as "heaven machinery"—was often used in Florentine religious theater. This wooden stage prop was covered and decorated to look like one or several clouds. The structure was used to transport actor-saints into higher regions that represented a closer adjacency to the divine, with the help of a hidden pulley system.[24] The cloud prop was a way of navigating the strict binary distinction between heaven and earth: adjoined but mutually exclusive realms. Although the point cloud is experienced only at the representational level of the interface and cannot be physically accessed like the cloud prop, it can be seen to play a similar role of accessing the intangible: It mediates between the non-physical realm of information, accurate beyond human perceptibility, and the physical world accessible to human perception. The cloud can thus be understood as a device of connection, as its responsive threshold permeates even unwavering boundaries. Krauss interprets /cloud/ as standing in for the "unknowable and unrepresentable,"[25] and operating "as the lack in the center of (...) knowledge."[26] I hope to show instead that the cloud is in fact a device of access, of mediation. Rather than an absence, the cloud is a site of generating possibility, new adjacencies and updated morphologies. The previously suggested "double stripping of meaning" is then a generative strategy for ever-renewing associations and interpretations.

The Geometry of Drama or The Meteorological Mode

In light of their manifold readings, there is *drama* in clouds and their representation. As early as 423 BCE, they inspired playwright Aristophanes to devise a leading role for these all-knowing, influential, and elusive entities, spectators and actors alike. Drawing an arch from this first comedy of ideas to the digital cloud of big data that governs today's information culture, the latter has recently been postulated as *drama* by digital media theorist Wendy Chun.[27] Chun delves into the role of the user, who has become social media's medium as the singular-plural YOU: "We are now characters in a universe of dramas putatively called Big Data."[28]

The theatrical, performative aspect of the spatiality of the digital cloud and its big data wafts, as well as of the meteorological cloud, has always held viewers with romantic and interpretive abilities, such as self-professed cloud-worshipper, artist, and writer John Ruskin, spellbound. In Andrea Mantegna's painting *San Sebastian* (1456–59) a cloud in the top left corner becomes the stage/actor for a hurried horseman, possibly an allusion to Saturn, the god associated with the destructive passage of time. The painter Casper David Friedrich, like his fellow Romantics, read the clouds as a spectacle of emotions. Clouds are drama, or rather, dramatic. These ever-changing, ever elusive and fleeting bodies, without surface and beyond linear time, share the realm of the divine with the somewhat opposite divine Platonic bodies of clearly delineated surfaces.

Clouds, be they digital, meteorological, or imaginary, exemplify what I call the meteorological mode: a spatiality of dispersal, a temporality of phasing and materiality of patterned particles. The cloud in all its manifestations—digital, meteorological, metaphorical—is unfathomable in its accuracy, its intangibility, and the continuous updates of its morphology. Despite the seeming dichotomy between clouds and architecture, which, despite such examples as those described above, is still largely perceived as static and contained by surfaces, these cloud-related characteristics have precipitated in the architectural discourse. For example, Keller Easterling's book *Extrastatecraft*[29] postulates architecture as moving away from the Cartesian object locatable in an absolute grid system towards the logic of infrastructure. This spatial mode is governed by disposition, flows, and the channeling of agencies, activities, information, and material that navigate space by correlation. The concern with architecture as a negotiation between an inside and an outside that has dominated modern architectural discourse gives way to a cloudy gathering of what traverses its responsive, updating, and adjusting thresholds, be it bodies without surfaces, withdrawing objects, or channeled resources.

In the meteorological mode, spatiality may still be governed by geometrical systems, yet this nebulous geometry is one that updates rather than dictates: The geometry of the cloud refutes the metaphorical holding still to consume a perfectly curated *trompe l'oeil* from the designated spot. Rather, the spatiality of the cloud *is* the drama, the stage, the illusion, the fact and its representation: clouds approximating a geometry that spatializes the multitudes of more-than-binary systems. A representational system based on the spatiality of the cloud could, unlike the postulated danger of the territory of sovereignty associated with the cloud of big data, result in a more fluid, less exclusive concept. This more adjustable approach could be oriented along Leonardo da Vinci's understanding of bodies without surface that "readily melt into and mingle with other thin bodies."[30] By consequence, da Vinci observes, their extremities "are mingled with the bodies near to them, whence by this intermingling their boundaries become confused and imperceptible."[31] Whereas lines suggest divisions and connections—in terms of above and below, right and left, inside and outside—the point clouds of architectural representation generate fields of adjacencies that withdraw from binary categorization. Cloud-space can be explored and sculpted but not flattened. This opens up questions with regard to the limitations of the plan. The spatial imagination of bodies that remain in a state of becoming—through exploration and variation—are beyond the scope of finite drawings. Clouds as a representation tool are a way of mediating the shortcomings of linear perspective, described by Damisch "as a structure of exclusion, the coherence of which is founded upon a series of rejections."[32] Clouds in the architectural discourse thus mark the threshold to an increasingly inhabited yet under-described spatiality of inclusive variability, fluid accuracy and responsive multiplicity.

1 Leonardo da Vinci, *The Notebooks of Leonardo da Vinci*, ed. and trans. Edward McCurdy (London: Jonathan Cape, 1938), vol. 2, 363–64.
2 Hubert Damisch, *A Theory of /Cloud/: Toward a History of Painting*, trans. Janet Lloyd (Stanford, CA: Stanford University Press, 2002), 123.
3 Rem Koolhaas' description of junkspace and Keller Easterling's extrastatecraft are characteristic examples. Rem Koolhaas, "Junkspace," *October* 100, Obsolescence (Spring 2002): 175–90. Keller Easterling, *Extrastatecraft: The Power of Infrastructure Space* (London and New York: Verso, 2014).
4 Beatriz Colomina, "Battle Lines," in *Rethinking Borders*, ed. John C. Welchman (Houndmills and London: Macmillan Press, 1996), 52.
5 Ibid., 51–52.
6 Ibid., 52.
7 Ibid., 52.
8 Samuel Y. Edgerton, *The Mirror, the Window, and the Telescope: How Renaissance Linear Perspective Changed Our Vision of the Universe* (Ithaca and London: Cornell University Press, 2009), 50–51.
9 Manetti quoted in Edgerton, *The Mirror, the Window, and the Telescope*, 46.
10 https://www.britannica.com/art/linear-perspective (accessed October 14, 2019).
11 Maurice Merleau-Ponty, *Phenomenology of Perception*, trans. Donald A. Landes (London and New York: Routledge, 2014), 347.
12 Albrecht Dürer depicted some of these in detail. Dürer's drawings that show drawing machinery relies on Leon Battista Alberti's instructions in his treatise *De pictura* (On Painting), written in 1435, published in 1450. Alberti was first to commit a perspectival method to text in *De pictura*. He can be seen to have merged the milky diffuseness of the cloud and the geometrical grid in the method of the *velo* (veil). There is an interesting analogy between this veil of accuracy—itself a dichotomy—and the point cloud.
13 John Durham Peters, *The Marvelous Clouds: Toward a Philosophy of Elemental Media* (Chicago, IL: Chicago University Press, 2015), 166.
14 Ibid., 166.
15 This vocabulary conjures the discourse of the topological turn, see for example jrebsame, "Gotthard Landscape | The Unexpected View," *Professor Christophe Girot* (blog), https://girot.arch.ethz.ch/research/gotthard-landscape-the-unexpected-view (accessed August 17, 2019).
16 For point clouds of landscapes, see Gotthard project by Prof. Girot at the ETH: ETH Chair of Landscape Architecture, "Gotthard Landscape | The Unexpected View," *Professor Christophe Girot* (blog), https://girot.arch.ethz.ch/research/gotthard-landscape-the-unexpected-view (accessed August 17, 2019).
17 Tiffany Fox, "Making the Past Present with Light, Warmth and a High-Tech Gaze," US San Diego News Center, February 24, 2015, https://ucsdnews.ucsd.edu/index.php/pressrelease/making_the_past_present_with_light_warmth_and_a_high_tech_gaze (accessed October 14, 2019).

8 Laurie Anderson, "Interview with lizabeth Diller and Ricardo Scofidio," in *canning: The Aberrant Architectures of iller + Scofidio*, ed. Aaron Betsky (New ork: Whitney Museum of American Art, 03), 147.

9 Diller + Scofidio, *Blur: The Making of othing* (New York: Harry N. Abrahams, 02).

0 Ibid., 33.

1 Rosalind Krauss, "The Grid, the / loud/, and the Detail," in *The Presence f Mies*, ed. Detlef Mertins (Princeton: rinceton Architectural Press, 1994), 34.

2 Diller + Scofidio, *Blur: The Making of othing*, 33.

3 Jessica Mairs, "Christian Kerez stalls Cavernous Cloud for Swiss avilion," *Dezeen*, May 27, 2016, https:// ww.dezeen.com/2016/05/27/christian- erez-cavernous-cloud-installation- wiss-pavilion-venice-architecture-bien- ale-2016/ (accessed October 14, 2019).

24 Alessandra Buccheri, *The Spectacle of Clouds, 1439–1650* (Farnham: Ashgate, 2014).

25 Krauss, "The Grid, the /Cloud/, and the Detail," 142.

26 Ibid., 142.

27 Wendy Hui Kyong Chun, "Big Data as Drama," *ELH* 83, no. 2 (Summer 2016): 363–82.

28 Ibid., 363.

29 Easterling, *Extrastatecraft*.

30 Leonardo da Vinci, *The Notebooks of Leonardo da Vinci*, trans. and ed. Edward MacCurdy (London: Jonathan Cape, 1938), 2:363–64 (C.A., 132rb); cited in Hubert Damisch, *A Theory of /Cloud/: Toward a History of Painting*, trans. Janet Lloyd (Stanford, CA: Stanford University press, 2002), 280–81.

31 Ibid.

32 Damisch, *A Theory of /Cloud/*, 124.

Fredrik Torisson

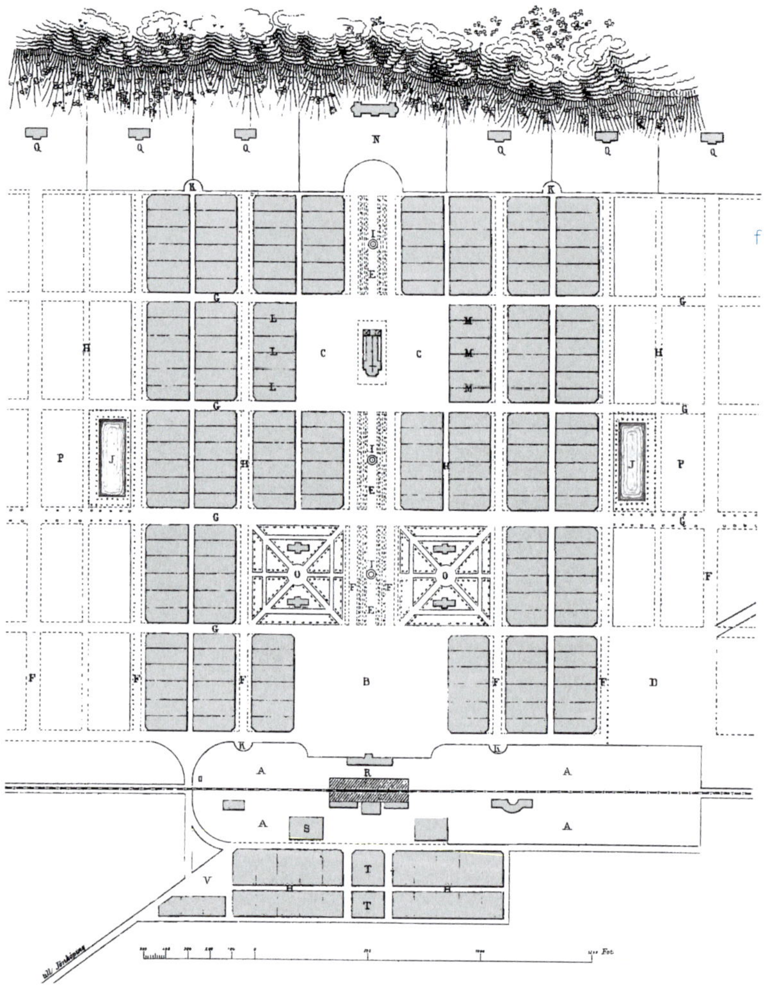

fig. 1

Plans for a Plentiful Future

ig. 2

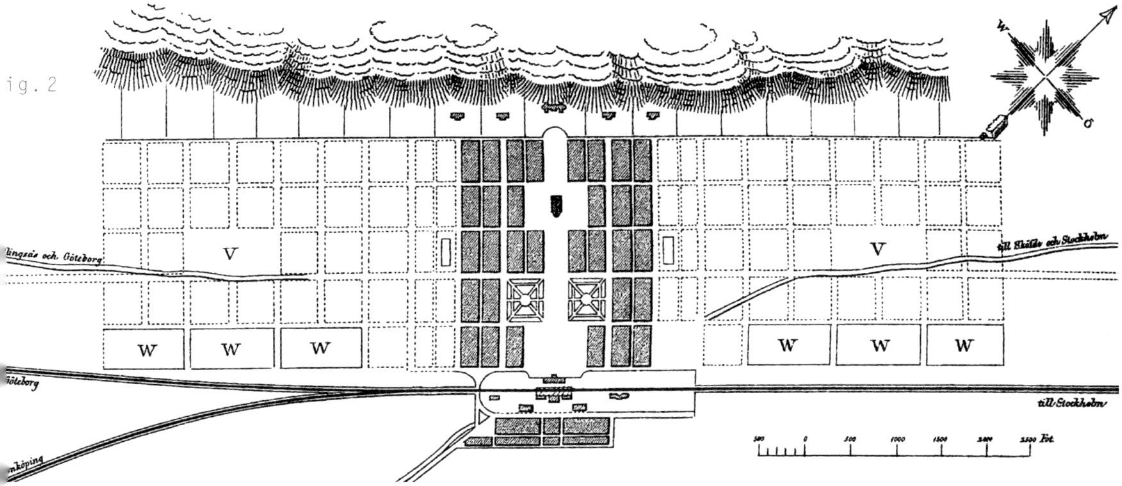

1 Adolf Edelsvärd, generic town plan, 1859. Published in *Tidskrift för Byggnadskonst och Ingeniörs vetenskap* (May 1859): Pl. XVII.

2 Adolf Edelsvärd, generic town plan, 1859. Published in *Tidskrift för Byggnadskonst och Ingeniörs vetenskap* (May 1859): Pl. XVIII, fig. 1.

The following will explore the notion of architecture in terms of what philosopher Sven-Olov Wallenstein has referred to as a "biopolitical machine," which he connects with the emergence of modern architecture, providing, simultaneously, both constraints and freedoms.[1] Its primary focus is the incorporation of what we could call a *growth paradigm* in the plan. This means, on the one hand, a freedom to expand, but simultaneously contains an imperative to do so, without reaching a final form. Growth could in this fashion be considered the condition of existence in the plan.

In this brief study, I will examine more closely two Swedish examples of both different times and different scales. What they have in common is precisely the possibility and imperative to grow over time. Consequently, the plans prescribe building a structure that would be considered perpetually incomplete, which is intended to be filled in over time.[2] This relation to growth is here associated with the biopolitical side of architecture as a way of ordering and controlling the life of subjects. However, as will become

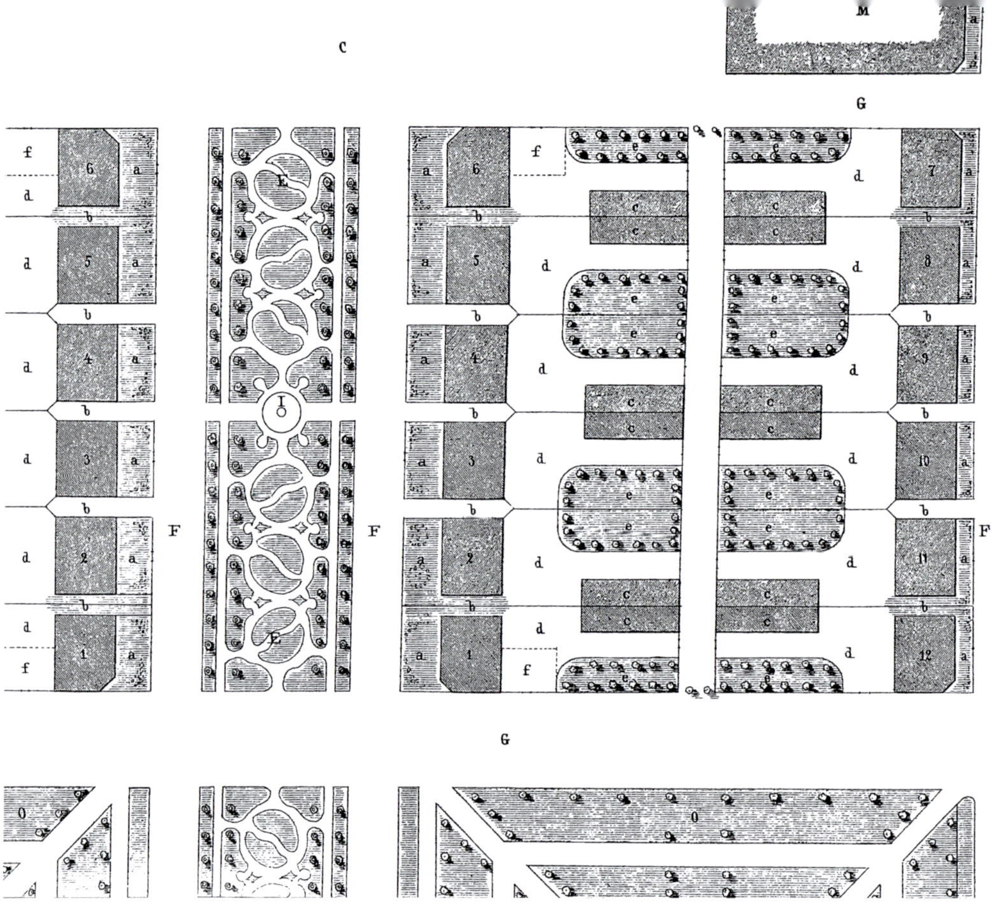

fig. 3

apparent, the notion of growth is translated in different ways, and the question of how growth should happen differs as well.

The first example is Adolf Edelsvärd's "generic town" from 1859, produced in connection with the establishment of a national rail network, and designed to be placed (almost) anywhere along this network where suitable resources could be found. The second project, Erik Friberger's *Däckshus* in Kallebäck, Gothenburg. This is a residential building constructed in 1960. It shares certain characteristics with Edelsvärd's generic town: both are based on a conception of individual freedom expressed in form within a structure defined by the architect (and the powers that be). Both are also based on the ability to grow, not simply expand outwards, but to fill out the structure provided by the architect. Both projects, furthermore, make use of the plan to establish the ordering principles of the project, suggesting a notion of the plan as something that orders rather than defines form, which is one important aspect of understanding architecture in terms of a biopolitical machine.

3 Adolf Edelsvärd, generic town plan, 1859. Published in *Tidskrift för Byggnadskonst och Ingeniörs vetenskap* (May 1859): Pl. XVIII, fig. 2.

Architecture and Biopolitics

Following Wallenstein, we can consider modern architecture as a "biopolitical machine," i.e., an architecture that no longer *represents* a societal order, but itself becomes a *tool for the ordering of society*.[3] Wallenstein's approach to biopolitics is based on the work of Michel Foucault, and biopolitics is then exercised on both the level of the population and of the individual through individualization.[4] These aspects are found in the projects discussed here, where both population and individualization can be considered vital points of reference in the making of the plan. Both plans can be considered in terms of a management of the future, a controlling of growth through architecture.

Architecture understood in these terms becomes a tool for subjectivization, for the production of subjectivities in a delicate combination of freedom and discipline.[5] Wallenstein argues, building on Foucault, that architecture, or modern architecture to be precise, works by producing specific forms of subjectivity. The subject experiences increased freedom if she accepts the proposed way of understanding herself and society, but she may choose to resist the forces of subjectivization, which, depending on how far from the norm one strays, will provoke a disciplinary response.[6] This is, according to Wallenstein's reading of Foucault, the principal way modern architecture functions.

One side of this biopolitical machine is of course the very physical regimentation of space, but another side—the topic of this article—is the redefinition of what a town is and how it works through transforming its fundamental principles of what it is, which here is analyzed through the plan. This is an aspect that was central to Françoise Choay, who in her book *The Rule and the Model* discusses this shift through an analysis of urban planner Ildefonso Cerdá and his book *General Theory of Urbanization*, first published in 1867, as well as his famous plan for Barcelona from a few years earlier, for which he coined the term "urbanism."[7] Pier Vittorio Aureli has argued in *The Possibility of an Absolute Architecture* (2011) (through the words of Giorgio Agamben) that Cerdá's plan shows the opening up of a "managerial paradigm," where economy replaces any notion of politics.[8] The rules of the plan in Cerdá's Barcelona plan here become "a totalitarian managerial process based on economy."[9]

Edelsvärd's Generic Town Recipe

In a 19th-century Swedish context, the expansion of railways connecting the major population centers redrew the map. Towns and villages along the principal railways were suddenly connected in new networks. The new railways also prompted a discussion on the construction of new towns at intersections or other advantageous sites along the tracks. The perhaps most famous proposition was published in the journal *Tidskrift för Byggnadskonst och Ingeniör vetenskap* by Adolf Edelsvärd in 1859 with the title "Plan och byggnadssätt för Landsortsstäder och Förstäder" (Plan and Construction Method for Small Towns and Suburbs). Edelsvärd was well placed to make such a proposition as he was head architect of Statens Järnvägar (National Swedish Railroad). The plan can, as Gunilla Linde Bjur notes, be referred to as a "principle plan," i. e., a plan that sets out a number of principles for how to organize the new town that are not connected with an ideal overall form.[10] The whole is not concerned with form, but focused on hygiene, fire safety, and, the most important aspect of all: managing growth in an orderly fashion. The article's very first paragraph stresses that the problem the author perceives in towns, in old ones certainly, but also in newly established towns, is that they have failed to take future growth into account.

The article is accompanied by two plates containing three illustrations [fig. 1–3], which show the organizational principle of the proposed town. The plates themselves are interesting, according to Edelsvärd, as they illustrate a generic plan that can be applied in the construction of new towns anywhere along the railroad. The proposition is in this sense a "recipe" of sorts for a new development. At the same time, the plans are proposed for the development of the Swedish village Falköping. The proposed town was not an expansion of the already existing village, but a proposed new town outside, in connection with the newly constructed railroad junction, central to the expanding national railroad network. The new town would have all the qualities the author found sorely missing in the existing Falköping, but the recipe was also meant to be repeated elsewhere.

Edelsvärd's article can be subdivided into four parts. The first discusses the problems of towns, and the perceived failure to accommodate growth, as well as a statement pertaining to the nature of beauty: "That which is useful and appropriate to its purpose is also the most beautiful."[11] The second part discusses the proposed principles of the town's construction in relation to the plates. Edelsvärd's concerns are on the scale of the town as a whole, stipulating that spaces for greenery should make up at least 18 % of the total area, that the city should reserve 9 % of the total urban area in the centrally located parts for future public administration buildings, to be completed when need arises, etc. Other concerns address details, e. g., outlining the principles for ventilation of basements in residential houses. The rules here are ordered in a numbered list that defines the rules of expansion within the plan's overall structure as presented in the plates, and they could be understood as annotations to the plates.[12]

The third part of the text discusses the conditions in Falköping, in terms of resources, opportunities, etc. This part deals with the situation of the project in Falköping and can be considered largely separate from the generic principles. The fourth and final part contains a recipe for how to go about founding towns of this sort. Here, Edelsvärd proposes a collaboration between the state and a limited company set up for this purpose. The state expropriates the land and leases it to the limited company for 50 years (approximately), and the company commits to follow the plan and to sell as many of the lots as possible during this period, and develop the infrastructure. At the end of the lease, the town and its amenities return to the state, save for those plots where the company itself has constructed buildings (in accordance with the plan), which will remain in their possession.[13]

Edelsvärd's plan is a plan based on statistics and considers practical as well as aesthetic questions (disguised in scientific language). That the plan's principal aim and constitution can be understood in context of industrial capitalism is clear, with the focus on managing growth as well as the very organization behind the town's founding being a corporation rather than a state entity. The state's role is to enable the corporation's land acquisition and to ensure that the corporation follows the rules outlined in the proposal.

Perhaps, in this sense, it is possible, at least from a present-day perspective, to regard Edelsvärd's proposed town as a kind of capitalist ideal town, if we take the liberty to redefine "ideal" not as a model but as a set of rules, not as a form but as a series of governing protocols.[14] There are a number of points in favor of such a perspective. First, the town is predicated on growth; this is its DNA. Second, it is generic, which means it can grow in number as well as in size and density; there will be many versions of the same distinguished only by form (which here is considered irrelevant to the operation as a whole). Third, the town is to be controlled by a corporate interest, nominally only during the first years, and will in an unspecified future (Edelsvärd's estimate of 50 years is merely a suggestion) be handed over to civic society, when it has grown enough. This is an interesting symbiosis between state and corporation: the town is established through the state's appropriation of land for the benefit of the corporation, which in theory, here, *is* the public good. Fourth, these towns are subsequently connected by the new railways, plugging each of the towns into a network structure. These are subsequently intended to replace the old town, the failed version of Falköping, unscientific and essentially obsolete in this brave new world.

In order to understand Edelsvärd's generic town as an ideal town, we need to modify how we understand the notion of the ideal town. The overall form of the town is meant to transform as the town expands, and the form of the town as a whole is invariably provisional. The form of the individual structures is equally secondary. Edelsvärd's text contains stipulations for the quality of specific buildings, but mainly in terms of material (stone in corner buildings, to give one example). The town's form is topological rather than defined by its boundaries. Form, of individual buildings, becomes a domain of the private realm, an arena of a certain liberty where the owner of the individual plot has a certain liberty, as long as he or she does not interfere with the overall structure of the whole.

In his role as head architect of the railway expansion Edelsvärd was very closely engaged in the proliferation of the different types of building necessary for the new communication networks, station buildings, hotels, canteens, etc. Part of planning the railroad network involved planning and placing different functions to maintain the system. If we regard the railroad network as one vast interlinked system that although extensive is compressed by the very infrastructure that is both its *raison d'être* and its connective tissue, this would then be a system that needs to be organized logically and planned in detail (but not in terms of form necessarily). From there, it would be but a short step to conceive of the town in terms of a system as well, and possibly the town could be considered a part of the larger system of the railroad itself.

The Open Form of Friberger's Däckshus

Almost exactly a century later, the question of architecture accommodating growth became central in parts of the architectural discourse. This is not to say that the question did not exist in the span of the century, but rather that the question assumed a more central position following the evolution of systems theory in postwar architecture. Here, I will only focus on one way of answering that question, which admittedly becomes somewhat decontextualized.[15] I am basically comparing two instances where the architect himself or herself, through the plan, provides a protocol for growth.

Open Form was introduced by Oskar and Zofia Hansen at the CIAM/Team 10 showdown in Otterlo in 1959.[16] CIAM, or *Congrès Internationaux d'Architecture Moderne,* was challenged by a younger generation of architects who, inspired by structuralism in linguistics and philosophy, sought to develop an architecture that was flexible, able to adapt to its users' needs and desires. The crisis of architecture at this time is portrayed by the Hansens as a crisis of the *Closed Form*.[17]

The Hansens contrasted *Closed Form*, characterized by rigidity and an overall form of the development, using Brasilia and Le Corbusier's *Unité d'habitation* as examples, with *Open Form*, which "does not exclude the energy of the client's initiative but on the contrary treats it as a basic, organic, and inseparable component element."[18] *Open Form* provides space for the individual to express himself or herself; the individual should be aided in "finding himself in the collective."[19] It is, we could surmise, about an architecture of potential to be developed rather than an architecture of form. This provides a new role of the architect: "The role of the artist-architect is altered from the previous exclusively personal and conceptional role (imposing Closed Form in the manifestation of which the form is defined beforehand and that most often for non-existing persons) to the conceptional-coordinating role."[20]

The architect would, simply put, provide not a form but a scaffolding (usually metaphorically speaking, sometimes literally: think of Yona Friedman's *Space Frame,* for example) that the user would fill with content. At the same time, the notions presented at the Otterlo meeting could possibly be associated as much with other discourses in a more complex configuration, in which I would certainly include Cybernetics.[21] All of these discourses organized space around principles that would govern future expansion, provision for which is now built in, and provided a certain amount of freedom to those within the organized domain.[22]

In a parallel development, in Sweden, the county architect of Gothenburg, Erik Friberger, was working on a project that was hailed at the time as a "unique project" that appears almost identical in approach.[23] In 1960, Friberger completed a building, usually referred to as *Däckshus,* in Kallebäck.[24] The principal idea is to construct detached houses or cottages stacked vertically on concrete decks or slabs. The individual cottage subsequently becomes independent of the larger whole, and able to expand or retract as needed. The restrictions imposed by the structure are limited to structural aspects and the location of services. The building is, to an extent, also shaped by the specific Swedish co-op ownership form of "bostadsrätt," where the occupier owns a share of an association that owns the building and the individual acquires the right to use and change the interior. *Däckshuset* is a four-story residential structure, a ground floor used for parking, and on top of this, three concrete slabs with railings around them (77.5 × 13.35 m). The three top floors are subdivided into a number of plots where residents could construct their own cottages.[25] The principle, again, is growth, where a family could update and expand their cottage as the family grew and/or acquired more means. The principal idea here is to provide individual freedom, and a kind of privacy, usually associated with the detached house but here applied vertically as well, but also a private sphere that is itself functioning through a logic of growth.

There is a structure that organizes this freedom, certain constraints that become visible in the plans. These constraints are primarily related to structure and to services. Growth will in effect also be bound by the very same constraints that determine how and what is possible to build on the individual plot. In terms of structural constraints, each deck or slab is supported by

fig. 4

fig. 5

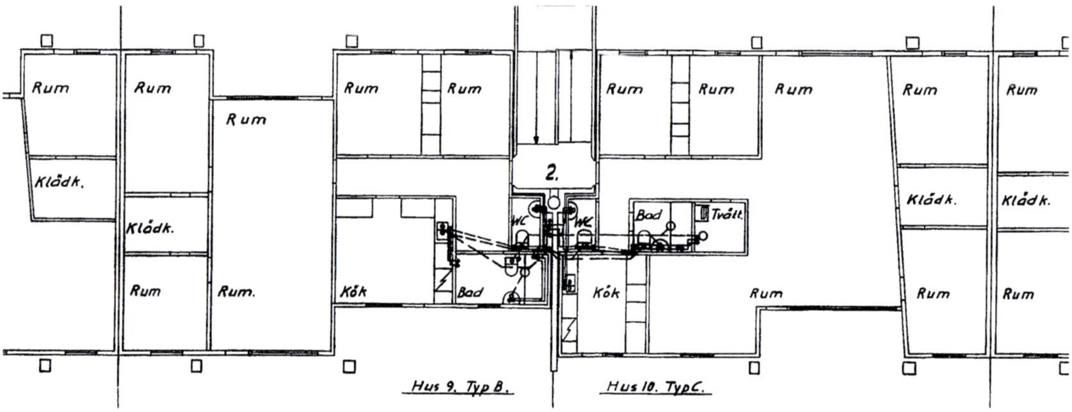

pillars every 5 m; these pillars are pulled in 1.8 m from the edge of the slab, which provides an edge for where it is possible to build, as the cantilevered part was not strong enough to support cottages. This leaves an open path that runs around the perimeter of each slab with a width of 1.5 m [fig. 4–6].

When it comes to constraints related to the services of buildings, the drains constitute a principal organizing element. All vertical services are located in three staircases along one side of the building. Each staircase serves two houses on each floor, making the total number of houses 18 in the development; the vertical services determine to a great extent both layout and placement of the individual houses. Plumbing provides a very definite organization, since each drain needs to slope downward, so the bathrooms and kitchens need to be placed within a certain distance of the staircases. As a consequence, bathrooms tend to be placed near the drainpipe that runs behind the staircase, and are consequently without natural light.[26] In the planning application, Friberger developed 18 different house type variations of different

4 Erik Friberger, *Däckshus*, Kallebäck, 1960. Photo 2015.

5 Plan of the two houses with one staircase. The drains are emphasized here as an organizing principle. Image from planning application.

ig. 6

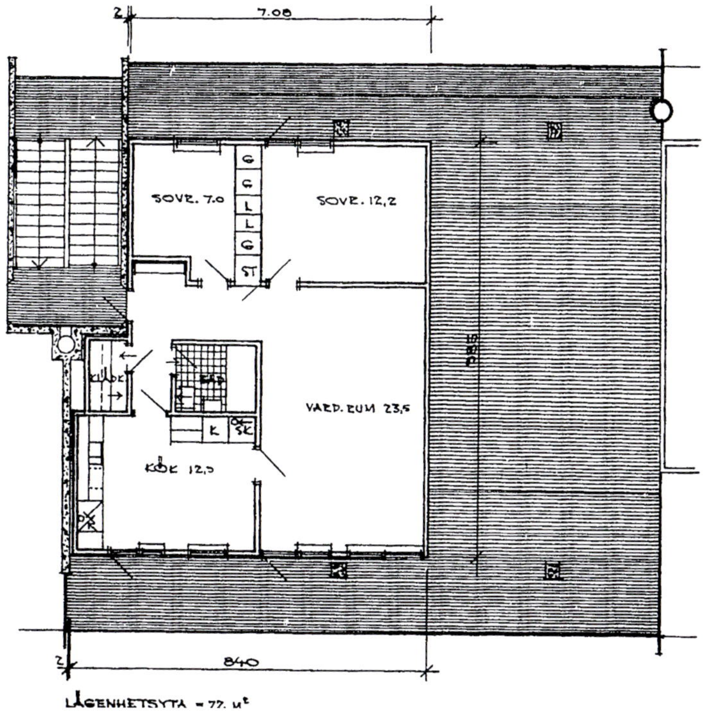

6 Plan of one of the smaller houses with a garden that was never constructed. All the tenants opted for the largest possible building on the site, leaving little space for gardens and communal areas. From the planning application.

sizes, from which the prospective resident could select. These were meant to be expanded over time, according to the needs and means of the household, but a few types covered more or less the entire allotted site. As it turned out, almost every inhabitant selected the largest possible house from the start, which to an extent went counter to the principle of the building itself.[27] Going through the planning application, we note that the few houses that did not occupy the entire site filed to expand to the maximum extent within a year or two. A later application for alteration filed (and granted) in 1971 also involves incorporating the concrete pillars within the wall of the house itself, suggesting an interesting conflict, or possibly a fusion between the two different orders of structure [fig. 7]. All of these alterations served to turn Friberger's *Däckshus* closer to a "normal" building, and what we could refer to in terms of an *Open Form,* after the Hansens' terms, became increasingly closed during the first years. Another setback for Friberger was that the developer, Skånska Cementgjuteriet (later Skanska), allegedly turned down their

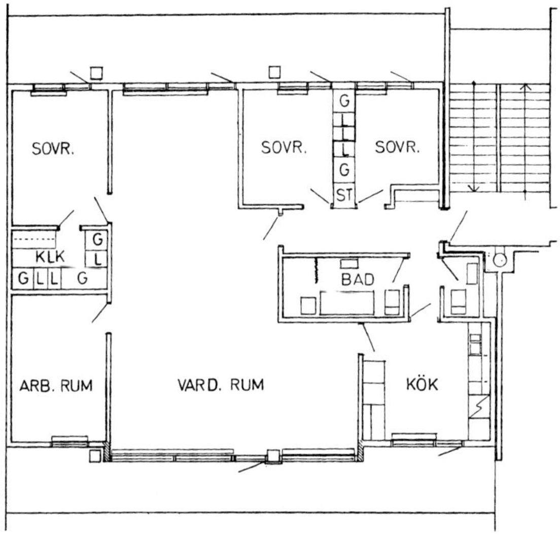

fig. 7

proposal of dimensioning the concrete decks and the distance between them for carrying 80 cm of soil on top of the concrete, which Friberger considered necessary for lush gardens.[28]

Friberger's *Däckshus*, although ultimately a rather mundane building as a result of all the rather restrictive limitations, remains one of the few examples from this time where the open form is actually constructed in an urban setting in combination with a self-build program. There are other projects on a similar theme, for example, Tadeusz Fuss-Kaden's proposal for structures with decks and small detached houses.[29] There are variations on the same theme in more recent architecture, notably in Elemental's well-published project for "incremental housing," in, among other places, Monterrey (2010), which have a different relationship between the structure and the tenant's self-build project. There, the two are integrated from the start rather than kept apart. Apart from this, there are echoes of Friberger in, for instance, Site's *Highrise of Homes* (1981), and other versions on the same theme.

7 Proposed plan from planning application filed in 1971, where the structure is proposed to be encased in the house itself, the exterior wall at the bottom of the image.

In some ways, another reference is rather particularly interesting: the section of Friberger's house resembles the drawing from *Life* magazine (1909) that Rem Koolhaas dubbed the "skyscraper theorem," which appears in his 1978 book *Delirious New York*, and which remains close in the architectural psyche [fig. 8].[30] Koolhaas, in *Delirious New York*, used the illustration to explain the concept of "schism," whereby each floor would be a pristine world of its own. Friberger's *Däckshus* could possibly be read as a Swedish, more collectively oriented version of the same dream, whereby a design program holds the overall coherence together.

Discussion

The two projects here introduced are both predicated on growth. They share certain characteristics, notably the built-in imperative to grow. This imperative does however have different nuances. In the case of Edelsvärd's generic town plan, it is the town that is meant to expand, while filling out the previously reserved central area as need arises. In Friberger's plan, it is the household, the private sphere that is expected to grow, whereas the collective structure remains static. To some extent, this is a result emerging from the scale of the plan: Edelsvärd planned a town, whereas Friberger designed a specific building. But, at the same time, it is interesting to ask whether such a shift in perspective could mean something else. Possibly, we could write this into a discussion of an industrial economy's focus on production in Edelsvärd's case, which then shifts to emphasize a consumer economy, visible in Friberger's plan. Framed in this way, the two projects would signify two slightly different biopolitical regimes, two different ways of organizing life that, while both predicated on growth, address this growth on different terms.

Turning to Friberger's building, the freedom to grow (coupled with the imperative to do so) is here shifted to the private sphere. The individual is provided with a very clear frame within which she can develop her own freedom: the development of the ideal home. At the same time, Friberger's building could be framed in a social democratic tradition aiming to provide working-class families with an opportunity to develop their own property.[31] Social democracy and the labor movement had experimented with this since the 1920s, also evident in the founding of building associations like HSB.[32] These are interesting as they simultaneously set out to improve the material situation of the working class (or, at least, certain parts of it), and thereby separate the interests of this group from the rest of the working class who still do not own property, thus theoretically making the wealthiest section of the working class less inclined to political radicalism.

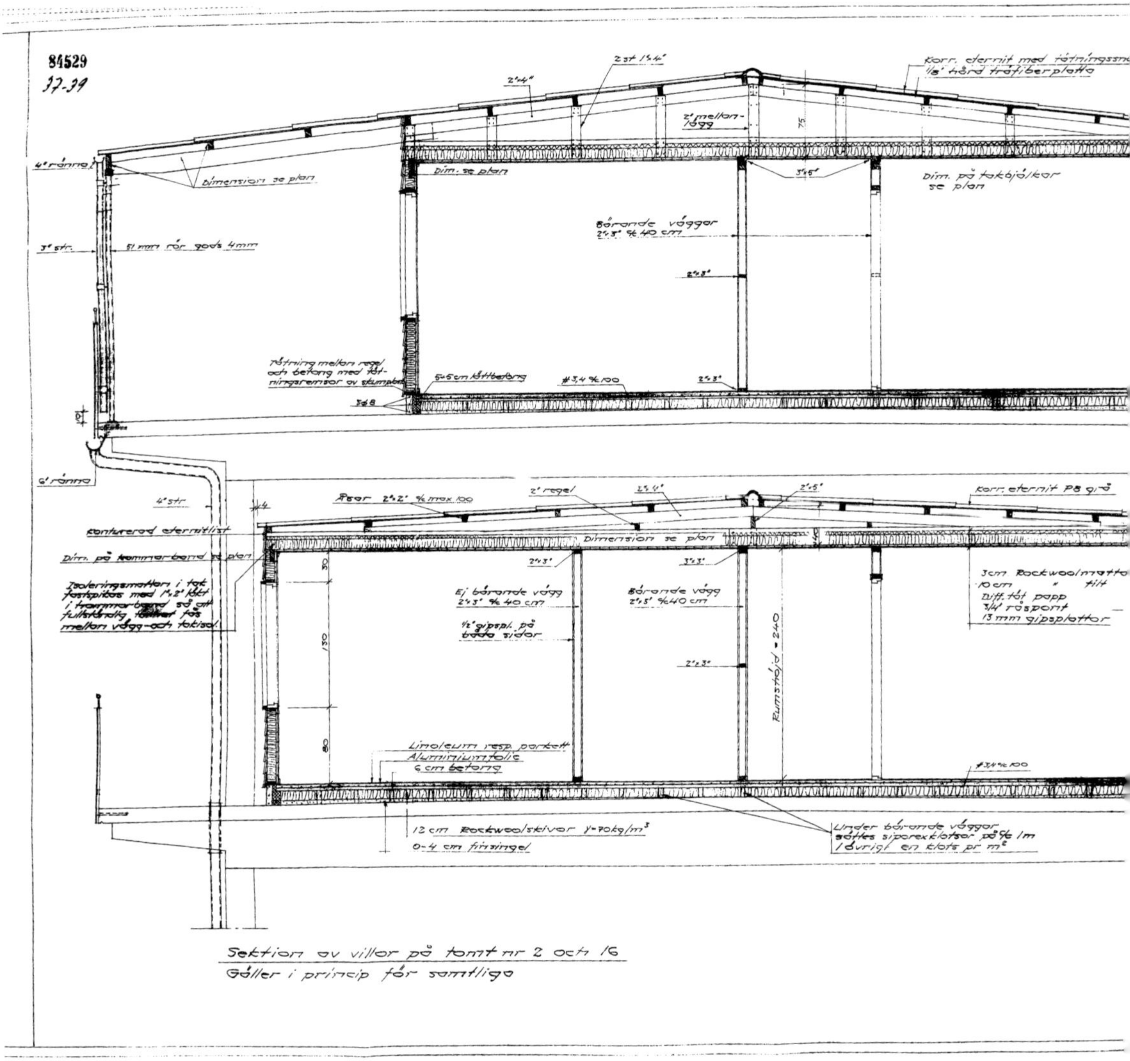

8 Section drawing of Friberger's *Däckshus* showing the two different orders of structures: the concrete decks and the houses constructed on the decks.

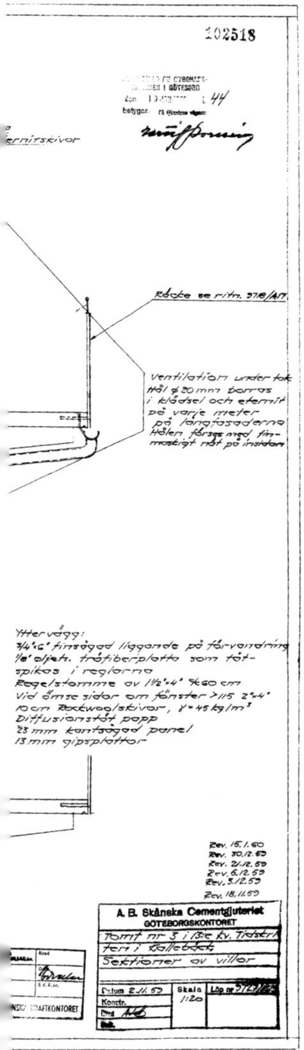

fig. 8

The double nature of freedom and control is, in Wallenstein's reading of Foucault, an indispensable aspect of architecture. Wallenstein interprets Foucault's answer in an interview by Paul Rabinow that liberty is what must be exercised rather than circumscribed by an enabling architecture. Any liberty produced through architecture is invariably accompanied by a degree of control. Foucault, according to Wallenstein, "locates (...) universals within a history that is neither simply empirical nor the gradual unfolding of Reason";[33] each freedom offered by the plan invariably exists in relation to constraints, and vice versa. The plan, then, becomes a medium wherein these juxtapositions of constraints and freedoms are played out. This interplay invariably actualizes questions of how the plan organizes life, and, in extension, on what principles these acts of organization can be analyzed.

1 I borrow the term "biopolitical machine" from Sven-Olov Wallenstein, *Biopolitics and the Emergence of Modern Architecture* (New York: The Temple Hoyne Buell Center for the Study of American Architecture & Princeton Architectural Press, 2008).

2 "Complete" is not a word that would be associated with either project, and if we do consider Friberger's house complete when all the detached houses have been completed, it is important to remember that the architect himself considered it a mistake.

3 Wallenstein, *Biopolitics*, 42. See also Pier Vittorio Aureli, *The Possibility of an Absolute Architecture* (Cambridge, MA, and London: MIT Press, 2011), 11.

4 Aureli, *The Possibility of an Absolute Architecture*, 10.

5 Wallenstein defines subjectivization as follows: "the totality of ways in which modern individuals have come to be formed, in terms of both a modeling from without and an inner response. That power is something productive means that it is always both power *over* (application of an external force that molds matter) and power *to* (the work of shaping a provisional self as a response to external forces); and its operations are always connected to a certain knowledge that is formed of the self." Wallenstein, *Biopolitics*, 5.

6 Ibid., 13.

7 Françoise Choay, *The Rule and the Model: On the Theory of Architecture and Urbanism*, trans. Denise Bratton (Cambridge, MA, and London: MIT Press, 1997). Sven-Olov Wallenstein, *Architecture, Critique, Ideology: Writings on Architecture and Theory* (Stockholm: Axl Books, 2016), 81–86.

8 Aureli, *The Possibility of an Absolute Architecture*, 11–13.

9 Ibid., 13.

10 Adolf Edelsvärd, "Plan och byggnadssätt för Landsortsstäder och Förstäder," *Tidskrift för Byggnadskonst och Ingeniörs vetenskap* (May, 1859), 65–69. This article has been discussed in a Swedish context on a few occasions, most exhaustively by Gunilla Linde Bjur, whose dissertation is a biography of Edelsvärd. See Bjur, "Arkitekt vid industrialismens genombrott: Adolf Edelsvärd en yrkesbiografi" (PhD diss., Gothenburg University, 1999), 302–308. See also Thomas Hall, "Urban Planning in Sweden," in *Planning and Growth in the Nordic Countries*, ed. Thomas Hall (London: E & FN Spon, 1991), 187–88.

11 Translated by Hall, "Urban Planning in Sweden," 187.

12 This use of rules and statistics appears to be similar to how Cerdá employed statistics as a means of managing growth. See Choay, *The Rule and the Model*, chapter 6: "The Theory of Urbanism."

13 Similar mechanisms were proposed in the establishment of garden cities in the United Kingdom.

14 Keller Easterling discusses a similar situation in Savannah, as outlined by James Oglethorpe in 1733. See Easterling, *Extrastatecraft: The Power of Infrastructure Space* (London: Verso, 2014), 79–81. Here, however, growth is in the multiplication of future "wards," whereas in Edelsvärd's case there is at the same time a densification of the central parts as the reserved land is put to use.

15 Other ways of dealing with the question of growth come in the form of Cybernetics, including the *Fun Palace* and Gordon Pask, with the counterculture movement in the United States, and later with the self-build movement. All of them see the building not as a static or complete object, but as something that evolves over time.

16 Oskar and Zofia Hansen, "The Open Form in Architecture: The Art of the Great Number," in *Ciam '59 in Otterlo*, ed. O. Newman (Stuttgart: Krämer Verlag, 1961).

17 There is a plethora of other definitions of the crisis of Modernism, depending on perspective. It is furthermore a crisis that, if it exists, is dated differently by different narrators. For the sake of convenience, I will here follow the Hansens' definition rather than analyze it in detail.

18 Hansen, "The Open Form in Architecture," 190.

19 Ibid., 190.

20 Ibid., 191.

21 See for instance Larry Busbea, *Topologies: The Urban Utopia in France 1960–1970* (Cambridge, MA, and London: MIT Press, 2007), 142–43.

22 On a side note, it is remarkable how persistent this idea has been in architecture since. We only need to recall Rem Koolhaas and Zoe Zenghelis' project *The City of the Captive Globe* from the early 1970s, where the grid serves as the organizing principle within which each individual block becomes an island free to shape its own world.

3 Torsten Frendberg, "Unikt projekt i öteborg," *Arkitektur* 3 (1959): 68–69.
4 The Kallebäck project appears in a ew publications, but usually in passing ather than with in-depth analysis. Erik igge also associates Friberger's project ith the Hansens' Otterlo presentation, ee Erik Sigge, *Architecture's Red Tape: overnment Building Construction in weden 1963–1973* (Stockholm: KTH, 017), 141–42; Erik Sigge, "From mpiricism to Structuralism: The ational Swedish Board of Housing," in *e-Scaling the Environment: New andscapes of Design, 1960–1980*, ed. kos Moravánszky and Karl R. Kegler 3asel: Birkhäuser, 2017), 223. See also laes Caldenby, "De stora programmens d, 1960–75," in *Att bygga ett land*, ed. laes Caldenby et al. (Stockholm: yggforskningsrådet, 1998), 145; and /hite Arkitekter, *Byggnadsminnes-tredning 2011-02-21 Erik Fribergers äckshus, Kallebäck* (Gothenburg: /hite/Göteborgs Stad, 2011).
5 In a structuralist manner, there is a eparation between the fixed basic ructure and flexible parts that respond the needs and desires of the dividuals.
6 White Arkitekter, *Byggnadsminnes-tredning 2011-02-21 Erik Fribergers äckshus, Kallebäck*, 20.
7 This is visible in the drawings as well noted as a point of disappointment by iberger in White Arkitekter, *Byggnads-innesutredning 2011-02-21 Erik ibergers däckshus, Kallebäck*, 16.
28 White Arkitekter, *Byggnads-minnesutredning 2011-02-21 Erik Fribergers däckshus, Kallebäck*, 16. In the article in *Arkitektur* (1959), Frendberg discusses the possibility of having 60 cm deep planters on the decks for the gardens, which does not appear to have been common. See Frendberg, "Unikt projekt i Göteborg."
29 This project is presented on the same page as Friberger's, but was presumably never realized. See Lennart Hård af Segerstad, "Småhus och hängande trädgårdar," *Arkitektur* 3 (1959): 69.
30 Rem Koolhaas, *Delirious New York: A Retroactive Manifesto for Manhattan* (New York: Monacelli Press, 1978); Robert Somol and Sarah Whiting, "Notes around the Doppler Effect and Other Moods of Modernism," *Perspecta* 33 (2002): 72–77.
31 Even if it technically never was their private property, as it was a "bostads-rättsförening" from the outset.
32 HSB (Hyresgästernas Sparkasse- och Byggnadsförening) was a building association founded in 1923. Its aim was to provide housing for the upper echelons of the working class that they would "own." See Kerstin Thörn, *En Bostad för Hemmet: Idéhistoriska Studier i Bostadsfrågan 1889–1929* (Umeå: Umeå universitet, 1997).
33 Wallenstein, *Biopolitics*, 41.

Anna Hougaard

fig.1

Real Berlin

Gentrification's Grip on Plans and Renderings

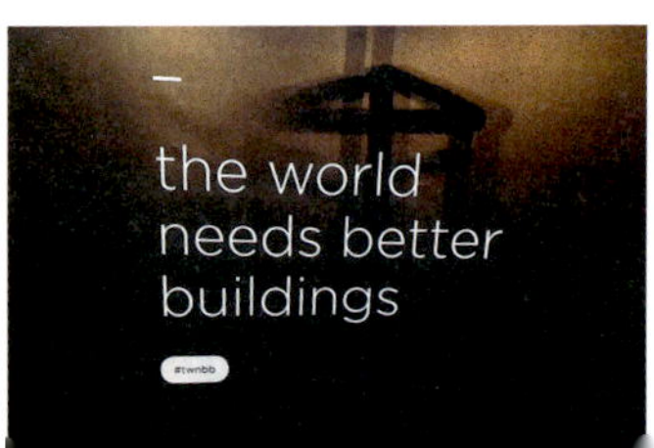

In early 2017, a billboard on a building site showing a large interior rendering caught my eye.[1] It was situated near Alexanderplatz in Berlin, proclaiming the construction of the *Grandaire* real estate project.[2] First, it was the small print on each rendering which said "nonbinding visualization," that puzzled me. Well aware of the bendable nature of renderings, I was surprised that this status was stated so clearly as a way of preventing legal problems for the selling part. I looked closer and noticed graffiti: "How antisocial. Millionaire projects, and who moves in? ANIMALS who are 0 % interested in the lives of others." Another said: "Social housing for renting ought to be built here" [fig. 2–3].[3]

The rendering carrying the graffiti shows a spacious eat-in kitchen offering a panoramic view on Berlin. The furniture is new and expensive and on the coffee table, books about fashion, interior design, and architecture are displayed, signaling a wealthy lifestyle.[4] Once an apartment in *Grandaire* has been taken, this is how a home might look like. And if this scenario is not

1 Billboards with renderings from various places in Berlin, 2017-19.

fig. 2

within economic reach, a rendering like this may provoke angry statements such as this graffiti.

Taking a closer look at real estate homepages offering housing, renderings are usually combined with floor plans. For instance, on *Grandaire*'s homepage the renderings played the most important role at that time, inviting browsing buyers into a luxurious scenario, while those seriously interested will eventually wish to look at the plans.[5] The plans shift the focus away from emotion, atmosphere, and lifestyle; contrary to the renderings, they require an understanding of scale and other architectural drawing conventions to be properly interpreted. The plans enable an understanding of room sizes and organization, and when accompanied with square meters and prize, their conventional meaning is tweaked towards an economically rational, spatially distributed investment. Emotion and lifestyle are communicated by the rendering, while the investment as such relies on the plan's statutory and measurable constitution. Together, the plan and the rendering create an

2 Building sign statin that the visualization is nonbinding, 2017.

3 Building sign next t *Grandaire* with graffiti, Berlin, 2017.

fig. 3

especially powerful medium communicating what could be called "emotio-economic" space, uncritically put to work as a tool of urban development, which often conduces to gentrification.

While this may be considered to represent a mainstream way of using renderings, the graffiti targets the rendering as a medium of communication. It comments on the larger wave of gentrification in which the rendering is put to work to communicate and sell the new building. The interior rendering communicates an urban feeling that has been transposed into the domestic space, and simultaneously the domestic scenario is being projected into real Berlin through the onsite building signs. This practice of "emotio-economic" communication on site constitutes a phenomenon that is sweeping through Berlin [fig. 1]. At the same time, there is another wave of urban development rolling through the city. Berlin is traditionally a tenants' city, and the *Mietskasernen* (tenement houses)[6] from the end of the 19th century have become objects of intense economic speculation. A typical scheme for increasing rents is that

fig. 4/5

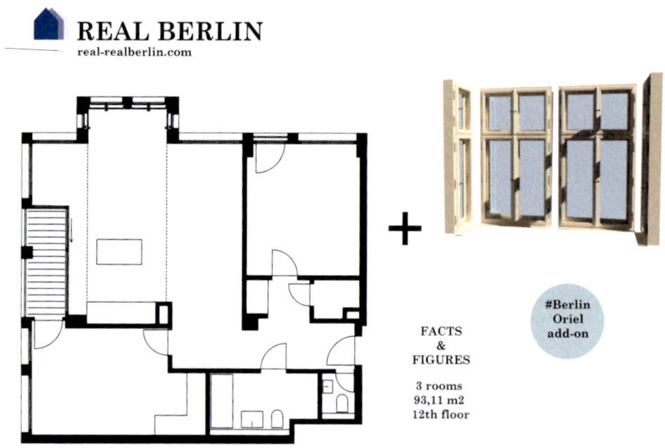

4 Anna Hougaard, *Real Berlin*, 2019. Plan with Berlin oriel add-on.

5 Anna Hougaard, *Real Berlin*, 2019. Rendering of corresponding room with Berlin oriel add-on.

fig. 6/7

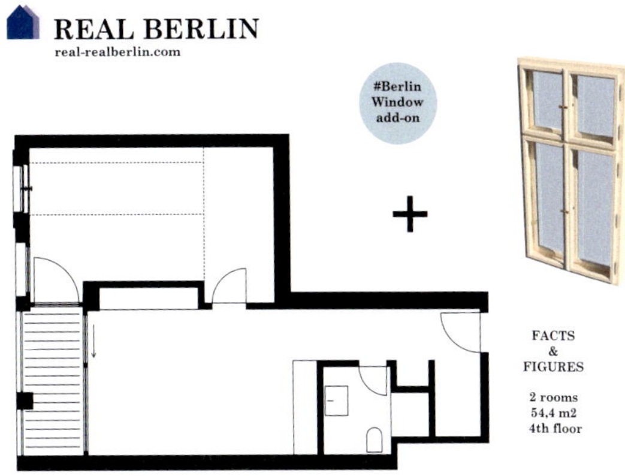

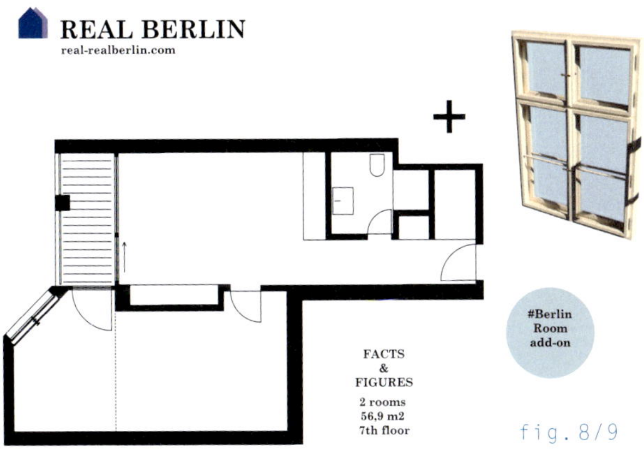

fig. 8/9

6 Anna Hougaard, *Real Berlin*, 2019. Rendering of corresponding room with Berlin window add-on.

7 Anna Hougaard, *Real Berlin*, 2019. Plan with Berlin window add-on.

8 Anna Hougaard, *Real Berlin*, 2019. Plan with Berlin window add-on.

9 Anna Hougaard, *Real Berlin*, 2019. Rendering of corresponding room with Berlin window add-on.

fig.10

10 Anna Hougaard, *Real Berlin*, 2019. Building sign, rendering.

of "sustainable modernization," and one of the most typical measures of modernizing is the replacement of the old, often original windows with new ones.[7] It is much debated whether replacing the original windows is at all sustainable,[8] all the more as aspects of social sustainability and architectural aesthetics are often not taken into account.

The project *Real Berlin* reflects on these two simultaneous waves of urban development and the role of plans and renderings within them [fig. 4–10]. Pages from a fictitious real estate project catalogue demonstrate that prospective buyers can choose to have original tenement house building parts placed in their new apartments. A kit of parts, including the Berlin tenement house window and other tenement house elements, makes it possible to customize a new apartment so that it emanates real Berlin atmosphere. The tall Berlin window type, with its slim vertical proportion fitting the generous ceiling heights in the *Mietskasernen*, might be built in just as it is [fig. 6–7] or by being expanded into a spatial add-on, such as an oriel [fig. 4–5], or as part of the characteristic *Berliner Zimmer*, with its extra-large window that creates a special, gloomy light atmosphere [fig. 8–9]. The human protagonists of these scenarios appear indirectly by way of the interior decoration targeting types such as the "single businessman or woman," the "young couple," and the "family with children."

While using the same medium, *Real Berlin* is a comment on the uncritical way in which rendering instrumentalizes human and spatial stereotypes as part of urban development processes. The scenography (of capitalization) is projected into the real Berlin through building signs, slowly turning the city into a city of renderings, a city whose realness is as bendable as its medium [fig. 10].

A rendering is a digital 2D perspectival ıage, usually photo-realistic, generated om a 3D model of a building. Although ırt of the architectural toolkit for eating architecture, renderings are ostly used to communicate a finished chitecture project to people who are ıfamiliar with architectural drawing nventions and communication. Cf. yle May, ed., *Clog Rendering*, (Brooklyn, Y: Kyle May, 2012), 29. Moreover, udies have shown that when renderings e photo-realistic, laypeople perceive em as more valid than other sorts of chitectural visualizations. Nada Bates-kljac, "Assessing Perceived Credibility Traditional and Computer-Generated rchitectural Representations," *Design udies* 30, no. 4 (2009): 415–37.

2 *Grandaire*, http://grandaire.berlin/de/ (accessed July 29, 2019).

3 My translation.

4 Studies show that when looking at renderings, both laypersons and architects look more at the entourage than the building. May, *Clog Rendering*, 57. *Entourage* expresses all the elements in a rendering that do not show the building, such as humans, furniture, greenery, bikes, cars, etc. May, *Clog Rendering*, 52–53.

5 *Grandaire*, http://grandaire.berlin/de/ (accessed July 29, 2019).

6 Johann Friedrich Geist and Klaus Kürvers, *Das Berliner Mietshaus 1862–1945* (Munich: Prestel, 1984).

7 This is being questioned in a current research project at the Technical University of Berlin, see Forschungsprojekt Fenstervergleich, http://fenstervergleich.archix.de/ (accessed July 29, 2019).

8 For instance, new windows often cause mildew, see "Mietrecht: Probleme mit den Wohnungsfenstern," *Mietrecht Lexikon*, https://www.mietrechtslexikon.de/a1lexikon2/f1/fenster.htm (accessed July 29, 2019).

Olivia Valentine

fig.1

Metropoliz Future Forest

Drawn Prospects

1 Fırat Erdim, Kim Karlsrud, Daniel Phillips, and Olivia Valentine, *Metropoliz Future Forest*, 2015, Rome.

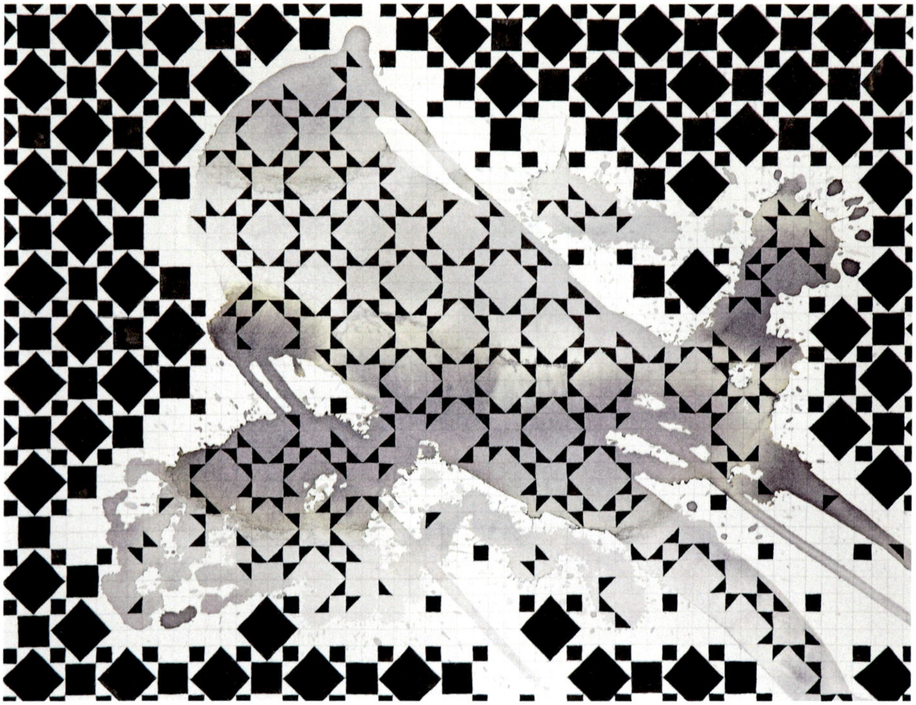

fig. 2

Metropoliz Future Forest is a 1:1-scale plan, drawn in situ at the Museo dell'Altro e dell'Altrove di Metropoliz, an informal immigrant community and art space located in an abandoned salami factory compound on the periphery of Rome. As a plan, this project both predicts and facilitates the growth of a future forest and garden, slowly created over an extended period of time by subsequent perforations in the concrete ground [fig. 1].

Metropoliz Future Forest grew out of a series of watercolor and graphite drawings, entitled *Interruptions*, based on floor tile patterns found in central Rome [fig. 2–4]. Referencing the tile patterns in a variety of spaces in Rome, the *Interruptions* drawings act as plans for imagined spaces and landmasses. Using water alongside watercolor pigments and graphite, these drawings are simultaneously improvisational and algorithmic in nature.

Stemming directly from *Interruptions,* an initial scaled plan for *Metropoliz Future Forest* was created in graphite and watercolor across several large pages [fig. 5]. The initial plan takes into account drainage, the

2 Olivia Valentine, *Interruptions (Santa Maria Maggiore)*, 2015. Watercolor and graphite on paper, 30 × 40 cm.

3 Olivia Valentine, *Interruptions (Carpet)*, 2015. Watercolor and graphite on paper, 42 × 56 cm.

4 Olivia Valentine, *Interruptions (Plaza Mayor)*, 2015. Watercolor and graphite on paper, 42 × 56 cm.

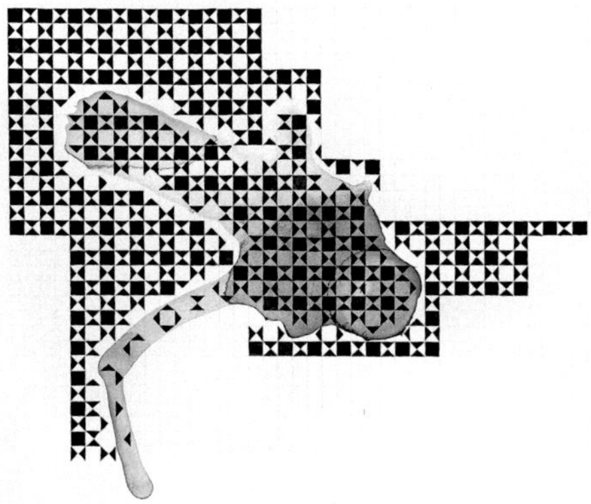

fig.3

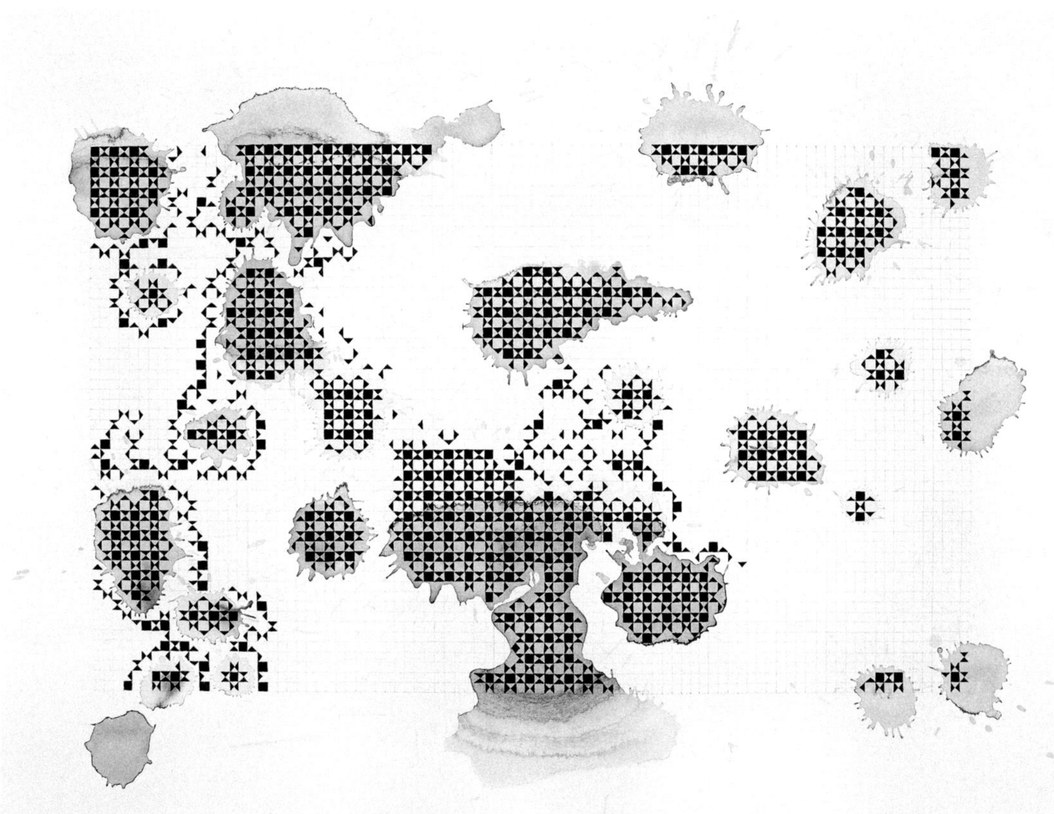

fig.4

presence of existing flora, and routes of passage across the site taken by the different immigrant and Roma communities that call Metropoliz home. This initial plan was then executed on site in chalk and paint, laying the groundwork for a series of perforations to the concrete intended to facilitate the natural reforestation process along geometric incised lines [fig. 6–7].

Rather than importing new vegetation for this urban garden and forest, we collaborated with the existing ecologies that already occupied the site—the grasses, trees, flowers, and weeds that have arisen spontaneously in the decades after the closing of the factory. By creating a series of perforations and cuts in the existing concrete, we were helping the seeds of these species to take root, and continuing to transform these spaces over the coming decades [fig. 8].

fig. 5

Metropoliz Future Forest was created in collaboration with Fırat Erdim, Kim Karlsrud, and Daniel Phillips in 2015. *Metropoliz Future Forest* was made possible by a project grant from the American Academy in Rome (AAR), the Museo dell'Altro e dell'Altrove di Metropoliz (MAAM), and dedicated volunteers, including Mac Casey, María Robles, Dave McKenzie, Paula Matthusen, Roger Camero, Stefania Tutino, and Adam Kuby from the AAR community, and Leslie Johnson, Lukasz Kowalczyk, and students from the College of Architecture at the Illinois Institute of Technology.

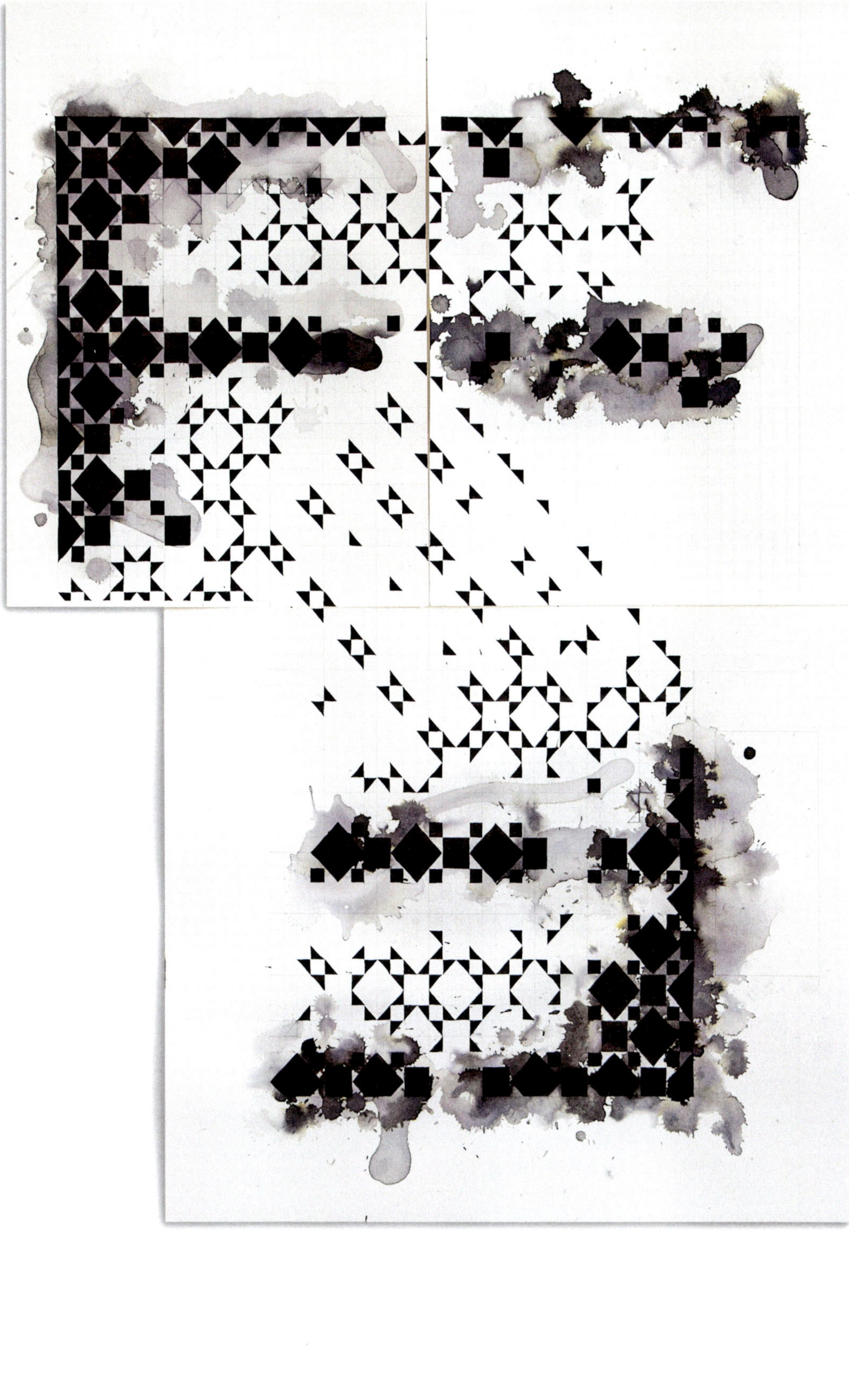

fig. 6

fig. 7

6 Fırat Erdim, Kim Karlsrud, Daniel Phillips, and Olivia Valentine, *Metropoliz Future Forest*, 2015, Rome. On-site drawing process.

7 Fırat Erdim, Kim Karlsrud, Daniel Phillips, and Olivia Valentine, *Metropoliz Future Forest*, 2015, Rome.

8 Fırat Erdim, Kim Karlsrud, Daniel Phillips, and Olivia Valentine, *Metropoliz Future Forest*, 2016, Rome. Evidence of growth, one year after completion.

fig. 8

Robin Schaeverbeke

Raw Plans

fig. 1

'No, I don't like work. I had rather laze about and think of all the fine things that can be done. I don't like work,—no man does—but I like what is in the work,—the chance to find yourself. Your own reality—for yourself, not for others—what no other man can ever know. They can only see the mere show, and never can tell what it really means.'[1]

– Joseph Conrad

Does it take, to turn to Richard Sennett's well-known statement, around 10,000 drawings to become an expert draughtsman—or architect for that matter?[2] Does it take 10,000 drawings to refine a formal or spatial idea? Does it take, as one of my colleagues, architect Koen Deprez, once suggested, at least 30 hours to elaborate a drawing?[3]

Architectural drawing concerns… then I got stuck. I intended to write something intelligent about the architectural drawing process, its learning and other processes—but the drawings I was working on demanded my full attention.

Perhaps I should provide some context. I trained as an architect. After some years of practical experience, I decided to teach and study architectural drawing as a full-time activity at an architectural faculty. In 2016 I successfully defended a PhD dissertation that investigated "drawing and improvised learning processes for architectural drawing."[4] After that I thought it was time to return to "the real thing" and find myself a real project,

1 Robin Schaeverbeke, heating, ventilation, and sewage, 2016. Axonometric drawing.

fig. 2

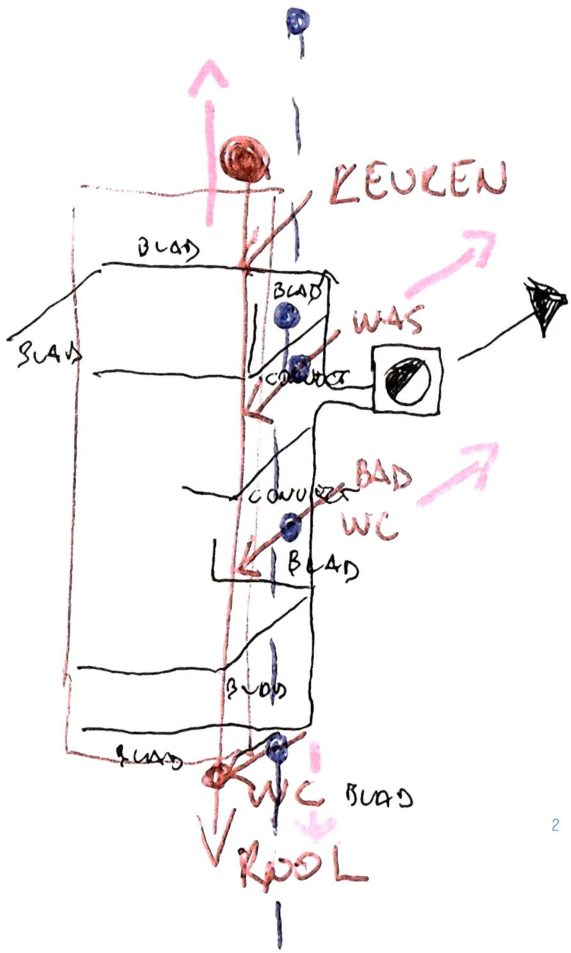

fig. 3

2 Aerial view, 2016. Photoshopped satellite view of th[e] house on the night w[e] discovered the opportunity on the real estate agent's site.

3 Robin Schaeverbeke, drains and heating (first sketch), 2016

4 Robin Schaeverbeke, unfolding of every room to calculate material needs, 2017

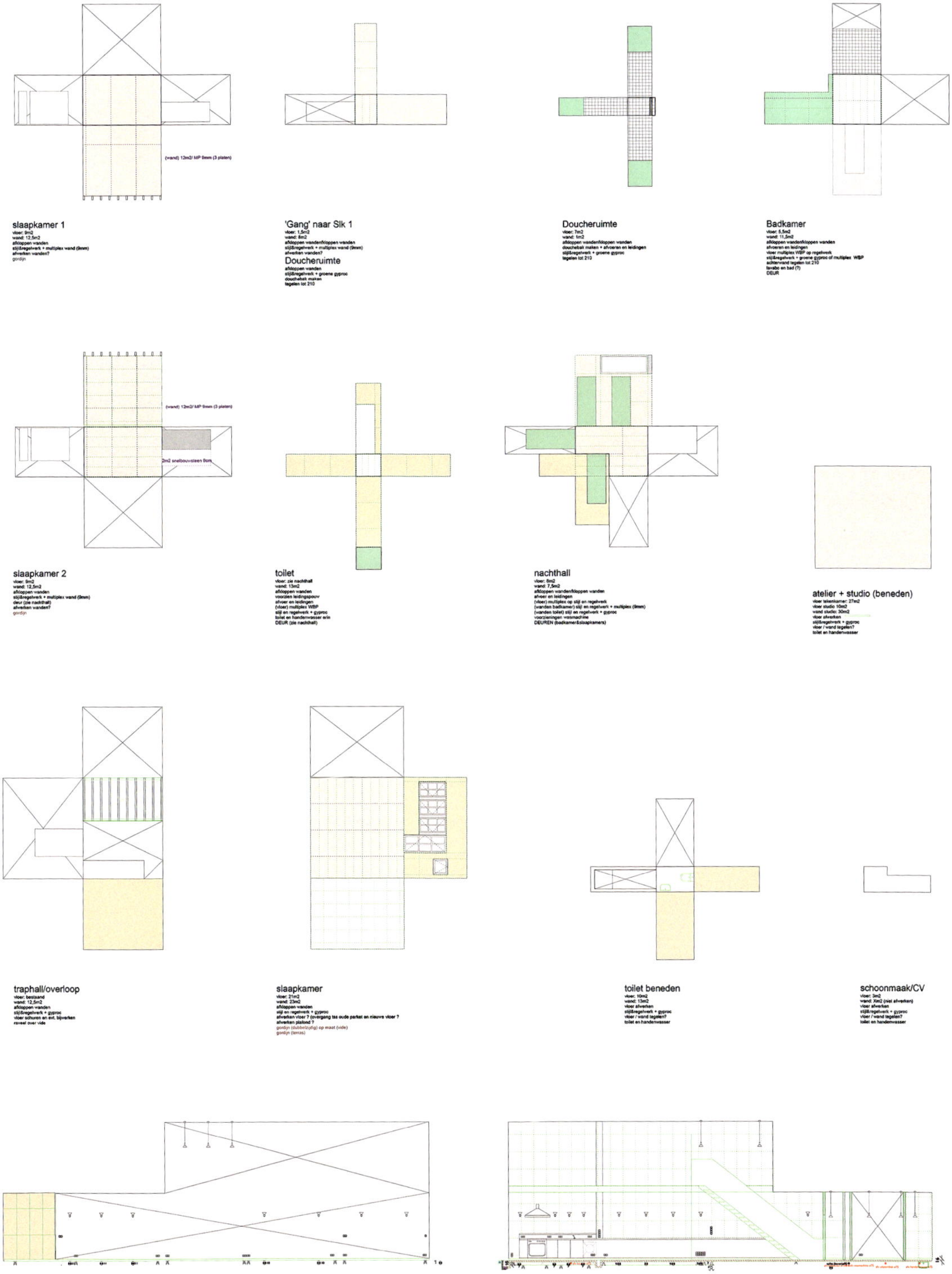
(wand) 12m2/ MP 9mm (3 platen)
slaapkamer 1
vloer: 9m2
wand: 12,5m2
afkloppen wanden
stijl&regelwerk + multiplex wand (9mm)
afwerken wanden?
gordijn
'Gang' naar Slk 1
vloer: 1,5m2
wand: 8m2
afkloppen wandenfkloppen wanden
stijl&regelwerk + multiplex wand (9mm)
afwerken wanden?
Doucheruimte
afkloppen wanden
stijl&regelwerk + groene gyproc
douchebak maken
tegelen tot 210
Doucheruimte
vloer: 7m2
wand: 1m2
afkloppen wandenfkloppen wanden
douchebak maken + afvoeren en leidingen
stijl&regelwerk + groene gyproc
tegelen tot 210
Badkamer
vloer: 5,5m2
wand: 11,5m2
afkloppen wandenfkloppen wanden
afvoeren en leidingen
vloer multiplex WBP op regelwerk
stijl&regelwerk + groene gyproc of multiplex WBP
achterwand tegelen tot 210
lavabo en bad (?)
DEUR
(wand) 12m2/ MP 9mm (3 platen)
2m2 snelbouwsteen 9cm
slaapkamer 2
vloer: 9m2
wand: 12,5m2
afkloppen wanden
stijl&regelwerk + multiplex wand (9mm)
deur (zie nachthall)
afwerken wanden?
gordijn
toilet
vloer: zie nachthall
wand: 13m2
afkloppen wanden
voorzien leidingspouw
afvoer en leidingen
(vloer) multiplex WBP
stijl en regelwerk + gyproc
toilet en handenwasser erin
DEUR (zie nachthall)
nachthall
vloer: 8m2
wand: 7,5m2
afkloppen wandenfkloppen wanden
afvoer en leidingen
(vloer) multiplex op stijl en regelwerk
(wanden badkamer) stijl en regelwerk + multiplex (9mm)
(wanden toilet) stijl en regelwerk + gyproc
voorzieningen wasmachine
DEUREN (badkamer&slaapkamers)
atelier + studio (beneden)
vloer tekenkamer: 27m2
vloer studio 10m2
wand studio: 30m2
vloer afwerken
stijl&regelwerk + gyproc
vloer / wand tegelen?
toilet en handenwasser
traphall/overloop
vloer: bestaand
wand: 12,5m2
afkloppen wanden
stijl&regelwerk + gyproc
vloer schuren en evt. bijwerken
raveel over vide
slaapkamer
vloer: 21m2
wand: 23m2
afkloppen wanden
stijl en regelwerk + gyproc
afwerken vloer ? (overgang tss oude parket en nieuwe vloer ?
afwerken plafond ?
gordijn (dubbelzijdig) op maat (vide)
gordijn (terras)
toilet beneden
vloer: 10m2
wand: 13m2
vloer afwerken
stijl&regelwerk + gyproc
vloer / wand tegelen?
toilet en handenwasser
schoonmaak/CV
vloer: 3m2
wand: Xm2 (niet afwerken)
vloer afwerken
stijl&regelwerk + gyproc
vloer / wand tegelen?
toilet en handenwasser

fig. 4

a renovation of some kind. In late November 2016 my partner and I bumped into the advert for a house: affordable, an abundance of space, a small garden, and a two-story workspace at the end of the plot [fig. 2]. We immediately fell in love with the possibilities of this structure and decided to "plunge into it."

Fast forward to a few months later. The structure officially became ours. I converted my calculation drawings [fig. 1, 4] into building permit plans [fig. 5] and called Michel, the contractor, to inform him when he could start. Very much to my surprise he answered: "What about right away?" This ignited a unique building process. "Right away" meant commencing construction without a building permit ("We'll start on the roof—no need for a permit for that!"), without an actual view of the building's soundness or overall state, and even without a clear view on any of the final materials. It flip-flopped the way I thought buildings were made and forced me to put on many hats at the same time: architect/client/draughtsman/layman/mediator. Suddenly I had to plan, prepare, strip, clean, think, solve, and help out—on site—all at the same time.

As we peeled the years from the walls and ceilings, the house and its structure started talking to us, revealing anomalies and opportunities difficult to imagine in advance [fig. 6]. Without a definite plan, building became a matter of discussing and resolving problems on the spot. Luckily, I was able to be present most of the time.

Nelson Goodman once compared the agency of architects' plans to composers' scores.[5] Engaging in this more or less improvised process challenges this view. When working with the materials and conditions at hand the result (the building) becomes a reflection of a series of (mediated) decisions, material opportunities and functional/structural rationales. In such a process, drawings become a lead, a suggestion from which to depart [fig. 6].

When I was selecting drawings for this presentation I realized that, apart from the building permit plans, I never really found time or urgency to actually fine-tune and finish drawings. I seriously doubt whether I should. Their raw state reflects the process and even the state of the building. Polishing them feels like hurting reality. The whole process was about getting things done, with or without drawings. Drawings were useful when they assisted the resolution of a problem—they proved to be hopelessly redundant after that [fig. 3, 7].

Fast forward again... We spent New Year's Eve in the house; after nine months of work we could move in. Of course it is far from finished but we are there, we have time. Would it be possible to enter a similar "improvised" process in a normal client-contractor-architect relationship? It would definitely be a juridical nightmare since the whole building process is governed by

5 Robin Schaeverbeke, building permit plans, 2017.

gevels best. situatie 1/100

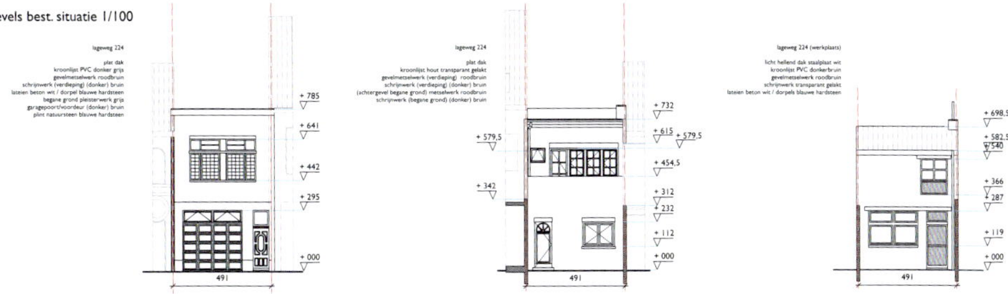

voorgevel (BS) achtergevel (BS) gevel werkplaatsen (BS)

plattegronden best. situatie 1/100

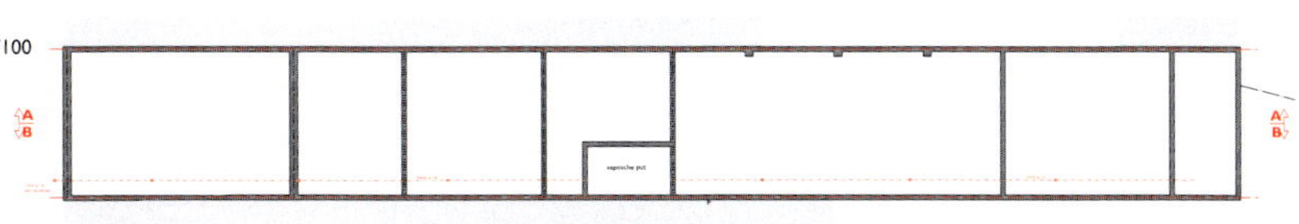

funderingsschema / riolering
(in ondergrondse sleuf)

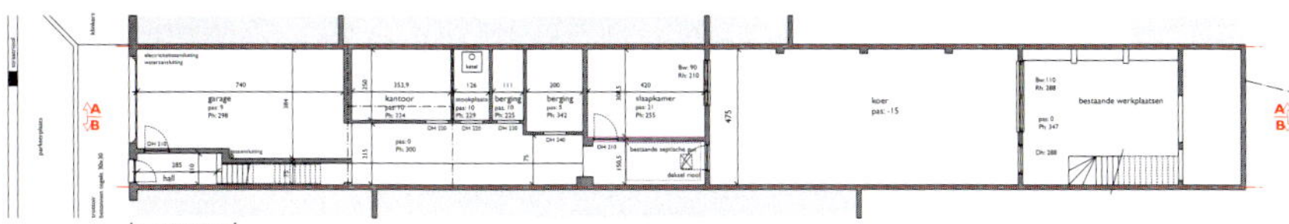

begane grond

fig. 5

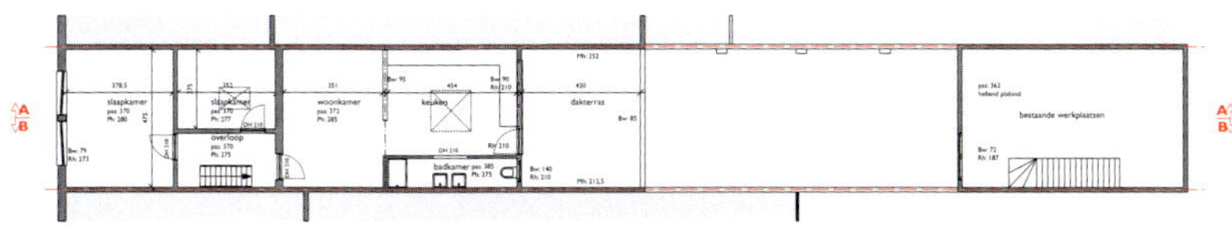

etage

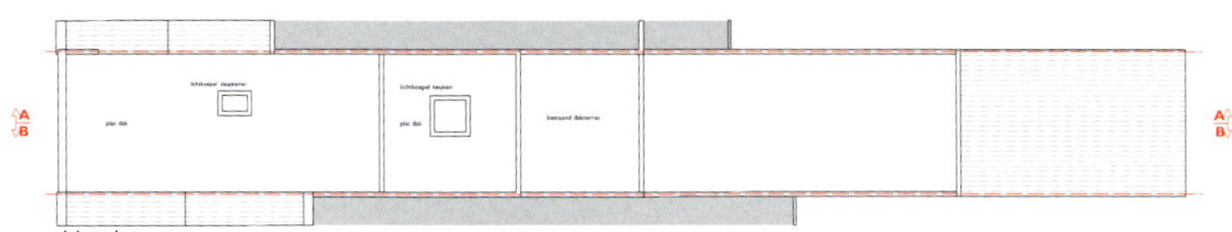

dakenplan

doorsnedes best. situatie 1/100

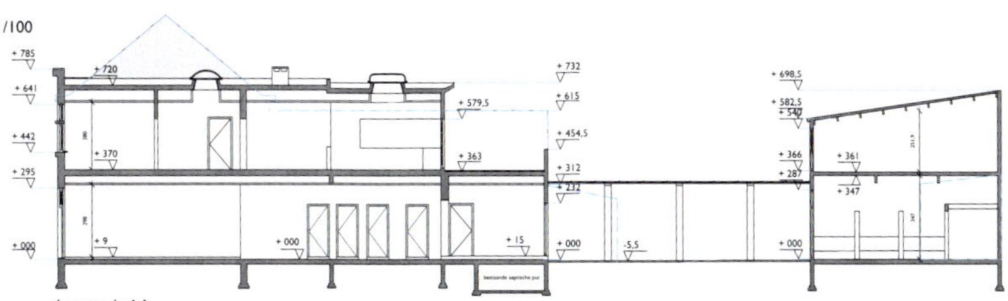

doorsnede AA

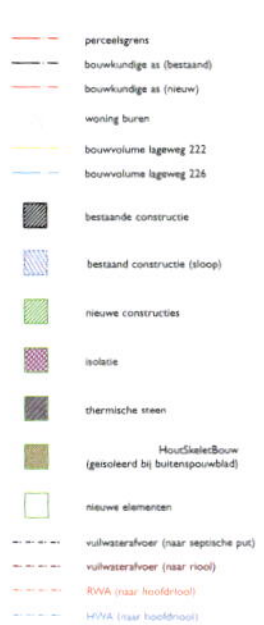

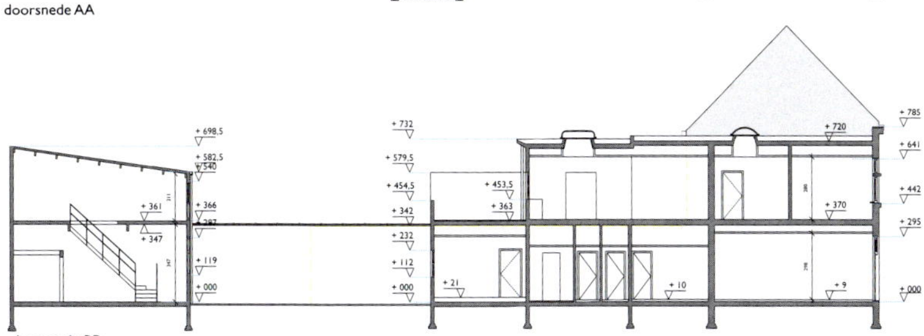

doorsnede BB

fig. 6

legislative demands, insurances, and guarantees. Improvisation—working with second-hand materials, listening to the building, changing things on the spot—challenges official consensus of how things are done. I would love to repeat this experiment with a third party. Finding someone crazy enough to participate. To be continued?

1 Joseph Conrad, *Heart of Darkness* (London: Penguin, 2012), 59–60.
2 Richard Sennett, *The Craftsman* (New Haven, CT: Yale University Press, 2009), 172.
3 Koen Deprez in conversation with the author, 2012.
4 Robin Schaeverbeke, "Extended Drawing" (PhD diss., KU Leuven, Faculty of Architecture, 2016).
5 Nelson Goodman, *Languages of Art: An Approach to a Theory of Symbols* (London: Oxford University Press, 1969), 122.

6 Robin Schaeverbeke, wall sketch, discussing a building knot with the contractor, 2017.

7 Robin Schaeverbeke, detail section to discuss the structure of the garden façade, 2017.

ig. 7

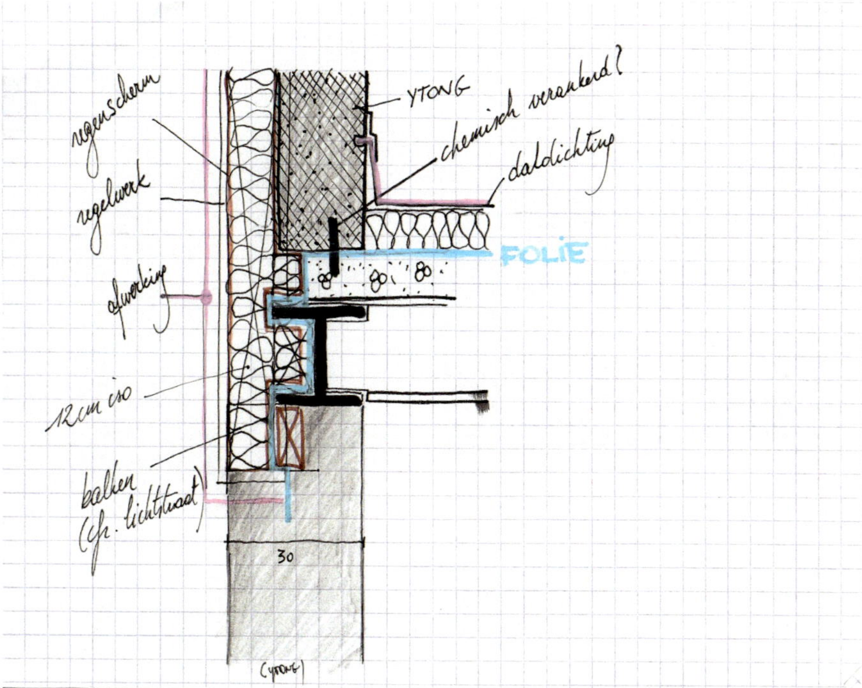
YTONG
chemisch verankerd?
daldichting
FOLIE
regenscherm
regelwerk
afwerking
12cm iso
balken
(cfr. lichtstraat)
30
(YTONG)

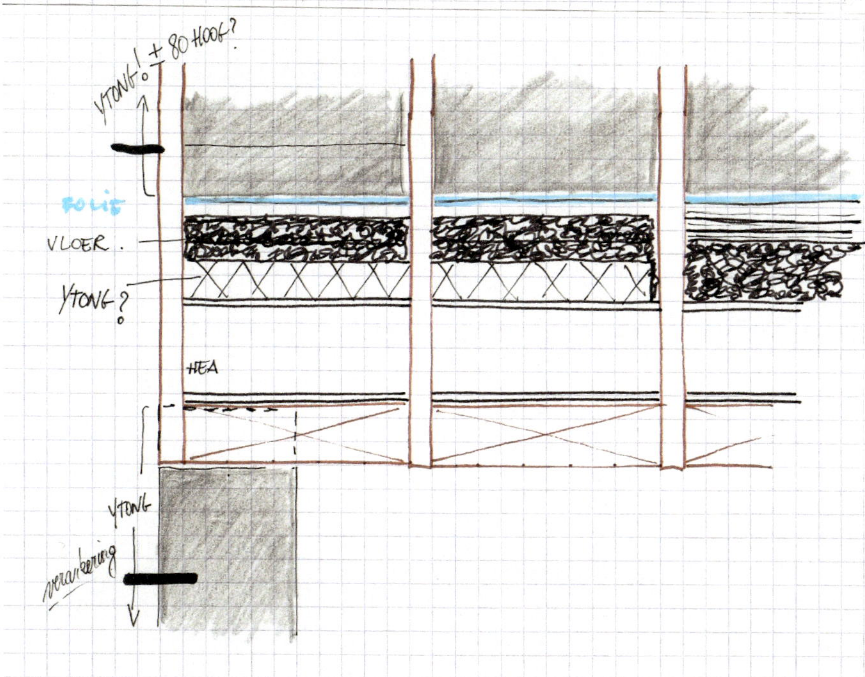
YTONG! ± 80 HOOG?
FOLIE
VLOER.
YTONG?
HEA
YTONG
verankering

Sean Griffiths

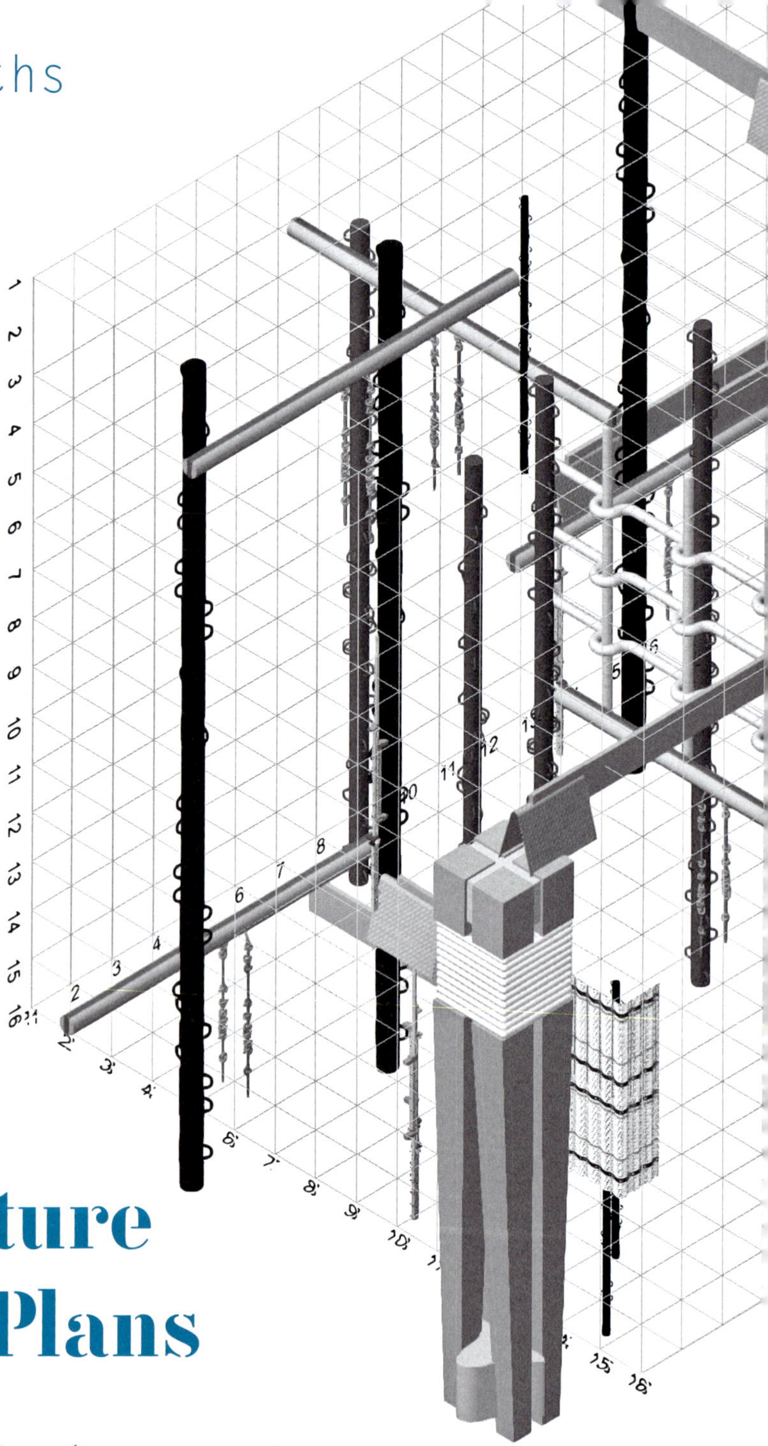

Architecture without Plans

Design Strategies Based on Chance Operations

fig. 1

The anthropologist Tim Ingold makes a distinction between "lines of habitation" and "lines of occupation."[1] Lines of habitation project outwards from a situation of *interiority*. A situation of interiority could be that of a hunter who, in following the scent of an animal, makes a path not mapped in advance, thereby creating a line of habitation. As he moves along the trail, the hunter is acutely aware of his surroundings. His senses are alive to sound, wind, smell, touch, and sight. His situationism might be described, in the words of composer John Cage, as "essentially non-dualistic, a multiplicity of centers in a state of non-obstruction and interpenetration."[2] For Ingold, certain drawn lines, such as those of Paul Klee, which in the artist's own analogy, "take a point for a walk,"[3] are also lines of habitation, created as one goes along without a destination or outcome in mind. They are open-ended processes, inclusive of experiences that unfold in time, that engage all the senses, that create new knowledge and are, for the most part, irregular in form.

1 Sean Griffiths, distribution of components along x-, y-, and z-axes, 2019.

By contrast, lines of occupation are *meta*-physical in character. They instrumentalize preexisting knowledge, connecting points the coordinates of which are determined in advance. They are lines of *exteriority*, arriving from the outside or from above. The tendencies they exhibit are those of a withdrawal towards a bounded interiority or territory. Lines of occupation are closed, controlled, and controlling. They give an overview of the entire territory at a single glance. Drawing on the work of philosopher Michel de Certeau, the examples Ingold gives include route maps and the lines of longitude and latitude. Lines of occupation are colonial in character.[4]

In recent times, even though the process of designing buildings is increasingly carried out using computers, the drawn line has remained the quintessential signifier and determinant of architectural space. Indeed, as Robin Evans discusses at length in his essay, "Translations from Drawing to Building,"[5] since the time when drawing began to shape the *modus operandi* of design, the act of determining architectural space has been conflated with the imposition of spatial difference through the drawing of the line. Architectural drawings derive from a Euclidean system that homogenizes space as a unified singularity, characterized by measurability, and organized in accordance with concepts that arise from measurability, such as symmetry and proportion. And yet concealed within this mathematical space are other territories that denote physical differences of material, of lighting, of temperature and humidity, of inside and out. But these lines inscribing compartmentations in physical reality also indicate spatial *caesuras* that demarcate the spaces of the sacred and the profane, the boundaries between the commonly held and the privately owned, the territories of social hierarchy, and the dominions of gender and ethnicity. The architectural line projects a boundary into real space, where the rules on one side will be different from those on the other [fig. 2]. An architectural plan is an arrangement of such signifying lines. They are, in Ingold's terms, lines of occupation. fig. 2

In respect of lines of habitation and lines of occupation, the wandering line of the nomadic wayfarer can be contrasted with the predetermined point-to-point movement of the modern-day traveler. The tradition of oral storytelling, in which the sound, tone, and general expression of the voice is as important as the meaning of the spoken words, is of a different order than the precomposed plot of the 18th- and 19th-century bourgeois novel, set down in orderly printed text. In the former, the voices of the narrators unfold in space and time. In the latter, the multiplicity of the voices is replaced by the singularity of a set of "word-objects"[6] signifying word-ideas. For Ingold, experience is rinsed out in these conversions of sensation to signification: "The attention of listeners is not drawn to the sounds of speech in them-

2 Matthew Crawford, *Two Squares Taped onto a Pavement*, London, 2014. Crawford taped the squares and observed that passersby avoided walking in them, thus suggesting that the lines had created an architectural boundary, where in the mind of the passerby, the rules on one side of the line were different from those on the other. The project seems to eloquently illustrate the power of a line that might usually be drawn on paper, by drawing it in real space.

selves but rather to the meanings conveyed by them and which they serve, in a sense, to deliver."[7]

The disjunction between the spoken and the printed word corresponds to that between the phenomenal reality of space as experienced and the manner in which it is signified in the architectural plan drawing. This compares to the difference between the acts of listening to music and of reading musical notation, related but entirely different experiences. And yet, while one would not confuse the differences between these latter practices in a musical context, as Evans points out, it is very common for architects to discuss plans (and sections and elevations) as if there were no differences between buildings and drawings of buildings.

While there exist identities between the geometries of orthogonal projection and those of buildings designed through their use, there is a difference in scale, and therefore of experience, in the way we encounter plans and buildings, respectively. The reader of the plan apprehends it in a single glance, but buildings are three-dimensional objects, with fronts and backs, often comprising several interconnecting spaces that can only be perceived by bodies moving through space in time. This temporal and sequential encounter with architectural space is fundamentally different from the process of viewing a plan. Comparing, for example, a building such as Andrea Palladio's Villa Rotonda in Vicenza with its drawn plan, the latter has a powerful, figural quality, containing repeating rotational symmetries that have something of the graphic qualities of a Hindu mandala. The multiple symmetries—diagonal and Cartesian—are preeminent components of the architectural concept and although it would be incorrect to claim that this concept is indiscernible in the experience of the building, the symmetries of the concept are only perceived from certain positions *determined* by the concept itself, which is a product of the orthogonal systems—plan, section, and elevation—used to develop it. For example, a full appreciation of one of the building's external symmetries is dependent upon the viewer standing on an axis perpendicular to one of the four identical façades. Standing at a 45 degree angle to one of the four corners of the building, the viewer will enjoy a bilateral meeting of two identical façades, either side of the corner. But the intensity of this perception of symmetry is much reduced if the view is taken from an oblique angle with no axial relationship to the façades or to the corner. My point is that while the experience of the building is not dependent on the plan, the perception of its concept is both dependent upon and determined by the plan.

Furthermore, one would have to be on the lookout for these crucial attributes, to be attentively studying the building, rather than casually inhabiting it. To do so would, in Ingold's world, be plotting a journey as a point-to-point preplanned encounter, along a line of occupation. The idea in the plan exists prior to and transcends the experience of the building. As we shall see, the use of experimental methodologies that are not reliant on plans, sections, and elevations have the potential to create very different conceptions of architecture.

Aural and Oral Spaces

It is stating the obvious that music is heard. But music is also felt. Sound is the way ears perceive airborne vibration and material resonances. Sound and touch are significant environmental experiences that architectural representations exclude. If we were to privilege these senses at the expense of the visual in the creation of architectural space, an entirely different conception of the latter would surely result.

In the 1960s, media theorist Marshall McLuhan argued that it was the form of media, rather than the message it carried, that had the greater effect on the construction of human subjectivity.[8] For McLuhan, a predominantly visual culture, such as that of the West, is a product of print technology. This culture constructs an "assembly line" type of subjectivity that is linear and fragmented, that through the use of concepts such as perspective, proportion, axiality, and symmetry encourages processes of idealization, centering and separation. Figure-ground conditions, which privilege singular, static, well-defined formal arrangements, are preferred to "field situations," which are not necessarily characterized by "strong" form and therefore cannot be assimilated in a single glance. Field situations—a term that might adequately describe the paintings of Jackson Pollock, for example—promote the movement of the eye across the field. If "strong" determinate form encourages the development of layered hierarchies of depth, "weak," indeterminate form fosters the emergence of multiplicities across a horizontal plane.

In oral cultures, sound and tactility create spatialities that are non-directional, interpenetrating, shifting, involving, and evolving. Sounds resist the imposition of boundaries. When a sound encounters a barrier, it changes its morphology via processes of absorption, reflection, and resonance. Similarly, tactility leads to its own form of spatial apprehension, which brings the architectural subject into an intimate but disinterested encounter with physical space. In a famous passage from "The Work of Art in the Age of Mechanical Reproduction," philosopher Walter Benjamin states:

> Buildings are (...) appropriated by use and perception—or by touch and sight. Such appropriation cannot be understood in terms of the attentive concentration of a tourist before a famous building (...) tactile appropriation is accomplished not so much by attention as by habit. As regards architecture, habit determines to a large extent even optical reception. The latter too, occurs much less through rapt attention than by noticing the object in an incidental fashion (...) For the tasks which face the human apparatus of perception at the turning point of history cannot be solved by optical means, that is, by contemplation alone. They are mastered gradually by habit, under the guidance of tactile appropriation.[9]

What Benjamin touches on here is significant. Critical discussion about architecture tends to focus, not on the long-term inhabitation of buildings, but on their visual attributes. One consequence of the privileged role that drawing enjoys in architectural design processes is that architectural criticism and writing are concerned with matters of appearance, composition, proportion, and form, encouraging a situation whereby the visual qualities of buildings often become the attributes by which they are judged.

The Capture of Sound

Just as space is fragmented in the plan, musical notation imprisons sound through a system of legal codifications that converts the qualities of a limited number of sounds from an acoustic to a visual dimension. Just as the plan evicts all spatial entities lacking in coherent form, proportional hierarchies, and figure-ground relationships from the realm of architecture, so the score excludes all sounds existing outside of the 12 tones of the harmonic scale from the jurisdiction of music. In musical notation, attributes that determine the precise character of musical experience, such as timbre, amplitude, intensity, and dynamics are underplayed in the foregrounding of tone and duration.

Music is expressed as a form of time that is transformed into something spatial in the score. As with the architectural plan, the ability the score bestows upon the musician to visualize the musical event before it is performed, at a scale that allows it to be digested as a total unity, encourages ambitions of an architectural nature. Thus, music takes on the attributes of structure, movement, repetition of motif, and variations on themes in ways that correlate with the attributes and concepts of architecture. Under these conditions, sounds cease to simply be themselves *as* sounds. In a way that reduces emphasis on their material character, they are transformed into signifiers whose aim is to communicate concepts rather than sounds. Just as the text transforms the spoken word into a visual code that emphasizes meaning over sound, the forms of Western music that have emerged since the invention of musical notation focus on concepts, structures, and ideas—characteristics of literary and visual systems—rather than sounds. As composer Toru Takemitsu, quoted by Ingold, puts it: "When sounds are possessed by ideas instead of having their own identity, music suffers."[10]

The Musical Philosophies of John Cage

Takemitsu is relating a sentiment that is very close to those that informed the ideas of John Cage. Cage wanted sounds to be nothing but themselves. Not signifiers, not representations, not components of a formal system, just sounds. He wanted sounds to emerge "in accordance with nature in the manner of her operation."[11] In this, he was not evoking a romanticized, transcendental nature. Rather, he was alluding to the purposeless creativity of nature. To this end he adopted chance as a compositional tool to create music without purpose, denuded of signification and free of recognizable form.

For Cage, scores were not the drivers of the compositional process. Chance operations were the creators of scores. Cage also had a deep interest in architecture. In the early part of his career he admired Gothic architecture because of the anonymous nature of its design.[12] In later years, he expressed his admiration for the "impersonal" architecture of Mies van der Rohe and in particular, the dematerializing, reflective qualities of those buildings whose extensive glazing allowed for the surrounding chance elements of changing nature and urban life to merge into the architecture itself.[13] By the same token, he was scathing about Le Corbusier's attempts to develop systems of harmonic proportion in projects like the *Modulor*, which according to Cage were essentially authoritarian in character.[14] For Cage, the only way to create was to endlessly experiment and to disregard *a priori* aesthetic systems. Legitimate experimentation was a process, the outcome of which is unknown. "I am trying to be unfamiliar with what I am doing," as he would put it with typical wit.[15]

Cage enjoyed close creative relationships with architects,[16] but evidence of the direct influence of his thinking upon architecture is rare. An exception is Yeoryia Manolopoulou's book *Architectures of Chance*, which investigates the role that various kinds of chance procedures, including those developed by Cage, play in the creation and understanding of architecture. Manolopoulou locates the ideas of Cage in a category she calls "active chance,"[17] which she claims is the most radical of a number of chance-based approaches that she uncovers in architecture. Significantly, she regards active chance as a condition in which the aleatory acts as "a critical part of all architecture (...) it asks how buildings and places perform in time and society, rather than how they are as objects."[18]

Manolopoulou contrasts this with what she calls "canned chance."[19] The latter, in her view, characterizes works such as *Open House* (1983) by Coop Himmelb(l)au, where a blind "automatic" drawing is simply converted into an architectural form, and subsequently developed, despite its apparently radical conception, in a manner that adheres to normative architectural processes. Notwithstanding Manolopoulou's cogent critique of *Open House*, her insistence that Cagean techniques are only appropriate for speculating upon social processes and cannot be translated into physical objects without becoming manifestations of canned chance does not take into account the profoundly materialist conception of sound that Cage's notion of "sounds in themselves" implies and the potential that this idea offers for the creation of physical objects. The latter, like sounds, have material attributes that can be unraveled and subjected to chance operations in a manner not unlike that which characterized the composer's first serious engagements with chance operations. Below, I attempt to set out how this might be done. But first we must describe the chance method that Cage developed for *Music of Changes*.

Music of Changes

Music of Changes (1951) was Cage's first realized composition based entirely on chance operations.[20] In this work, Cage undertook a detailed deconstruction of the attributes of each potential sound into the components of frequency, timbre, morphology, amplitude, and duration. Each of these categories was mapped onto a grid chart of eight rows and eight columns so as to create 64 squares corresponding to the 64 hexagrams of the Chinese *I Ching, or Book of Changes* [fig. 3]. Following the book's traditional method, Cage tossed coins in order to generate one of the numbered hexagrams, having in advance attributed musical values, including silences, to the particular numbered hexagrams generated. By doing this for each of the categories of tone, amplitude, duration, dynamics, and morphology, he was able to determine the complex and variable character of each acoustical moment within the composition. So, for example, the duration of a sound would be determined on a scale of 1:64 (with 1 representing the shortest time and 64 the longest). Then its amplitude would be deduced in the same way and so on for the remaining categories. Because sounds were generated through this process of chance and were not part of preordained composition, each sound emerged as an "in-and-for-itself" component, operating outside any human-determined, transcendental system, and enjoying a relationship to other acoustical moments in the generated set that was completely accidental. fig. 3

Music of Changes was eventually set down in the form of a traditionally notated score. However, importantly, the score was the result, not the primary generator, of the compositional process. The latter emerges along a line of habitation, created as the composer goes along, alert to the complex attributes of the new musical environment as it develops, but not knowing its destination. Such a process has profound consequences for what we understand as a creative process. Notions such as composition, representation, meaning, intentionality, and authorship are all brought into question.

A Cagean Design Method for Architecture

By reprising Cage's deconstruction of sounds, it is possible to develop a method for generating physical elements through an analogous technique that breaks down material objects into their constituent attributes. By creating small components one at a time, just as Cage generated sounds one at a time, we follow a line of habitation, the destination of which is unknown and not determined by a plan or concept. But while there is a clear difference between the conception of the musical or material properties of a single sound and that of an idealized arrangement of sequences of sounds, it remains the case that in music, single sounds still exist alongside other sounds, even if the adjacent sounds are not conceptually related. As music is inescapably durational, a sound must necessarily be preceded by a sound

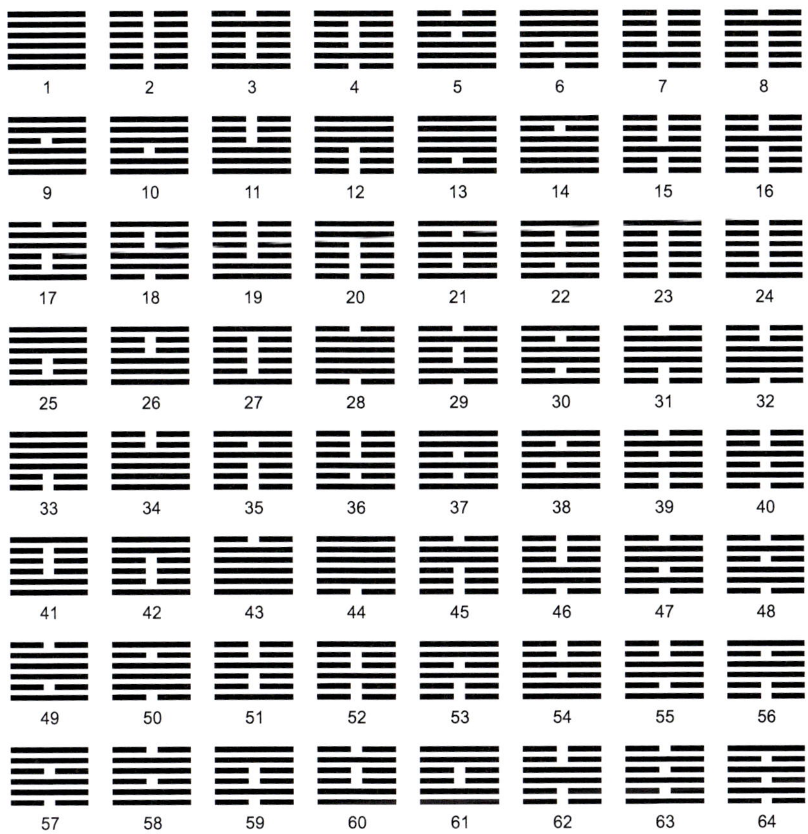

3 Sean Griffiths, *I Ching* hexagrams.

and be followed by another. By mimicking this note-to-note procedure in the generation of a series of "single note" physical objects which, like Cage's sounds, emerge one at a time outside of any compositional structure, it becomes possible to conceive of making a collection of architectural objects that might eventually coalesce into a spatial proposal in much the same way. This is a way of making an architecture without plans.

If we read the properties of sound—tone, timbre, amplitude, dynamics, duration, time signature—as corresponding to properties existing in a physical object, such as, say, numbers of component materials, types of material, scale of elements, articulation of elements, actions to be performed on materials, methods of combination, and so on, we can use precisely the same method that Cage employed in utilizing charts and the *I Ching* to determine values for musical attributes via the tossing of coins. In doing so, it is possible to determine material (or other) properties of objects that might subsequently become architectural components.

Cage generally used the *I Ching* as a way of generating numbers between 1 and 64, to which he could apply a value. Tossing three coins six times would generate the six broken or unbroken lines that make up each hexagram. Each time the three coins are tossed, a majority of heads (two or all) will create an unbroken line and a majority of tails (two or all) will create a broken line. The particular hexagram generated can then be read off a chart to find its corresponding number, which would then be used to determine the value of one of his musical attributes. So, when replicating Cage's numerical technique for an object, questions that might be asked of the *I Ching* might, for example, include:

> On a scale of 1:64, what size is this object?
> How many different materials are used in the composition of the object?
> How many parts does the object have?
> What materials are used? (e. g., 1. Wood, 2. Metal, 3. Glass, 4. Paint and so on to 64).
> What actions shall be performed on this or that material? (e. g., 1. Bend, 2. Plane, 3. Drill, 4. Saw, 5. Notch, 6. Paint, 7. Gouge and so on. Possible actions could, of course, be determined by some random measure).

In instances where 64 options might be too many, the number of choices might be reduced by using factors of 64. For example, a straight binary choice can be generated by reducing the choice of hexagrams between those with odd or even numbers. Dividing 64 by 8 gives a range of numbers (e. g., 1–8, 9–16, 17–24, etc.) each of which might refer to one of eight choices. By acting in accordance with the numerical values obtained through the *I Ching*, a physical object can be generated that corresponds to the given values for scale, combinations of materials, actions undertaken and so on, whose emergence is therefore the result of chance operations [fig. 4].

However, this algorithmic technique is not the only way *I Ching* might be used to derive an object's attributes. In his introduction to Richard Wilhelm's 1923 German translation,[21] psychologist Carl Gustav Jung outlines an alternative procedure for generating answers to questions via the method of chance, this time making use of the texts that append each of *I Ching*'s hexagrams. Jung describes the dilemma he is faced with in being asked to introduce the Oriental *I Ching* to the Western mind. He is concerned that an ancient book of Chinese wisdom, offering chance-generated commentaries on life's dilemmas, will fall into disrepute if exposed to a Western sensibility that, in seeking rational solutions to problems, gives priority to the mechanisms of cause and effect on the assumption that an analysis of the cause of a problem

fig. 4

will suggest its solutions. Jung worries that the *I Ching*'s intuitive and apparently irrational approach to dealing with a dilemma will be the subject of ridicule by Western minds in thrall to rational causality.

Jung therefore asks the *I Ching* to pass judgment on his proposal to write an introduction for Western readers. As Cage would later do, Jung tossed three sets of coins six times in order to obtain one of *I Ching*'s 64 six-line hexagrams. In Jung's case the answer arrived at was *No. 50, The Cauldron*. The texts that accompany each hexagram in the *I Ching* offer rather cryptic advice on the situation or dilemma posed. As Jung demonstrates in his introduction, in being interpreted by the reader, the text can act as a prism, outside of the questioner's own prejudices, through which to view the question or dilemma posed, thereby giving a different and unexpected perspective from which to consider it. Jung goes on to explain how his interpretation of the text helped him to come to the conclusion that he should indeed write the introduction to the German edition of the *I Ching*.

4 Ciaran Linane, *Timber and String Composition*, 2017.

Where the question concerns creating an object, the text that accompanies the hexagram offers a way to intuit solutions that might not have otherwise occurred to the individual generating it. To run through an example: charts are established for the following criteria in the development of an object, and following the tossing of coins and the cross referencing of the resultant hexagrams, the following outcomes are generated:

Number and type of material:	3
Number of parts to the whole:	19
Size:	3
Articulation:	Complex

However, additional characteristics of the object might also be obtained by asking more idiosyncratic questions of *I Ching,* for instance:

> What other characteristics does this object have?
> Answer: 29 K'an/ The Abysmal (Water).

> Water follows Water, spilling over any cliff, flowing past all obstacles, no matter the depth or distance, to the Sea.[22]

fig. 5

The texts that accompany this hexagram in the *I Ching* relate to plunging water, to danger, to protection through accustomization, to learning from mistakes, and to symmetry. It suggests, on the one hand, a process of making through which "mistakes" will be made and, on the other, an object in which is embodied a danger of falling (plunging water) to which one eventually becomes accustomed, or perhaps learns to accommodate. Recall that we are working with an object made from three materials with 19 parts, which is complex and articulated. Could the object be made from pieces of wood and pebbles, stacked and tied together with string (three materials) and assembled to a height of 3 m (danger of falling)? This would suggest attributes for an object which correspond to those described by the texts related to hexagram 29 in the *I Ching*. In attempting to make a thing with these materials in this way, there would be a clear danger of the stacked stones collapsing as they mimicked the tendency of water to follow the forces of gravity. The collapse would therefore result from a fluidity not unlike falling water. But in undertaking repeated attempts to erect this object, the maker would perhaps begin to develop a knowledge about how best to combine these elements in a manner true to the hexagram's texts, such that eventually it might be possible to get the object to stand up. Perhaps by tying the pebbles together in some ingenious way that uses the tensile properties of the string, the object could be erected. On the other hand, the wisdom inferred from the process

5 Molly De Courcy Wheeler, *Compositions*, 2014. Stone, string, and sticks.

6 Angus Smith, *Balustrade Detail*, 2017.

fig. 6

might be that such an object can never stand up, and hence its nature will always be to be in a state of collapse and as such, it will exist in such a state. Whatever the outcome, an object is created which will have required an accommodation with the tendencies of the materials as assembled in this particular combination and under these particular circumstances. It is my contention that such an object is highly unlikely to have been imagined without the aid of this chance process [fig. 5].

Purpose without Purpose, Composition without Composition, Program without Program

The purpose of the sounds in works by John Cage is to be purposeless. They are not meant to form part of transcendental system, to lead anywhere, or to convey ideas. Objects can also be purposeless. But in architecture, even an object that is generated to be without purpose will have a function bestowed upon it. In an architectural design process whose aim is to obviate intentionality and purpose as generators of architectural elements, there is a danger that this ambition might be undermined by the assigning of use-values to objects in a determinate fashion, based on normative assumptions about its physical characteristics.

To avoid such a danger, which would be antithetical to Cagean philosophy, it is important to provisionally understand the physical objects that arise out of chance procedures as what I will call *objects-without-assignments*, the nature of which is given only by their physical and material properties and not by any functional or architectural role that may be conventionally intuited on the basis of those properties. The basis of Cage's aim to compose "in accordance with nature in the manner of her operation" is that forms in nature are the products of endless sequences of purposeless processes whose multitudinous outcomes result from the organism's subjection to chance-generated mutations. And yet, for our purposes, it is worth noting that, like entities found in nature that are appropriated by other organisms for food, shelter, and reproduction, the purposeless objects generated out of chance operations might also be appropriated for uses for which they were not "consciously" designed. In other words, although the objects are assigned to uses *a posteriori* because of their qualities, their qualities are not specifically "designed" for those uses.

However, this "intuitive" approach might yet be replaced with an experimental one. If, for example, the function of the *object-without-assignment* is also determined by chance, it is forced to undergo a new series of transformations, because the use conditions imposed by chance might enforce a performative role that may or may not be in intuitive agreement with its physical properties [fig. 6]. Thus, a linear object that might, following a pragmatic intuition, be designated an architectural role as, say, a column, may have assigned to it an unexpected role by chance. If, for example, a chance procedure determines that the object is a light switch, in adapting the object to this unexpected role, the possibility for the development of an entirely unforeseen form of light switch thus emerges.

Having been assigned performative roles in this way, we can begin to think of our objects as architectural components that act as parts in a larger architectural composition existing in real space. The real space will perhaps be a site with its own specific attributes. Alongside those other contingent but commonplace elements that inform the development of architectural projects—the client, the program, the budget, and so on—the site introduces another set of chance relationships. Issues of topography, orientation, access, and climate are further examples of conditions not determined by architects but which impact significantly on the design of architecture. Furthermore, by establishing values for the number of occurrences of particular objects and their positional values along the notional x-, y-, and z-axes of a virtual lattice grid representing the proposed field of distribution within the given site, and then subjecting them to chance operations, an arrangement of objects is created that forms the outline of an architectural composition over a three-dimensional field into which possible forms of habitation can be projected [fig. 1].

Within our notional composition, the objects themselves, their number, their scale, the extent and manner of their combinations, their functions, and their arrangements in three-dimensional space are constituted aleatorically. If we consider the conditions of site to also constitute a chance operation, it still remains the case that the project remains unaffected by any architectural program. The relationship between architecture and program has often been thought of as axiomatic. Form supposedly, to one extent or another, follows function. And yet arguably this is rarely the case. Buildings designed and built for a particular use are regularly put to new uses unforeseen at the time of their original design and construction. We might even reasonably speculate that the majority of existing buildings in any given place are no longer used for the purposes for which they were designed. When older buildings are put to new uses, notwithstanding any necessary adaptations, it is often the case that the forms and organizational attributes of the existing building attenuate the new use to which it is host. In these situations, chance inflections that arise out of the relationship between the nature of habitation and the constraints of the existing building are liable to promote inventive adaptation [fig. 7].

Architecture without Plans

What is significant in Cage's procedure for *Music of Changes*, whereby each sound is developed independently of those that precede and succeed it, is that the sounds have no necessary relationship with any of the other sounds in the piece, other than that of haphazard proximity. There is no concept, no structure, no meta–narrative, no teleological import, and no representative meaning beyond the sounds themselves. The procedure of *Music of Changes*, in which each sound is developed individually in sequence as the piece goes along, accords with a way of being in the world that recalls Ingold's lines of habitation. With Cagean methodologies, we are making an architecture originating in an interiority in which each element is both encountered and created one by one as the inhabitant and/or designer goes along. There is no overview of the entire territory, no idealized form, no plan, no line of occupation. The design process itself unfolds slowly in time and mimics the inhabitant's experience of architectural space as he or she would progress through it, no doubt in blissful ignorance of its plan. Here, architecture is not given as the singular object presented by the architectural drawing.

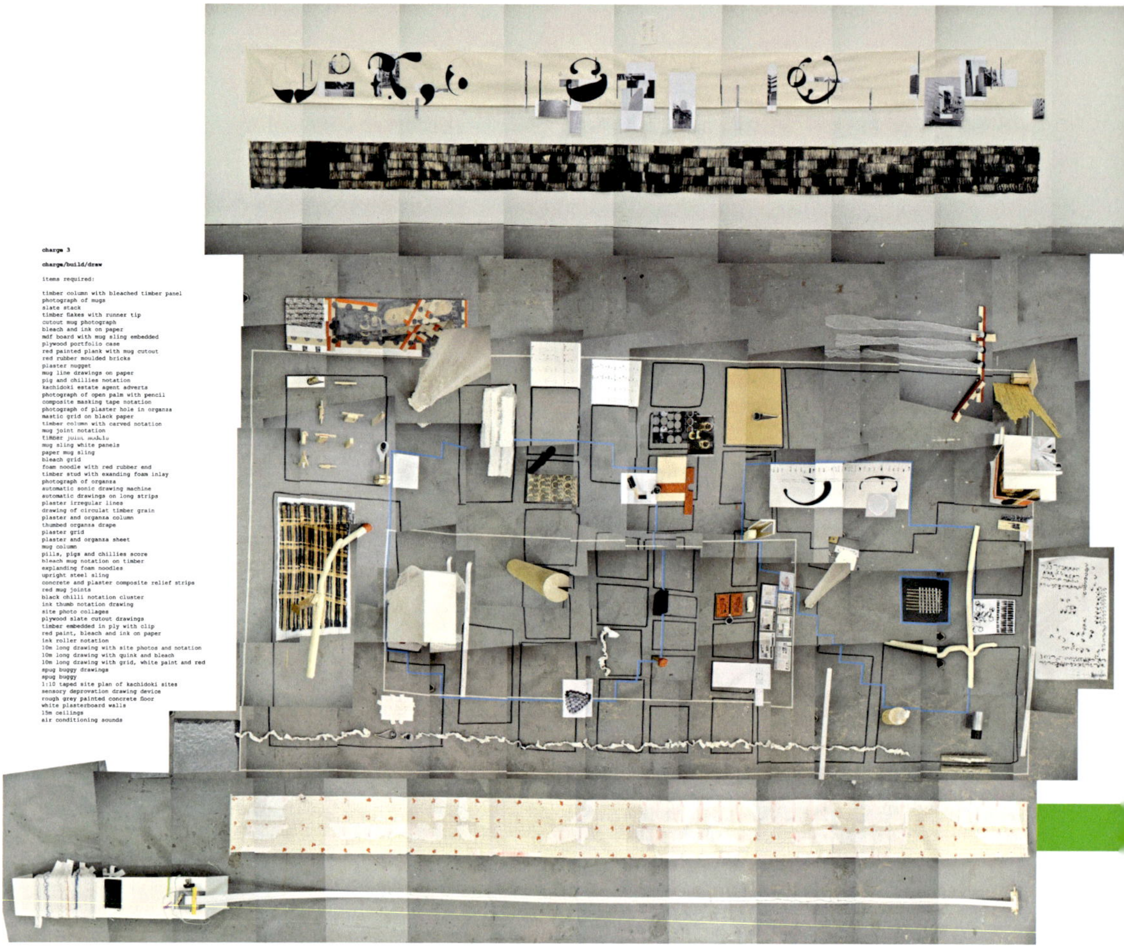

charge 3

charge/build/draw

items required:

timber column with bleached timber panel
photograph of mugs
slate stack
timber flakes with runner tip
cutout mug photograph
bleach and ink on paper
mdf board with mug sling embedded
plywood portfolio case
red painted plank with mug cutout
red rubber moulded bricks
plaster nugget
mug line drawings on paper
pig and chillies notation
kachidoki estate agent adverts
photograph of open palm with pencil
composite masking tape notation
photograph of plaster hole in organza
mastic grid on black paper
timber column with carved notation
mug joint notation
timber joint models
mug sling white panels
paper mug sling
bleach grid
foam noodle with red rubber end
timber stud with exanding foam inlay
photograph of organza
automatic sonic drawing machine
automatic drawings on long strips
plaster irregular lines
drawing of circulat timber grain
plaster and organza column
thumbed organza drape
plaster grid
plaster and organza sheet
mug column
pills, pigs and chillies score
bleach mug notation on timber
explanding foam noodles
upright steel sling
concrete and plaster composite relief strips
red mug joints
black chilli notation cluster
ink thumb notation drawing
site photo collages
plywood slate cutout drawings
timber embedded in ply with clip
red paint, bleach and ink on paper
ink roller notation
10m long drawing with site photos and notation
10m long drawing with quink and bleach
10m long drawing with grid, white paint and red
spug buggy drawings
spug buggy
1:10 taped site plan of kachidoki sites
sensory deprovation drawing device
rough grey painted concrete floor
white plasterboard walls
15m ceilings
air conditioning sounds

ig.7 fig.8

Max Martin, Conor Sheenan and Angus Smith, *Event Elevation*, 2017.

Max Martin, Conor Sheenan and Angus Smith, *Event Plan*, 2017.

fig.9

9 Pip Phillips, *Window Component* and *Architectural Composition*, 2014.

10 Alex Nqai, Alexandra McCluskey, Daniel Rymer-Trenholme, *Tactile Elements, Floor Piece*, 2017.

ig. 10

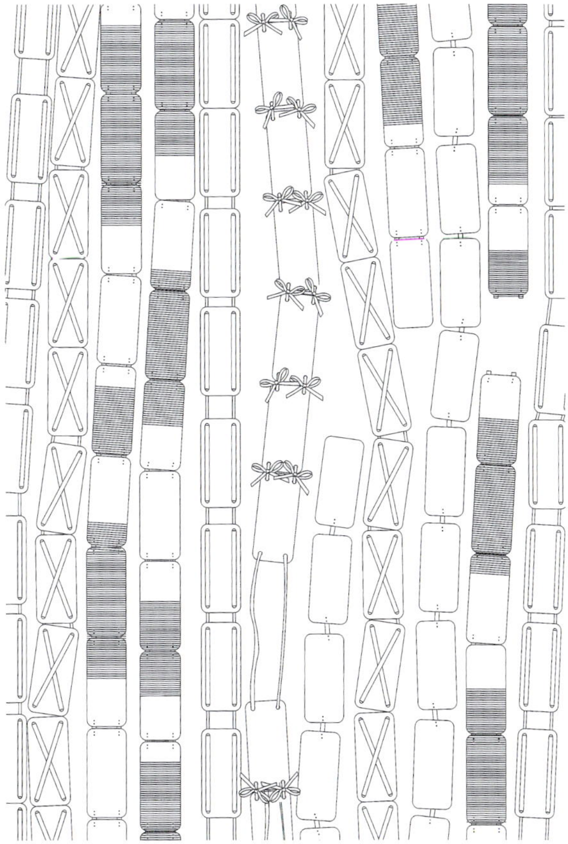

Space is not apprehended all at once in a single totalizing glance, but rather, it is experienced sequentially, or as philosopher Henri Bergson might have put it, durationally.[23]

Architecture and space unfold in time as multiplicities comprising objects, openings, gaps, and material combinations, which are encountered in turn just as the individual sounds in the *Music of Changes*. And just as the latter implies a speculative materialism of sound, our chance-generated architecture also frees itself from its idealist concepts and their manifestation as a plan. In the process, any plan is a result of the process, not the driver of it [fig. 8]. The plan is no longer the generator. In the use of chance operations, the normative processes of rational causality, intentionality, and authorship that architecture claims as part of its *modus operandi* are impaired.[24] An architecture arising out of chance places emphasis on the relationship between how architecture is designed and how it is apprehended in time. It changes the scale at which architecture is conceived from one in which it is thought of as a singular, totalizing object, to one in which it emerges as a set of unrelated parts placed in a field arrangement, each of which originates at the scale of 1:1 encounter [fig. 9]. As such, the importance of coherent form diminishes as sequence, time, and duration become more the dominant characteristics of a *promenade accidentelle*. Contrary to writer and philosopher Johann Wolfgang von Goethe's famous conception of architecture as "frozen music,"[25] chance-generated architecture resembles a resolutely unfrozen music of changes, whose "will" to inconsistency discourages notions of hierarchy, order, and teleological finality. The latter conditions are those that McLuhan identified as the characteristics of a literary culture of the printed word that privileges the visual sense. These characteristics also manifest themselves in the structures of the perspectival image, of the novel and the symphony, all of which are significant typologies in the culture of the West. They are also present in the architectural plan, which favors, in its conception and the appreciation thereof, proportion, order, and systematic composition over inconsistency, randomness, and heterogeneity. Notwithstanding the significant changes wrought by the advent of digital technology, the dominating characteristic of our culture in the West remains primarily visual. By contrast the world of chance offers the ecstasies of chaos, unpredictability, and incongruity, arising from an oral/aural culture of immersive, multidirectional, and non-hierarchical fields, a paradigm for a culture that is perhaps more in tune with the kind of society that McLuhan so presciently predicted would develop in the light of electronic technology.

Could the process we have described here open the door to architectures conceived and orchestrated in terms of sounds, smells, and touch [fig. 10]? These are some of the ways in which thinking about architecture might open up when we think of the environment in terms of a physical encounter with objects, and in doing so, escape the visual biases of the plan.

Tim Ingold, *Lines: A Brief History* \bingdon: Routledge, 2016), 85–87.

John Cage, "Indeterminacy," in *ilence, Lectures and Writings.* (London: arion Boyars, 2011), 36.

Paul Klee, *Notebooks—Volume. 1: he Thinking Eye*, ed. Jürg Spiller, ans. Ralph Manheim (London: Lund umphries, 1961), 105.

Ingold, *Lines*, 85.

Robin Evans, "Translations from rawing to Building," in *Translations om Drawing to Building and Other ssays* (London: Architectural ssociation, 1997), 153–93.

Ingold, *Lines*, 9.

Ibid., 6.

Marshall McLuhan, *Understanding edia: The Extensions of Man* (London: outledge, 1994).

Walter Benjamin, "The Work of Art in e Age of Mechanical Reproduction," in *uminations: Essays and Reflections*, l. Hannah Arendt, trans. Henry Zohn lew York: Schocken Books, 1985), 240.

As quoted in Ingold, *Lines*, 8.

John Cage, "45' for a Speaker," in *lence, Lectures and Writings* (London: arion Boyars, 2011), 155.

Branden W. Joseph, *Experimenta-ons: John Cage in Music, Art and rchitecture* (New York and London: oomsbury Academic, 2016), 137.

John Cage, "Experimental Music: octrine," in *Silence, Lectures and Writings* ondon: Marion Boyars, 2011), 8.

Branden W. Joseph, "John Cage and e Architecture of Silence," *John Cage ctober Files)*, ed. Julia Robinson ambridge, MA and London: MIT Press, 11), 74.

John Cage, "On Robert Rauschen-rg, Artist, and His Work," in *Silence, ctures and Writings* (London: Marion yars, 2011), 106.

Cage's relationships with the chitects Richard Buckminster Fuller d Paul Williams are documented at ngth in Joseph, "John Cage and the chitecture of Silence," 73–93.

17 Yeoryia Manolopoulou, *Architectures of Chance* (Farnham: Ashgate, 2013), 193.

18 Ibid., 223.

19 Ibid., 120.

20 Although Marcel Duchamp had created his piece for three voices, *Erratum Musical*, in 1913 by randomly pulling notes out of a hat, Cage's developed chance operation procedures exhibited a level of intricacy and complexity that reflected a much fuller understanding of the properties of music. Joseph, *Experimentations, John Cage in Music, Art and Architecture*, 138.

21 Ibid, 159.

22 *I Ching, or Book of Changes*, trans. Richard Wilhelm (London: Penguin Books, 2003), xxi–xxxix.

23 Henri Bergson, *Time and Free Will: An Essay on the Immediate Date of Consciousness*, trans F. L. Pogson (London: George Allen & Unwin, 1950). This work was Bergson's doctoral thesis in which he sought to establish the notion of duration, conceived of as experience of time as lived, in opposition to the scientific conception of time as spatialized in, for example, the form of a clock.

24 In bringing into question rationality, causality, intentionality, forms of idealism, and the transcendent through the endorsement of chance processes, and thereby attempting to draw attention to objects *as* objects, conceived as being freely generated *without* ideas, and without any ambition to signify, symbolize or indulge in any form of communication or to be part of a wider system of order or communication, I am at pains to assert that in placing emphasis on the direct experience of objects, I am not endorsing phenomenology as the "true" mode of being. The phenomenological position, after Husserl, asserts that human subjectivity is the ground of being, an idea that I reject. That does not mean that experiences themselves do not have phenomenological qualities, which are, in the context of this, a legitimate subject of discussion. However, I contend that the use of chance, precisely because of the deflection of subjective agency it entails, makes a step in the direction of indexing an objective reality. This is philosophically significant because it lights a potential route to overcoming Immanuel Kant's distinction between noumena (things-in-themselves) and phenomena (things as they are perceived by us). Kant's assertion that the latter are knowable to us via our senses, but the latter are not, underpins philosophies that philosopher Quentin Meillassoux has condemned as "correlationist," by which he means the idea that being is dependent upon, and therefore a correlate of, thinking. Meillassoux and others (Alain Badiou, Ray Brassier, and Slavoj Žižek, for example) have, in recent years, ferociously contested this anti-realism. See Quentin Meillassoux, *After Finitude: An Essay on the Necessity of Contingency*, trans. Ray Brassier (London: Bloomsbury, 2008), which underpins not only phenomenology, but many of the various postmodernisms that have a strong foothold in architectural theory. It can be argued that Cage's *I Ching*-derived chance operations are algorithmic in nature and can be thus be related to the development of forms of machine learning, which are likely in the future to bring into question the very definitions of subjectivity and objectivity. There is no scope for exploring this notion and its consequences for architecture here, but it is a subject to which it is my intention to return in future work.

25 Johann Wolfgang von Goethe, *Maxims and Reflections*, trans. Elisabeth Stopp (London and New York: Penguin Books, 1998), 143.

5

The Plan and the Expanded Field of Architectural Drawing

Martin Søberg and Anna Hougaard

Uncertainty seems to haunt *and* liberate contemporary architectural drawing. Our hybrid, post-digital condition has disrupted architectural representation and now allows a million different ways of drawing, millions of plans.[1] In this final part of the book, we primarily lean towards this final conclusion: Being positioned in a new digital media space liberates architectural drawing and our main protagonist, the plan. We argue for an expansion of what it means to practice architecture.

Contemporary architectural culture is full of work that profoundly questions the nature of architecture, its modes of research, materiality, and disciplinary boundaries. The artful plan transmutes into and opens up new practices relating to other kinds of visual expression, whether art, film, or photography, in a transmedial and expanded field of aesthetic possibilities.[2]

One aspect of this expansion and reconfiguration concerns how drawings are generated and what generative powers they possess. This suggests a notion of architecture as an intense network of meanings and sensations that are open for interpretation and play, an ambiguity that implies certain challenges. In his book *Languages of Art*, philosopher Nelson Goodman describes the conventional architectural plan drawing as a "digital diagram."[3] Goodman conceives of this digital diagram as a notational medium, which is able to form an unambiguous translation between drawing and building. This would ensure that a message is passed on accurately when traveling through a medium, from idea to actual built edifice in the case of architecture. Yet while drawing has been perceived as a notational device aiming for precise, unambiguous communication, this has never been possible. Precise communication is certainly needed in architectural practice, but the inherent translational malfunction of drawing is also apt for creative exploration and sparking inspirations. It implies questioning the very idea of representation as sameness, while allowing for an artistic "alteration of resemblance."[4]

Suggestiveness rather than exactness nurtures the development of architectural ideas and their materialization. This is a peculiar aspect of sketching in particular: intuitions and sensations are captured and transformed by the process of drawing itself.[5] Maybe these inputs are not explicable and are still in the making, yet they can be extremely precise and can form a basis for detailed project and working drawings later on. In this conception of sketching as a practice of artistic and generative becoming, digitally generated drawings can also be understood as sketches. They can enter the crossover zone between sketching and diagramming, encompassing logic and intuition, rules, and subjective moves. The generativity of architectural diagrammatics allows an openness in direction and the iconicity of the sketch allows oscillating readings of meaning.[6]

Another aspect concerns architectural drawing and its role within a range of specific architectural approaches—drawing as a means of research and communication as well as a material and social document. The projects and articles in this part of the book use the plan as a medium for hybrid and transmedial forms of creation and interaction. While many of the projects in this book explore the aesthetic and sensitive aspects of architecture in and through drawing, this last part concentrates more closely on the plan's artful aspects in reflected artistic practices.

The plan allows us to develop and understand new ways architecture comes into being and takes part in the production of the world in which we live. Architectural representations and media play various roles for architects. An individual interplay of media conditions their particular architectural practices and their reflection on architecture. Within this setting, architectural media interact with other media of different capacities. The communicative and performative aspects of contemporary architectural representation highlight the notion that drawing *does* something, that it operates with an effect and agency that takes part in social processes as an epistemic, material, and sensorial object.[7]

We have previously mentioned the material aspects of drawing as a conditioning factor of what it is possible to think and express. This is no less important considering the influence of digital technologies on contemporary architectural culture. Technical tools inflect how we perceive and produce architectural representation, not just in their capacity as technologies, but as materially present objects that we engage with physically and that are closely tied to ideological agendas and desires.[8] In this context, the drawing may function as an epistemic artifact, on which and through which its makers reflect. Drawing thus opens up new ways of understanding, new lines of thought, however entangled with the sensorial aspects of the medium, its appearance and materiality.

This approach is closely related to an understanding of the drawing as a diagram that condenses and presents certain forces and relationships, and to mapping strategies that strive to collect information and impressions in synthetic, often layered visual objects.[9]

Disarraying Projection

With its concept of "the architectural virtual," Sophia Banou's article "The Architectural Virtual: From Language to Experience" overcomes a simplistic discussion concerning architecture's media future as either analog or digital. Instead, she conceives of architectural "drawing" as a post-digital phenomenon in which the digital has given architecture a large potential of working practices. The challenge is to carefully consider ways in which architecture is conceptually invented and mediated, something that Banou describes as the "utopic" modes of architectural design, in which real and imaginary aspects of architectural space intermingle. The cartographic drawings by Guro Sollid, presented here in the project *Artificial Landscapes*, attest to such an overlapping of projection and imagination. Sollid operates in contemporary landscapes and cityscapes dense with multilayered flows and currents. Her aim is not to reduce this complexity, but to develop drawing forms that can respond to it and to the shifting situations it encompasses. The drawings reflect an inventive sketching process, which is an analog-digital hybrid. In Sollid's mapping strategy, drawing is conceived as a sketch that records the iterative process of its own making and adaptation.

Fırat Erdim works with projection in a performative manner. His projects *Yeryüzü + Gökyüzü and Peregrine Projections* relate political developments in the cities of Istanbul and Segovia to projection. He investigates monuments in these cities in an interplay between them and himself as a moving subject who draws while changing positions in pursuit of monuments that symbolize the cities' various political regimes and history. Erdim choreographs his own positions in relation to larger collective movements of protesters or military parades, and includes the monuments as projections of the city's profiles. He thus develops an inverted form of triangulation: Instead of drawing a city map, he records a subjective experience of movements and trembling in the city through projections.

In her article "The Veiled Matrix of Architectural Drawing," Penelope Haralambidou investigates the projective construction of the human gaze inscribed in perspective and orthogonal drawings. The human gaze is often directed by geometrical projections that are concealed and far from neutral. Capturing and exposing how geometry conditions our gaze and our desires in spatial installations and drawings constitutes a research practice in which existing artworks, films, and drawing techniques are reappropriated towards new ends, exploring architectural semantics and sensibilities. Maja Zander Fisker also pursues a transmedial practice generative of a plan universe, which is intertwined with photography. In the project *You Wouldn't Have Known Her* Zander uses prose, photography, and montage techniques to start generating diagrammatic plans. This allows her to establish a layering of time and space aligned with particular narratives. This story—together with other media—contributes to her palette of drawing and is further articulated by the incorporation of photos and montage.

Artful Communication

The plan grants social visual communication. This communication is not necessarily about design or construction. The plan can activate other topics of communication related to architecture, for instance, making participants emotionally involved. Depending on the topic and the initiator's intention, this involvement can be directed towards different ends and use different visual techniques. As mentioned before, plan drawings comprise signatures that convey conventionalized meaning, enabling others to read and interpret them as meaningful signs. The use of signatures is reworked by Katica Pedisic, who questions their conventional form in transformational drawings of the plan of a hearth. In her project *Four Ways to Occupy a Hearth*, Pedisic questions the line and its potential to be more than a way of setting boundaries and giving directions. Instead, she alienates the line work of the drawing, developing a sense of spatial depth and occupational intensity in plans by overlaying these dense moments.

Julia Sedlock and Joseph Altshuler focus on a creature-based understanding of the world in their article "Creaturely Plans: Reorienting Ground and Subject." Introducing zoomorphic shapes and cartoonish elements into drawings and, more specifically, into plans may, they argue, awaken human empathy with other living creatures by way of association. Built architecture pursues this aim by establishing new points of view for the human body. Emotional involvement may heighten awareness of the impact of human superiority in the Anthropocene and enable new approaches to the animate living environment. Reversing the dictum that seeing is believing, Sedlock and Altshuler make the point that believing also influences what we see, in and through drawing. The cartoonish as a communicative potential in architectural drawing is also addressed by Kassandra Nakas in her article "SANAA's Playtime: Communication and Interaction in Kazuyo Sejima's and Ryūe Nishizawa's Architectural Drawings." While SANAA's drawings employ more subtle and introverted figurative styles, Nakas finds animistic metaphors here as well. SANAA dismiss spatial images as a starting point for their drawing practice, in favor of a vaguely suggestive diagrammatic register in simple line drawings. Readers are encouraged to lend life to the drawing, filling in the simple but iconic sketches using their own imaginations. "Lesser specificity leads to more imagination," Nakas points out, a visual approach very characteristic of sketching. She concludes that SANAA's subtle hand drawings succeed in featuring space itself as a means of communication.

What we have termed "the artful plan" in this book—and which could be expanded into a field of "artful drawing"—is not simply generative in one direction, i.e., towards building, but in a diversity of directions. This approach to drawing sets off different trajectories towards different modes of invention and communication: Towards describing spaces that are otherwise hard to grasp because they are plastic and in a flow situation, towards describing photographic and poetic space, towards the implications between aesthetic communication and social empathy, and towards projected spaces. More than anything, the artful plan holds the promise of architectural practices being multiple, layered, and maybe confusing, but also able to reconfigure architectural conventions, matter, ideas, and imaginaries—which is, after all, where all new beginnings occur.

1 "Drawing Millions of Plans" is the title of the conference that formed the starting point for this book. It was held at the Royal Danish Academy of Art, School of Architecture in Copenhagen, November 1–3, 2017.
2 The notion of the expanded field was developed by Rosalind Krauss in her assessment of Postminimalist sculpture during the 1970s. Krauss, "Sculpture in the Expanded Field," *October* 8 (Spring 1979): 30–44. For more recent perspectives on this notion, see Spyros Papapetros and Julian Rose, eds., *Retracing the Expanded Field: Encounters between Art and Architecture* (Cambridge, MA, and London: MIT Press, 2014).
3 Nelson Goodman, *Languages of Art: An Approach to a Theory of Symbols*, 2nd edition (Indianapolis: Hackett, 1976), 219, 221.
4 Jacques Rancière, *The Future of the Image*, trans. Gregory Elliott (London and New York: Verso, 2007), 6–7.
5 Martin Søberg, "The Oscillating Sketch" (PhD diss., Royal Danish Academy of Fine Arts, School of Architecture, 2013); Anna Katrine Hougaard, "The Animate Drawing" (PhD diss., Royal Danish Academy of Fine Arts, School of Architecture, 2016).
6 Anna Katrine Hougaard, "Sketch Diagrams," in *Refractions: Artistic Research in Architecture*, ed. Anna Katrine Hougaard, Martin Søberg, et al. (Copenhagen: Architectural Publisher B, 2016), 137–67.
7 Cf. Levi R. Bryant, "Machine-oriented Architecture: Oikos and Ecology," in *Architectural Materialisms: Nonhuman Creativity*, ed. Maria Voyatzaki (Edinburgh: Edinburgh University Press), 161–75.
8 Claus Peder Pedersen, "Digital Imperfection: Polemical Outline of a Digital Form of Drawing," in *Cartography, Morphology, Topology*, ed. Cort Ross Dinesen (Copenhagen: Kunstakademiets Arkitektskoles Forlag, 2009), 83.
9 Peter Bertram, "The Diagrammatic Inquiry of Architectural Media," *Footprint: Delft Architecture Theory Journal* 12, no. 1 (2018): 33–50.

Sophia Banou

The Architectural Virtual

From Language to Experience

fig. 1

1 Adolfo Natalini, *Architettura Riflessa*, 1970. From Sketchbook No. 14. Ink on paper, 18 × 25 cm. Drawing Matter Collections.

In recent decades, architecture has persistently engaged with redefining its identity through a tormented relationship with digitization. A series of digital-related architectures have been announced as the future of the discipline: "digital," "algorithmic," "parametric," "data-," "smart," "responsive," and so on. In this pursuit of the next paradigm shift, the role of architectural drawing has been often questioned, at times presented as an unnecessary intermediary between the architect and their craft,[1] as a nostalgic remnant of times past. Digital iterations of drawing emerge, eager to announce the salvation of the drawing but only to invoke new rebuttals.[2] Yet, as Sam Jacob suggests in his discussion of a "post-digital" drawing practice,[3] what is at stake in any such discussion of "drawing's" death or resurrection is not the question of what the thing *looks* like as an image but what it entails, that is, what it *does*, for architecture and architectural design.

In this debate that seems to counter not distinct "styles" of architecture, but architecture's own role between the image/object and the situated

fig. 2

experience of space and therefore architecture's own ends and means, both sides of the battlefield—the digital and the representational—emerge as equally contested terms. The double character of architectural drawing as visual artifact and conceptual process,[4] as figure and notation,[5] has been widely discussed. Yet it seems that it is still this double character that we have not yet come to terms with; a doubling that does not suggest polarities but instead highlights drawing's hybrid nature and raises the equally ambivalent nature of architecture itself.

In his celebrated essay "Translations from Drawing to Building,"[6] Robin Evans responded to an overproduction and over-idealization of visually "consumable" drawings by making a case for drawing's "peculiar" ability to operate between the abstract and the corporeal. We can perhaps consider the recent "digital" contestations of architectural drawing as pertaining to the same question: the question of mediation. The digital rejection of drawing, as multifarious as it is—ranging from the power of algorithmic calculation to

fig. 2

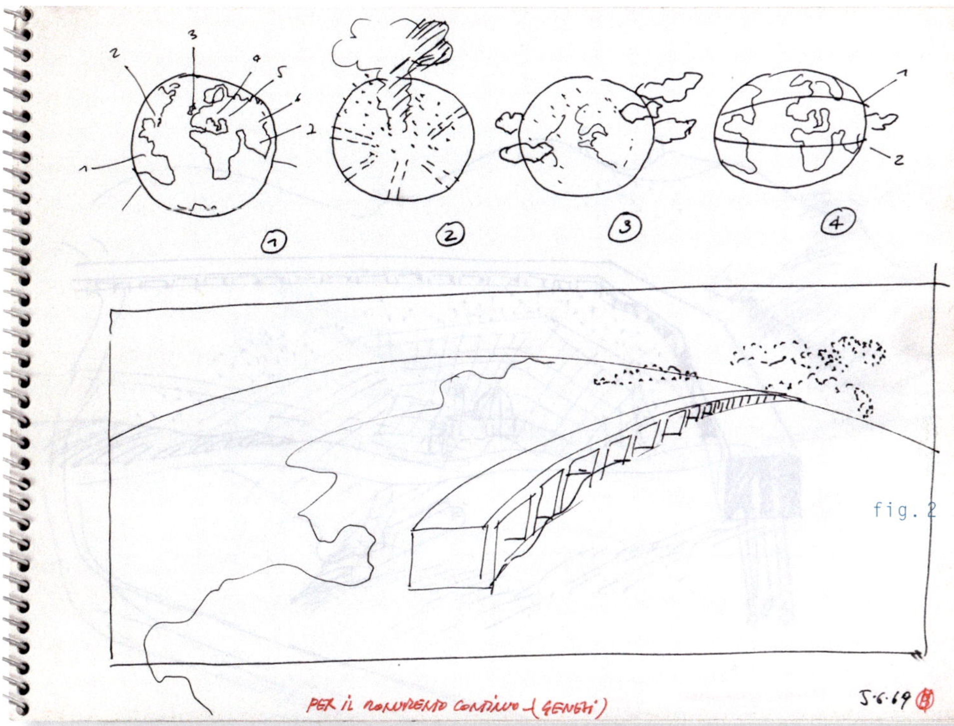

fig. 3

2 Adolfo Natalini, *The Continuous Monument*, 1969. From Sketchbook No. 11. Ink on paper, 17.5 × 25 cm. Drawing Matter Collections.

3 Adolfo Natalini, *The Continuous Monument: Genesi*, 1969. From Sketchbook No. 11. Ink on paper, 17.5 × 25 cm. Drawing Matter Collections.

the drawing-like simulations that emerge from the domination of architectural practice by 3D modeling and even BIM processes—involves the appraisal of architecture and the architectural work through an evaluation of degrees of (only phenomenal) immediacies: of a new kind of disembodied corporeality that only operates on the level of the visual through a digitized virtual. This article suggests that the question of architecture's future does not lie between the digital or the analog, and perhaps not even between the representational or the simulative, but rather on where we locate architecture's ability to neither mediate nor represent but to *produce* architectural spaces. Ultimately, in both analog and digital realms of design, architecture is never really liberated from the mediation of an un-built process. The potential of the digital relies largely on its ability to simulate a (digital) virtual spatiality. However, drawing similarly constitutes a field of mediation for itself. Architectural design always emerges through a mediation that calls into question not only the media at hand, but also the very definition of architecture's own claim upon the *virtual* before the real, as built.

To consider this contested relationship between the mediation of representations and the unmediated built, it is necessary to understand how this "architectural virtual" manifests before, or rather in spite of, digitization. The winning point for the primacy of the digital relies on its ability to simulate and thus resemble the built as architecture's end, in terms of either form or other structural and calculative attributes.[7] This, however, raises the question of where architecture's true locus lies. A critical moment of recent architectural history and historiography that highlights this dilemma was the 1988 exhibition *Deconstructivist Architecture,* curated by Mark Wigley and Philip Johnson at the New York City Museum of Modern Art. The exhibition offered a review of a body of work that, according to Wigley, proposed a "contamination" of form that although intrinsic to architecture had been repressed by convention. In the texts accompanying the exhibition, the common ground of Deconstructivist Architecture was summarized as regarding a formal exploration of built structures. The destabilizing of the geometric purity and formal unity that had been tightly welded with architectural tradition and pivotal to the architectural production of High Modernism was there attributed by the curators to formal strategies that were akin to those of the early-20th-century Constructivist movement of the Russian avant-garde.[8]

Johnson and Wigley both suggested that the deconstruction that takes place within deconstructivist architecture concerns a dismantling that concerns structure as form. To further highlight this, Wigley claimed that the works included in the exhibition engage with the "center" of architectural tradition in that, unlike other conceptual works, they were concerned with the relation between building and structure, that is, they aimed outside drawing and towards building:

> This work carries out the kind of subversion usually regarded as possible only in realms distanced from the reality of built form. (...) Critical work today can be done only in the realm of building: to engage with the discourse, architects have to engage with building; the object becomes the site of all theoretical inquiry.[9]

Wigley's statement celebrates the possibilities of a representational virtuality but only because of how it is articulated within a built form. It is easy to locate in his interpretation of both deconstruction and architecture the echo of architecture's persistent insecurity about (representational) mediation and the consequent false hope of the liberation from it.

The underlying definition of the architectural object as building is a proposition that seems to perpetuate the dualism of the corporeal and the abstract, as reflected in the built and the drawn. Building, according to this interpretation of deconstruction, is about concrete form, while mental concepts remain immaterial. Unable to propose any valid criticism of the "real," they remain remote from the challenges of the built (the modes of practice and construction, the institutions involved). This debate over architecture's real object is, of course, longstanding.[10] What arises, however, from Wigley's statement is not only the contradiction between the material and the conceptual, but also an evaluation of the intentionality of the concept that emerges through the insistence on the built. Bernard Tschumi argues that in the built execution, architecture becomes liable to be "mystified" by the powers that implement it.[11] It is in its built instantiation that architecture becomes appropriated and absorbed, and thus ceases being critical. We can find instances of this in late capitalism's spectacular buildings of "deconstructivist" architecture. Yet, in Wigley's terms, architecture remains synonymous with its object; that *built* structure in which the concrete and the corporeal regard the pure material presence of the building as object rather than the experience of the building.

Nevertheless, in his later essay "The Translation of Architecture,"[12] Wigley engages with deconstruction in its original philosophical sense, which concerns not a purely formal de-Constructivism, but a "non-method" of inquiry deriving from the writings of Jacques Derrida. Drawing from the structuralist linguistics of Ferdinand de Saussure and pointing out the purely conventional relation between "signifier" and "signified," Derrida's concept of deconstruction challenges the fixed hierarchies of representational thinking and through it the rational basis of Western metaphysics and the dualisms it asserts.[13] What the concept of deconstruction fundamentally reveals is the instability of representation and consequently the question of language within architectural practice. Wigley associates the architectural with the philosophical by interpreting structure as an architectural metaphor of built form. The point of departure for Derrida, however, is not form as figure, something concrete and fixed, but as a sign; that is, not form as image but as *writing*.[14] According to Derrida, deconstruction is revealed in the written instantiation of language as a process of representation, within the slippage that occurs between the form and the content of the sign. This instability of representation then renders the opposition between the two, the signifying and the signified, unsustainable.[15]

And here is where the complication of the crossover between architecture and the poststructuralist linguistic paradigm lies, placing under further scrutiny the possible "language-like" qualities of both architecture and drawing.[16] What brings together philosophical thinking and architecture is not structural integrity but the spatiality and mutability of language and writing;

a semiotic play that entails a mode of situated experience; a mode of dwelling. This takes place in architecture both in the building and in the representational processes that precede it, which although fixed in terms of form, are similarly "slippery" and unstable. Architecture requires not only the participation of the dweller of the built, but before that of the designer as the dweller of a possible real (the built) through the interpretive participation of an architectural virtual. Architecture's object may regard the concept of architectural space as form, yet this form cannot be considered independently of the processes and media that produce it. These processes constitute the passage, the way across the conventional "fissure"[17] of the conceptual and the material, through which a multitude of spatial dimensions and manifestations, real, virtual, conventional, and institutional,[18] enter architectural design. This passage unfolds through a series of not simply semiotic but also phenomenological actions such as experience, observation, memory, and recollection. Deconstruction, therefore, does not concern the structural "integrity" of form as an architectural object but of form as process and medium. The subversion that Wigley describes is inherent in architecture's representational tools and tactics, but it is equally inherent in and liable to the reconsideration of its referents: of presence itself.

What deconstruction ultimately offers to architecture is a new approach to the understanding of the modes and capabilities of architectural drawing as a means and a site of architectural design in itself. For Derrida, writing, before enunciation, is the field of operation. Equally, architectural drawing can be understood as a process of creation that takes place prior to "representation" as the instruction of a physical experience of building. Hierarchy, "harmony," and order are substituted by the disjunctions that nestle in the textuality of space as a web of relations both real and representational. The deconstruction produced out of these disjunctions is not to do with the structure of the building or the drawing, but with a form of occupation entailed in the appropriation of the intermediary representational structures (such as architectural drawing), which require the participation of a designer as reader.

Hard Goodbyes

In the postmodern field, the emergence of the textuality, of the openness and density entailed in the written rather than the linguistic, ironically coincides with the domination of the image and the consequent crisis of representation that evolves into a crisis of language. This, however, concerns more than a language of words: it concerns the dispersal of textuality and the "flirtation" with a new visual sensibility, which responds to the dominant position of visuality and a recourse to the virtual. In order to consider this clash between representation and visuality it is perhaps useful to take a brief excursus to cinema through film director Jean-Luc Godard's *Goodbye to Language*. This film engages with the destiny of language as drawn out of the poststructuralist debates of the 20th century, and particularly through the very medium that to a degree enabled the emergence of the very visual culture that now contests it: film.[19]

The title of the film is suggestive of the conflict between the word and the image while it can also be considered to refer to the concept of *langage* as discussed by linguist Ferdinand de Saussure: not as a systematic, self-contained convention of signification but as the innate faculty of speech that manifests between the systematic convention (*langue*) and the individual enunciation (*parole*).[20] In the film, it is the language of cinema as representational medium that Godard revisits through prototype 3D filming techniques, the asynchronicity of sound and image, the location of action outside of the frame. At the same time, however, the questioning of the narrative structure and its articulation cannot be separated from the questioning of language as *langage*, that is, as a cognitive faculty that surpasses cultural constructions and therefore binds the immediacy of experience to processes of representation.

Godard's film is an essay on a crisis of representation as a crisis of communication. The film unfolds through the mirroring narratives of two couples under the titles "Nature" and "Metaphor." The narratives are disrupted and sutured by a wide range of film clips, print citations, and references spoken by the characters, offering commentary on a range of issues, from politics to philosophy. But the recurring commentary is on the Spectacle—referring to cinema, television and their collateral industries, which by now expand into the digital—and its effects on language.[21] It is indeed today in cinema—not simply as a medium but as a wider mode of cultural production—and in turn in the digital as a subsequent form of mass mediation,[22] that we can still trace the origins and present of the Spectacle.[23] Emerging from the Situationist discourse of Guy Debord, the Spectacle highlights the beginnings of the current polarization between the displacement into the visual and the corporeality of situated experience, as manifestations of the conceptual and the material.

A major influence on the Situationist theory, sociologist Henri Lefebvre proposed the understanding of space as the result of concrete processes of social production, referring to the inadequacy of architectural representation to account for the complex interaction between humans and their environment. Lefebvre's theory on the production of space, despite his critique of the linguistic theories of poststructuralism,[24] suggests that the production of space emerges through three distinct yet always interrelated conditions of space. "Conceived space" is related to representations of space that emerge from the practice of architects and other "technocrats" who "administer" space.[25] The conventional "conceived" presents geometricized, quantifying impressions of space through which architecture appears to dominate the lived—depriving the user of their authority over space.[26] On the other hand, the "lived" is too grounded within representation by producing symbolic meaning through "use," while the "perceived" is in turn unfolded through the enactment of social relations as "deciphering." Sociologist Christian Schmid traces this triad of spaces to Lefebvre's earlier triadic analysis of linguistic dimensions: the syntactic, the paradigmatic, and the symbolic,[27] suggesting a deep connection between the ways in which space and language are "practiced."

Language, in its wider, holistic sense of *langage*, and respectively space, appear to emerge not only from the syntactic and the systematic (the paradigmatic) but also from the poetics of connotation and ambiguity that lie in the symbolic value of the spoken or the lived. There is therefore an expression of language to be discovered in the preverbal in the same way that there is a concrete spatiality emerging from the immateriality and ephemerality of inhabitation. At the interplay of its three dimensions, space remains a "concrete abstraction" that may be irreducible to concrete form, but not possibly to representation, as it is always produced from relevant acts of translation. Like the metonymic, it is born out of a constant metamorphosis of the "real" lived into an abstracted spatiality, and of the perceived and the conceived to concrete reality. As such, it acquires a "reality" of its own inasmuch as it has a direct effect on social reality. Directly referring to the very literal representational space of architecture through drawing, Lefebvre's "conceived space" brings to the fore the agency of not only designed space but also architectural conceptions and representations, and places them equally alongside, rather than against, the eternal opposition of the concrete materiality of the "real."

Similarly, in Godard's film, despite the complex juxtaposition of verbal and visual references through the constant disjunctions of the mirroring narratives, focus is inevitably placed on the event of the cinematic image itself: its constituents and the constellations of meaning that it produces beyond the narrative.[28] As film theorist David Bordwell remarks: "We are moved (...) by beauty (...) Instead of feeling with the characters, we feel with the film."[29] We thus feel through *the medium* rather than the content. The distinct narratives are bound by the presence of Godard's dog, Roxy, as the messenger for the celebration of the preverbal immediate experience of the animal, roving across color-saturated landscapes in the phenomenal stereoscopic immediacy of the 3D image. Experience as nature, and language as metaphor, are tangled together as nested representations that equally construct and deconstruct one another. Godard's "goodbye" can be interpreted as signifying the eventual redundancy of representation as *langage*. Yet, it could suggest a reconsideration of the very notion of language as well, of formalisms and conventions, through which representation could come to constitute a kind of nature of its own due to involving a kind of experience itself. Language and image are there unable to oppose one another any longer, as the rise and decline of representational thinking.

Utopias of the Virtual

Lefebvre's theories of language, the urban, and space contributed to a wider discourse around the sociopolitical nature of the spatial that took place in the 1960s. The questioning of the role and capabilities of architecture within capitalist society was already evident in speculative architectural projects that questioned and criticized the way in which cities and societies functioned,[30] speculating for the first time on the death of both drawing and architecture, and foregrounding representation as an outlet for the construction of architectural utopias. However, if somehow architecture has survived until today, what is commonly questioned is not so much drawing itself, but its modes of operation and primarily the concept of architectural design as a mode of representational thinking.[31] The ambivalence of both terms, the drawn and the digital in architecture, is itself indicative of the predicament, which, I would argue, involves not the tools but a questioning of representation altogether and its relation to the production as well as experience of architectural space. What seems to be questioned is the survival of drawing as a systematic language itself and with it the concept of abstract ideation, traditionally expressed in the abstract partiality of the conventions of parallel projections such as the plan and the section. Its quantifiable measurability has been often considered insignificant compared to the pseudo-scientific approach of "datascapes"[32] or the performative simulations of structures within the virtual world of the screen. Perspective, on the other hand, is revived and glorified as foreshadowing the simulation of an embodied experience. This opposition echoes Godard's questioning of the dominance of image over language, b ut it also echoes far more familiar and longstanding oppositions. Leon Battista Alberti, for instance, situates his analysis of perspective in his treatise *De pictura* (*On Painting*, 1439–41) rather than *De re aedificatioria* (*On the Art of Building*, 1454) while proposing, in his own approach to design, the geometric line as attaining a virtuality that is internal to the drawing as a system of signification.[33]

In the glossary of the digital, simulation alludes to the concept of the virtual as the simulation of a concrete experience as real.[34] Yet the notion of the virtual, referring to both the projected building and drawing's own intangible spatiality, has been fundamental to architectural thinking, relying on the dual nature of architecture and of drawing itself as physical craft and intellectual calculation. Yet how does architecture's representational virtual relate to this newly found digitized virtuality that seems to contest the very purpose of representation? Philosopher Louis Marin's understanding of the utopic can perhaps shed some light onto what we might define as the "representational virtual." Marin traces the association between language and space through Thomas More's "utopian text,"[35] proposing the utopic as a signifying practice of spaces, where meaning is produced within the text at the interplay of a multiplicity of spaces, real and imagined. These spaces, although multiple, are engendered in the unity of the narrative as a form of representation,[36] which in true virtual manner negates both reality and mimesis. Marin's idea of the utopic brings into play diverse concepts of spatiality, derived by what theorist Fredric Jameson describes as a "duality of registers"[37]: an internal discontinuity that emerges from the clash of the figural (physical and imaginary) and the textual (symbolic). The play of meaning proceeds through description and narrative, in a combined process of poiesis and projection that suggests a kind of spatial experience.

Marin pays particular attention to maps as instantiations of such a dual register. The incongruity of the utopic, the spatial play of difference, takes place within this textual milieu at a moment of alienation or interference, which signifies the negation of place as a failure of utterance: a failure of the syntagmatic convention where space and text become interchangeable. This negation of a referent place can therefore be considered as establishing the space of the map or the plan and, by extension, as the triumph of representation. The failure of the syntax takes place in the understanding of the utopic text as a descriptive form rather than an abstract sign that requires further interpretation. This offers a point of transgression to a representational utopia; that is, a place that, because it is neither real nor imaginary, is therefore equally real and imaginary. The opposition between representation and simulation, between systematic convention and (a phenomenally immediate) experience, stumbles on the equally contested notion of the virtual, which has been persistently appropriated by expressions of the digital as a neutralized mediation. Its value lies in that in simulating it does not represent or mediate. It does not entail an abstraction of the real, nor a concrete experience, but a real "semblance" of an unreal experience.[38]

This can be further considered in relation to the digital through a utopic text of the late 20th century: *The Neuromancer*.[39] William Gibson's 1984 novel introduced the concept of "cyberspace," to describe "machine-generated" virtualities meant to be perceived as real. Jameson points out that although an invention, cyberspace has not only become hugely relevant to the understanding of postmodern society, but also that its historical roots "greatly transcend the technological fact of computer development or the invention of the Internet."[40] Cyberspace reflects effects of information technology on the social that are currently prominent (such as alienation and fakeness). However, the definitions of virtuality that it provides assign it a representational function. Originally the term described a (quite literally) utopic immaterial "space" that humans experience through a direct docking of the brain and nervous system onto a global network of information. Proposed as such, this digital virtual does not fetishize the real or the technological, but instead proposes an extreme idealism where the body is considered as pure matter (as "meat")[41] and physical experience becomes irrelevant. Nevertheless, this imaginary non-place is described by Gibson in both abstract and concrete terms. Its back end (that is, the part of the system which, although infrastructural to the effects of the set up, is not visible to the user) takes on the form of a "city of data," where the code can be navigated in a cinematic manner. But its essence is concluded on the "simstim," a simulation of stimulus that allows an "operator" to experience something through someone else's body and mind[42]: a digital *kino-eye*,[43] phenomenally bypassing mediation.

Despite liberating the subject from the constraints of a physical ground, this imaginary datascape is still described and understood in visually consumed, spatial terms that ground their simulation onto the illusion of the code, "experienced" through a first-person cinematic gaze. This second degree of abstraction is what becomes specific to the postmodern, and finds correspondence to the fusion of the digital desire with the cinematic mode of perception, as defined through media theorist Jonathan Beller's "cinematic mode of production."[44] The cinematic suggests an extreme embedment of visuality and of looking not as a discursive act, but rather as one that directly reaches and produces consciousness by simulating it.[45] Cyberspace's first degree, on the other hand, regards the masking of its image-like quality through the use of the code's skeuomorphic city-morphing. Contemporary iterations of cyberspace in architectural visualization take on both of these forms: the skeuomorphic allusion to drawing as a form of representational language is present within CAD, and performative and visual simulations such as renders pursue the phenomenal lack of mediation, entailed in the direct attachment of the cinematic image—in this case, not to the nervous system but to consciousness. Is it therefore possible to consider that there is a genealogical correlation between the utopics of the plan and the utopics of the architectural image?

In "The Global Neuromancer," Fredric Jameson suggests that it was the 20th century in which "utopian dreams were displaced by dystopian ones," but in architecture it has often worked the other way around, especially with regard to the scaremongering discourse of ends that we have already discussed. A prime example of this was architectural collective Superstudio's "negative utopia" of the *Continuous Monument*, itself a direct reaction to globalization [fig. 1–3]. As member of the group Adolfo Natalini has said: "It was quite difficult, we found, to make a revolution in the world. So we thought well, maybe we can try and make a revolution in architecture."[46] This they practiced by demonstrating its absurdity, its utopic nature. In the *Continuous Monument* one is easily mesmerized by the apparent iconicity of the over-familiar images of landmarks that seemingly ground the scene to a possible reality. Yet it is easy to miss the hand-drawn orthographic construction of the grid structure that describes the architecture of the *Continuous Monument*. Persistently holding on to a language of abstraction, despite its perspectival structuring, the grid structure adds to the image something of the quality of an impossible global plan, revealing the back end of architecture's own mediality by grafting the spectacular image with the abstraction of a Cartesian linearity.

We can perhaps consider this work as a moment in architecture where its two distinct utopic modes of operation converge: the representational, derived from the inhabitation of the deep structure of its geometricized conventional language, and the "spectacular," derived by the very iconic modes of visual consumption that Superstudio and their contemporaries critiqued, as plan and perspective come together in a hybrid mode of a utopic architectural text. If we were to unravel from that point a genealogy of the architectural virtual, we would certainly stumble on the later segregation of these along distinct paths. At its representational end we would find architecture's cartographic turns, as defined by Mark Dorrian,[47] and through the work of architects such as Peter Eisenman and Daniel Libeskind, which reveal drawing as an experience of participation; of dwelling in the real from within the virtual. At its digital end we might instead consider the datascapes that David Gissen describes through architecture's geographic turn, yet in more recent examples we would often find ourselves in the purely spectacular world of 3D modeling and rendering but we would also reach the spectacular environments of Point Supreme or Sam Jacob.

In *Goodbye to Language*, the Professor announces: "Interior experience is now forbidden by society in general and spectacle in particular."[48] Yet the failure of language and representation as form that this statement declares, by relating the domination of the iconic to the loss of interiority, is quickly upended by the film itself. As Roxy turns her animalistic perception towards the colorful wilderness of nature, Godard calls the viewer to turn to metaphor as nature, to observe language and form with the pre-objective gaze of the animal.[49] Superstudio's example, from the *Monument* to *Supersurface*, similarly illustrates that rather than its abandonment, the crisis of language can become its proliferation by discovering its own syntactic, paradigmatic, and symbolic interiority: a metanarrative of its own formalizations that operates at the interplay of predefined conventions and narrative situations. For if the utopic is placeless, it is not a-spatial but multi-spatial. The key, then, to reinstating drawing's contested prevalence is perhaps the reinstatement of its virtuality as a utopic multiplicity: as encompassing both language and experience. The medium that we *feel through* there is the drawing not as artifact, but as *architecture*. The inhabitation of the image as a kind of textual architectural experience does not offer the descriptive accuracy of a plan, but it can be as artful and cunning as a plan. As Superstudio write in the dystopic *Continuous Monument* storyboard, for drawing too, architecture is the only alternative.[50]

1 Mario Carpo, *The Alphabet and the Algorithm* (Cambridge, MA, and London: MIT Press, 2011).
2 Mario Carpo's recent article on the resurrection of collage presents a direct response to Sam Jacob's post-digital collage drawings, presented in the same publication. Mario Carpo, "Post-digital 'Quitters': Why the Shift towards Collage is Worrying," *Metropolis*, March 26, 2018, http://www.metropolismag.com/architecture/post-digital-collage/ (accessed October 1, 2019).
3 Sam Jacob, "Architecture Enters the Age of Post-digital Drawing," *Metropolis*, March 21, 2017, http://www.metropolis-mag.com/architecture/architecture-enters-age-post-digital-drawing/ (accessed October 1, 2019).
4 See Robin Evans, "Translations from Drawing to Building," in *Translations from Drawing to Building and Other Essays* (London: Architectural Association, 1997), 153–93.
5 See Stan Allen, "Notations + Diagrams: Mapping the Intangible," in *Practice: Architecture, Technique + Representation* (London: Routledge, 2009), 41–67.
6 Evans, "Translations from Drawing to Building."
7 See Mario Carpo, "The Ebb and Flow of Digital Innovation: From Form Making to Form Finding – and Beyond," *Architectural Design* 83, no. 1 (2013): 60.
8 Wigley makes wide reference to the works of El Lissitzky, Kasimir Malevich, and Vladimir Tatlin. Mark Wigley, "Deconstructivist Architecture," in *Deconstructivist Architecture*, ed. Philip Johnson and Mark Wigley (New York: MoMA, 1988), 11–16.
9 Ibid., 12–13.
10 Ibid., 34.
11 Bernard Tschumi, *Architecture and Disjunction* (Cambridge, MA, and London: MIT Press, 1996), 12.
12 Mark Wigley, "The Translation of Architecture, the Production of Babel," *Assemblage* 8 (1989): 6–21.
13 Jacques Derrida, *Of Grammatology*, trans. Gayatri Chakravorty Spivak (Baltimore: Johns Hopkins University Press, 1997).
14 Jacques Derrida, "Writing Before the Letter," in *Of Grammatology*, trans. Gayatri Chakravorty Spivak (Baltimore: Johns Hopkins University Press, 1997), 75–149.
15 Derrida, *Of Grammatology*, 20.
16 Evans, "Translations from Drawing to Building," 154.
17 From Derrida's discussion of the Heideggerian *Riss* (from German: 1 – sketch, design, outline, or 2 – tear, crack, cleft, breech). Derrida finds architecture is an imitation of the *Riss* as a deconstructive bridging between concept and matter that takes place between drawing and architecture. See Jacques Derrida, "Architecture: Where the Desire may Live," in *Rethinking Architecture: A Reader in Cultural Theory*, ed. Neil Leach (London and New York: Routledge, 1997), 322.
18 Sophia Banou, "Deep Surface: On the Situation of Drawing," *Inflection* 2: Projection (2015): 76–83.
19 Sophia Banou, "Drawing the Digital: From 'Virtual' Experiences of Spaces to 'Real' Drawings," in *Drawing Futures: Speculations Contemporary Drawing for Art and Architecture*, ed. Laura Allen and Luke Caspar Pearson (London: UCL Press, 2016), 20–27, http://www.ucl.ac.uk/ucl-press/browse-books/drawing-futures (accessed July 29, 2019).
20 Ferdinand de Saussure, "The Object of Linguistics," in *Course in General Linguistics*, trans. Wade Baskin (New York: Philosophical Library, 1959), 7–17.
21 Guy Debord, *Society of the Spectacle*, trans. Donald Nicholson-Smith (New York: Zone Books, 1994).
22 Jonathan Beller, "Kino-I, Kino-World: Notes on the Cinematic Mode of Production," in *The Visual Culture Reader: Second revised edition*, ed. Nicholas Mirzoeff (New York and London: Routledge, 2002), 60–85.
23 Banou, "Drawing the Digital," 20–27.
24 Lefebvre specifically refers to "Julia Kristeva's σημειωτική, to Jacques Derrida's 'grammatology', and to Rolan Barthes' general semiology." Henri Lefebvre, *The Production of Space*, trans. Donald Nicholson-Smith (Oxford and Cambridge, MA: Blackwell, 1991), 5.
25 Ibid., 38.
26 Ibid., 361–62.
27 Henri Lefebvre, *Le Langage et la Société* ([Paris], 1966).
28 See film theorist David Bordwell's review in David Bordwell, "Adieu Au Langage: 2 + 2 × 3D," *Observations on Film and Art*, September 7, 2014, http://www.davidbordwell.net/blog/2014/09/07/adieu-au-langage-2-2-x-3d/ (accessed October 1, 2019).
29 Ibid.
30 In parallel to the critique of the "Spectacle" in Constant Nieuwenhuys' *New Babylon* in the Netherlands, Archizoom's ironic proposal of the catatonic and featureless *No Stop City* in Italy was presented as an instrument towards a society freed from its own alienation, emancipated from the rhetorical forms of humanitarian socialism and rhetorical progressivism, while Archigram's visions of futuristic nomadic cities in England despite the lack of any clear ideology often made claims for an architecture that would allow for greater personal freedom or freedom of choice.
31 From William Mitchell's 1989 piece o the obsoleteness of pencil drawing, to Michael Graves's 2012 article in the *New York Times*, and Mario Carpo's discussio of the redundancy of the intermediary t the craft representation, the scope and definition of drawing appears to be suffering under the weight of the digita ranging from mimetic environments suc as 2D CAD drawing to "post-digital" iterations. William J. Mitchell, "The Death of Drawing," *UCLA Architectura Journal* 2 (1989); 64–69; Michael Graves "Architecture and the Lost Art of Drawing," *New York Times*, September 1 2012, https://www.nytimes.com/2012/09/02/opinion/sunday/architecture-and-the-lost-art-of-drawin html (accessed October 1, 2019); Mario Carpo, "The Art of Drawing," *Architectural Design* 83, no. 5 (2013): 128–33.

2 A term originally introduced by the utch architectural practice MVRDV. On *atascapes* see James Corner, "Eidetic perations and New Landscapes," *ecovering Landscape: Essays in ontemporary Landscape Theory*, ed. ames Corner (New York: Princeton rchitectural Press, 1999), 165.
3 Leon Battista Alberti, *On the Art of uilding in Ten Books*, trans. Joseph ykwert, Robert Tavernor and Neil Leach ambridge, MA, and London: MIT Press, 988).
4 Gilles Deleuze, *Difference and epetition*, trans. Paul Patton (London nd New York: Columbia University ress, 1994), 208.
5 Thomas More, *Utopia* (Cambridge, K: Cambridge University Press, 2002).
6 Louis Marin, "Utopia of the Map," in *topics: Spatial Play*, trans. Robert A. ollrath (Atlantic Highlands, NJ: umanities Press 1984), 233–38.
7 Eugene D. Hill, "The Place of Future: ouis Marin and his *Utopiques*," *Science iction Studies* 9, no. 27 (1982), http:// ww.depauw.edu/sfs/backissues/27/hill. tml (accessed July 8, 2019).
8 Slavoj Žižek, "Cyberspace, or the irtuality of the Real," *Journal of the entre for Freudian Analysis and esearch* 7 (1996), http://jcfar.org.uk/ p-content/uploads/2016/03/Cyberspace- nd-the-Virtuality-of-the-Real-Slavoj- izek.pdf (accessed July 29, 2019).
9 William Gibson, *The Neuromancer* lew York: Ace Books, 1984).
0 Fredric Jameson, "The Global euromancer," in *The Ancients and the ostmoderns: On the History of Forms* lew York: Verso, 2015), 222.
1 Ibid., 226.
2 Ibid., 234.
3 Dziga Vertov, *Kino-Eye: The Writings f Dziga Vertov*, ed. Annette Michelson 3erkeley: University of California Press, 984), 17.
4 Beller, "Kino-I, Kino-World," 60.
5 Ibid., 63–64.
6 Adolfo Natalini, "Adolfo Natalini on rawing," *Drawing Matter*, February 4, 016, https://www.drawingmatter.org/ ets/portfolios/adolfo-natalini-drawing/ ccessed October 1, 2019).

47 Mark Dorrian, "Architecture's Cartographic Turn," in *Figures de la Ville et Construction des Savoirs*, ed. Frédéric Pousin (Paris: CNRS Editions, 2005), 61–72.
48 *Adieu au Langage*, dir. by Jean-Luc Godard (StudioCanal, 2014), 00:13:54 [Amazon Video].
49 Godard dubs Roxy's views with an expert of Rainer Maria Rilke's *Eighth Duino Elegy* (1923): "It is not animals who are blind/Man, blinded by conscience is incapable of seeing the world/What is outside, wrote Rilke, can only be known by the gaze of the animal." Godard, *Goodbye to Language*, 00:27:14.
50 Superstudio, *The Continuous Monument*, 1969, scene by scene storyboard for film. Drawing Matter Collections.

Guro Sollid

Artificial Landscapes

fig. 1

1 Guro Sollid, *Artificial Landscapes – Isola di San Michele*, 2017. Digital print on paper, 110 × 140 cm.

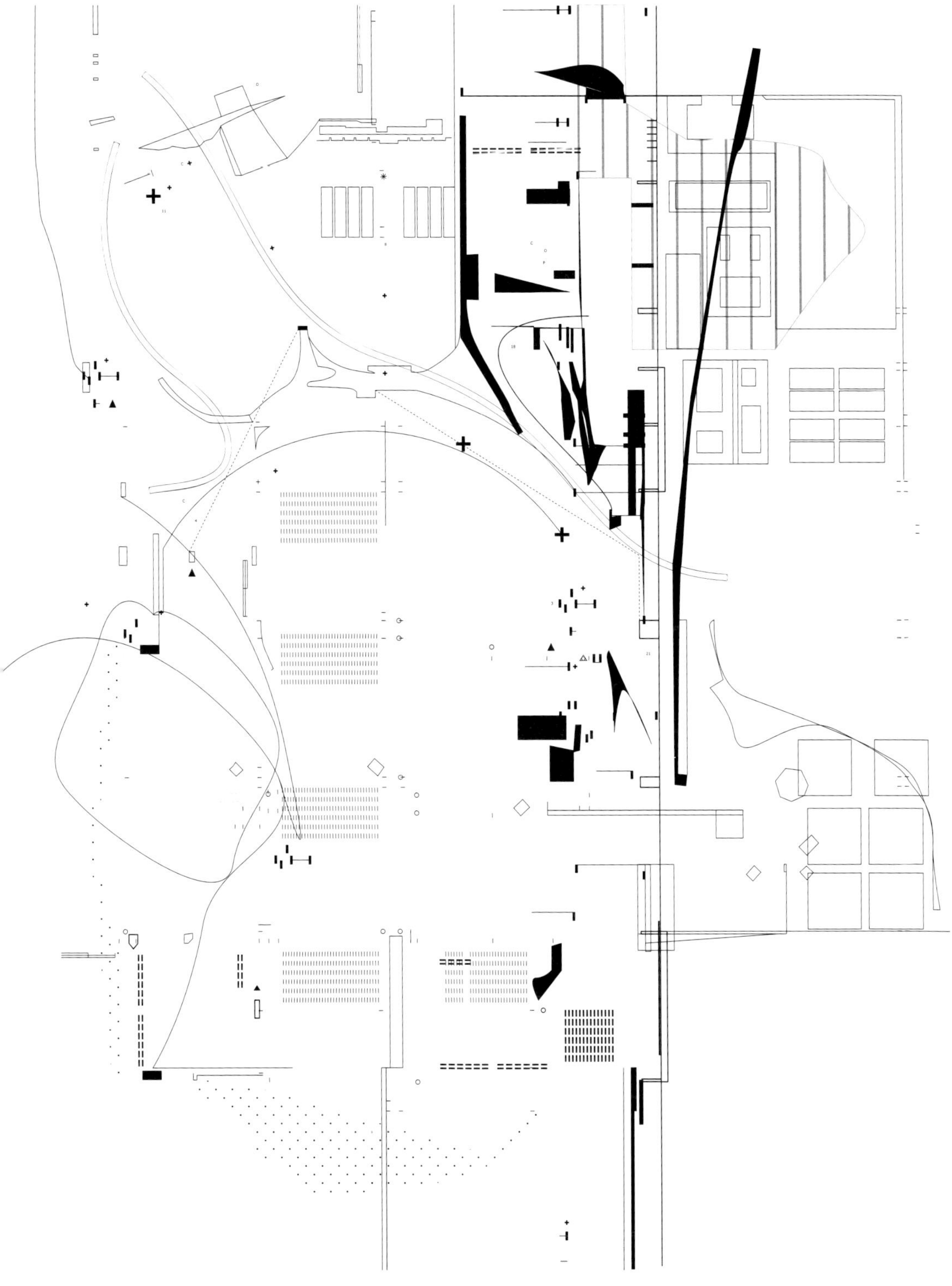

In an effort to investigate the basic conditions of representation, the project *Artificial Landscapes* examines the architectural drawing's capability to engage *virtual* as well as *actual* processes.[1] By challenging traditional architectural tools such as cartography and the diagram, this project aims to establish a drawing practice that can absorb some of the dynamics and complex systems that surround us. Acknowledging both visible and invisible dynamics at the same level—such as historical, socio-economic, geopolitical, and technological dynamics—the aim is to develop a drawing practice that is able to exploit and induce potential in the seemingly intractable. Rather than reducing complexity through unambiguous tools whose main objectives are to measure, categorize, and put into order, the aim is to develop our concepts and drawing tools' abilities to operate in a shifting state of spatiotemporality.

The survey consists of a set of cartographic and diagrammatic drawings exploring the cemetery island Isola di San Michele in Venice [fig. 1–2]. It deals with a particularly heterotopic type, the cemetery island, and a particularly artificial city, Venice. Aware of Michel Foucault's notion of "elsewhere," characterized as "a sort of simultaneously mythic and real contestation of the space in which we live,"[2] the project sets out to render visible a series of artificial landscapes. It is important to acknowledge that all maps are constructions, and that every attempt to define distinct elements or currents in a map will leave a multitude of others behind. By addressing both actual and virtual processes, the cemetery is not treated as an overall descriptive form or a figure, but is regarded as a fluctuating model—an artificial landscape of multiple currents, visible and invisible. The mathematical term *topology* helps us to address this issue. In a topological survey, the qualitative properties of an object stay intact even when subjected to continuous transformation. As the cartographic drawings undergo various steps of transformation and displacement, attention is brought to processes and internal connections rather than to the shape of individual elements. The dynamic interaction between questions of rising sea levels, burial limitations, trade, tourism, and occultism is manifested in drawings that are at once precise and explorative. Contrary to the representative and exact drawing, the intention is to seek ways to express space, time, and movement. For example, how do we capture the fact that, every 10 years, the graves on the cemetery island are dug up and the remains relocated to the mainland? Or how do we portray the immense efforts made to preserve the city of Venice, dealing with sinking foundation pillars and rising sea levels?

Looking at Isola San Michele and Venice as artificial landscapes, the drawings address different questions of laminar movements. Symbolic references embedded in the carnival mask or the water surface come to mind.

The mirror—itself a heterotopic model in being simultaneously absolutely real and absolutely unreal—has also proven useful. In attempts to expose, mask, and yet again reveal potential, the drawings are constructed and disassembled in a continuous movement. They are considered to represent different positions of an iterative process, like siblings or mirror images of each other, and each recurrence in the process is used as the outset for the next iteration.

The cartographic drawings are developed in an intuitive and analog manner, but with digital tools. The aim is to contain to some extent the immediate lightness of the analog sketch, while digital shortcuts are rendered visible through acts of stretching, copy-pasting, scaling, and layering, in the seemingly infinite digital interface. The complexity manifests itself in the accumulation of iterative layers, of acts of adding or subtracting information, and by way of abstraction itself. The drawings' qualities and limitations are tested in their ability to identify difference and to function as diagrams. Following the theoretical traces of Charles Sanders Peirce, Gilles Deleuze, and Félix Guattari, the diagram is not considered a representation of a reality, yet is rather self-producing by virtue of its abstraction.[3] As such, the drawing process seeks ways not to represent space, but to generate thought. The question is no longer, "what does it look like?" but "how does it work?"

1 The project is part of an ongoing artistic research practice that investigates the architectural drawing's ability to configure new morphological entities, and that recognizes the architectural drawing as an essential tool for creative reflection. The subject is considered relevant to both architectural practices and educational purposes. The artistic research is developed in close relationship with the Master's program Architecture, Space and Time at the Institute for Architecture, Urbanism and Landscape at the Royal Danish Academy of Fine Arts, School of Architecture (KADK).

2 Michel Foucault, "Of Other Spaces: Utopias and Heterotopias," *Architecture/Mouvement/Continuité* 5 (October 1984): 46–49.

3 Malene Busk, "The Diagrams of Peirce and Deleuze," in *Cartography, Morphology, Topology*, ed. Cort Ross Dinesen (Copenhagen: The Royal Danish Academy of Fine Arts, School of Architecture Publishers, 2009): 170–73.

fig. 2

2 Guro Sollid, *Artificial Landscapes - Isola di San Michele*, 2017. Digital print on paper, 110 × 140 cm.

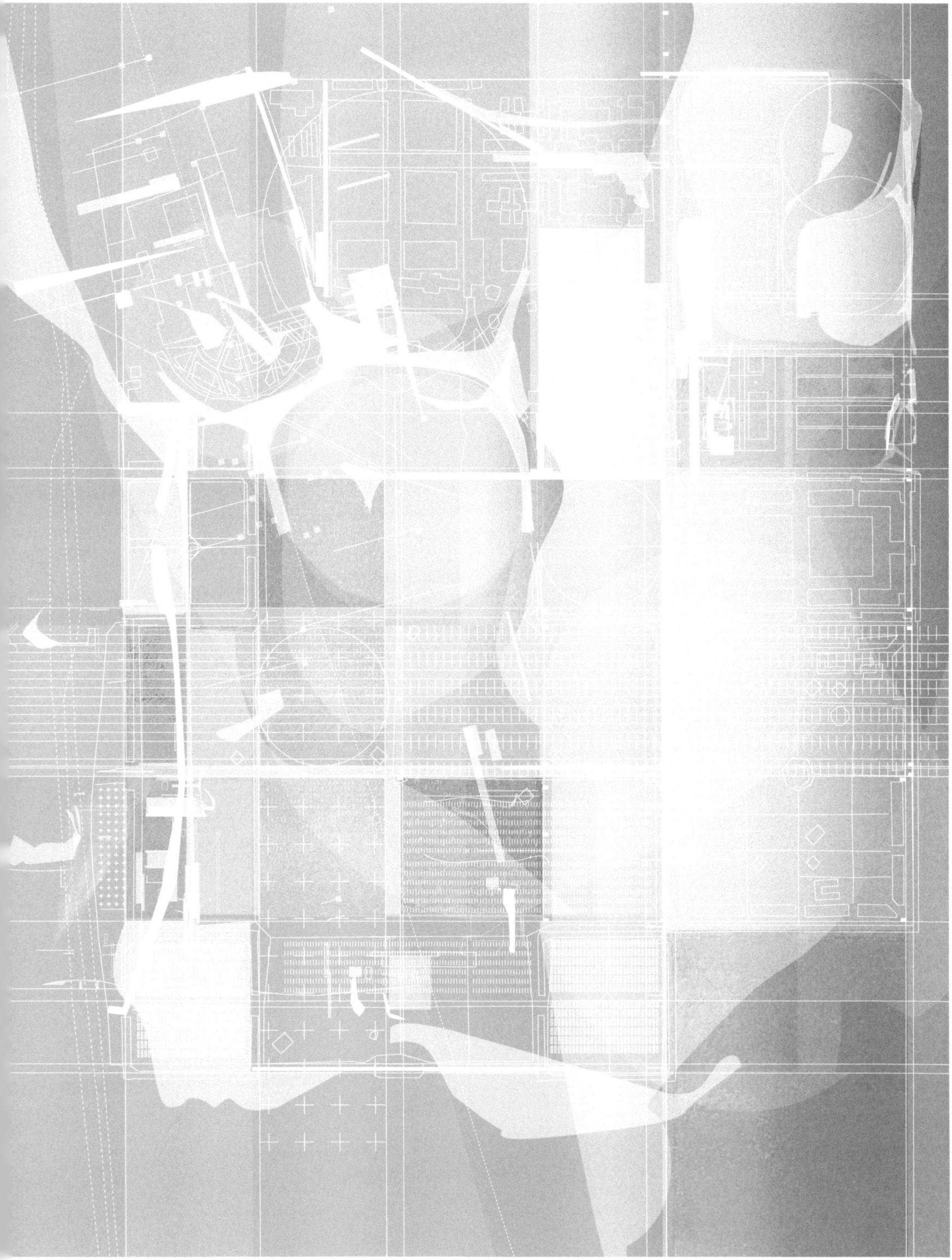

Fırat Erdim

Yeryüzü + Gökyüzü and Peregrine Projections

The Liberated Potential of Projection

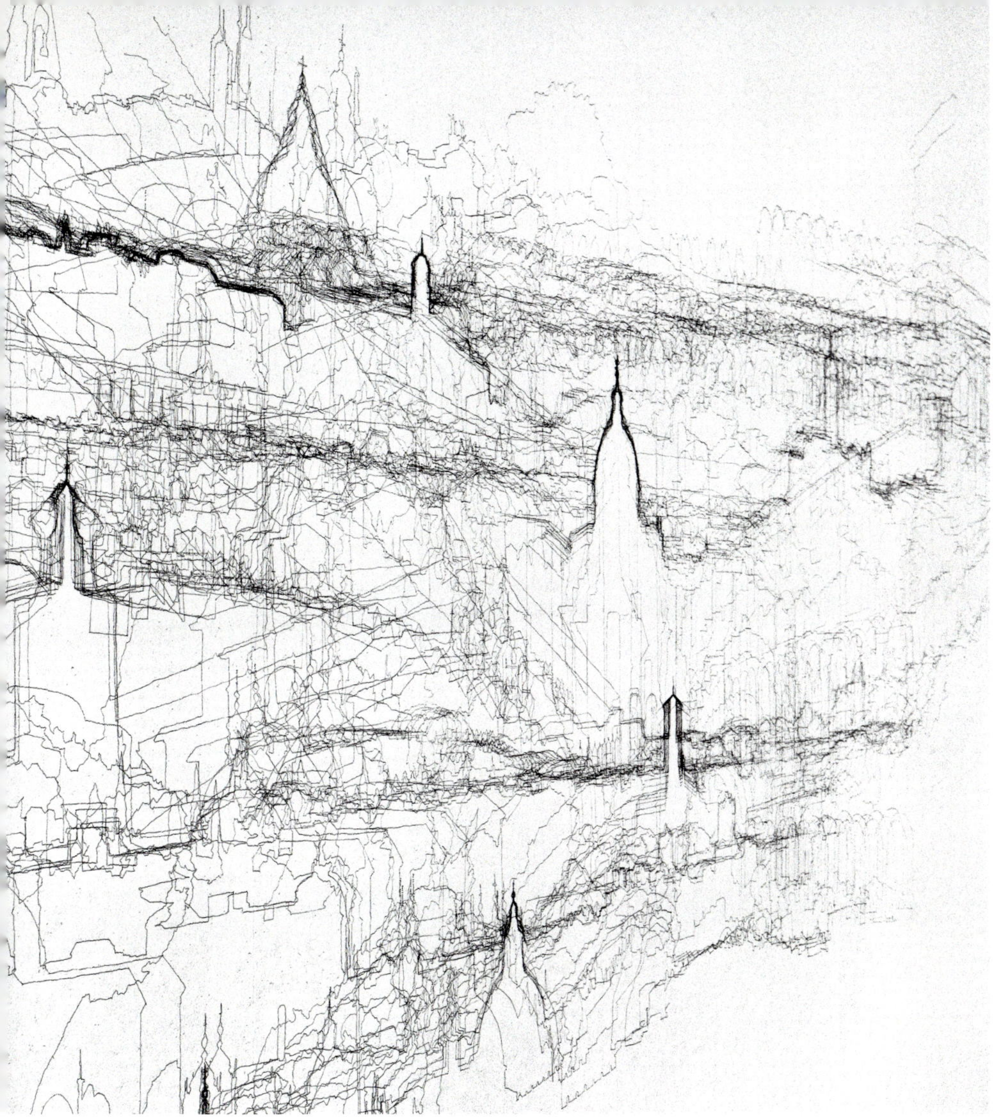

fig.1

1 Fırat Erdim, *Peregrine Projections: Palatine Hill + Forum*, 2015. Detail, graphite on wall, 490 cm wide.

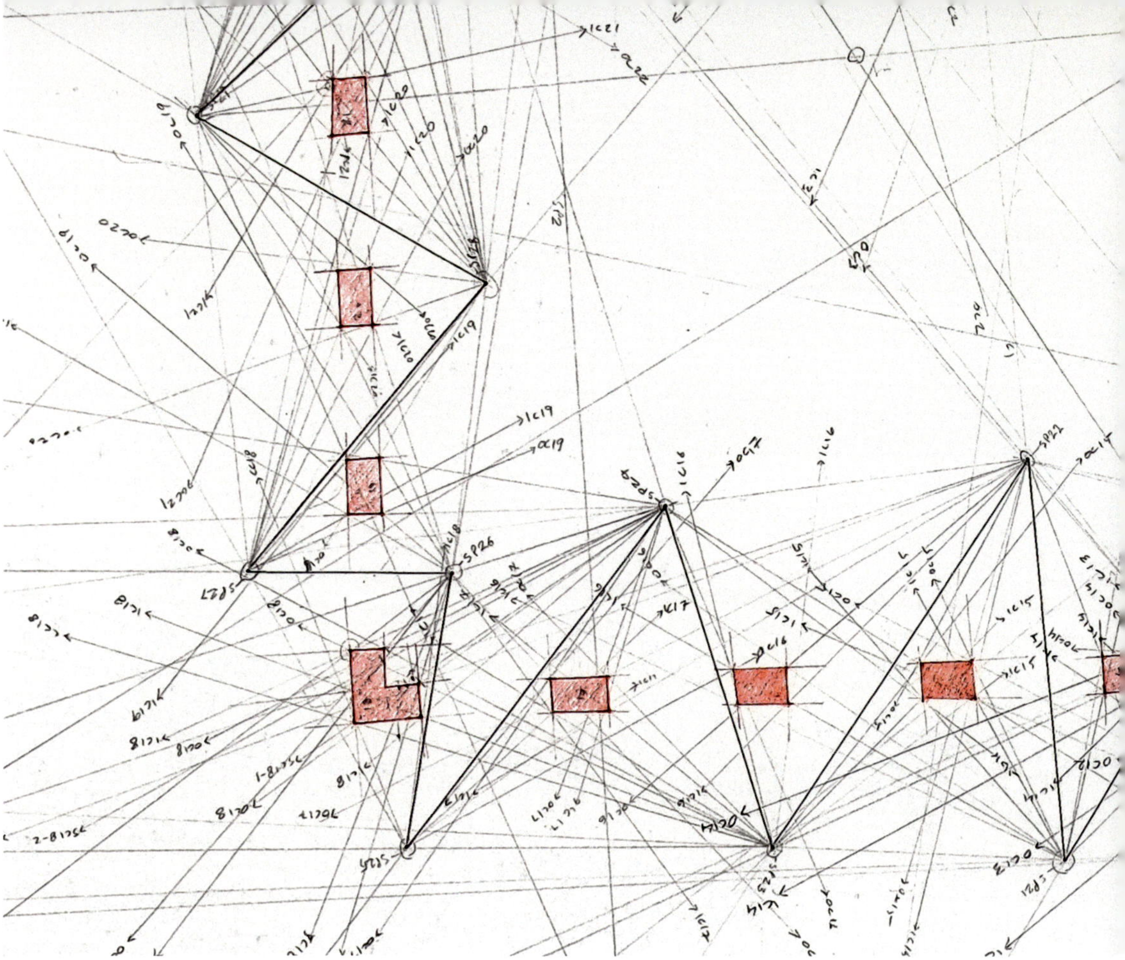

Today, as the instrumental links between design and fabrication are streamlined through digital modeling and CNC tools, the instrumentality of projection in architectural thought is increasingly questionable. This text is an account of two related projects that explore the potential of projection as liberated from its conventional role in the architectural imaginary.

The two projects, *Yeryüzü + Gökyüzü* and *Peregrine Projections*, follow the premise that orthographic projection, rather than conventionally rotating an object to reveal different views, could instead be seen as the navigation of a nomadic subject around a sedentary object. Both projects employ methodologies derived from plane table surveying, which utilizes the principle of stereoscopic vision to survey space. In plane table surveying, a plan is constructed through extending the visual sense of the body to the measure of architecture. The drafting table, made mobile, becomes a literal vessel of navigation and measurement [fig. 4]. The nature of a plan delineated through such a stereotomy of sight lines is situational, depending on the order of movement and duration of time between station points along a journey [fig. 2].

The two projects use similar means to unfold the dialogue between the nomadic and the sedentary. This dialogue encodes how the significance of monuments is continually reactivated or transformed by the occupation of their territory through processions, marches, pilgrimages, and parades. Such ambulatory actions are usually collective, arising from and expressing shared identities and concerns within a community. In both projects, the particular dialogue with a monument unfolds through the actions of a single protagonist within collective space.

Yeryüzü + Gökyüzü took place in Izmir during the Gezi Park Protests of 2013. Initially, the protests were aimed against the government's plans to redevelop Gezi Park, one of the few remaining green spaces in Istanbul, into a shopping center. The brutality of the police response led to a much larger wave of protests throughout the country, voicing discontent with the autocratic and authoritarian attitude of the government toward public space and public life. The Duran Adam (Standing Man) form of protest, emerging in response to police brutality, was emblematic of the tension in public space at that time. Whether there were one, five, or 100 people at the plaza, each individual stood apart from and did not speak to others. By standing upright, still and silent in the plaza of a monument, each person made themselves a part of the space of that monument. *Yeryüzü + Gökyüzü* took on this idea of becoming a "satellite monument," with a plane table circling the Izmir Clock Tower and surveying the path of the sun across the sky on the summer solstice of 2013.

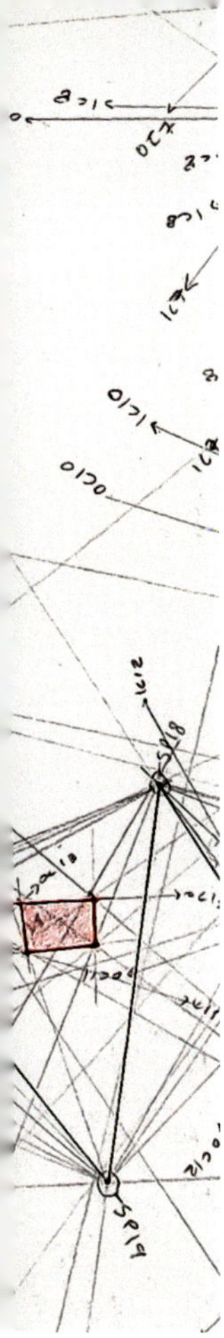

fig. 2

2 Fırat Erdim, detail of plane table survey drawing, 2014. Graphite and color pencil on paper, 56 x 76 cm.

The Clock Tower stands in Konak Square, at the center of state authority in the city. It was a gift, in 1901, from Emperor Wilhelm II to Sultan Abdul Hamid II, who abolished the fledgling Ottoman Constitution and Parliament. It complements the investment made by both rulers toward the construction of railroads across the Ottoman Empire to the Arabian Peninsula. As much as a symbol of modernization and westernization, connecting the East to the West spatially and relating them temporally, it is also emblematic of the role of autocratic rule in this modernization. Over the last two decades, the plaza has been widened and pedestrianized, isolating the clock tower in a square surrounded by headquarters for the governor, mayor, police, and government ministries. Ironically, widening the plaza has opened up the alternative possibility that the clock tower could function in a more archaic manner, as a sundial.

During the performance on the summer solstice, I used the radial pattern of the paving in the plaza as regular intervals by which to circle the tower and record the shadow cast by a small, souvenir version of the tower

fig. 3

fig. 5

fig. 4

3 Fırat Erdim, *Yeryüzü + Gökyüzü*, 2013. Plane table, plumb bob, compass, souvenir clock tower graphite on paper. Documentation of surveying performance at the Izmir Clock Tower.

4 Fırat Erdim, *Yeryüzü + Gökyüzü*, 2013. Plane table, plumb bob, compass, souvenir clock tower graphite on paper. Detail of surveying performance at the Izmir Clock Tower.

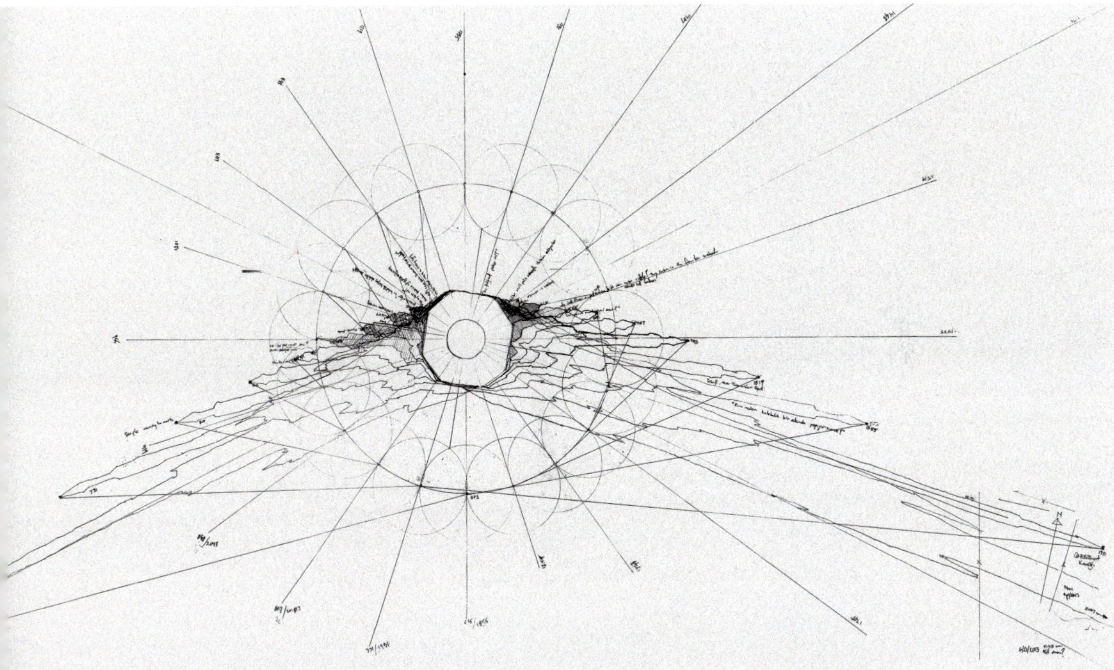

Fırat Erdim, *Yeryüzü + Gökyüzü*, 2013. Graphite on paper. Completed survey drawing.

placed on a surveying table [fig. 3–4]. The drawing utilized the same intervals to notate conversations with journalists, passersby, undercover policemen, and fortune-tellers on the plaza over the course of that day [fig. 5]. These artifacts were then used to construct an installation, re-projecting the path of the sun across the sky that day, weaving together the geometries of encounters, my revolution around the tower, and the earth's rotation about its axis [fig. 6].

Peregrine Projections was initiated in the Spanish city of Segovia, where, in the incessant cycle of parades and marches, the numerous bell towers act as navigation points across the city, structuring routes of procession, while the bells count time through day and night. These communal processions seemed to me to engage the city in a way that touched on something at its core, able to read or "play" the city as a turntable plays a record. Being a resident yet an outsider in the city, it seemed appropriate to invent my own processions. The drawings document these solitary walks,

each stalking a single tower from within and beyond the city walls. Each drawing generates an "automatic cartography" of the city, an accumulation of horizons traced from photographs taken at regular intervals during each walk [fig. 1, 7]. The process of tracing is a secondary walk, in the space of the projection, with pencil across the horizon [fig. 8].

This project was continued and developed further in Rome.[1] While the drawings from Segovia are centered on individual points of reference, this more complex, labyrinthine context led to a multipoint drawing that combined numerous walks centered on different monuments throughout the city [fig. 1]. Over time, walking became analogous to drawing, as if I were the tip of a pencil moving along the edge of a parallel ruler or drafting triangle. The anticipation of drawing started to direct the walk itself, driving me to roam the city through unlikely paths, while remaining tethered to the steeple, dome, or obelisk by the tenuous thread of a sight line.

fig. 6

6 Fırat Erdim, *Yeryüzü + Gökyüzü*, 2013. Plane table, drawing from surveying performance, souvenir clock tower, weaving thread. Documentation of installation at 49A, an artist-run project space in Izmir, Turkey.

1 This phase of the project was supported by a Rome Prize Fellowship at the American Academy in Rome.

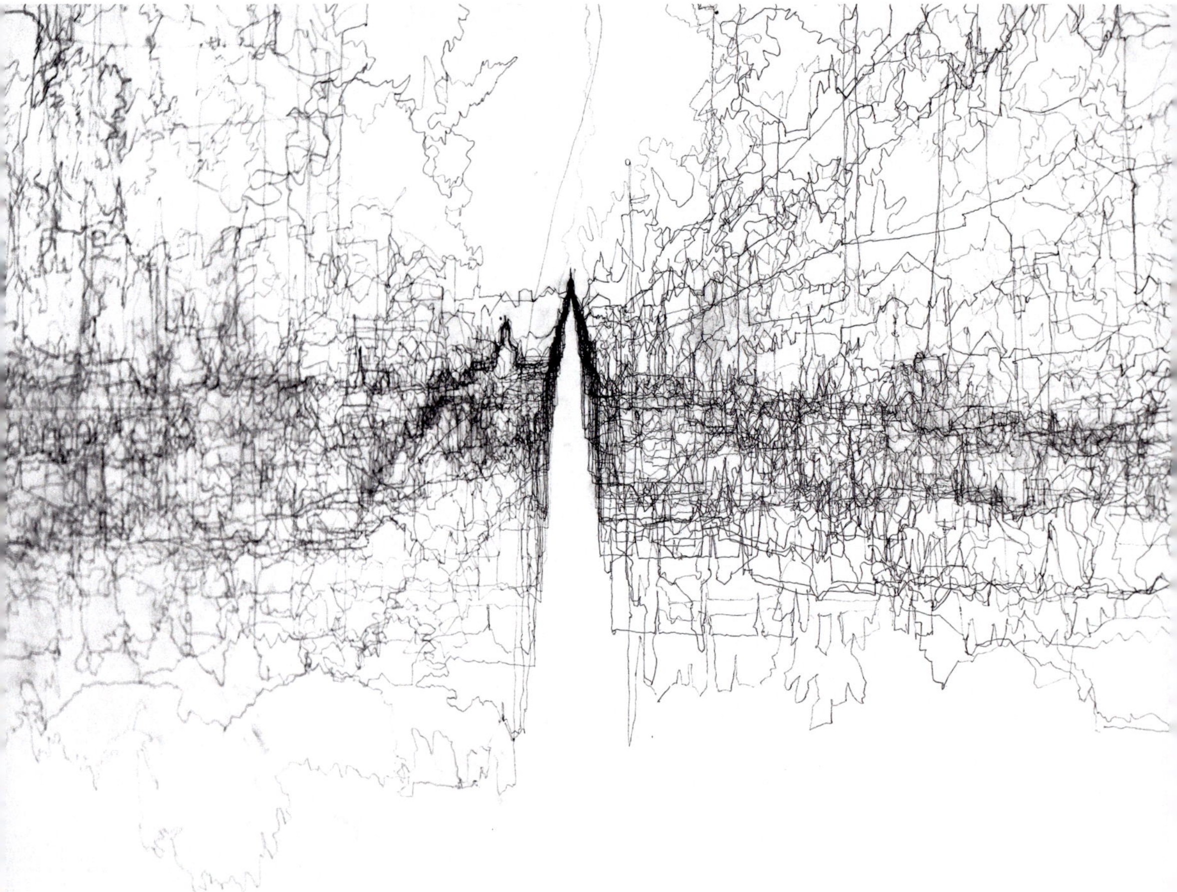

7 Fırat Erdim, *Peregrine Projections: Cathedral of Segovia (Circumnavigation)*, 2014. Detail, graphite on paper, 150 × 250 cm.

8 Documentation of the process of tracing projected photographs to accumulate horizon lines.

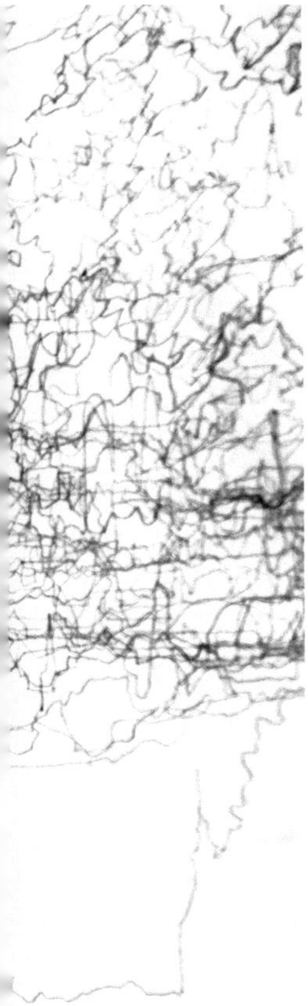

fig. 7

fig. 8

Penelope Haralambidou

fig. 1

The Veiled Matrix of Architectural Drawing

1 Penelope Haralambidou. *With-drawing Room on Vellum*, 2016. Red and black ink, watercolor, shell gold, shell lapis lazuli, and digital projection on parchment, 23 × 30.5 cm.

fig. 2

Even in its present digital phase, architectural drawing is still under the hegemony of orthographic projection, established by the matrimony between the drawing of the plan and the section, and instituted during the Renaissance. An earlier Greek projection system—based on an understanding of vision as spherical and measured in degrees of angles—gave way to a novel concept. Best described by philosopher and architect Leon Battista Alberti in his abstract diagram of perspective construction, this innovation consisted of dissecting the visual pyramid with a notional rectangular surface: the flat picture plane. As a result, linear projection allowed the Vitruvian *ichnographia* and *orthographia* to come together and give birth to *scenographia*, rendering monocular visual space homogenous and measurable for the first time, but splitting it from the dimension of time and leading to a Cartesian conception of space. Orthographic projection is a potent, and often unquestioned, underlying syntax of visual representation, an efficient but also unavoidably limiting instrument for organizing space. It constitutes an

fig. 3

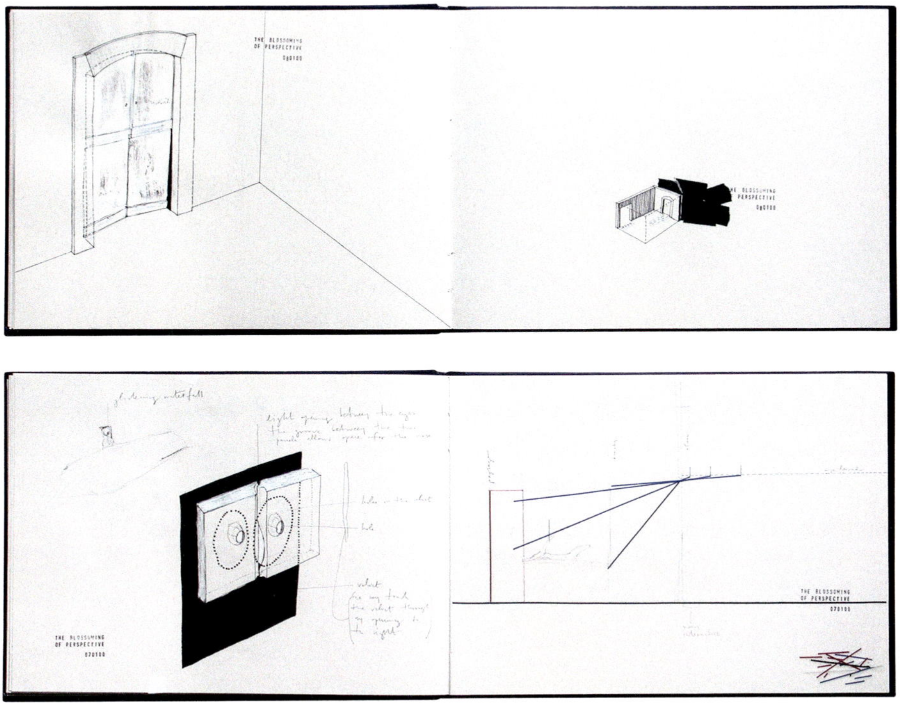

2 Penelope Haralambidou, *Stereoscopic Pair of Given*, 2000. Digital collage of images taken through the two peepholes.

3 Penelope Haralambidou, *Philadelphia Sketchbook*, 2000. Pen, pencil, ink, acrylic, black tape, and Letraset Letraline tape on paper, A4 landscape spreads, 21.7 × 60 cm.

invisible "matrix" dominating spatial thinking throughout the Modern period and up to today, not only in architecture, but also in fine art and cinema. As it is intertwined with all modes of representation on the page, the drawing surface, the computer, and the cinema screen, it is very difficult to break through and see beyond it. So how can this veiled matrix be exposed and questioned?

In my work, I have tried to identify the limitations of the matrix of architectural representation by using the drawing itself. I present three works, which I conceive of as drawings, that deal with forgotten, implicit or taken-for-granted aspects of orthographic projection: the other eye, the lost surface, and time.

These works are not directly plans, but representations that challenge and expand what I see as a reductive underlying matrix. The act of drawing offers glimpses of alternative figurations that depart not only from the plan, but also from the Cartesian understanding of space.

The first work, *The Act of Looking* (2007), redraws an art piece, *Given: 1. The Waterfall, 2. The Illuminating Gas ...* (1946–66), a built diorama by the artist Marcel Duchamp [fig. 2].[1] Performing an architectural analysis of *Given*, my drawing is the culmination of a wider research on the link between architectural thinking and Duchamp's work. By focusing on the role of stereoscopy in Duchamp's oeuvre, my drawing exposes the omission of "the other eye," which underlies monocular perspective and orthographic projection.

The second work, *Déjà vu: Restaging Resnais's Last Year at Marienbad* (2009), redraws another enigmatic piece of work, this time a film by filmmaker Alain Resnais entitled *Last Year at Marienbad* (1961).[2] My drawing aims to analyze the film and disrupt the singular picture plane by splitting it, thereby exposing the overlooked dimension of time and opening up the narrative potential of architectural representation.

fig. 4

Finally, *With-drawing Room on Vellum* (2016) is a twofold drawing that reflects on the recent vanishing of the architectural drawing surface, both physically and notionally.[3] Drawn on vellum, the piece is informed by historical examples of medieval architectural working drawings, as well as illuminated manuscripts, and is matched by a digital back projection. By bringing together vellum—as the forgotten, visceral past—and digital projection—as the uncertain, evanescent future of architectural drawing surface—*With-drawing Room on Vellum* aims to probe and challenge the current tendency for drawing to withdraw from the skin of the world.

The Act of Looking

The Act of Looking is part of my wider research on Duchamp and architecture, where I employ design, drawing, and making—the tools of the architect—to perform an architectural analysis of Duchamp's *Given*.[4] My drawn investigation serves as a research methodology able to grasp meaning beyond textual analysis. This novel reading of Duchamp's ideas and methods aims to add to, but also challenge, other art-historical interpretations. Through three main themes—desire, allegory, and visuality—I perform, define and theorize an alternative drawing practice positioned between art and architecture.

The link between *Large Glass* (1915–23), another of Duchamp's major pieces, and architectural drawing is perhaps evident—one could say, transparent. *Large Glass* and its allegorical narrative of an exchange between a bride and her bachelors, coded in Duchamp's accompanying notes, have inspired many architectural readings that focus on drawing and architecture's connection with Eros and desire.[5] *Given* could not be more different in form—

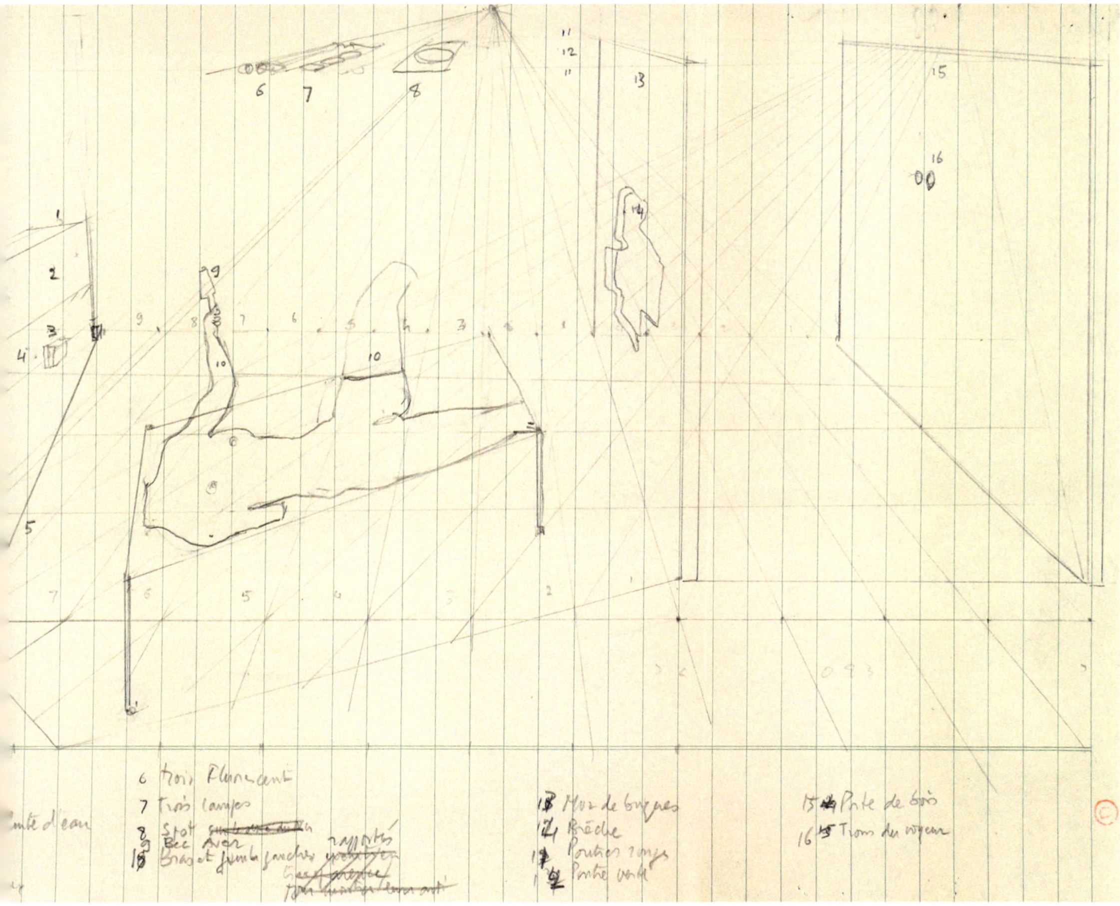

Jean-François Lyotard, *Vue cavalière d'Étant donnés* (Approximate View of Given), 1976. Pencil on lined paper, 29.5 × 18 cm. Bibliothèque Littéraire Jacques Doucet, Paris.

it is veiled and opaque—but I believe it shares the same themes.[6] For a start, it has a very real bride at the center of its conception, Duchamp's lover Maria Martins: in 1946, when Duchamp started work on *Given* and their affair was secret, Duchamp gave Martins a work entitled *Faulty Landscape* (1946), the medium of which was later disclosed by chemical analysis to be seminal fluid.[7] So, *Given* is undeniably the construction of a daydream, an architecture that Duchamp built to house "his" desire.[8] However, analogously to *Large Glass*, *Given* can also be seen as a meticulous drawing of desire, while also being compellingly "architectural."

Given is permanently installed at the Philadelphia Museum of Art and was opened to the public in 1969. Published images present two aspects of the piece—a door with two peepholes and a pornographic view beyond. However, its particular spatial arrangement is not always fully understood [fig. 3–4]. As my sketches from my visit to the museum show, *Given*'s door is installed at the far end of a dark vestibule positioned off the main Duchamp gallery [fig. 3]. The door hides the view of the brightly illuminated three-dimensional diorama behind it, which is only visible when you approach and look through the two peepholes.[9] Jean François Lyotard's sketch of the interior best describes this peculiar topology and reveals that the piece consists of a staged vista and an architectural structure composed of different layers [fig. 4].[10] Furthermore, my reading of *Given* stems from Lyotard's observation that its *mise en scène* is a physical incarnation of Alberti's abstract diagram of perspective construction. Inspired by Lyotard, I also began to see *Given* as Duchamp's attempt to expand and construct Alberti's diagram in full scale. But how exactly does *Given* expand the rules of perspective and thus the Cartesian understanding of space?

fig. 5

The start of my investigation was triggered by the observation that the door in *Given* features not one but two peepholes.[11] This led me to research the stereoscope, a 19th-century device that foregrounds normal binocular vision by staging the view of two slightly different images for each eye. Stereoscopic viewing offers a particular sensation of depth, similar to normal binocular depth perception, which is in addition to perspectival diminution, as if the flat image *blossoms* in our mind.[12] Duchamp was very fond of the technique—as is obvious from earlier pieces, such as *Handmade Stereopticon Slide* (c. 1918–19), and also his very last work, *Anaglyphic Chimney* (1968)—regardless, or perhaps not least because, stereoscopy was also linked to pornography.[13] Duchamp uses the term "blossoming," *épanouissement*, to describe the explosion of the bride's desire, but Paul Matisse has also linked the use of the term to Duchamp's interest in four-dimensional geometry and in particular mathematician Esprit Jouffret's description of the passage into dimensional fields of higher orders.[14]

5 Penelope Haralambidou, *Stereoscope*, 2007. Wall-mounted steel support, photographs, front surface mirror.

6 Penelope Haralambidou, *The Act of Looking*, 2007. Steel, Perspex, nickel silver, and waxed twine, 153 × 105 × 300 cm.

Through the term "blossoming," therefore, in my research, I link Duchamp's interest in stereoscopy to his fascination with the fourth dimension. To test the connection between *Given*, the stereoscope, and Duchamp's playful search for a fourth dimension, I took two images of the interior scene, one from each peephole, and constructed my own wall-mounted stereoscope to display the images [fig. 5]. When viewed in the stereoscope, the fusing of this pair of images allows the nude to blossom in visual space.[15] This close study of stereoscopy made me wonder: Can this mentally constructed depth, this visual fourth dimension, be measured and fleshed out in physical space?

A full-scale representation of *Given* in steel and waxed thread, *The Act of Looking* gives material substance to the act of looking at Duchamp's piece [fig. 6]. It is a ghost image of Duchamp's assemblage, where all the main constituent elements—door, wall, naked body, and illusionistic landscape—are stripped bare, while the hidden architecture of the gaze, the expansion of

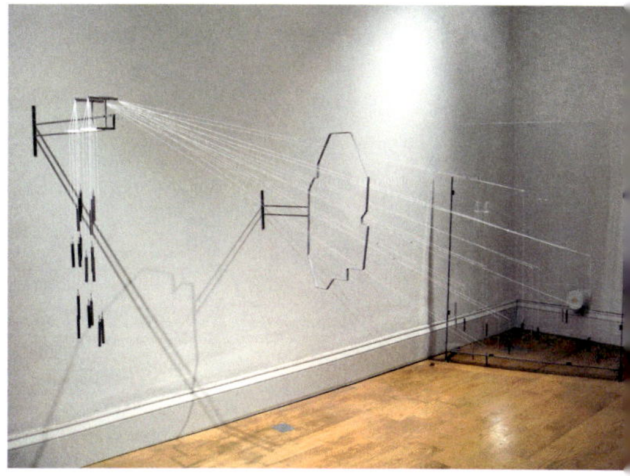

fig. 6

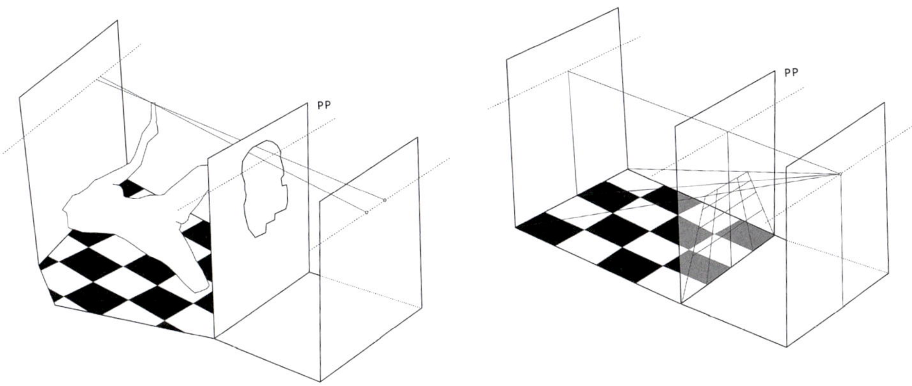

fig. 7

7 Penelope Haralambidou, comparison between *Given*'s spatial arrangement and Alberti's diagram of perspective construction, 2007.

Alberti's diagram, acquires subtle substance. By redrawing it in space my aim was to foreground *Given* as a meticulous drawing. Its components directly reference the constituent elements of *Given*: the door and its two peepholes becomes a steel structure carrying binoculars and spectacles; the breach on the wall is an irregular steel frame; selected points in the scene are marked by nickel silver discs; the illusory landscape at the back becomes a perforated Perspex sheet; and finally the visual rays emanating from the eyes of the viewer/voyeur that tie all the elements together are drawn weighted strings [fig. 7].

For the strings, I used whipping twine—a material for securing the loose ends of ropes in sailing—in white, which makes the strings glow when lit, in subtle contrast to their shadows on the grey wall at the DomoBaal gallery, where the piece was first installed.[16] My use of waxed twine to represent notional visual rays in *The Act of Looking* was inspired by the portrayal of visual rays as strings or threads in Renaissance perspectivists' treatises. It also relates with the portrayal of a drawing exercise by

8 Salomon de Caus, *Drawing of a Cube*, 1612. Published in Salomon de Caus, *La perspective, avec la raison des ombres et miroirs* (London: Norton, 1612), Plate 6.

Salomon de Caus—a process of drawing a cube with a string performed in a small room by two men [fig. 8]. The embodied nature of this process has led Stan Allen to suggest that every operation could be carried out by a "blind man," as this drawing technique is primarily tactile.[17] The drawing is formed point by point on a hinged picture plane from a specific point of view. This point of view is clearly not the one held by the instructor, nor the helper. The single "eye" constructing the drawing on the picture plane is the hook, the eyelet on the wall, marked with the letter H, and the taut string represents the visual ray tracing the object this eye is looking at. Therefore, the woodcut portrays not only a drawing technique but an *act of looking* embodied in an inanimate object. Drawing performed by a bodiless single eye epitomizes the perspectival understanding of visual space, which since the Renaissance has dominated most representation apparatuses. Inspired by this embodied drawing technique from a disembodied eye, my own redrawing of Duchamp's *Given* asks: what about the forgotten, second, other eye?

As we have seen, the door in *Given* has two peepholes, so, instead of a single string hanging from an eyelet on the wall, I have designed two tubes, which I call binoculars, that represent the two peepholes on the door. The binoculars suspend a complex web of strings to draw points in space; each tube collects nine strings representing visual or light rays. The strings are analogous to the process of "drawing" a line between two points and are kept taut by weights on both ends. Installing the piece is a slow spatial weaving of lines, creating a three-dimensional spider's web with the intention of catching a volumetric trace of the desirous gaze. In *The Act of Looking* I was seeking the precision of the attentive look delineating a form that we find in de Caus.

fig. 8 De Caus's string, starting from the single cyclopean eyelet on the wall, intersects with the picture plane to form a point and slowly render a two-dimensional drawing. In *The Act of Looking* the picture plane is absent and each pair of strings—the two visual rays that start at the binoculars crossing and ending at specifically drilled pairs of holes on the Perspex sheet—establish the location of each point as an intersection in space. Etched nickel silver discs slot into the intersections to act as markers of all the points floating in space. As with an asterism—where figures of deities are plotted in the sky—the nickel silver discs—like stars—tether the drawn constellation of *Given*'s interior in suspension.

In orthographic projection, the plan and the section are necessary prerequisites to produce a three-dimensional form. Through a slow weaving of threads by hand, *The Act of Looking* begins to reconstruct the hidden volumetric diagram of *Given*, without the need for a plan or a section; instead the work blossoms out by combining pictorial information found in the two retinal images forming in our two eyes [fig. 9].

By negating *Given*'s visceral materiality and figurative rendering, *The Act of Looking* attempts to isolate and expose the geometry of the voyeuristic gaze that it generates. In comparison to the physicality of *Given*, which is often described as vulgar, my adaptation is by contrast delicate and ethereal. Yet it is also a drawing that treads the world of things: drawn not on paper but in space, in steel, Perspex, and waxed thread, *The Act of Looking* is a full-scale diagram rendered in matter.

Although coded as a constellation of points in space, this central allegorical motif of both *Given* and *Large Glass*, the bride is seemingly absent or not there yet. Her absence, the missing bride, laments what I see as a lost, or perhaps repressed, dimension in the Cartesian visual space: the lost "other" eye, which, as Duchamp infers, could also be the locus of an either forgotten, or not yet discovered, fourth dimension.

fig. 9

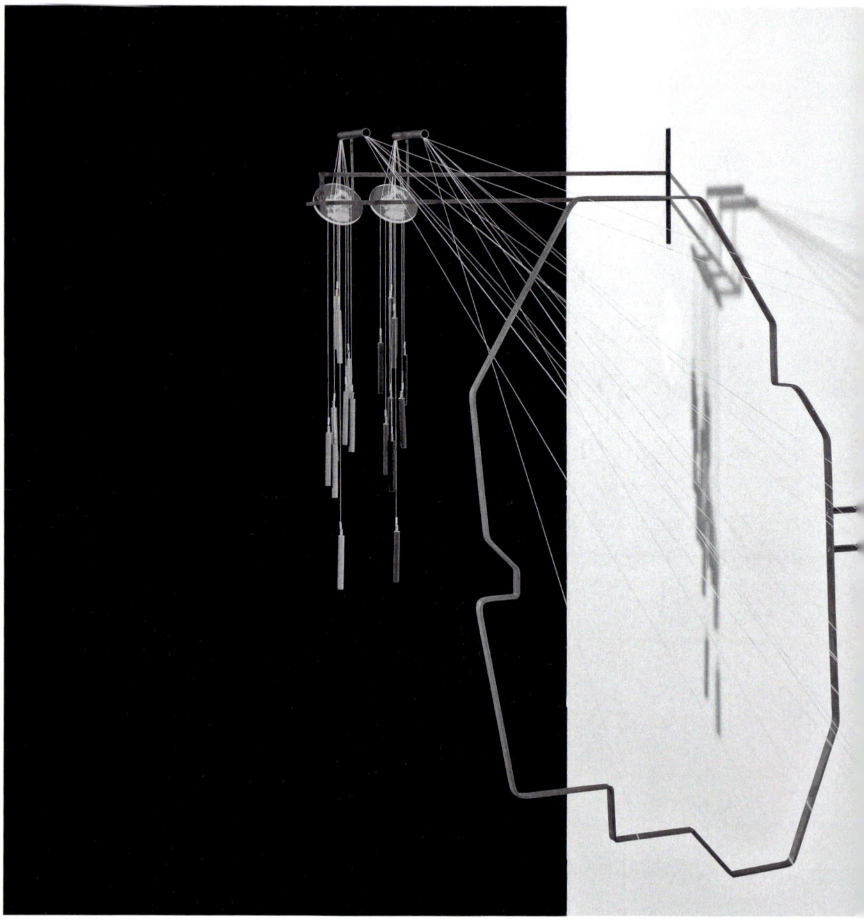

fig. 10

9 Penelope Haralambidou, *The Act of Looking*, 2007. Steel, Perspex, nickel silver, and waxed twine, 300 × 153 × 105 cm.

10 Penelope Haralambidou, *Déjà vu: Restaging Resnais's Last Year at Marienbad*, 2009. Paper, wood, and digital projection, 116 × 114 × 167 cm.

11 Penelope Haralambidou, *Déjà vu: Restaging Resnais's Last Year at Marienbad*, 2009. Detail of the screens without projection. Paper, wood, and digital projection, 116 × 114 × 167 cm.

fig. 11

Déjà vu: Restaging Resnais's Last Year at Marienbad

The second drawing, *Déjà vu*, restages a film through the means of architectural drawing conventions with the aim of exploring narrative and the notion of time [fig. 10].[18] This was my first dive into the world of film, using the moving image as a drawing technique and questioning the architecture of the cinema and the big screen. The film I chose to "redraw" was Resnais's *Last Year at Marienbad* (1961), which was based on Alain Robbe-Grillet's screenplay. The film takes place in a labyrinthine Baroque hotel, where X, the male protagonist, meets A, the female protagonist, and confronts her with descriptions of their romantic involvement a year ago, of which she has no recollection.[19] The unfolding love affair happens under the gaze of another mysterious protagonist M [fig. 11]. An enigma of seduction, the narrative of the film flips between present and past, memory and imagination, and has been described as a love story, abstract thriller or even a philosophical puzzle.[20]

I was seduced by its story of seduction and its portrayal of remembrance and oblivion in architecture, and interested in how a building can

12 Penelope Haralambidou, *Déjà vu: Restaging Resnais's Last Year at Marienbad*, 2009.

become the locus of a repressed memory or the cradle of a false recollection. Furthermore, I was attracted by the manner in which Resnais films architecture, how his camera's desirous gaze caresses the ornate surfaces of the hotel and treats it like another protagonist, whose intentions are ambivalent. Furthermore, the film is notoriously inscrutable, addressing the audience as a riddle. Captivated by the unresolved puzzle of its *mise en scène*, I decided to restage it, or draw it out, with the aim of portraying and unraveling its temporal and spatial organization of clues.

Déjà vu consists of an abstract paper model of the fictional Baroque hotel, and a digital reworking of selected scenes from the original film specifically designed to be projected on the model. For the base of the piece, I used an old library table. I laid the table with sheets of paper and, making careful incisions, I cut rectangular shapes and folded them out to form structurally robust, but delicate, paper screens that flicker with slight air movements. A series of specially designed wooden pieces painted white

helped to raise the paper screens to a second level, while others acted as vertical elements, as pawns on this cinematic game board.

In an attempt to break the flatness of the single screen and the linear delivery of the plot, *Déjà vu* redraws the film in light and time but also space. The three-dimensional arrangement of the screens relates to selected scenes of different durations that I digitally isolated: the garden; the theatre *mise en abyme*; the game of *Nim*; the endless corridors; the enigma of the bedroom; as well as close-up scenes for each protagonist. The looped scenes become metaphorical hotel "rooms" that play themselves, appearing and disappearing in sequence [fig. 12].

The paper substrate explores the hinge between the plan and the
fig. 12 section, how the planar mark making creates a vertical surface for projection through incision and rotation. Its crisp simplicity—folded paper and white-painted blocks of wood—reflects the contrast between the austere Modernism in the elliptical storyline of Robbe-Grillet's screenplay and the camera's love affair with the Baroque embellishments of the fictional hotel's skin.

A cinema screen is always perceived as a large window, a vertical picture plane that transports the viewer to fictional other worlds, while physically pinning her or him in a single viewing position. Placed on a table in the middle of a gallery, the model, dressed with the luminous imagery of the film, allows the viewer to circulate around it and inhabit this fragmentation of the picture plane at an intimate level. The film in *Déjà vu* is not only distributed in space but can also be seen from the back (I specifically chose the paper for its back projection quality). The positioning of the piece on a table creates a sense of familiarity. By encountering the fragmented action on its surface, the viewer merges the visual appreciation of the moving image with her or his tactile memory of handling things on tables: on library tables, drawing tables, dinner tables, or tables where board games are played.

Important in *Déjà vu*'s conception and delivery was the handmade nature of the process: the "drawing out" of the piece. The composition was derived through trial and error, cutting, folding, and moving pieces of paper while adjusting the projection digitally, but in real time. I was also invested in entering the space created by the projection with my whole body and sculpting within it a drawing in light.

Resnais's film is a faithful adaptation of Robbe-Grillet's exceptionally precise screenplay.[21] As one of the main advocates of the *nouveau roman*, Robbe-Grillet's displays a writing style that is methodical and geometric, focusing on often compulsive and repetitive descriptions of objects and spaces. Repetitions combined with the fractured timeline and the enigmatic plot produce an effect equivalent to a collage or a Cubist painting. The screenplay's lack of chronological indications led the script supervisor Sylvette Baudrot to draw an elaborate graph, which organizes the film sequences on an x- and y-axis in relation to changes of set, as well as time [fig. 13].[22] At the bottom of the graph we find scenes that describe the present, at the top the past (last year), and in between an intermediary area with long blocks that represent shots that had no precise date or were timeless.

I tried to replicate this diagrammatic delineation of time in the arrangement of the folded paper screens, here in relation to focal range. In cinema, the surface of the large projection screen obviously coincides with the sharpest focus. In *Déjà vu* the projector is positioned at an angle so that the projection on the whole arrangement on the table is oblique. Emerging from a single projector, all the images of the rooms were designed anamorphically on a single plane, to geometrically match the screens in different depths.[23] As they are projected in different locations within the focal range, the paper screens interrupt the projection pyramid in and out of focus. The selected scenes of "the present" (the embellished ceilings and views of lavish corridors) are positioned in the middle of the table, where the projection is in sharp focus, while the past, "last year" (the mysterious bedroom scene) and "timeless" (the garden scene), appear out of focus at the back and front of the table, respectively [fig. 14]. Pertaining to memory or imagination, these scenes are blurred, in contrast with the sharpness of the present.

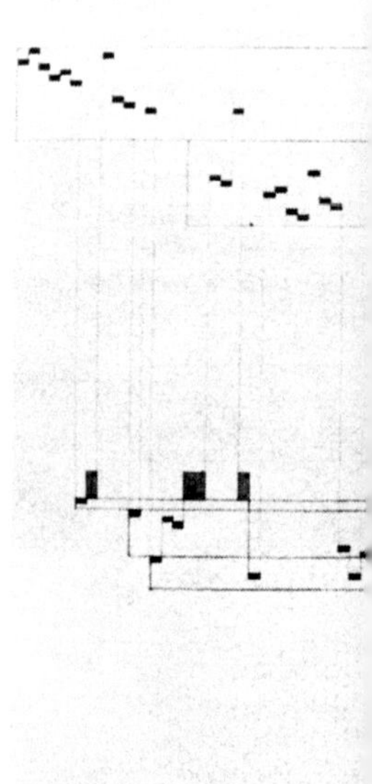

The *décor* of the bedroom, where key scenes of the film take place, starts as a stark interior bathed in a blinding white light, but gradually blossoms into a suffocating, complex, flowery pattern. This blossoming represents the opening up and unfolding of either a repressed memory or a newly constructed event in the imagination. By digitally reworking the image of the bedroom and creating a short animation, I was able to accentuate this blossoming of the architecture, which I also see as a representation of desire.

In *Déjà vu* I combine model making with projection mapping as drawing tools to create and perform a critical essay on Resnais's *Last Year at Marienbad*. I use design and drawing as an analytical language. The work harnesses the communicative possibilities of architectural representation and uses it to suggest a practice-led approach to film criticism. This restaging of the film uncovers the architectural significance of the themes in Resnais's film: how the plot links architecture to memory, imagination, and desire; the significance of pairing the minimalist narrative to a lavish location; and the portrayal of the labyrinthine hotel as one of the protagonists.

Finally, *Déjà vu* is a redrawing of a film in the form of a model, in this case a model for an allegorical Baroque hotel, using film as a drawing technique—light on paper, where the play of black and white seeps through and tempo-

13 Diagram by Sylvette Baudrot of the scrip for the film *Last Year at Marienbad*, 1961. Published in *Cahiers du Cinéma* 12 (September 1961): 9.

14 Penelope Haralambidou, *Déjà vu: Restaging Resnais's Last Year at Marienbad*, 2009. Paper, wood, and digital projection, 116 × 114 × 167 cm.

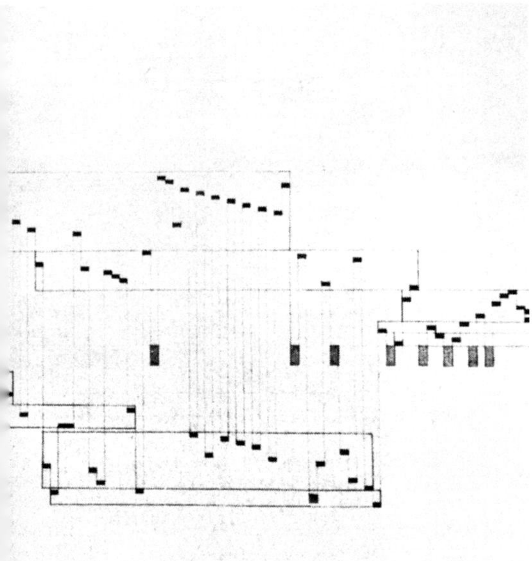

fig. 13

fig. 14

rarily stains the multiple screens like ephemeral ink. Cut out of matter—the paper dressing the table—the plan folds out and becomes a screen able to display duration, storytelling, and desire. By casting recorded time on its surface, the drawing becomes alive, flickering in the light of a doomed love story for a short while, fading out and disappearing before being born again in a cycle.

With-drawing Room on Vellum

With-drawing Room on Vellum is the start of a larger project that studies the current status of the architectural drawing surface by looking at its origins in history and by imagining its future.[24]

One of the earliest surviving examples of an architectural plan on a membrane, dating from the early 9th century, the *Plan of Saint Gall*, depicts a monastic compound drawn in fine red lines on five pieces of parchment sewn together [fig. 15]. The plan does not seem to correspond to a specific built monastery and most scholars agree that it is rather a "two-dimensional meditation on the ideal early medieval monastic community."[25] The plan is

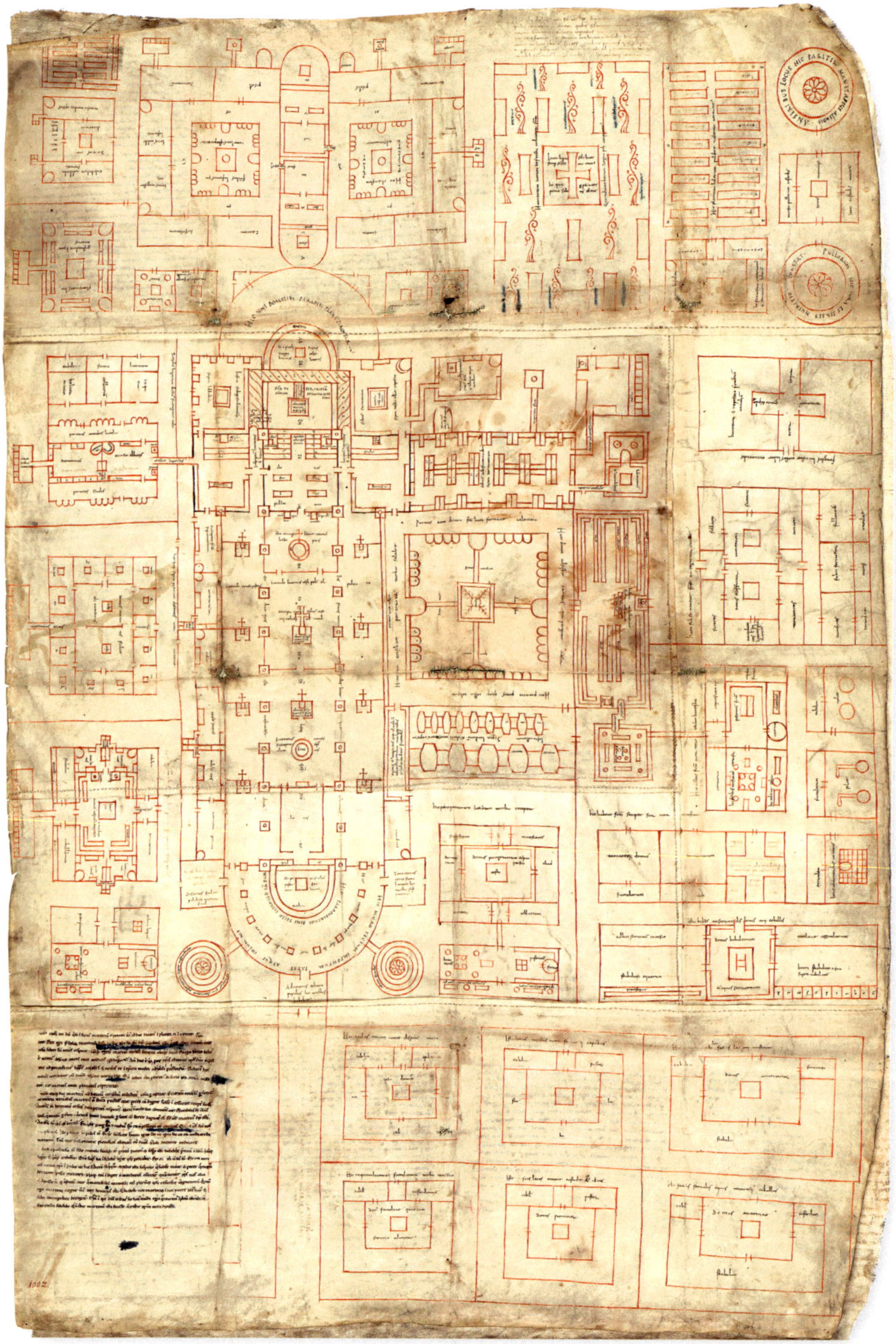

fig. 15

the only major surviving architectural drawing from a nearly 700-year period up to the 13th century. In fact, the drawing's durability is due to its remarkably resilient drawing surface, parchment, which predates paper—a thin membrane made of animal hide, prepared for use as a surface for drawing and writing.

Vellum is a finer quality parchment made specifically from calf, off-white, soft, and semi-translucent: a painting and drawing surface that has been revered by architects and artists throughout history. A rich source of information about architectural practice during the Middle Ages is preserved in the form of "illumination" on vellum pages bound in manuscripts. In these pages, elegant architectural forms drawn laboriously by hand in gold gilding and lapis lazuli frame the narrative of the depicted religious scenes [fig. 16]. Drawings on vellum have remained tethered to not only inert, but also organic animal matter for more than 1,150 years. Fixed on animal skin, the past of architectural drawing could not be more visceral.

In sharp contrast, advancements in digital technology have led contemporary architectural drawing to withdraw from the skin of the world. On a luminous screen, points and lines are defined with mathematical precision that can never be touched. But where is the drawing surface and what is its matter?

To answer this question, *With-drawing Room on Vellum* combines research in the medieval use of vellum for representing architecture with the making of a composite drawing. Marrying two unlikely techniques—drafting on vellum and projection of digital animation—separated by 12 centuries, I aimed to establish a fecund tension for questioning their conventions. The use of drawing as a research method opens up a series of questions as the often-intuitive links that happen through drawing hold ideas that are yet unnamable.

Architectural designs on a membrane were a technological innovation in the Middle Ages. Drawing on vellum is a paradox: it constitutes the first materialization of architectural representation and at the same time is a significant step away from matter. Before the Renaissance, architectural drawings, as they are known today, were rare, if not non-existent. Architectural knowledge was embedded in the traditions of making and building. It was a collaborative process transmitted orally, and the control of the form of a building did not belong to a single individual but was spread up the hierarchical ladder of the guild.[26] Medieval drafting was often executed in situ by the master builder on a layer of plaster of Paris on the floor of the lodge's "tracing house."[27] Drawing was a physical act where the draughtsman performed the design with his whole body, full-scale. The equivalent of the drawing surface was a tracing floor, a spatial feature incorporated inside the building that was being built.

15 Unknown, *Plan of Saint Gall*, c. 830 CE. Red ink on vellum, approx. 112 × 77.5 cm. St. Gallen, Stiftsbibliothek.

The use of a stand-alone flat membrane turned the drawing surface into an abstract projection plane able to hold a measured image of the building in scale. Its high cost meant that architects used it only for presentations, and they scraped drawings to create clean surfaces for new designs, so vellum was used as a palimpsest.[28] Vellum also fulfilled a need for "transmission": drawings incised on floors and models lack portability but drawings on parchment or vellum rolled or assembled in folios could travel. A significant example belonged to a traveling draftsman: Villard de Honnecourt.[29] So vellum not only kept the drawing safe on its surface but also became a repository of design information in a way that is uncannily similar to digital practices in drawing today.

The emergence of masterly draftsmanship that started in the late 13th century allowed the architect to link the invisible geometric relationships of the building into a single image through pen on parchment.[30] This coincided with the improving status of architects, who were now more in control of their designs as distinguished from those who worked with hands and tools. Vellum, therefore, gave birth to not only architectural drawing, as we know it today, but also to the contemporary architect. fig. 16

Another medieval graphic representation of architecture on vellum can be found in illuminated manuscripts—text that is illustrated, "lit" by the way light catches on the burnished gold and silver adorning the dazzling drawings and embellishments accompanying the text. Illuminated manuscripts offer a unique insight into the significance of built form during the medieval era.[31]

But architecture played another, perhaps more unexpected role. Medieval illuminators saw knowledge as a mental edifice and used building elements as decorative motifs to frame and organize texts, images, and charts. This architectural decorative vocabulary was so rich that turning the pages of the manuscript approximates an extraordinary architectural tour.[32] Pointedly, architecture was also important in organizing the narrative structure in scriptures and books of hours.

So where is the drawing surface today? Caught in the whirlwind of technological advancement, has its extinction gone unnoticed? Behind the screen, the tactility of the drawing surface and the infinitesimal materiality of the line and texture have all been lost. What has been gained is a dynamic, three-dimensional digital simulacrum of a building, which, after loosening its ties to a physical membrane or sheet, can come to life. I am particularly interested in the new time-based media and their promise for a new cinematic drawing.[33]

To start the drawing, I ordered two pieces of vellum from the last remaining manufacturer of parchment in the UK, who has used the same traditional techniques since 1870.[34] Apart from the tell-tale shape, the pure

16 Unknown, Michael Lupi de Çandiu, *Initial A: Two Men before a King and A Man Speaking to a Family*, c. 1290–1310. Tempera, gold leaf, and ink on parchment, leaf, 36.5 × 24 cm. Los Angeles, The J. Paul Getty Museum.

17 Penelope Haralambidou, details of handling and painting on vellum, 2016.

fig. 17

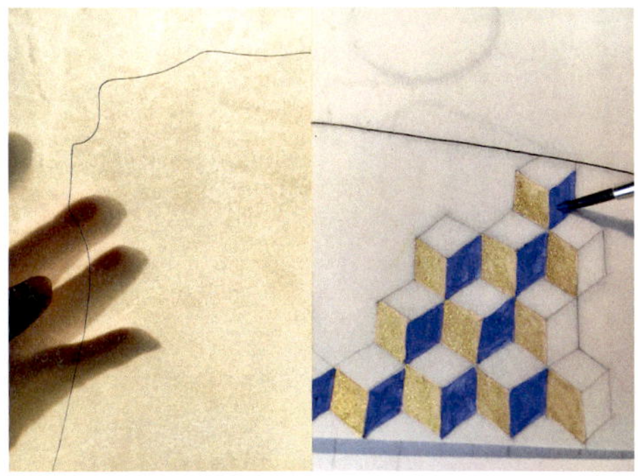

whiteness of this membrane has very little to suggest its animal descent at first sight. Held against the light, however, it has an amazing translucency and the anatomy of the animal is revealed: spine, hip, and shoulder pressure points become visible. Closer inspection also reveals a network of veins.

The decision on the building that I chose to depict in the drawing was somewhat autobiographical: the Bartlett School of Architecture at 22 Gordon Street in London, our home, where we returned in January 2017 after it had been refurbished. The drawing, which was completed just before our return, does not seek to accurately represent the physical form of the new/old building. Rather, it attempts to portray the intangible identity of the institution that it houses. Inspired by both architectural working drawings and illuminated manuscripts on vellum, *With-drawing Room on Vellum* takes the form of an illuminated manuscript page, a preface or a test, but also the design of a larger future drawing on a larger, whole skin. This drawing within a drawing is a synecdoche: the part refers to the whole.

To draw on the skin I used shell gold and lapis lazuli, the pigments often adorning illumination manuscripts, as well as other inks and watercolor.[35] Vellum is one of the most rewarding drawing surfaces I have used, affording a satisfying gliding of the metal nib or brush [fig. 17]. At the top left corner is an intricate rendition of the letter B. The general shape follows the Bartlett School of Architecture's logo, replicating medieval examples of decorated monograms. At the bottom edge of the drawing, the illusionistic cubic motif represents both a tile floor pattern often found in illumination and a visual reference to the virtual world of the digital voxel.

The symmetry of the body of the animal inspired a strong symmetry in the overall composition that also brings my own symmetrical body into the foreground [fig. 1]. Flanking the skin in the center, left and right, two pico-projectors are decipherable—throwing their projections onto the front and the back of the skin, respectively. The projectors are connected with cables to two open laptops below. Caught between the twisting cables, peculiar geometric architectural ornaments blossom, similar to the complex decorated margins of illuminated texts flowering with botanic as well as architectural patterns. This part of my drawing touches upon the proliferation of motifs that constitute "a Bartlett drawing," a trademark visual language that rarely fails to seduce. I see this potent drawing idiom as part of the identity of the Bartlett.

Finally, the central part of the composition hosts a short animation drawn by T. J. Brook Lin, whom I commissioned to contribute to the piece.[36] It shows a fictional cinematic rendition of 22 Gordon Street, where the façade of the new building, drawn in shell gold, opens up to reveal a colorful imaginary interior. It rotates and withdraws from the flat plane into alternative versions reminiscent of the shades and forms found in illuminated manuscripts. The arrangement requires real-time matching of the projection with the vellum, introducing a dialogue between the hand-drawn piece and the digital insertion. The two become a pair and depend on each other for the completion of the composition.

One could say that the true essence of architectural representation is never tethered on a surface, instead residing in the imagination or in the finished building itself. By bringing together vellum—as the forgotten, visceral past—and digital projection—as the uncertain, evanescent future—of the architectural drawing surface, *With-drawing Room on Vellum* aims to probe and challenge its disappearing.

In April 2016, the majority of Members of the House of Commons voted to continue to print Acts of Parliament on vellum, a tradition that goes back to the drafting of the Magna Carta, as there were concerns about the longevity of archival paper and long-term security of digital technology.[37] Does the ongoing vanishing of the architectural drawing surface signify that it was a blip in the history of architectural representation? Not drawn on vellum, will the plans that we draw today survive for the next 1,150 years, and if so, where will they lie?

Conclusion

Searching for and foregrounding some unconscious assumptions on the veiled matrix of architectural representation, the three drawings that I present expose blind spots: the other eye, the lost surface, and time. Looking at disciplines and methods beyond current architectural practice, in fine art, filmmaking, and the drawing techniques of the past, helps to define these blind spots. By using mostly analog hand drawing as a method, I enter the space of representation and assimilate the practices first of an artist, then of a filmmaker—both of whom can be found either in the center or at the periphery of the Modernist canon, depending on how you look at it—and finally of a medieval draftswoman, at a time just before Cartesian space had taken control. The act of drawing becomes an investigatory technique challenging the accepted syntax of architectural drawing in search of alternative methods for representing space beyond the plan: my drawings add binocular depth and duration, and remove the flat intersecting picture plane.

The recent emergence of immersive technologies, of virtual and augmented reality, has created an unprecedented spatial drawing experience: lines and shapes made out of illusory light can now be drawn by a softly mechanized hand in stereoscopic deep space and in real time.[38] Does this mean that we have already broken away from the invisible matrix of architectural representation and that we are now able to enter the drawing and mark space through storytelling? If so, where exactly is this act of drawing and its result taking place and how will they affect not only the way we design and build architecture but also the structure of our thinking and intellectual space?

Although hand-drawn elaborately over long periods of time using traditional and somewhat ancient techniques, my drawings directly question and aim to foreground contemporary advancements in spatial representation brought by the digital and computation. As technologies develop at even faster speeds, it is perhaps even more important today than ever before to reverse-engineer, to engage with the speculative dimension of projection, visuality, surface, and time, and try to understand representation in an excruciatingly slow manner, through our bodies and manually, by hand.

1 The title of the piece in French is: Étant donnés: 1° la chute d'eau, 2° le gaz d'éclairage… For more details and images see the Philadelphia Museum website, .http://www.philamuseum.org/collections/permanent/65633.html?mulR=860108392|27 (accessed 5 March, 2018). For an in-depth analysis of *Given* see Michael R. Taylor, *Marcel Duchamp: Étant donnés* (Philadelphia: Philadelphia Museum of Art; New Haven and London: Yale University, 2009).
2 For more details of the work see, Penelope Haralambidou, Déjà vu: *Restaging Resnais's Last Year at Marienbad*, 2016, https://issuu.com/bartlettarchucl/docs/haralambidou_01_deja_vu_s05_update (accessed July 29, 2019).
3 Penelope Haralambidou, "With-drawing Room on Vellum: The Persistent Vanishing of the Architectural Drawing Surface," in *Drawing Futures*, ed. Laura Allen and Luke Caspar Pearson (London: UCL Press, 2016), 82–89, http://www.ucl.ac.uk/ucl-press/browse-books/drawing-futures (accessed July 29, 2019).
4 For more on this research see Penelope Haralambidou, *Marcel Duchamp and the Architecture of Desire* (London: Routledge, 2013).
5 For other architects discussing Duchamp's work and architecture see Bernard Tschumi, "Architecture and its Double," *Architectural Design* 48, no. 2–3 (1978): 111–16, and Alberto Pérez-Gómez, *Built upon Love: Architectural Longing after Ethics and Aesthetics* (Cambridge, MA: MIT Press, 2006), 101.
6 Haralambidou, *Marcel Duchamp and the Architecture of Desire*, 230.
7 Marcel Duchamp, *Faulty Landscape*, 1946. Seminal fluid on Astralon, backed with black satin. Toyama, Museum of Modern Art. The chemical analysis took place in 1980.
8 For a discussion on the relationship between Duchamp, architecture, and desire, see the podcast of "Architecture and Eroticism," a talk I contributed to at Royal Academy of Arts, 2017, https://www.royalacademy.org.uk/event/architecture-and-eroticism (accessed 5 March, 2018), and Penelope Haralambidou, "Eroticism, Architecture and the Desire to Grasp the World Visually in the Work of Marcel Duchamp," *AArchitecture* 33 (January 2018): 22–29, https://issuu.com/aaschool/docs/aarchitecture33 (accessed 29 July 2019).
9 In the top sketchbook spread in figure 2, note the tilted bottom panels of the door creating a recess for the feet, so as to allow closer contact of the body. In the bottom spread on the left, see a close-up detail of the peepholes and the groove between the two upper panels allowing space for the nose, making the door fit like a mask. On the right, a simple section shows the plane of the door, the breached wall, and the visual rays, starting at the peepholes and looking down at the nude, which is positioned horizontally.
10 Lyotard's study of *Given* and Duchamp's *Manual of Instructions* was published in Jean-François Lyotard, *Duchamp's TRANS/formers*, trans. Ian McLeod (Venice, CA: Lapis, 1990).
11 I have recently explored *Given*'s door and its two peepholes in an article in the Canadian magazine *Public*, for an issue entitled *Attendant A to Z*, ed. Serkan Ozkaya and Robert Fitterman. See Penelope Haralambidou, "C for Camera Obscura (Reversed)," *Public* 56 (2017): 22–31.
12 For more on the stereoscope see Jonathan Crary, *Techniques of the Observer: On Vision and Modernity in the Nineteenth Century* (Cambridge, MA, and London: MIT Press, 1990). For the relationship between *Given* and the stereoscope see Haralambidou, *Marcel Duchamp and the Architecture of Desire*, 65–97.
13 A photograph by Man Ray entitled *L Dernier Œuvre de Duchamp/Cheminée Anaglyphe*, 1968, shows Duchamp's attempted physical construction in wire of the geometric shape described in his anaglyphic drawing. See Chrissie Iles, "Marcel Duchamp, Man Ray and the Desiring Machine," in *Marcel Duchamp—Man Ray: 50 Years of Alchemy* (New York: Sean Kelly Gallery, 2004), 88.
14 See the drawings in Esprit Pascal Jouffret, *Traité élémentaire de géométr à quatre dimensions et introduction à la géométrie à n dimensions* (Paris: Gauthier-Villiars, 1903).
15 Note that, unlike all published image of *Given*, the photograph on the left doe not show the lock of hair.
16 *The Act of Looking* is the culminatio of this research and is informed by my study of stereoscopy and stereo-photogrammetry. It was the central piece I designed specifically for my solo show *The Blossoming of Perspective* at the DomoBaal Gallery in 2007, and was shown again in *Speculative Models*, a two-person show at London Gallery West in 2009. For more images visit the Domobaal website, https://www.domobaal.com/exhibitions/39-07-penelope-haralambidou-01.html (accessed July 29, 2019).
17 See Stan Allen, *Practice: Architecture, Technique + Representation* (London: Routledge, 2000), 10.
18 *Déjà vu* was exhibited in *Speculativ Models: Air Grid and The Blossoming o Perspective*, a two-person show at London Gallery West in 2009, where it was shown next to *The Act of Looking*. See also Ro Spankie, "Speculative Models: Air Grid and the Blossoming of Perspective," *The Journal of Architecture* 14, no. 4 (2009): 533–37.
19 Penelope Haralambidou, "The Act o Looking and Déjà vu: Notes on a 'Figura Theory,'" *KTHA* 2 (2011): 2–9.
20 Although it received mixed reviews, the film was winner of the Golden Lion award at the 1961 Venice Film Festival. Jean-Louis Leutrat, *L'année dernière à Marienbad* (*Last Year in Marienbad*), trans. Paul Hammond (London: British Film Institute, 2000).

1 Alain Robbe-Grillet, *Last Year at Marienbad*, trans. Richard Howard New York: Grove Press, 1962).

2 Quoted in Leutrat, *L'anneé dernière*, 1, and François Thomas, *L'atelier 'Alain Resnais* (Paris: Flammarion, 989), 152. The diagram was published Cahiers du Cinéma 123 (September 961): 9.

3 Anamorphosis is technique using istorted projection to render an image hat can only be deciphered from a pecific vantage point.

4 *With-drawing Room on Vellum* was riginally prepared for Drawing Futures, conference at the Bartlett School Architecture, UCL in 2016. See aralambidou, "With-drawing Room," 2–89.

5 For more on The St. Gall Project visit he website, http://www.stgallplan.org/n/index_plan.html (accessed July 29, 019).

6 Alberto Pérez-Gómez and Louise elletier, *Architectural Representation nd the Perspective Hinge* (Cambridge, A, and London: MIT Press, 1997), 8.

7 An example of a "tracing floor" urvives in York Minster. In a confused ass of intersecting lines engraved into e floor, the full-scale drawing for the ady Chapel's window can still be istinguished and the walls are also overed with physical wooden templates r drawing other parts of the building. on R. Shelby, "The Geometrical nowledge of Mediaeval Master asons," in *The Engineering of Medieval athedrals*, ed. Lynn T. Courtenay ldershot: Ashgate, 1997), 41.

Nancy Wu, "Facade of Strasbourg athedral (Plan A1)," in *Pen and archment: Drawing in the Middle Ages*, d. Melanie Holcomb (New York: etropolitan Museum of Art, 2009), 134.

29 The album was discovered in the mid-19th century. See Carl F. Barnes, *Villard de Honnecourt—The Artist and his Drawings: A Critical Bibliography* (Boston: G.K. Hall, 1982), and Nikolaus Pevsner, "Villard de Honnecourt," in *Pevsner on Art and Architecture*, ed. Stephen Games (London: Methuen, 2002), 61–69.

30 Wu, "Facade of Strasbourg Cathedral," 134.

31 Christine Sciacca, *Building the Medieval World* (Los Angeles: J. Paul Getty Museum; London: British Library, 2010).

32 Melanie Holcomb, "Strokes of Genius: The Draftsman's Art in the Middle Ages," in *Pen and Parchment: Drawing in the Middle Ages*, ed. Melanie Holcomb (New York: Metropolitan Museum of Art, 2009), 21.

33 I have explored the potential of cinematic drawing in the Masters Unit 24, Bartlett School of Architecture, UCL, which I teach with Michael Tite. For examples of the students' films see the Unit 24 website, http://www.unittwenty-four.com/ (accessed March 5, 2018).

34 See the William Cowley website, http://www.williamcowley.co.uk (accessed March 5, 2018).

35 Useful details of illumination techniques can be found in Patricia Lovett, *Illumination: Gold and Colour* (London: L. Cornelissen and Son, 2015), 68.

36 See Ting Jui Brook Lin, http://www.tjblin.com/ (accessed July 29, 2019).

37 "Printing Acts of Parliament on Vellum," in *The Public Whip*, April 20, 2016, http://www.publicwhip.org.uk/division.php?date=2016-04-20&number=245 (accessed October 1, 2019).

38 See Unit 24 student Jasper Stevens, drawing in virtual space, https://www.youtube.com/watch?v=9bAO0O5mKi8 (accessed July 29, 2019).

Maja Zander Fisker

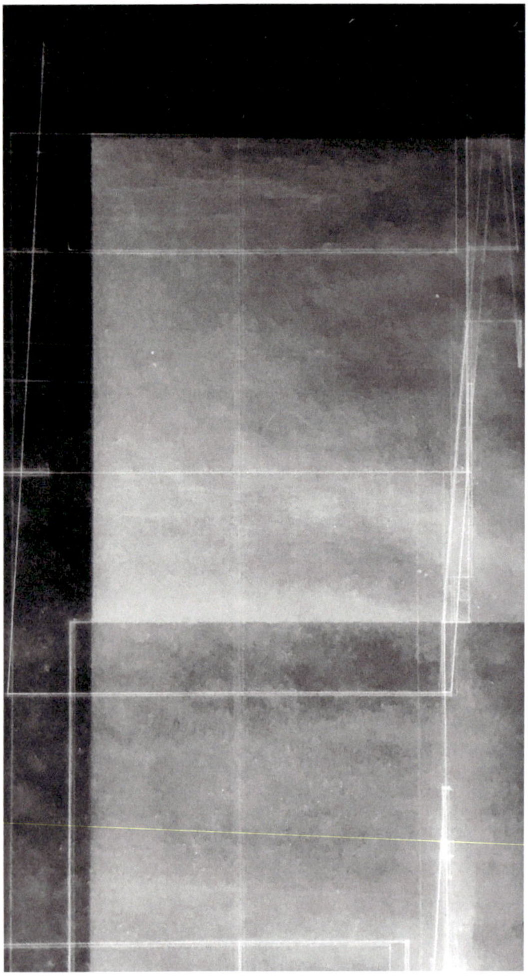

fig. 1

You Wouldn't Have Known Her

Plans, Prose, and Photography

1 Maja Zander Fisker, *You Wouldn't Have Known Her*, 2017. Photographic fragment. Photography on paper, 15 × 21 cm.

2 Maja Zander Fisker, *You Wouldn't Have Known Her*, 2017. Photographic fragment. Photography on paper, 15 × 21 cm.

fig. 2

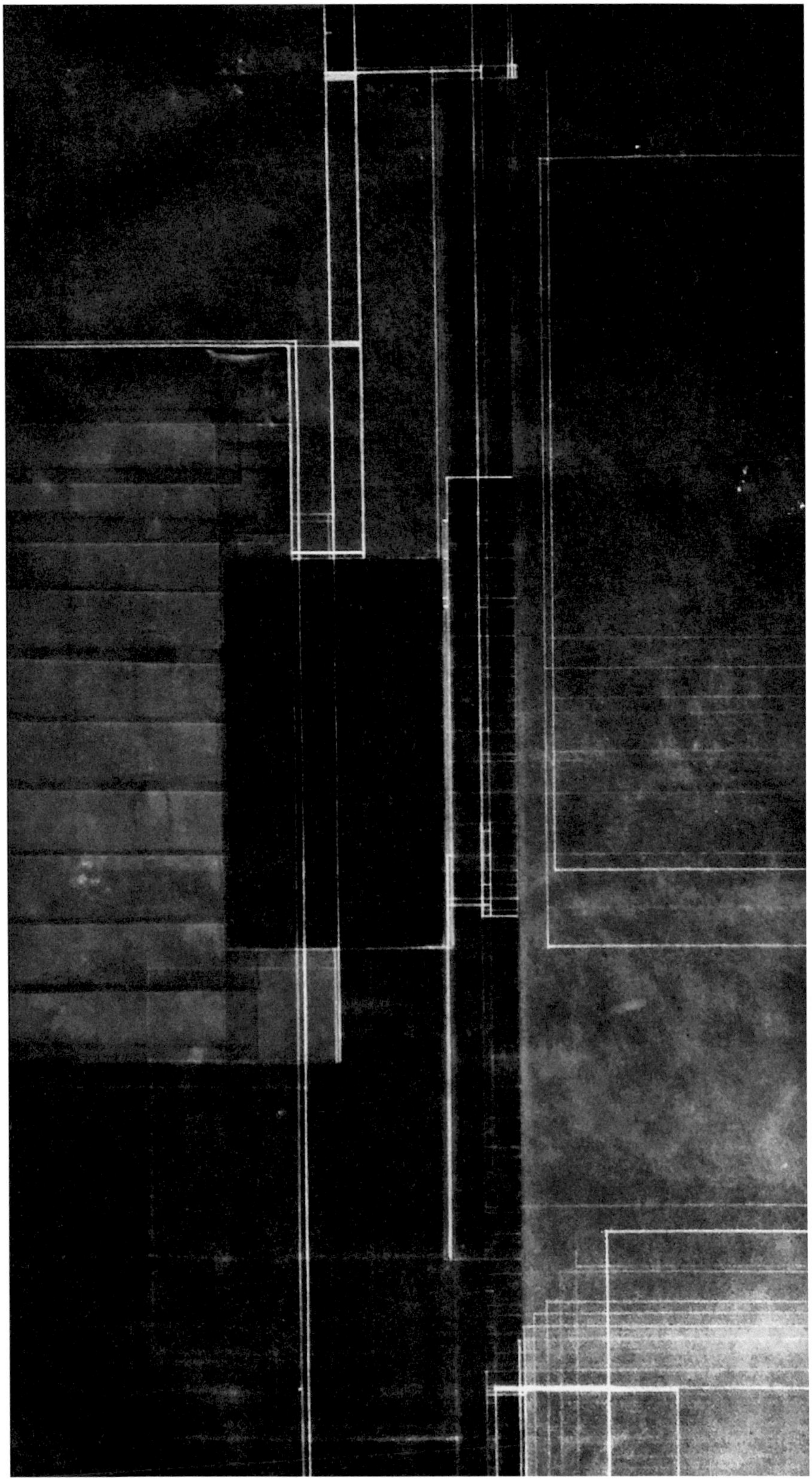

"You wouldn't have known her, you'd have seen her everywhere at once, in a hotel, in a street, in a train, in a bar, in a book, in a film, in yourself, your inmost self." So they go, the opening lines in Marguerite Duras's 1982 book of prose, *The Malady of Death*.[1] This specific textual situation opens a possible time and space and evinces the possibility of every imaginable time-space. It is particularly the articulated conjunctions of imagined space and time that makes this literary text relevant to a creative practice of architecture.

In contemplation of these lines, the project *You Wouldn't Have Known Her* addresses the architectural drawing as a process that articulates spatial thinking and imagination [fig. 1–4]. It inquires into architectural becoming through development of plan drawings, deriving from a transmedial practice including text, drawing, and photography. Within distinct iterative drawing series, the project investigates how medial transpositions can work as an operational resource in the architectural creation process as a way to incept new experiences of spatial construction.

The project examines how the specific media of text, drawing, and photography together are able to articulate relations and events, and how transpositions between those media contribute to reformatting architectural configurations of time-space. In each medium a new place is revealed, and here "place" is not a matter of metric sizes as much as a set of relations. A new situation. It is, however, in the transitions between the different media that the medial affordances become generative.

The investigation's premise is a set of chosen medial characteristics used to structure and generate the work. For the text: enunciation and scene; for the analog drawing: layers and transparency; and for the photograph: framing and light. The work is situated in Duras's text, and its possible relations to other media. The text thereby establishes a contextual situation that constitutes a field of simultaneous times and multilayered spaces that work as agents causing a creative moment.

3 Maja Zander Fisker, *You Wouldn't Have Known Her*, 2017. Photographic fragment. Photography on paper, 15 × 21 cm.

The subject of the plan drawings coming into being is derived from the text, which is a contextual framework for the drawing, defined not as a geographical place, but as a complex situation—a space constituted by a manifold evoking of material and immaterial scenarios—which instigates the focus of the drawing. When this is related to photography, the purpose becomes to investigate how the drawing in interaction with the photograph enables a juxtaposition of relations between social, spatial, and temporal conditions. Working with multiple transparent layers, the drawing is developed through the order of the plan, informed by the temporal and spatial events of the context, and, secondly, through a continuous addition of layers that operates an incremental negotiation of the order setting the plan.

fig. 3

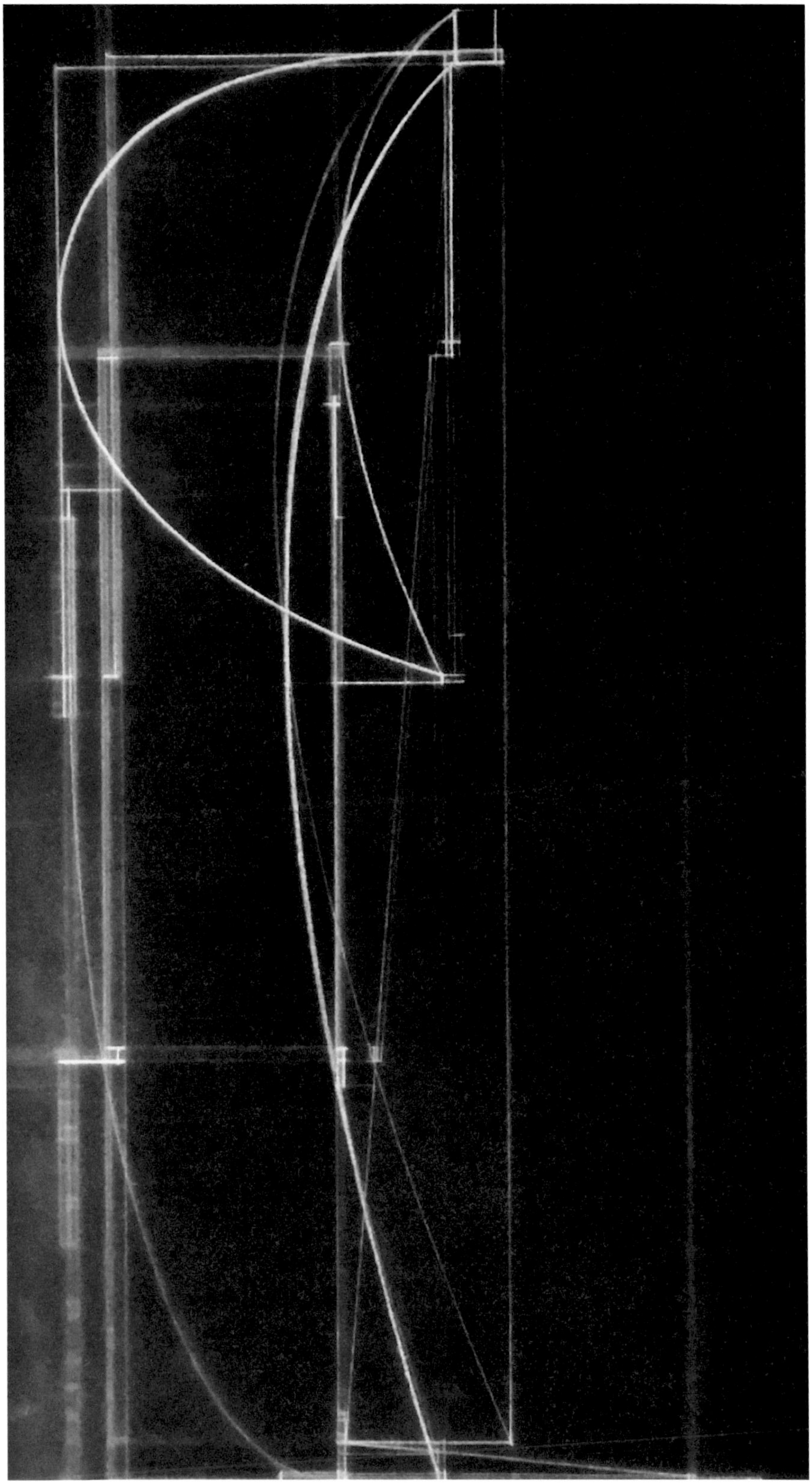

The photograph is an incision in the world. Based on the process of the analog drawing and its successive layering, the project presents a series of photographic fragments of the drawn plan. The photographic series works with assemblage and montage as another act of translation, creating new views on the drawing, which is no longer represented as a whole. The photographic series thus explores the initial text, as a variance of what is experienced and what is experienced through. The photograph here works as an incision in the layered drawing, and together these incisions form the montage: a continuity with an intrinsic discontinuity—a new gathering or reenactment of sets of relations.

Inspired by the poet Lucretius' idea of "clinamen,"[2] understood as the downward movement of atoms, caused by gravity, and their arbitrary deviations from the straight line of the fall, their swirl, the montage introduces a *fall* due to its verticality. All the phases of this process within the different media can be considered consistent in themselves, but there is also a desire to consider them as *related*. The awareness of the medial differences and their interference permits a return to each stage of the process, as situations, as a fall through them, and as new constellations of appearance. New spatial constructions.

In sum, the project inaugurates a process where the generative logic of the medial differences sets the work in motion; not by pursuing equalization within uniform appearances, but by acknowledging the different modes and powers of significance imbuing each medium: questions of both temporality and spatiality, matters of time, space, and place are at work.

4 Maja Zander Fisker, *You Wouldn't Have Known Her*, 2017. Photographic montage. Photography on paper 75 × 140 cm.

1 Marguerite Duras, *The Malady of Death*, trans. Barbara Bray (New York: Grove Press, 1986).
2 Lucretius, *On the Nature of Things*, trans. Cyril Bailey (Oxford: Clarendon Press, 1948).

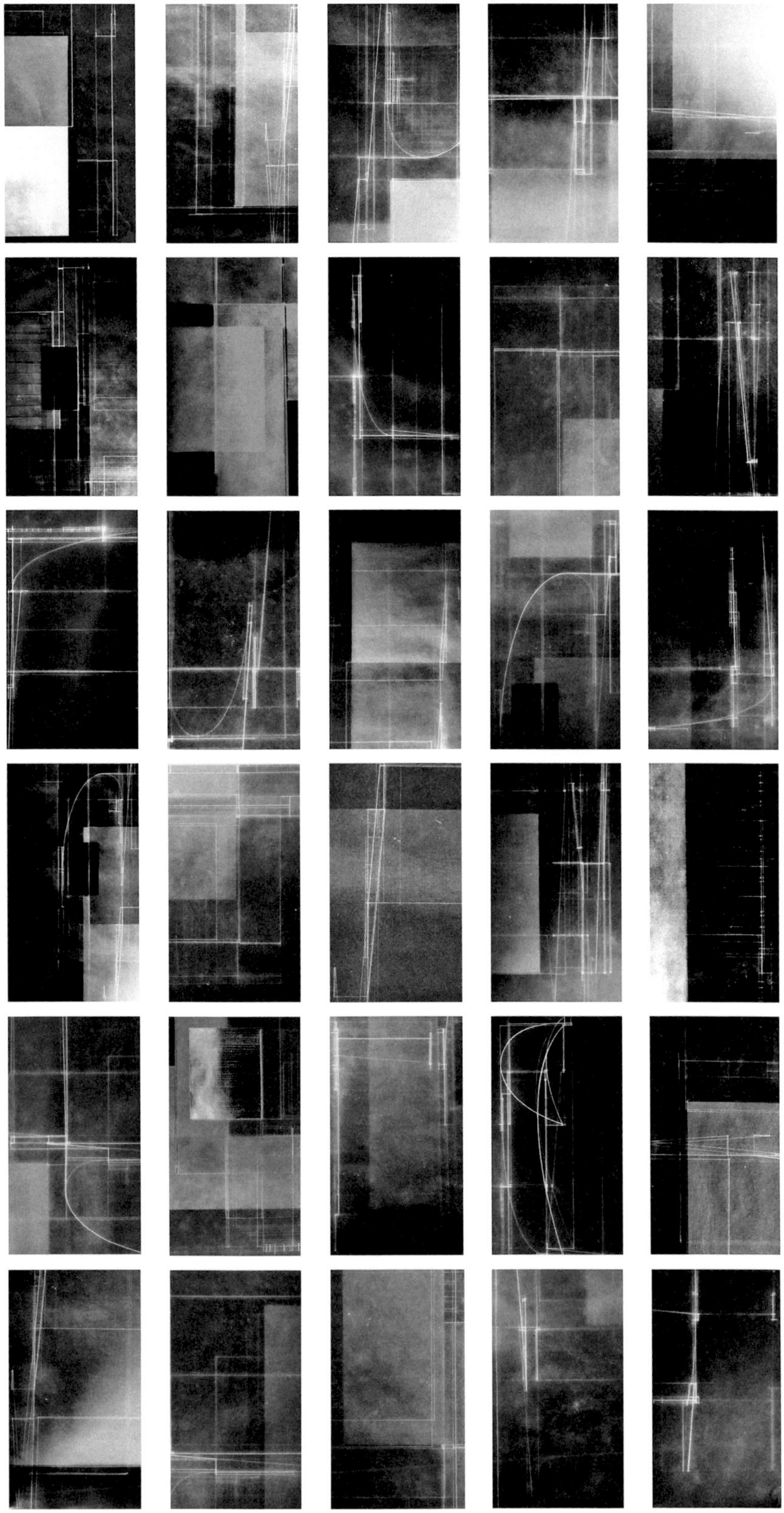

fig.4

Katica Pedisic

Four Ways to Occupy a Hearth

On Conceiving the Invisible

fig. 1

As the primary mechanism making up an architectural plan, the line is a potent device. Struck like a tuning fork, it resonates—a tether setting off a trajectory for the future life of that line. Compressed in the line is resource: future incarnations of industry; people laboring at bringing about built forms (in the cold, the heat) and, ultimately, the line guides the everyday struggle and prospective joy of occupants as they go about the minutiae of their daily lives... the end-point, perhaps, of the line. Before that, a flashback if you will, to a beginning: the toil of a pencil moving across a surface, someone drawing out a plan. We live in drawings.

Writing on the work of spatial artist Marie-Jeanne Hoffner, Joana Neves observed: "The illusion of architectural space in a drawing is based on a very simple structure, which is why it works: the eye is directed into a space the body cannot traverse and which the imagination must thus people."[1] Although Neves spoke of architectural drawings in general, it may be the architectural plan that demands the greatest imaginative leap. Perspectives,

1 Katica Pedisic, *Four Ways to Occupy a Hearth*, panel 2 (detail), 2017. Ink, pencil, and compressed charcoal on Arches paper, 59.4 × 42 cm.

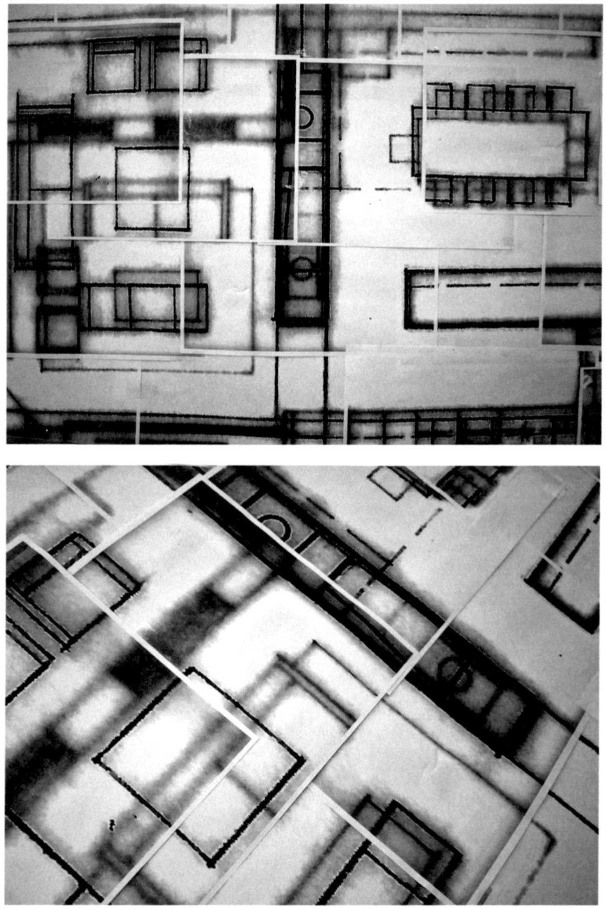

fig. 2

sections, and elevations contain greater depth than plans and additionally are viewed from a horizontal, upright position, aligning with the way we usually see the world. A plan, however, asks us to view from above, vertically, a way of looking that is common in architecture (but less common outside the profession), requiring an imaginative embodiment to orient between spatial markers. The "peopling" of a plan demands continual causal appraisals behind each line placement. Yet what do lines on a plan actually represent? Conventionally, they delineate space, describing its boundaries, a condition of edge, that precise spot where a surface changes direction or ends. But point to "space" in a drawing? It is usually white and almost certainly blank.[2] Lines demonstrate how an interior might be, but they are not that space. A plan attends to space inversely—if space is there—it is there by implication. Bruce Nauman's cast of the "space" under his chair and Rachel Whiteread doing similarly (though more neatly) in casting the void under hers explore space manifested inversely, and petrified. Space here is a mute reflection of its container.

A Line Made by Walking (1967) is a drawing Richard Long made by walking across a field. Long articulates space, not as container, but as matter fluctuating in relation to the temporal, embodied activities it enables. Long proposed that our occupations of space are perceived by recursive transgression, which "draws" our presence on the spaces we inhabit. Long's "line" is temporal, appearing as the trace of a mobile subject.[3] It relies not on a static instance of a cut, but an unravelling of ongoing, lived moments connected to one another.

What if the mechanisms of the line could describe space, not as an abstract notion of extent, but as matter fluctuating in relation to the temporal, embodied activities it enables, and which ultimately come to define it? The work discussed here—four pencil and charcoal drawings titled *Four Ways to Occupy a Hearth*—are explorations prompted by this question.

Based on the overlapping spatial geometries for additions to two residential projects, the four drawings converge around the central motif of the hearth. Two of the drawings correspond with the kitchen and dining areas of each residence, the other two with the living area on the other side of the hearth. The plans are then superimposed, not just aligning one residence with the other but also compressing time, collating one set of design decisions against the other [fig. 2].

In addition to the counterpoint set by the two plans, the four drawings are composed at an angle, using a 1 cm isometric grid. While the plans are drawn on two-dimensional planes, the presence of the grid as background and its oblique angle suggests that the plans contain a potential for a further dimension. Overlaying the isometric grid, the line-work is primarily comprised of charcoal dust. Charcoal is a medium that lends itself perfectly to accumulation, and also to removal, to making and unmaking. The charcoal areas identify the parts of the plans where most time is accumulated, so that the most extended and repeated occupation correlates with the darkest areas of the drawings. Fixed joinery and architectural elements such as walls or windows are left blank. After masking part of the drawing, the charcoal is applied in the form of dust, darkening with each application [fig. 3]. Tape is then placed over the charcoal and further lines are scribed onto and through the tape. When the tape is removed, it removes with it the charcoal below [fig. 1, 3–4]. The densities of charcoal are coded in terms of habitual durations and intensity, and the further layer of gridded line-work articulates nuanced daily activities: paths of travel; lines of sight from one room to the other; the centralized configuration of a television as focal point; the optimal seating position whilst dining, nearest the hearth and at the same time allowing views into the garden or a distant tree [fig. 5–6].

2 Katica Pedisic, *Four Ways to Occupy a Hearth*, process drawings and detail 2017. Collaged photocopies, 96 × 82 cm.

fig. 3

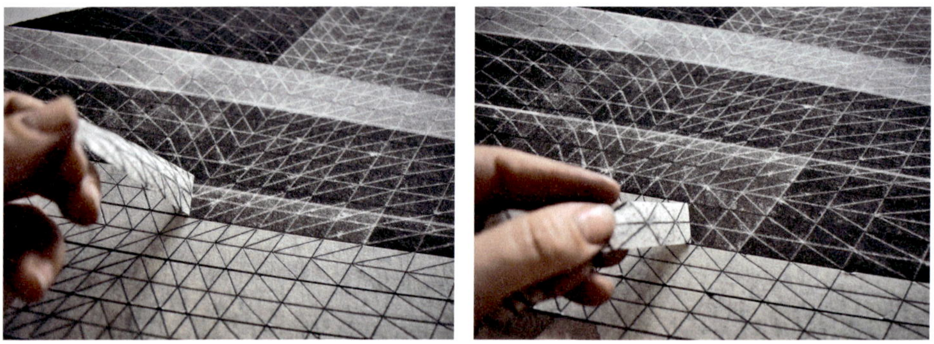

fig. 4

3 Katica Pedisic, *Four Ways to Occupy a Hearth*, panel 4 (detail), 2017. Ink, pencil, and compressed charcoal on Arches paper, 59.4 × 42 cm.

4 Katica Pedisic, *Four Ways to Occupy a Hearth*, tape transfer process (detail), 2017.

fig. 5

5 Katica Pedisic, *Four Ways to Occupy a Hearth*, panel 4 (detail), 2017.

6 Katica Pedisic, *Four Ways to Occupy a Hearth*, panels 1, 2, 3 and 4, 2017. Ink, pencil, and compressed charcoal on Arches paper, each 59.4 × 42 cm, overall dimensions 122.8 × 88 cm.

fig. 6

The line-work marks out daily registers, recurrent details of habitation rather than indicating physical structures. The resulting set of drawings propose an architectural plan in reverse: occupational understanding affecting, rather than affected by, spatial allocation. The accumulated lines saturate the plan with a million moments (or thereabouts) of temporal instances, lending a dimensional presence to space.

A further exploration of a plan's spatial measures is proposed by placing the plan not within a usual x/y axial, rectilinear arrangement, but over a background of an isometric grid which introduces a perspectival skew [fig. 7]. Douglas Huebler's conceptual and seminal *Xerox Book* drawings (1968)[4] demonstrated that much about architectural drawings operates on faith—the capacity of a flat page to evoke depth—positioning the drawing between the registers of two and three dimensions and always fluttering between the two.

What could an alternative mode of drawing plans reveal—plans as accumulations of lines? What might a plan look like when its space is described, not by its parameters, but the accumulated saturation of occupation? The plan becomes the site of an ongoing conversation, where the possibilities of the line play out their potentials across time and across dimensions. Defined by a temporal unfolding, *Four Ways to Occupy a Hearth* suggests alternative ways in which plans could be explored as an unfolding phenomenon in flux, as space suffused with time.

fig. 7

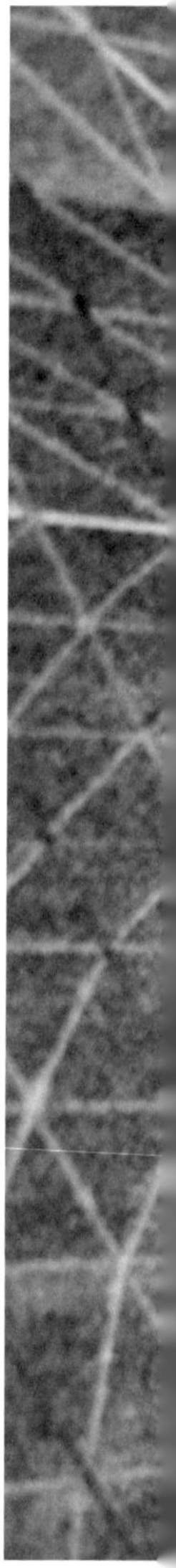

7 Katica Pedisic, *Four Ways to Occupy a Hearth*, panel 3 (detail), 2017.

1 Joana Neves, "Anamorphoses," in *Plans: Marie-Jeanne Hoffner*, ed. Marie Ange Brayer, Joana Neves, and David Sanson (Paris: Roven, 2010), vii.
2 Jeremy Till, *Architecture Depends* (Cambridge, MA and London: MIT Press, 2009), 118.
3 Brian Hatton, "Motive and Motif," in *Mobility of the Line: Art, Architecture, Design*, ed. Ivana Wingham (Basel: Birkhäuser, 2013), 214.
4 Seth Siegelaub, *Xerox Book* (New York: Seth Siegelaub, John Wendler, 1968).

Julia Sedlock and
Joseph Altshuler

fig.1

Creaturely Plans

Reorienting Ground and Subject

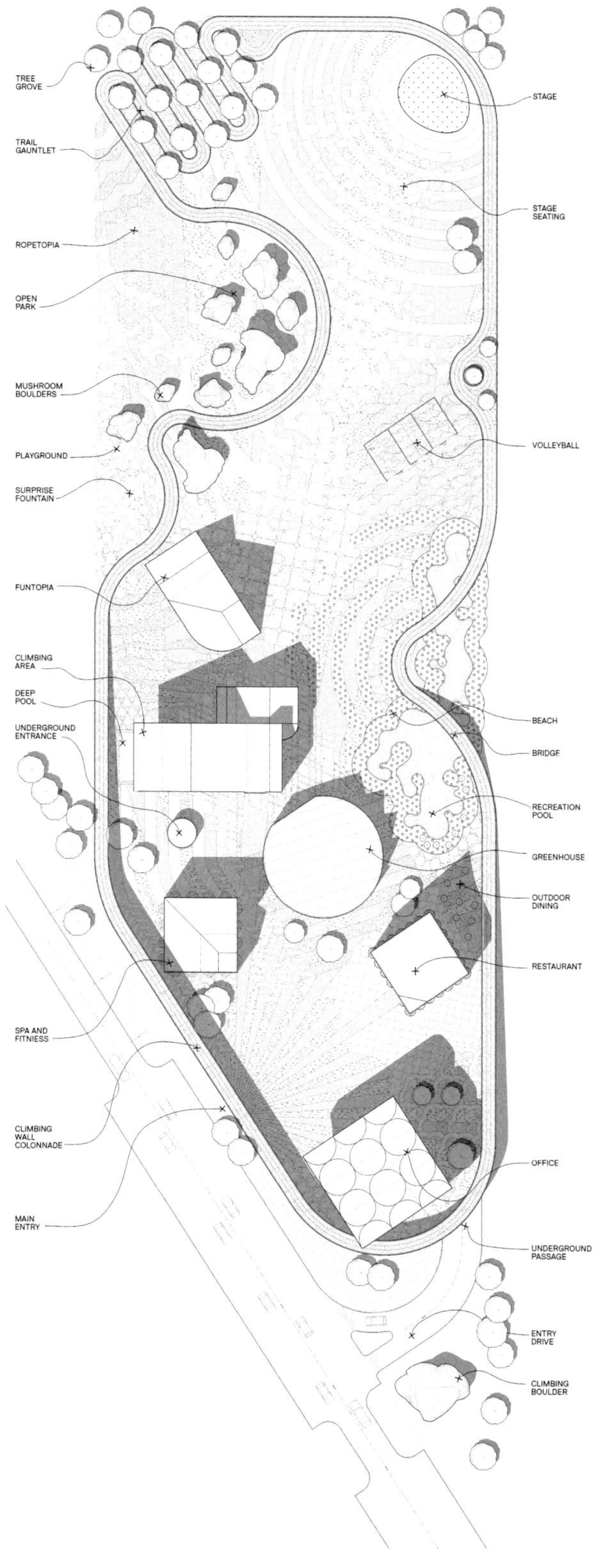

fig. 2

1 Design With Company, *Collider Activity Center*, 2013, site plan.

2 Design With Company, *Collider Activity Center*, 2013, site plan.

This study of the post-anthropocentric plan is part of a larger body of design research for a forthcoming book with the working title *Creatures are Stirring*. The book explores how zoomorphism[1] and animism in contemporary architectural practice contribute to an expanded subjectivity and agency in political, environmental, and economic activity. The project argues that animate architectural form is endowed with a subjectivity of its own, rendering architectural objects as companions that cohabitate our urban and rural landscapes, charting a course towards a post-anthropocentric and post-capitalist condition that empowers human and nonhuman subjects alike.

Architectural creatures—that is, buildings that resemble real animals or fictional beasts—are often dismissed as gestures of whimsy, yet represent an opportunity for architecture to intensify its performance in the world. From Jean-Jacques Lequeu to John Hejduk, a genealogy of architectural precedent demonstrates how creature-like form and character interacts with context and audience. In contemporary practices, the predecessor of architectural creatures is "shape architecture," as theorized by R. E. Somol and embodied by the work of Rem Koolhaas, among others.[2] While creature architecture samples from Somol's ideas about shape, logo, and "graphic expediency" as a means of audience building,[3] it differentiates itself from shape architecture through its relationship to context and engagement with its surroundings. Somol describes shape architecture as otherworldly, an aloof and disinterested monolith landed from another planet, and clearly indebted to the Koolhaasian "f**k context"[4] ethos. In contrast, creatures are inner-worldly and gregarious. Emerging from the depths of dreams and fantasies, they are monsters in closets or from our favorite horror stories, as well as imaginary friends. They are defined by intensity, intimacy, immediacy, and interaction, and consequently, by an investment in context—not necessarily an interest in fitting in or replicating, but rather a commitment to engage and enact a new narrative with their surroundings. Despite this clear distinction between the creaturely and their shapely predecessors, these formally articulated architectural creatures shape architecture's tendency to operate formally, with a strong emphasis on section and elevation in a way that provides an opportunity to perceive these buildings as animate beings with their own character and personality. However, this focus on section and elevation diminishes the important role of plan in manifesting a critical facet of our creature-based ontology: the enactment of the human subject as a creaturely being through an augmented interaction with context. Creature-based ontology suggests that beyond developing the perception of a creaturely building as a companion being with its own subjectivity, we might also adjust the perception of our own human personhood to acknowledge all that we have in common with these creature companions, which the conventional built environment rarely recognizes, and so that we might understand ourselves, nonhuman people, and built things as companion creatures inhabiting a shared and expanded environment.

The case studies in this article use architectural conventions and assumptions about the meaning of and relationship between plan and section to simultaneously draw attention to and question our dominant place in the world as bipedal upright organisms, by presenting alternatives to our "right-side-up" orientation. Through their fluid relationship between plan and section, these projects deconstruct our "right-side-up" definition of plan in order to construct environments that reorient our relationship to ground, in much the same way that airborne, aquatic, or sticky-footed creatures inhabit the world. All three projects use plan to prompt us to suspend our human disbelief and to enter into the fictional world of the creature.

From a Donkey's Figure to Its Hooves

Le Corbusier's notion of plan as generator asserted his reverence for human rational planning, as well as his disdain for the pack donkey's way.[5] For us, the chaotic meandering line that defined the pre-Modern city may provide a point of entry for our interest in the suspension of human disbelief, and a potential re-entry for the perspective of the creature. Far from the chaos implied by Le Corbusier's donkey path, the case studies below embrace the sensibility of the nonrational through their unabashed privileging of figural form over geometric order, specifically in plan.

Plan has a reputation as the strong and silent type. As generator, it typically plays the role out of sight and out of mind, imposing organizational authority upon us at the volume of a whisper, or as a subliminal command that operates on both the body and the unconscious. Sections and elevations tend to "speak" more loudly than plans—they communicate through visual cues like shape, volume, light, material, color, etc., that are immediately accessible to human perception. Conversely, plans communicate through quieter tactics. Not always perceived consciously through sensory stimuli, plans establish organizational structures, circulation patterns, programmatic sequence, and contextual relationships to construct an architectural narrative that is generated through the accumulation and cognitive processing of perception, engagement, and experience. The plan positions the human subject within the story of a project.

Like the meandering path of a donkey, the figural condenses conventional meaning with an indirect and sometimes surprising outcome, as opposed to the precision and truth of rational geometry. The term *figure* is broad and versatile, applied to many cultural disciplines including painting, sculpture, linguistics, mathematics, landscape, and architecture. Even within architecture, the term is fluid with multiple meanings and uses. Its origins connect to the makeup, proportions, and shape of the human body, and for Western architects, the figure became a proportional system to delineate relationships between parts and wholes. In its many applications, from human "scale figure" to figure-ground, the term generally connotes the representation of an idea that is extracted from reality or truth and made common in use through assigned definitions and cultural understanding. Alan Colquhoun's 1978 essay "Form and Figure" notes examples where the rhetorical use of figure contains a synthetic power to "crystallize" a "series of complex relationships (...) to suggest the richness and complexity of reality."[6] Colquhoun's point helps to articulate this essay's interest in the way figural plan strategies draw attention to themselves as legible or semi-legible translations of complex contextual relationships and storylines.

The Good, the Bad, and the Nonbinary

The specific architectural figures Colquhoun references come laden with the heavy baggage of historicist postmodernism and the traditional meanings assigned to particular configurations of architectural elements. In his 2005 essay "Go Figure," Ron Witte of WW Architecture resuscitates the figure for contemporary architecture by differentiating what he calls the "good figure" from the "bad," i. e., the historicist and representational tendencies of postmodernism.[7] Witte's update pushes the figure towards abstraction, privileging legibility over resemblance, and introducing new qualities such as multiplicity, resonance, and density in its definition of "good figure" as a means to achieve a deep integration of systems through the coupling of floor, wall, and ceiling with program, form, and technology. Witte's 21st-century update added a useful layer of performative potential to the figure's repertoire, yet this position manifested in the early aughts as a series of projects that were heavily dependent on the use of fillet, or rounded corners, in plan as a means to achieve the level of figural abstraction that Witte deems appropriate. Apologetic for their overuse of the fillet, Witte defends its efficacy in plan for its ability to "control a far greater bandwidth of architectural relationships" than the sectional-fillet which "rarely, if ever, escapes narcissistic (...) pronouncements of itself" and is "heavily dependent on the semantics and narratives that bogged down the 1980s."[8]

Alternatively, in "Plan v. Section," a story by Jimenez Lai of Bureau Spectacular, two protagonists debate the pros and cons of the two orthographic projections, with one defending his love of section because "it's like cloud watching (...) I can imagine anything,"[9] while lambasting plans

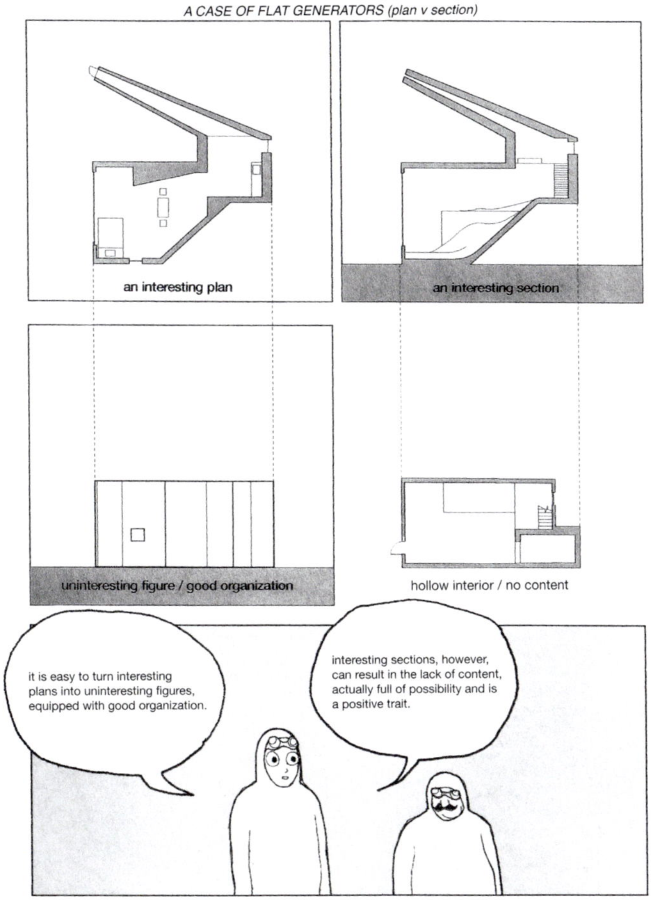

fig. 3

3 "Plan v. Section," excerpt from Jimenez Lai, *Citizens of No Place: An Architectural Graphic Novel* (New York: Princeton Architectural Press, 2012), 99.

because they rely on the unattainable "god's-eye view that humans can never experience" and complex plans become simple box-like extrusions when viewed from the ground [fig. 3]. However, other projects by Bureau Spectacular offer a third way out of the plan-versus-section debate, where qualities of plan and section are interchangeable. In several of his stories, Lai uses the conceit of outer space's zero-gravity condition to assert this possibility, and then tests its potential in small installation projects such as *Phalanstery Module* (2008) and *White Elephant* (2012), where occupiable follies are untethered from ground and endowed with the freedom to rotate their orientation such that the distinction between plan and section becomes irrelevant [fig. 4]. Our interest is to find ways that translate this concept of fluidity between plan and section from a special effect only possible without gravity or on other planets, to an earthly effect that can be achieved through disciplinary means.

While figural strategies in section often privilege symbolic communication and expression, the figural plan offers an opportunity to leverage

fig. 4

more operative and organizational effects. We are interested in figures that provide a loose fit between legibility on the ground and the identity or activities that they contain or enable. In particular, we appreciate figural plans that initiate overlapping and the traits of simultaneous identities and characters, and that prompt people to make decisions about how they affiliate with and occupy these various positions. Graphics on the ground, landscape patterns, shapely walls, and other built edifices all play an equally important role in choreographing a participatory and nonauthoritarian occupation of the ground.

The projects discussed below rebrand figural gestures in plan through analogies to creaturely cognition, locomotion, and subjectivity. These analogies challenge assumptions about the fixed relationship between plan and section and suggest more fluid, nonbinary, and companionable ontologies for inhabiting possible worlds. While the analogies to known creatures (worms, birds, and ticks) may harbor existing anthropocentric biases about power relationships among humans and animals, we believe that the fictional and biological familiarity of these animal positions will help push out the existing species-based hegemony of the human position and invite non-bipedal-based worldviews to expand the architectural imagination.

Worm's-Eye Plan

> When my ancestor on the East African savanna hoisted herself for the first time onto her hind legs, it was a journey of far more than a few feet. It was a journey into a new world. She was immediately a creature whose world was framed not by the top of the grass and the baked mud of the ground, but by the far horizon and the stars. The Genesis account was suddenly true: she had visual dominion over the things that crept and crawled. She saw them in a way that they did not see her: they looked up to her, and she couldn't help looking down on them (...) She saw their backs, their contexts, and the patterns of their lives.[10]

In this description of our ancestors' transition from quadrupedal to bipedal locomotion, writer Charles Foster captures a condition of human evolution that defines the anthropocentric perspective through which our relationships to both culture and the environment are defined—that the view from our upright position is the basis of our ability to see the contexts and relationships of all other species in a way that they cannot see themselves, and which provides the basis for our presumed supremacy. The idiom, a "worm's-eye view," meaning a limited or narrow-minded understanding, is shackled in an anthropocentric cognition of the world in which only a conventional human perspective, with a vantage point six feet above the ground, can produce meaningful comprehension. In architectural representation, the worm's-eye projection, and the worm's-eye axonometric in particular, challenge the limitations associated with the colloquial usage of this term Worm's-eye projection offers a revelatory and seemingly impossible view of a space, effectively removing the presence of the opaque ground plane that most other architectural viewpoints assume, yet, at that same, interrogating the makeup of the ground itself.

4 Bureau Spectacular, *Phalanstery Module*, 2008.

Bureau Spectacular's *Pool Party* elevates nine found swimming pool basins above the open triangular courtyard at the museum MoMA PS1 in New York City. Each pool is a different industry standard model that exhibits a distinctive figural shape: kidney bean, L-shape, chevron, etc. With most of the pools positioned right side up and a couple positioned upside down, the variety of figural shapes and concavities create an array of figural character traits, high in the air for everyone to see. In effect, the project re-enacts the

fig. 5

viewpoint of a worm's-eye plan drawing, casting the human occupants into the role of virtual earthworms, wriggling their way through the invisible substratum of simulated soil, place-held by squiggly benches and meandering patches of sod. The high perimeter concrete walls of the museum's courtyard reinforce the fiction that the audience is exploring a subterranean world [fig. 5].

Pool Party literally removes the ground within which swimming pools are typically embedded, replacing it with a diaphanous structural grid. By reorienting our optical imagination into a kind of virtual "underworld" suggested by a worm's vantage point, the project challenges us to reconsider the planes of human creaturely inhabitation and perception that we frequently take for granted. By amplifying the spatial presence of shadows, removing our typical reference to the horizon, and teasing if not completely denying our access to pools of desire, the project reminds us that the sensory inputs and contextual cues for how we apprehend our environment are a cognitive construction of our subjective viewpoint.

fig.6

fig.7

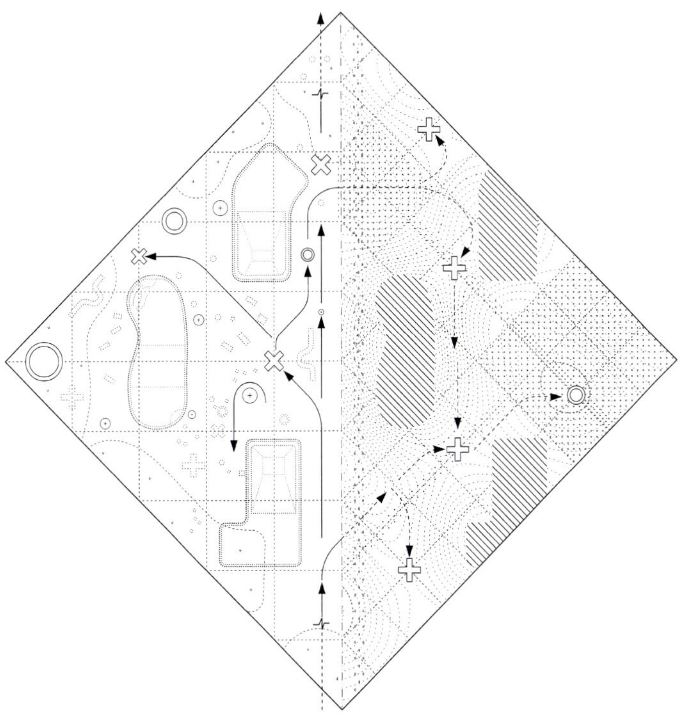

5 Bureau Spectacular, *Pool Party*, 2016, perspective.

6 Bureau Spectacular, *Pool Party*, 2016, plan concept.

7 Bureau Spectacular, *Pool Party*, 2016, plan.

Pool Party also employs its simulation of a worm's-eye view to reveal that the assumption of human uprightness defines plan as opposed to section. For a creature with sticky feet or locomotors like earthworms, the orientation of plan seamlessly transitions into section and vice versa, with little regard for gravity. The project privileges cognition over experience, reorienting the spatial qualities that we typically associate with section such as vaulted or sculptural ceiling contours, empathic relationships between the body and proportions, symbolic expression and, most of all, the eye-level perception of simultaneous spaces, into the gravity of plan [fig. 6]. The figural character, e. g., that seductive kidney bean shape, of the swimming pools is delineated in plan, but if you swim according to a conventional swimming stroke technique in a pool, the body is reoriented such that the planimetric shape of the pool is temporarily registered as "section" relative to the horizontal orientation of the swimmer. As a result, the pools provide an instructional catalyst for transposing occupational spatial qualities that we associate with section into the organizationally instrumental potentials of floor plan [fig. 7]. The purpose of this reorientation is not to regress to a pre-evolutionary position on four legs or belly, but to remind us of our capacity as human creatures to occupy a variety of positions and therefore perspectives, rather than remaining fixed to our upright view that separates us from other species and perpetuates our destructive myth of planetary dominance.

Bird's-Eye Plan

Pita & Bloom's project *The New Zocalo* transposes Augustus Woodward's 1805 masterplan for Detroit into a colorful architectural plan for a contemporary cultural complex set upon a large figural plinth. The project engages visual and figural sampling at a variety of scales, vantage points, and orientations, extracting familiar colors, shapes, and profiles from the surrounding neighborhood and abstracting and recombining them into strange new configurations and assemblages. The site plan samples the hexagonal pattern of triangular blocks with major and minor intersections from Woodward's plan and transposes them upon the triangular boundary of a given site in southwest Detroit [fig. 8]. By shifting, magnifying, and reorienting fragments of the urban plan's fabric, Pita & Bloom generate a figural plinth with a jagged, irregular edge that exaggerates the sampled influences and provides a counterpoint for the site's more rigid geometry. In effect, the plinth's elevated surface becomes a kind of caricature or cartogram of the urban influences that underpin the geography and culture of the place, inviting people strolling on its colorfully patterned paving to encounter strange abstractions and distortions of their local context.

The plinth is punctuated by six separate cultural and commercial buildings [fig. 9]. Each building's form is generated by the three-dimensional extruded intersection of two section figures and one plan figure, sampled from nearby buildings [fig. 10]. According to the architects, the "tracings of these typical Detroit buildings are merged both to produce new wholes and to define space with figural contours."[11] By extruding figural silhouettes in multiple directions to produce compound figures, these buildings start to equivocate and even confuse the figural capacities of plan and section; there is a sense that these buildings might rotate into a different plane, substituting plan for section at a moment's notice. To enhance this effect even further, the sphere of influence of each building cluster is made explicit by a shadow-like graphic projection on the ground that articulates the individual sectional profiles required to produce the 3D figural form, cast from each side. In effect, the sectional figures are reproduced directly as graphic plan figures, saturated with sampled colors and textures.

New Zocalo challenges the conventional construction of human subjectivity by offering something akin to a bird's-eye view. A bird's-eye view is closest to true plan with its vantage point from the sky. However, a bird also experiences a continuously shifting perspective as it takes off from ground to sky, transitions from vertical to horizontal motion, and then returns to ground or to perch in a treetop or a roof. In this way, its relationships to figure and ground are always changing—at one moment a building's elevation looms above, at another the building's roof is ground, or the elevation drifts by alongside as it flies down the street. The sampled urban fragments of *New Zocalo* build an immersive experience that reproduces this alternative construction of the city. Elevation is projected onto ground, ground is projected onto elevation; solid figural extrusions bleed into transparent figural frame structures. Ground is layered upon ground. And in the process, new kinds of urban architectural space are created. Unlike the Nolli plan's black and white figure-ground representation of public and private, or inside and out, Pita & Bloom's urban experience is defined by multiple grounds at several elevations and scales, and multiple thresholds that extend and distort transitions between inside and out.

By physically treading on these familiar fragments in plan as opposed to viewing them elevationally in an exhibit display, the content becomes experiential rather than interpretative. The fragments cannot be readily dissected, classified, or analyzed, but as a series of overlapping ground figures, they become a living diagram suggesting other ways to occupy the ground. In this sense, the project operates like a full-scale occupiable map of a fictional cityscape [fig. 11]. As opposed to a GPS that directs you along a specific path to reach a fixed endpoint, this map exposes the construction and logic of possible pathways to discover new and open-ended routes, while revealing that the urban ground itself (a plinth after all!) is a fabrication of the imagination.

fig. 9

fig. 8

8 Pita & Bloom, *The New Zocalo*, 2016, site diagram.

9 Pita & Bloom, *The New Zocalo*, 2016, site axonometric.

10 Pita & Bloom, *The New Zocalo*, 2016, axonometric.

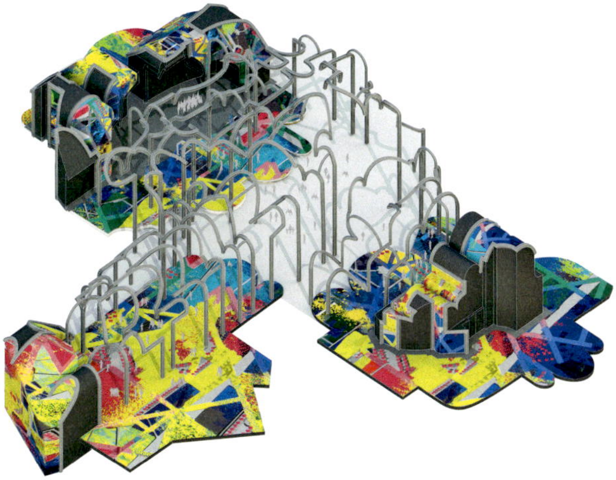

fig.10

fig.11

11 Pita & Bloom,
The New Zocalo, 2016,
diagram.

fig. 12

fig. 13

Tick's-Eye Plan

Design With Company's proposal for the *Collider Activity Center* in Sofia, Bulgaria (2013), circumscribes its site with a 0.75 km figural pedestrian track that collects multiple zones of activity into a coherent masterplan. As the headquarters for a rock-climbing company, the entire project serves as a billboard for and demonstration of alternative forms of human engagement with ground, meaning the surface on which we locomote and from which we orient ourselves to the rest of the world, whether it be horizontal, vertical, or somewhere in between. Most literally, this includes climbing walls on the exterior skins of the buildings and perimeter wall, a boulder field, pools and water features, and a ropes course and playground. Like a tick that nestles on the side of a deer's body, the relative "ground" surface for humans fluctuates relative to gravity as humans climb their way across the architecture's vertical and canted surfaces.

12 Design With Company, *Collider Activity Center*, 2013, aerial perspective.

13 Design With Company, *Collider Activity Center*, 2013, site diagram.

Even the most straightforward inhabitation of the horizontal ground plane is translated into a locomotive adventure that is narrated by the plan

fig. 14

drawing, specifically the figural pedestrian track that loops its way around the entire site. At one end of the site, the track parallels the tapering property line and rises above the ground as an elevated walkway, while at the other end, it twists and meanders along labyrinthine coils at grade. The result is a super-scaled planimetric figure that, from an aerial vantage point, evokes the silhouette of a cartoonish cetacean fluttering its caudal fin [fig. 12]. For a pedestrian walking or jogging on the track, the experience of moving along a sequence of sweeping radial curves, oblique straightaways and winding slalom produced by the coiled "trail gauntlet" provides an ever-changing perspective and relationship to the ground, prompting bodies and buildings to cohabitate within the campus loop [fig. 13].

The totality of the aquatic creature is never visible to human visitors scurrying along the ground plane, and in turn, the pictorial reference provides a logo-like graphic for the would-be campus map, as opposed to a physically present symbol laden with meaning for visitors to interpret. Inside the ring of the super figure, the ground is coated with brightly colored materials and patterns that solicit multiple uses and associations. The material applications are organized according to an oblique 30 m^2 grid that also accommodates six different buildings within its graphical matrix. While each material and pattern is centered within a given grid cell, some patterns bleed into, overlap, and underlap patterns in other cells, creating rich and unexpected connections and affiliations between disparate regions of the ground [fig. 1]. So too do, the footprints of the six buildings exhibit fluid alignments to the grid. The oscillating synchronicity of the buildings, material patterns, and superfigure create an ongoing sense of checks and balances for the identity and power of any given component of the plan. This is a figural patchwork of lines, surfaces, volumes, and people moving in space, where each entity exerts a mutual and egalitarian force upon the others [fig. 2]. The buildings within the campus are clustered towards one end of the track, distributed within the oblique grid. However, their relationships are casual, shifted to one side or the other of the grid cell they occupy, sometimes rotated at 45° angles to one another, and nestled closer to one neighbor than another. Furthermore, each building is a character with a personality and presence of its own, defined by a uniquely expressive silhouette, with idiosyncratic features composed by architectural elements—a leggy colonnade, a coiffed saw-tooth roofline, an oversized heady gable.

As formal creatures in their own right, the buildings' spacing and orientation in relationship to one another is not just a matter of plan organization, but of plan-based storytelling. The site plan that fixes the footprints of these creatures to the ground also determines who will face each other and at what proximity. In other words, it suggests who are friends and who are enemies. These relationships are determined by both the fixed location of the structures, but also the constantly changing location and perspective of the viewer. As a human cohabitant moves around the figural track, their view of the creature cluster is always shifting—at moments brushing up against the underbelly or seeing a pink head peeking out from behind the massive grey rhino-like body to spy on you [fig. 14]. Or rounding another corner to see that the other side of the pink head is too preoccupied to spy on you because she is kissing buddies with the jolly green-peaked gryphon. While on the far side of the track, you are no longer a companion to the crew of creatures, but rather an observer, watching as they move together and then apart, like the fickle love stories of a tawdry telenovela.

14 Design With Company, *Collider Activity Center*, 2013, perspective.

Conclusion

Philosopher Timothy Morton states that "a functional definition of 'child' is 'someone who is still allowed to talk with an inanimate stuffed animal as if it were not only an actual life-form but also conscious.'"[12] What we see is one thing, and how we process it is another. The experience of seeing an architectural creature—an object that re-presents itself as a friend and potential companion or the representation of such object—grants permission to an adult human to engage with an inanimate object the way they once did with a stuffed toy. In this case, architecture's capacity to transform human subjectivity operates through a "seeing is believing" framework. That is to say, "if you do not believe that architectural objects are animate subjects, then I will show you how a building that looks like an animal will make you feel like you can empathize with it, that it has personality and character, that you can interact with it." Alternatively, the projects in this article operate through the mechanism of "believing is seeing," where belief fueled by perceptual and cognitive experience translates into seeing the world through a new lens, specifically through the lens of the creaturely human subject.

Our current lens is one that separates and elevates us as human subjects above the mute objects of buildings and the lesser bodies of other species, and through that separation justifies our dismissal or often violent mistreatment of objects and bodies that are not our own. Emancipation from this violence of anthropocentrism requires us to unlearn the spatial and ontological cognition of how we see and understand the world from our upright position, and recognize our capacity to share an alternative subjective perspective with the buildings and creatures who are our companions in the world. Perhaps counterintuitively, a creature-based ontology invites us to adopt a bit of animism in order to catalyze this broad perceptual shift in our human personhood. The discipline of architecture is well aware that the floor plan as an architectural representation assumes great power in enacting how the spaces we inhabit organize and operate. In turn, the projects analyzed in this article demonstrate how plan-based creaturely techniques apply perceptual pressure that reminds human subjects that their vertical orientation to ground plane is one of many options. Plans like these challenge the anthropocentric assumptions of the status quo that dictate a specifically upright position as the dominant and privileged point of view. Whether it involves a non-terranean simulation that pushes out our supreme human privilege or a narrative choreography that casts our existing humanity into novel fictionalized roles, creaturely plans initiate new modes of companionable existence.

Zoomorphism refers to forms that esemble the shape, image, or likeness of nimals.

R. E. Somol, "12 Reasons to Get Back n Shape," in *Content*, ed. OMA and Rem Koolhaas (Cologne: Taschen, 2004): 6–87; and R. E. Somol, "Green Dots 01," *Hunch: Berlage Institute Report* 11 Winter 2006–7): 35. Somol's definition of hape architecture is summarized by his ve points for "how to do logo buildings":) Intensify an element; 2) Extend the ne; 3) Develop a precise but vague ilhouette; 4) Saturate with a monotone reatment; 5) Bore through it. These oints describe shared qualities of rojects such as OMA's Casa da Musica nd CCTV headquarters, MVRDV's Mirador Housing, and Neutelings Riedijk's Sphinx Housing and Shipping nd Transport College.

Somol, "12 Reasons to Get Back in hape," 86–87.

Rem Koolhaas, "Bigness (Or the Problem of Large)," in *S, M, L, XL: Office or Metropolitan Architecture, Rem Koolhaas and Bruce Mau*, ed. Jennifer igler (New York: Monacelli Press, 1995), 95–516.

5 Le Corbusier, *The City of Tomorrow*, trans. Frederick Etchells (Cambridge, MA: MIT Press, 1971).

6 Alan Colquhoun, "Form and Figure," *Oppositions* 12 (Spring 1978): 28–32.

7 Ron Witte, "Go Figure," *Log* 5 (Spring-Summer 2005): 76–81.

8 Ron Witte, "Let's Get Figural," *Fresh Meat* 3 (Fall 2010): 33.

9 Jimenez Lai, *Citizens of No Place: An Architectural Graphic Novel* (New York: Princeton Architectural Press, 2012).

10 Charles Foster, *Being a Beast* (New York: Metropolitan Books/Henry Holt and Company, 2016), 17.

11 Pita & Bloom, "The New Zocalo," *Log* 37 (2016): 74.

12 Timothy Morton, *Humankind: Solidarity with Nonhuman People* (London and New York: Verso, 2017), 15.

Kassandra Nakas

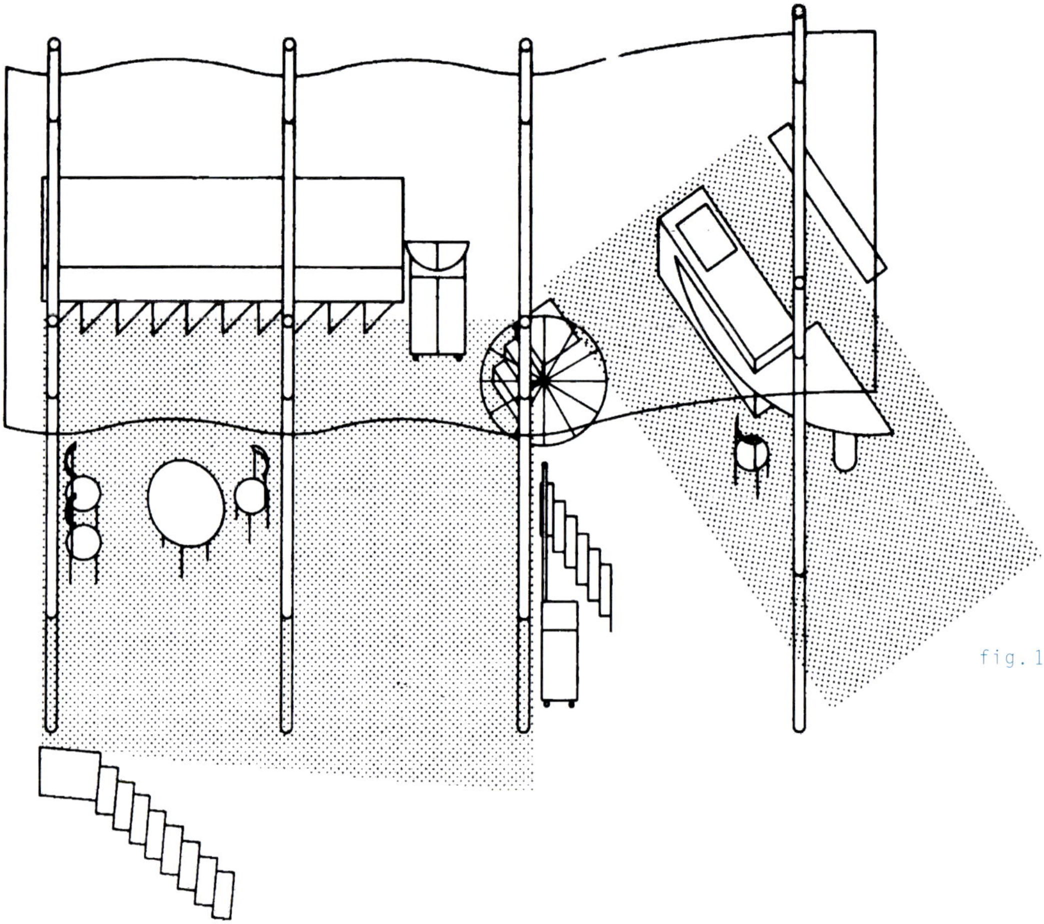

fig. 1

SANAA's Playtime

Communication and Interaction in Kazuyo Sejima's and Ryūe Nishizawa's Architectural Drawings

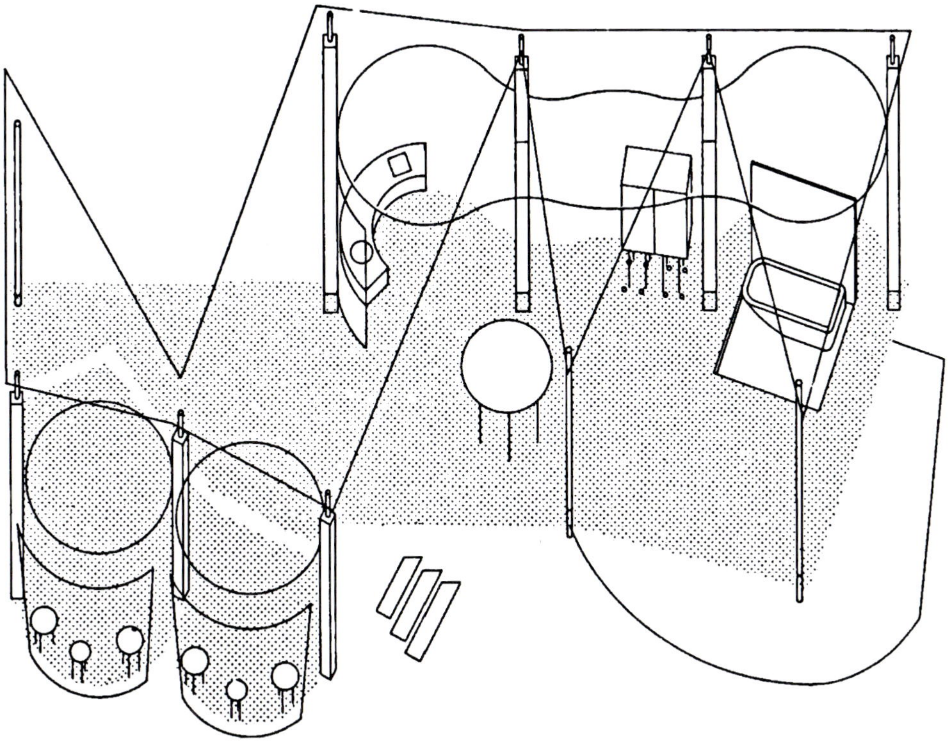

fig. 2

1 Kazuyo Sejima and Associates, *Platform I*, 1987/88.

2 Kazuyo Sejima and Associates, *Platform II*, 1988/90.

Contemporary Japanese architecture is most commonly associated with abstract, Minimalist aesthetic features and a penchant for technologically advanced construction projects. However, for all its cultural-technological savviness, the country's architectural scene exhibits a remarkable predilection for representational media that stress the analog, or rather, the manufactural, handicraft aspects of their creative processes. It is not the digital imagery of computerized representational techniques that dominates the (visual) discourse of contemporary design practices from Japan, but a "strong presence of manual tools," as Olivier Meystre put it in his book *New Representations of Japanese Architecture*.[1] The author, an architect and designer of "architectural depictions"[2] himself, examines drawings, pictures, and models that were created in the design processes of renowned Japanese offices such as Toyō Itō, Kazuyo Sejima, Ryūe Nishizawa and SANAA, Junya Ishigami, Go Hasegawa, Kazuo Shinohara, Hideyuki Nakayama, and others over roughly the past two decades. Meystre's book adds to a growing number of publications that reflect upon the role of drawing and mediation techniques in contemporary design processes.[3] As he says, "a complex interplay of influences [is operating] between the reality of a projected building, and its representation in the form of drawings and models."[4] And while the pioneering work of SANAA, the Tokyo-based office founded by Kazuyo Sejima and Ryūe Nishizawa in 1995, forms a major part of his discussion, it is the interplay between two- and three-dimensional working tools in the process and the reliance on traditional aspects of Japanese design in which Meystre's chief interest lies.

In the following remarks, however, I propose a somewhat different approach to some key features of the office's practice. It will situate the office's drawing practice within the architects' general design processes and the genealogical development of their projects, but also look at the functional statements these drawings address, and the aesthetic implications they convey and effect. I will focus on the somewhat cartoonish quality of some of their most memorable working drawings, and reflect upon their specific function with regard to the office's aesthetic and conceptual program, that is, to create spaces that support human communication and interaction. In SANAA's and Kazuyo Sejima's and Ryūe Nishizawa's individual practices (which they maintain alongside their collaboration), the practice of hand drawing seems, at first sight, somewhat detached from the otherwise restrained, Minimalist architectural vocabulary. Still, the drawings, together with the production of an often immense number of physical models, form the basis of a thoroughly experimental design process, as Kazuyo Sejima outlined in 1996:

> Explanations are often applied to describe the final product once a piece of architecture has been completed. What I am experimenting with is the design process itself, and the variety of possibilities one can discover within it. For me, design is a continuous process of discovery. I focus on two stages within a basic design. In the first stage, there is *no spatial image*, since I do not determine my goals or methods ahead of time. I take a lot of the various elements before me, such as the wishes of the client, the condition of the plot, and whatever ideas I myself might have, and organize them. I put all these together in a system, and then try moving forward into the basic design stage. At this stage, I'm still trying to develop any new possibilities that come into view. In many cases, I still won't have arrived at a definitive sense of what the theme of the structure will be. However, as I continue to pursue all of the possibilities, I and my staff somehow manage to settle on the theme. Precisely how it all comes together I don't exactly know. But this is where basic design really begins.[5]

Sejima's candid remarks reveal a conceptually open and fairly playful approach to her projects, which manifests itself in the collaborative projects with Ryūe Nishizawa as well. The drawing process in these early stages of designing is characterized as a space of multiple possibilities and a realm where manifold narratives may evolve—as a *Möglichkeitsraum*, as you would say in German.[6] Sejima's earliest projects after leaving the office of Toyō Itō, where she had been working from 1981 until 1987, clearly expose these features of openness and flexibility. Tellingly, they are entitled *Platform I* and *II*, 1987/88 and 1988/90, respectively [fig. 1–2]. While the technical term "platform" might not have been as ubiquitous for virtual structures within the operating system of a computer in the late 1980s as it is today, it surely indicated, and still does, the plan or design of a place (or surface) for interchange, exchange, and discussion. Accordingly, the initial drawings for these two housing and studio projects in the rural areas of the Chiba and Yamanashi Prefecture, respectively, show sparse structures that primarily allow for immediate access to and interaction with the surrounding nature. The architect intended to create a "dynamic [and] fluid space,"[7] a space that cautiously intertwines with the natural environment. We can see that there is indeed "no spatial image" in these early stages of designing, as the black-and-white drawings, while offering axonometric projections of the pavilion-like projects, operate on a decidedly diagrammatical and flat formal register. The vertical and horizontal structures seem to float as weightlessly on the paper's surface as the stairs, the built-ins, the stools, chairs, and tables. The equivalence of the drawn lines implies no hierarchy whatsoever between primary (built) and secondary elements (such as the furnishings). There is no defining outline of the plan, and the hatched (rect-)angular areas only subtly indicate the existence of a grounding floor or structure. Yet while the drawn architectural elements insist on an utmost level of abstraction, the simplified forms of furnishing suggest the presence of an inhabitant. His or her (imaginary) actions within the building and interactions with its surroundings are given a maximum of creative leeway, and a high degree of vividness is expressed in the cartoonish drawing style.

Filling the Space

Using the term "cartoon/ish" might seem, for one thing, somewhat inappropriate to describe an architectural language (and its development) that has been recognized for its bold and persistent Minimalism. After all, Minimalist styles in art and architecture have been identified with rather isolating modes of expression, which insist on the "objectness" of its entities and keep the beholder at a distance. Art critic Michael Fried accordingly coined the notion of the "theatricality" of Minimalism, discussing sculptural works of the 1960s which, to his mind, denied any transcendental content and instead confined themselves, in the works of Robert Morris, Donald Judd, and others, to a "presentness" and "literalness" that involve the beholder in his or her corporeal, participating presence.[8] More recently, art and architecture critic Hal Foster has reiterated this argument to some extent in his book *The Art-Architecture Complex* (2011). He argues that Minimalism, as the dominant current aesthetic style besides Postmodernism (as an extension of Pop), "marked the moment when, once again in architectural discourse, attention to surface began to be as important as an understanding of space, and a reading of skin as important as an understanding of structure (...) a scenographic surface of images."[9] The strategies of spatial dissolution in Minimalist works—especially in light installations that challenge one's physical, sensory or temporal spatial experience, as in architectural interventions by James Turrell or Robert Irwin—might indeed seem comparable to the over-exposed, diffuse light that distinguishes some of the most remarkable interior shots of Sejima's and Nishizawa's projects, be it the model photographs of the latter's Screening pavilion in Naoshima (2002), of SANAA's Rolex Learning Center in Lausanne (2010), or artistic approaches such as Walter Niedermayr's images of Nishizawa's Moriyama House in Tokyo (2006).[10] Moreover, emphasizing the scenographic character of Minimalist spaces, which encourage the beholder/attendee to "make use" of the given situation, tempts us to draw another parallel between them and Sejima's and Nishizawa's projects, as will be further expounded in the following remarks.

Then again, using the term "cartoon/ish" and referring to the cultural complex of cartoon imagery when discussing SANAA's drawing practice might not appear as odd as it initially did. Etymologically, the term derives from the French "*carton*," thus hinting at a basic material prerequisite of drawing, (stout) paper. From there, the word denotes 1) a preparatory drawing on solid paper that will serve as a plan for another work of art or design in different media, but of same size, or 2) a humorous or topical illustration in a paper or periodical, often relating to current events.[11] Given the simplistic, abstract, and unrealistic nature of cartoon imagery, it nevertheless—or rather consequently—invites its creator to expand and create narrative structures out of single cartoon images, to generate an animated cartoon that projects bodies in action and their movement in space. If we believe comics theorist Scott McCloud, who has offered the most comprehensive analysis of the visual vocabulary and the logic of the line in cartoons so far, their "simple style" of drawing and their figures' status as a "blank slate" are determining factors for the reader to be able to "give life" to its content, to "fill up" the iconic form.[12] *Lesser* specificity leads to *more* imagination regarding how to "fill" the space "up" with (fictional) life and activity. The depiction of figures follows this same path of reduction and abduction—to use a term coined, for the semiotic discourse, by linguist Charles Sanders Peirce.[13] The less defined a given space or a character is, the more easily we identify with them: "when you enter the world of the *cartoon*, you see *yourself*"; "*Who* I am is irrelevant. I'm just a little piece of *you*," as Scott McCloud introduces his cartoonish alter ego in his book.[14]

Communicating Space

While Anna Hougaard has explored the relationship between abductive and diagrammatic reasoning in architectural drawing processes,[15] my focus here is on the potential for identification that lies in the abstract quality of cartoon style—the "little piece" in which the average beholder can, figuratively speaking, recognize himself or herself, to which they can relate—and which allows them to extrapolate a built construction from a given hand or computer drawing on paper. Or, as Sejima put it, "to jump from the two-dimensional field, to the three-dimensional world."[16] With this statement, the architect admits to the architectural thinking of Toyō Itō, who, in turn, characterized his former associate's work as "diagram architecture."[17] In his own design practice, Itō operates on a similar plane, as the drawings for the Sendai Mediathèque (1995–2001) demonstrate. Here, the defining features are a clearly shaped cubic structure with open and seemingly continuous vertical tubes that perform a multitude of functions from structural support to vertical circulation. Toyō Itō's media-savvy architectural approach, which is also manifest in his writings—his collection of essays *Tarzans in the Media Forest* is a case in point[18]—surely had an impact on the work of Kazuyo Sejima, who often emphasizes her endeavor to reflect upon architecture's potential to engage with what she addresses as the "invisible" structure of information society.[19] The flexible organization of space, the variable dimensions of volumes and the thinness of structures are operative tools within these efforts.

As a result, it seems fair to say that the idea of "space as a means of communication"[20] is the driving force behind the architecture of Sejima, Nishizawa, and their collaborative practice SANAA, and a simplistic, abstract drawing style is supportive of conveying this idea. In this sense, the early concept sketch for SANAA's 21st Century Museum of Contemporary Art in Kanazawa, finalized in 2004, envisioned the basic structure of a transparent circle with vertical boxes within.[21] Both hand- and computer-drawn plan are characterized by spherical and rectangular units within the circle. Thin partitions and evenly allotted gaps in between suggest a free-flowing fluctuation of the museum's visitors; ultimately, exhibition planning and the public's needs determine the volumes and shapes of the passageways. Visitors are free to access the building through four opposing gates, as the museum has no formal front or back. With this projected flow of people through the building and the isolated units of temporary *aggregation* and, then again, *disaggregation* (in the passages from one unit to the other), the layout for Kanazawa metaphorically invokes the pattern of an electronic circuit. In these everyday technical configurations, flows of data (or information or simply energy) in conductive tracks are fed into a system where they coalesce in circuit boards, from where new impulses or signals emerge. Similarly, the architects conceive of their building as a "powerful creative tool" for communal activities, constantly fed in by the input of the visitors and their experiences.[22]

In a similar, even if less complex scope the Glass Pavilion of the Toledo Museum of Art (2001–06) organizes courtyards and functional areas within a clear-cut rectangular plane. However, the rounded-off edges of the thin glass partitions distinguish the drawn plan as a playful, almost speech bubble- or thought bubble-like arrangement, which somewhat stands out against the crystalline serenity of the built structure. The formal tendency towards a jaunty, animated drawn foundation for a built structure is even more stunning in SANAA's initial design for the 2009 Serpentine Gallery Pavilion in London. While the final shaping of the mirror-finished aluminum sheets on thin stainless steel columns connects to the form of a smoke cloud lingering between the trees of Hyde Park, as conveyed in the renderings and construction drawings of the project, an early concept sketch [fig. 3] playfully alludes to a cartoonish, dog-like figure reminiscent of Jeff Koons's iconic balloon dog sculpture (which happens to be made from mirror-finished steel as well). The dynamic organic shape in the early conceptual drawing is rooted in an aesthetic attitude that also informed the architects' object design activities; see the "rabbit chair," which avoided, as Nishizawa put it, a "mathematical, scientific line" in favor of "a hand-drawn line."[23]

3 SANAA, *Serpentine Gallery Pavilion*, London, 2009, concept sketch.

Recapitulating these projects from the 2000s, Sejima's and Nishizawa's design processes reveal, at least on the level of the hand-drawn sketches, drawings, and plans, a bias towards cartoonish style principles. This bias is pretty much obliterated when it comes to the final appearance of their works, especially in its mediated form, in photographs of buildings that are praised for their simplicity and somewhat detached elegance. Yet I would claim that the strategies of simplification, identification, and amplification (of a mood or expression), which are inherent in the stylistic features of cartooning, may be seen as intricately related to the office's pursuit to develop, in their drawing practice, a design vocabulary that compensates for a seemingly aloof elusiveness and that meets the needs of today's technologically advanced culture of communication and interaction.

fig. 3

Let us take a closer look at the architects' project for the municipal Theatre and Arts Centre in Almere, near Amsterdam. The building, part of a master plan developed by the Office for Metropolitan Architecture, is located on the bank of a small lake in the city center. Seen from the city side front, the complex, finalized in 2007, is a rather enclosed structural shell that does not instantly reveal the lightness of its interior. Three blocks appear to float on water, each housing a theater auditorium seating 1,050, 350, and 150 people, respectively. Given the role of the building complex as a site of defining and developing the city's cultural identity, the architects' focus in the design process was on creating spaces for a multitude of possible activities. Accordingly, they created a sort of landscape of adjacent rooms for different purposes. An early sketch of the ground plan shows, from a bird's-eye perspective, the variety of actions and events [fig. 4]. Next to an elongated exhibition space there is a lobby for receptions, a concert hall, a sound studio, meeting rooms and classrooms, co-working offices, workshops and artists' studios, recreation

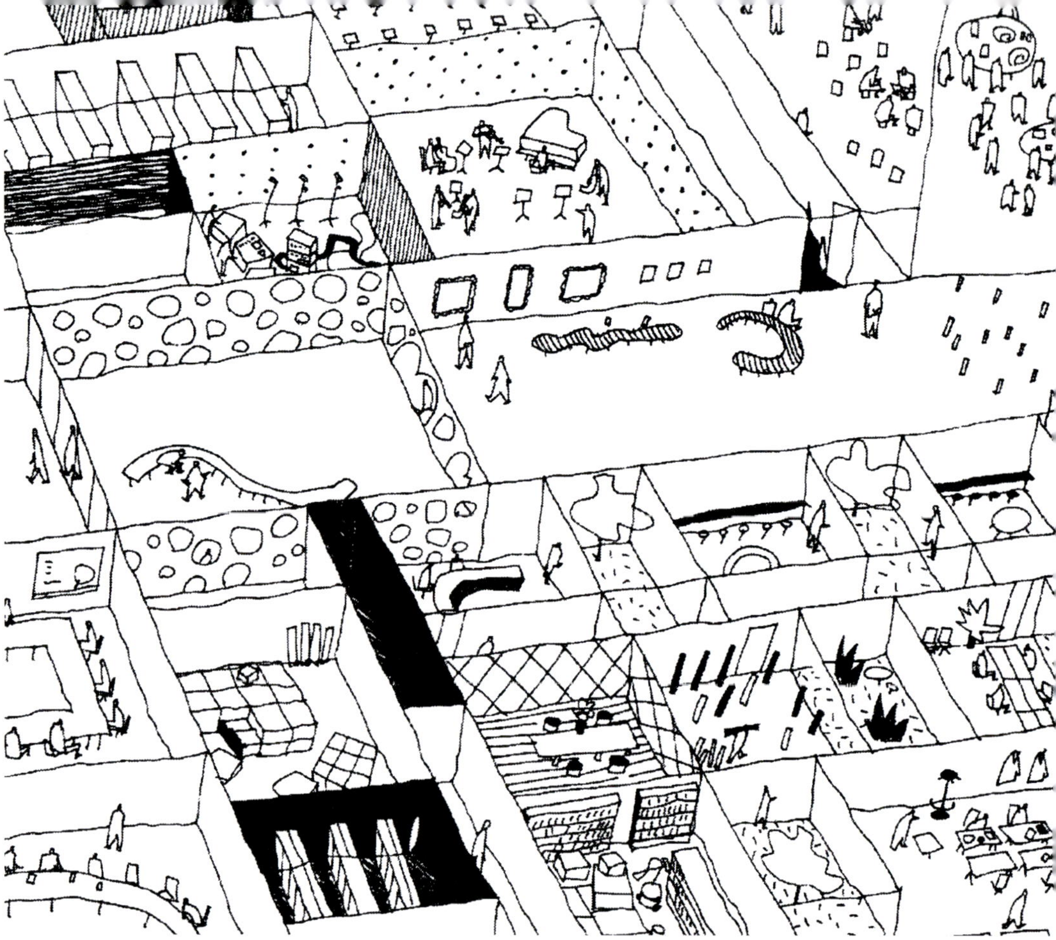

rooms, and more. Every space is distinguished by size and interior design, in an attempt to aesthetically address individuality and diversity. In contrast to the Kanazawa museum, there are no passageways or corridors that separate the spaces for activities, which stresses even more the overarching idea of encounter and communication that defines the building. The plan is hand-drawn in a cartoonish style with simple lines and clear contours.[24] With its highly personal, even idiosyncratic note, it underscores the architects' predilection for the medium: "The reason why we like hand-drawing is because the abstraction it allows is more personal than that on computer," as Ryūe Nishizawa states.[25] Even though it offers a three-dimensional outline of the envisioned array of spaces, it conveys a rather two-dimensional impression, making it easier for the viewer to relate to a conceived sequence of movements through the different zones. He or she will imagine following the roughly drawn human figures with their different activities and interactions. While the dense arrangement of smaller and bigger spaces seems to contradict

4 SANAA, *Municipal Theatre and Cultural Centre*, Almere, 1998 – 2007, isometric sketch.

fig. 4

Sejima's unwillingness to conceive a building from an initial "spatial image," it becomes clear from the drawings that it is the "human factor" that defines the programming of spaces. The free-hand sketches combine linear accuracy with spatial illogicalities such as transparent walls and rooms without openings. Two-dimensionality is stressed by the mosaic-like pattern of spaces and by superposing elements such as the outlined trees. Populating these rooms with schematic yet acting figures emphasizes their respective, and variable, functionalities; the lively rendering of the characters is a far cry from, say, Atelier Bow-Wow's analytical approach to an inhabitant's behavior in architectural space.

The depicted figures are reminiscent of the proverbial Everyman. Given their ageless and faceless contours, they address the "little piece" of each of "us," they are proxies. In their abstract uniformity they stand for the multifaceted modes of usage that this building is supposed to offer. Seen from a Western European perspective, the figures also seem reminiscent of the average type main character in Jacques Tati's famous movies from the late 1950s and 1960s, Monsieur Hulot. Tati's movies—*Mon Oncle* (1958) and *Playtime* (1967) are the most pertinent examples—may be best characterized as filmic meditations on the impact of modernization and mechanization on society and culture, especially architecture.[26] In a mixture of fascination and mockery, they send their protagonist on desperate journeys into technically advanced and highly standardized environments such as private houses that today trade under the name *smart home*, or urban spaces that we came to associate with "non-places," such as airports, shopping malls, and traffic zones.[27] As such, the visual comedies of Jacques Tati offer a vivid reflection upon the potentials and challenges of a highly technologized postmodern culture and society.

Inhabiting Space

Obviously, the Almere drawings, which were created at a very early stage of the project to convey the complex inner organization of an externally monolithic building and its multifaceted functional dimensions, cannot genuinely be read as tongue-in-cheek depictions of the restraints of a post-modern culture of self-discipline and self-modeling—even if a recent essay on SANAA has argued that an overall disciplining demand be a driving force behind their Minimalism[28]: Matthew Allen developed this argument with regards to Nizhizawa's Moriyama House in Tokyo (2005), which, again, has been represented by computer drawings that prominently stress the different usages of the house's individual compartments.[29] Yet the early hand drawings for Almere, which later made way for more abstract and Minimalist models and drawn plans while their communal spirit was taken along throughout the process, seem like literal formulations of an idea that Kazuyo Sejima expressed with regard to the later project for Lausanne, the Rolex Learning Center (2010): that "the space only appears with people. It is just some nondescript space, and if people meet or start to do something, the space appears."[30] In this sense, the cartoonish figures and spaces in the mediation of SANAA's projects are markers of a respective "use value." As such, the practice of their drawn representation seems to have been heavily reduced, if not abandoned, in recent years: given the office's impressive résumé of different types of public buildings, their compensatory function with regard to Minimalist representations of finalized projects seems dispensable.

Yet to fully appreciate these animated sketches it is worth reflecting their relation to the "diagrammatic" character of the office's architecture, as far as it keeps up with some of the most distinctive features of Sejima's early practice. Toyō Itō's much-cited coining of the term from 1996 highlighted a particular quality of the diagram in Sejima's design process. For him, her spatial diagrams are able to convey "the daily activities for which the building is intended in abstract form." Even more, the "building [becomes] essentially the equivalent of the kind of spatial diagram."[31] Her distinctly clear drawings express, in all their formal simplification, a sensitive engagement with the potential uses of the space. This is worth mentioning since—as later authors have pointed out—Sejima's use of the diagram thus differs from the more "scientific" diagrammatic design practices that seem to be more interested in the *process* of designing than in the final, built structure (and its uses).[32] So, while the representational genre of the diagram is, from a historical perspective, burdened by its association with a rationalist architecture indifferent towards the needs and desires of its inhabitants, the diagram in Sejima's and SANAA's practice openly addresses those human requirements. The cartoonish figures populating the floor plan sketches for Almere thus allow a glimpse, even if transitory, into their commitment to an accessible and communicative understanding of architecture.

Olivier Meystre, *Pictures of the*
'oating Microcosm: New Representa-
ons of Japanese Architecture (Zurich:
ark Books, 2017).
See Meystre's website, https://
iviermeystre.com/a-propos (accessed
ıly 29, 2019).
See, among others, Laura Allen and
ıke Caspar Pearson, eds., *Drawing*
ıtures: Speculations in Contemporary
rawing for Art and Architecture
ondon: UCL Press, 2016), http://www.
cl.ac.uk/ucl-press/browse-books/
rawing-futures (accessed July 29, 2019);
nna Katrine Hougaard, Martin Søberg,
ristine Annabell Torp, et al., eds.,
efractions: Artistic Research in
rchitecture (Copenhagen: Architectural
ıblisher B, 2016); Daniel Gehtmann
ıd Susanne Hauser, eds., *Kulturtechnik*
ıtwerfen: Praktiken, Konzepte und
'edien in Architektur und Design
cience (Bielefeld: transcript, 2009);
nna Katrine Hougaard, "The Animate
rawing" (PhD diss., Royal Danish
cademy of Fine Arts, School of
rchitecture, 2016).
Meystre, *Pictures*, 92.
Kazuyo Sejima, "Conversation with
ɔji Taki," *El Croquis* 77, no. I (1999): 22,
terview Tokyo 1996, my emphasis.
The German term *Möglichkeitsraum* is
ıly unsatisfactorily translated into the
ıglish *possibility space*. It designates
physical and psychosocial space of
ıter-)action that conceives reality as a
ollectively) malleable construction.
Sejima, "Conversation with Koji Taki," 30.
Michael Fried, "Art and Objecthood,"
rtforum 5, no. 10 (1967): 12–23.
Hal Foster, *The Art-Architecture*
ɔmplex (London and New York: Verso,
11), 107.
Cf. Meystre, *Pictures,* 53–83 (with
ages of the abovementioned projects).
Oxford English Dictionary Online, s.v.
artoon," http://www.oed.com/view/
ıtry/28312?rskey=QrOmT4&re-
ılt=1&isAdvanced=false#eid (accessed
ɔril 1, 2018).

12 Scott McCloud, *Understanding Comics: The Invisible Art* (New York: Harper Perennial, 1994), 36–37.

13 For a discussion of Peirce's concept of abduction with regard to cartoons and comics, see Stephan Packard, *Anatomie des Comics: psychosemiotische Medienanalyse* (Göttingen: Wallstein, 2006), 121–58.

14 McCloud, *Understanding Comics*, 37.

15 Hougaard, "Animate Drawing," 59–119.

16 Kazuyo Sejima, cited in *Kazuo Sejima, Ryūe Nishizawa, The Conversation Series, 26*, ed. Hans Ulrich Obrist (Cologne: Verlag der Buchhandlung Walther König, 2012), 85.

17 Toyō Itō, "Diagram Architecture," *El Croquis* 77, no. I (1996): 18–24.

18 Toyō Itō, *Tarzans in the Media Forest* (London: AA Publications, 2011).

19 Sejima, "Conversation," *El Croquis* 77(I)+99+121/122 (2007), 16

20 Sejima, cited in Pedro Gadanho and Sarah Resnick, eds., *A Japanese Constellation: Toyo Ito, Kazuyo Sejima, SANAA, Ryūe Nishizawa, Sou Fujimoto, Akihisa Hirata, Junya Ishigami* (New York: The Museum of Modern Art, 2016), 79.

21 An image of this sketch is reproduced in *El Croquis* 121/122 (1999), 60.

22 "A Conversation with Kazuyo Sejima and Ryūe Nishizawa," in "Sistemas de Continuidad/Continuity Systems: SANAA 2011–2015," *El Croquis* 179/180 (2015): 23, cited in: Phoebe Springstubb, "SANAA. 21st Century Museum of Contemporary Art, Kanazawa, Japan, 1999–2004," in Gadanho and Resnick, eds., *A Japanese Constellation*, 107.

23 Ryūe Nishizawa, cited in *Kazuo Sejima, Ryūe Nishizawa, The Conversation Series,* 85.

24 An image of this plan is reproduced in *El Croquis* 77 (I)+99 (2001): 285

25 Ryūe Nishizawa, cited in *Kazuo Sejima, Ryūe Nishizawa, The Conversation Series*, 66.

26 On Tati's films and architecture see, among others, François Penz, "Architecture in the Films of Jacques Tati," in *Cinema & Architecture: Méliès, Mallet-Stevens, Multimedia*, ed. François Penz and Maureen Thomas (London: British Film Institute, 1997), 62–69.

27 See Marc Augé, *Non-Places: Introduction to an Anthropology of Supermodernity*, trans. John Howe (London and New York: Verso, 1995).

28 Matthew Allen, "Curate yourself," in *Architecture at the Edge of Everything Else*, ed. Esther Choi and Marikka Trotter (Cambridge, MA, and London: MIT Press, 2010), 22–34. Ryūe Nishizawa seems to confirm this claim when he defines one most important function of architecture as expressing each era and culture's lifestyle: Ryūe Nishizawa, cited in *Lives of the Artists, Lives of the Architects*, ed. Hans Ulrich Obrist (London: Allen Lane, 2015), 470.

29 Cf. Meystre, *Pictures*, 157, fig. 86. The hand drawing on the opposite page (156, fig. 85) features a highly summarized conceptualization of the building's program. A recently completed movie by artist-filmmakers Ila Bêka and Louise Lemoine, *Moriyama-san*, 2017 (France, 2017, HD, color, 63'), equally focuses on domestic life within the building's characteristic volumes; http://www.bekalemoine.com/moriyama.php (accessed April 6, 2018).

30 Kazuyo Sejima, cited in *Kazuo Sejima, Ryūe Nishizawa, The Conversation Series*, 89.

31 Toyō Itō, *Diagram Architecture* (1966), cited in Anthony Vidler, "Diagrams of Diagrams: Architectural Abstraction and Modern Representation," *Representations* 72 (Autumn, 2000): 3.

32 See Oya Atalay Franck, "Architekturdiagramme und diagrammatische Architektur. Das Diagramm: erklärende Illustration oder Mittel zur Formfindung?" *Tec21* 128, no. 8 (2002): 17.

About the Editors and Contributors

Martin Søberg, PhD, Assistant Professor of Architectural History at the Institute of Architecture and Culture at the Royal Danish Academy of Fine Arts, School of Architecture and President of the Danish Association of Art Historians. He holds a Master (mag.art.) in Art History from the University of Copenhagen and a PhD in Architecture from the Royal Danish Academy of Fine Arts, School of Architecture. Main research interests include architectural representations and poetics, particularly in the 20th and 21st centuries. He is coeditor of the books *Refractions: Artistic Research in Architecture* (2016) and *What Images Do* (2019).

Anna Hougaard, PhD and architect MAA, is a practising architect, visualizer, and curator. She is specialized in new developments in architectural drawing. Her PhD project, *The Animate Drawing* (published 2016), investigates diagrammatics in architecture as being both intertwined with the digitalization of conventional drawing and with artistic research methodology. She has taught architecture for several years at the Royal Danish Academy of Fine Arts, School of Architecture and at the TU Berlin. She is coeditor of the book *Refractions: Artistic Research in Architecture* (2016) and a contributor to *Drawing Futures* (ed. Allan and Pearson, 2016).

Joseph Altshuler is co-founder of Could Be Architecture, a Chicago-based design practice, and the founding editor of *Soiled*, a periodical of architectural storytelling positioned between a literary journal and a design magazine. He teaches architecture at the School of the Art Institute of Chicago and the Illinois Institute of Technology. He curated *The Unsolicited Sideshow* at the 2017 Chicago Architecture Biennial. Journals publishing his writings include *Log, MAS Context, Clog, Pidgin,* and *Plat.* His winning entry to the first international Fairy Tales competition was published in the book *Fairy Tales: When Architecture Tells a Story* (2015).

Sophia Banou, PhD, is a Lecturer in Architecture at the UWE Bristol. She has studied architecture in Athens and Edinburgh. Her doctoral research at the Edinburgh School of Architecture and Landscape Architecture (published 2016), funded by the Bodossaki Foundation, examined architectural representation and the status of architectural drawing conventions through a critical-historical approach to urban representation. She has practiced architecture in Greece and taught architectural design and theory at the Newcastle University and the University of Edinburgh. She is currently an editor for *Drawing On: Journal of Architectural Research by Design* and *Charrette.* Her recent research is concerned with questions of representation, media, and mediation in architecture.

Bernadette Devilat, PhD, is a practicing architect and has a Master in Architecture from the Catholic University of Chile. She holds a PhD in Architectural Design from the Bartlett School of Architecture, UCL, where she teaches 3D laser scanning workshops, leading BScan. Bernadette is co-founder of DLA Scan – Devilat + Lanuza Architects, an architecture studio focusing on the critical understanding of built environment recording technologies, such as 3D laser scanning and photography. Her research interests include their application for heritage intervention and re-construction after earthquakes in Chilean heritage areas. Her design and research work has received awards and has been exhibited internationally.

Paul Emmons, PhD, is an architect and Associate Dean of Graduate Studies at the Virginia Tech College of Architecture and Urban Studies, based at the Washington-Alexandria Architecture Center where he coordinates the PhD program in Architecture + Design Research. His book *Drawing Imagining Building: Embodiment in Architectural Design Practices* was published in 2019; he has co-edited *Confabulations: Storytelling in Architecture* (2016) and *Ceilings and Dreams: The Architecture of Levity* (2019).

Fırat Erdim is an Assistant Professor of Architecture at Iowa State University. He holds a BArch Degree from the Cooper Union School of Architecture and an MArch Degree from the University of Virginia. His work has been exhibited internationally at venues including the Roy Boyd Gallery, Spartanburg Art Museum, Urban Institute for Contemporary Arts, Elmhurst Art Museum, Museo dell'Altro e dell'Altrove di Metropoliz, The Windor in Madrid, as well as 49A and Maquis Projects in İzmir. His awards include the 2014 Founders Rome Prize in Architecture from the American Academy in Rome and the 2016 Santo Foundation Award for Individual Artists.

Athanasiou Geolas investigates relationships between well-mannered bodies and unwieldy institutions at the turn of the 20th century. Trained at Rhode Island School of Design, he is currently a PhD Candidate at Cornell University.

Sean Griffiths is a practicing architect, artist, and academic. He is Professor of Architecture at the University of Westminster in London and currently practices as Modern Architect. He studied architecture at Manchester Polytechnic and the Polytechnic of Central London, graduating in 1991. From 1991 to 2014 he was a founding director of the London-based art and architecture collaborative FAT (Fashion Architecture Taste). His writings have been widely published and his works as both FAT and Modern Architect have been exhibited and published internationally.

Penelope Haralambidou, PhD, is Associate Professor and Director of Communications at the Bartlett School of Architecture, UCL. She coordinates MArch PG24, which studies the link between architecture, film, and digital time-based and immersive media. Her research employs architectural drawing, model-making, and digital film as investigatory tools to analyze ideas and work, not only in architecture but also in visual representation, politics of vision, art, and cinema. She is the author of the monograph *Marcel Duchamp and the Architecture of Desire* (2013) and has published widely on themes such as allegory, figural theory, stereoscopy, and film.

Mette Johanne Hübschmann is an architect with her own practice in Copenhagen, collaborating with other young practices across Europe. She holds an MArch from the Royal Danish Academy of Fine Arts, School of Architecture and the École polytechnique fédérale de Lausanne (EPFL). Hübschmann has worked in architectural practices in Copenhagen, Berlin, and London since 2012, including Adam Khan Architects, where she led competition-winning domestic schemes, and more recently in practices in London and Copenhagen with a focus on small-scale projects, including spaces for artists and galleries. She was a studio leader at undergraduate level at Kingston School of Art, London, and has taught at the Royal Danish Academy of Fine Arts, School of Architecture since 2017.

Rachel Hurst, PhD, is Senior Lecturer and Design Coordinator in Architecture at the University of South Australia (UniSA). Her research investigates transformative practices in contemporary architecture, including the role of the everyday, analog craft, and the curatorial agency. She has an extensive exhibition and publication background in practice-based design and architectural criticism, with over 25 shows and 100 text works. Her PhD by project at RMIT was awarded three national awards for art book publishing. She is a contributing editor for *Architecture Australia* and regular juror in national and international awards and competitions. In 2019 she was made a Fellow of the Australian Institute of Architects.

Poul Ingemann is an architect and Associate Professor Emeritus at the Royal Danish Academy of Fine Arts, School of Architecture. He has run his own practice since 1987 with completed projects including residential housing in Blangstedgård, Odense; two exhibition buildings at the Johannes Larsen Museum, Kerteminde; Viking Museum at Ladby, Kerteminde; Local History Archive, Kerteminde; Urban renewal at Istedgade, Copenhagen; new building for Rudbjerggård manor house, Lolland; villa in Gråsten; TERMINI, an installation in Ringe; and several art-installation objects exhibited in various museums. He is a recipient of the C. F. Hansen Medal, the Royal Danish Academy's highest acclaim.

Natalie P. Koerner, PhD, is Assistant Professor at the School of Architecture at the Royal Danish Academy of Fine Arts, School of Architecture. She also holds a research position at the Centre for Privacy Studies at the University of Copenhagen. Combining research with practice, she has an architecture studio in Berlin and has worked for several firms, including the artist Studio Olafur Eliasson. Natalie studied at University of Cambridge and ETH Zurich. Her PhD research, completed in 2019, at the Royal Danish Academy of Fine Arts, School of Architecture, linked notions of a planetary imaginary to the archival modes of data centers and the cloud. She investigates spatialities that extend beyond the Cartesian and negate binary systems.

Maya Lahmy is an architect and PhD within digitally driven artistic design processes from Aarhus School of Architecture. She studied architecture at the Cooper Union, Irwin S. Chanin School of Architecture in New York and took her master from the Royal Danish Academy of Fine Arts, School of Architecture, where she also taught architecture for seven years. Maya has specialized in exhibition architecture among other work; over the years she has taken part in the realization of nine exhibitions at the Louisiana Museum of Modern Art. At present she is an exhibition architect at the Danish Architecture Centre in Copenhagen.

Felipe Lanuza, PhD, is a practicing architect trained at the University of Chile. He holds a Master in Architecture from the Catholic University of Chile and a PhD in Architectural Design from the Bartlett School of Architecture, UCL. He is co-founder of DLA Scan – Devilat + Lanuza Architects, an architecture studio focused on the critical understanding of built environment recording technologies, such as 3D laser scanning and photography. As a researcher, he explores the agencies of absence in the understanding, representation, and design of the built environment. He has taught and exhibited internationally and is presently a post-doctoral researcher at the UCL Urban Laboratory.

Marian Macken, PhD, teaches design and media in the School of Architecture and Planning at the University of Auckland. She trained in architecture, landscape architecture, and visual art and holds a PhD, by thesis and creative work, from the University of Sydney. Marian's research examines histories and theories of spatial representation, temporal aspects of architecture, and the book form as spatial practice. Her work has been acquired by international public collections of artists' books, including those at Tate Britain, the Victoria and Albert Museum, the Canadian Centre for Architecture, and the Kunstbibliothek of the Staatliche Museen zu Berlin. Her book *Binding Space: The Book as Spatial Practice* was published in 2018 as part of Routledge's Design Research in Architecture series.

Kassandra Nakas holds a PhD in art history from the Freie Universität Berlin. She currently teaches at Technische Universität Braunschweig, Institute of Media and Design (IMD). Prior to this, she was a Guest Professor at Universität der Künste Berlin and taught courses at Leuphana Universität Lüneburg and Köln International School of Design. Current research fields are at the intersections of art and architecture, concepts of nature in contemporary art, architecture, and design, and correlations of (new) materialistic theories and images of the body from the 19th century to today.

Katica Pedisic, PhD, is an academic, architect, and artist, and Lecturer in Architecture at the University of South Australia. Her research explores architectural sites through making drawing and digital film works with an emphasis on their storytelling potential. Her drawings have been published internationally and exhibited at the Bartlett and the Royal Danish Academy of Fine Arts, School of Architecture, and her architectural work has received numerous AIA awards for design excellence. She has spoken at public colloquia in Australia, such as the Parlour salon series and most recently MPavilion's MTalks on the role of new and inclusive narratives for public space.

Robin Schaeverbeke, PhD, situates himself in his practice in-between designer, researcher, draughtsman, and improviser. He inquires and teaches architectural drawing and media at the KU Leuven Faculty of Architecture (Brussels-Ghent). Currently Robin is exploring extensions of the geometric foundations of architectural drawing in design processes to include movement, time, as well as sensory and subjective aspects of form and space, searching for a fusion of geometry and experience. In addition to that, he collaborates in a design-driven project to explore and resolve design paradoxes and conflicting views, using a combination of BIM, physical models, extended drawings, and design-based artifacts.

Julia Sedlock is a co-founder of Cosmo Design Factory, an architectural design practice focused on residential and civic projects in and around New York's Hudson Valley. In addition to several completed house projects, her current work in Philmont, NY, leverages architectural practice as a form of community development and activism, working with neighbors and local government to transform a small rural village into a model for a more equitable and inclusive society. She and her partner collaborate with existing non-profit organizations and have co-founded new grassroots and cooperative organizations. Julia holds an MArch and MA in Design Criticism from the University of Illinois at Chicago. Selected writing has been published in *Plat, MAS Context, Soiled, Conditions,* and *Log.*

Guro Sollid is an architect and Teaching Associate Professor at the Royal Danish Academy of Fine Arts, School of Architecture, and Head of the master's program Architecture, Space & Time at the Institute of Architecture, Urbanism and Landscape. She is engaged in challenging the architectural drawing, exploring boundaries between architectural representation and architectural reflection. Evolving around artistic research in architecture, her practice explores the synergy between research-based teaching and teaching-based research. She has been involved in the recurrent summer school *Hydra,* which employs cartography, morphology, and topology as means of questioning contemporary architectural drawing practice. This research has led to numerus publications and seminars.

Martino Tattara, PhD, is Assistant Professor of Architectural Design at KU Leuven, Faculty of Architecture, and a practicing architect. After graduating from the Università iuav di Venezia, he obtained a postgraduate Master degree at the Berlage Institute in Rotterdam and a PhD in Urbanism at the Università iuav di Venezia with a dissertation centered on Lúcio Costa's project for Brasilia. His main theoretical interest is the relationship between architecture and large-scale urban design. Together with Pier Vittorio Aureli, he is the co-founder of Dogma, an office based in Brussels and focused on the project of the city.

Fredrik Torisson, PhD, is a postdoctoral researcher at the Centre for Privacy Studies at the University of Copenhagen and at the Royal Danish Academy of Fine Arts, School of Architecture. His research focuses on renegotiations of privacy and the private in early modern Europe, with a particular focus on the development of new institutions and their spatial transformations in this era. He has a background in architectural theory and defended his doctoral dissertation, *Utopology: Re-thinking the Utopian in Architecture,* at Lund University in 2017.

Olivia Valentine is a visual artist working in drawing, photography, and textile construction, exhibiting internationally at galleries and museums. She is currently Assistant Professor of Art and Visual Culture at Iowa State University. She received her MFA from the School of the Art Institute of Chicago and her BFA from the Rhode Island School of Design. She is the recipient of a Fulbright Fellowship for Installation Art in Turkey and the Brandford/Elliott Award for excellence in Fiber Art.

Maja Zander Fisker is an architect and Doctoral Fellow at the Royal Danish Academy of Fine Arts, School of Architecture. Her work examines medial affordances and processes of architectural creation, including the generative properties of the architectural drawing. Her PhD project, *Reflexive Practice: Trans-medial Process and Method in Architectural Education,* is funded by a three-year grant from the Independent Research Fund Denmark.

Illustration Credits

Cover illustration by Maya Lahmy

Changing Plans
From Footprints as Indexes of Construction to Horizontal Sections
Paul Emmons

Figure 1
© 2018 Artists Rights Society (ARS), New York/VG Bild-Kunst, Bonn.

Figure 2
Bpk Bildagentur, Vorderasiatisches Museum, Berlin, Olaf M. Tessmer, Art Resource, New York.

Figure 3
© RMN-Grand Palais, Art Resource, New York. Photo by René-Gabriel Ojeda.

Figure 4, 7–10
Public domain.

Figure 5
Drawn by Paul Emmons after Francis Ching, *Architectural Graphics,* 4th edition (New York: John Wiley & Sons, 2003), 39.

Figure 6
Ferrara, Biblioteca Comunale Ariostea.

Figure 11
© 2019 Photo Scala, Florence.

Passage
Reading John Hejduk's Wall House 2
Marian Macken

Figure 1–4
Photo by Darren Glass.

Figure 5–6
Marian Macken.

My Plans for the Future
Poul Ingemann

Figure 1–6
Poul Ingemann.

"Manner of Working"
Robin Evans, the Drawing, and a Theory of Practice
Athanasiou Geolas

Figure 1, 4, 5, 8
Public domain.

Figure 2
© Pinacoteca di Brera, Milan.

Figure 3
© 2019 Photo Scala, Florence. Courtesy of the Ministero Beni e delle Attività Culturali e del Turismo.

Figure 6–7
Courtesy of Penguin Random House.

Plans of Ideas
Exploring the Spatial and Figurative Qualities of Plans
Mette Johanne Hübschmann

Figure 1–2
Students and teachers at Studio 2.6, 2016–17, Kingston School of Art.

Figure 3
Alexander Houze.

Figure 4
Sandro Hernando Rosales.

Floor Plan Diagrams and the Typology of Difference
Martin Søberg

Figure 1
The Royal Library, Copenhagen.

Figure 2
Public domain.

Figure 3
Courtesy of the Kay Fisker estate.

Figure 4
Courtesy of the Steen Eiler Rasmussen estate.

Figure 5
Collection Centre Canadien d'Architecture/Canadian Centre for Architecture, Montréal.

Figure 6
Courtesy of Christ & Gantenbein.

The Project of Mapping
The Design Agency of Drawing City Plans
Martino Tattara

Figure 1
Royal Collection Trust / © Her Majesty Queen Elizabeth II 2019.

Figure 2–4
Stanford Digital Forma Urbis Romae Project.

Figure 5
Ministero dei Beni e delle Attività Culturali e del Turismo, Italy.

Figure 6
Public domain.

Figure 7
ETH Zurich.

A Million Hours of Plans
Exploiting Time and Transparency
Rachel Hurst

Figure 1, 6–8
Rachel Hurst.

Figure 2–5, 9, 13–18
Photo by Rachel Hurst.

Figure 10–12
Photo by Steve Wilson.

Figure 19
Photo by Steve Wilson. Assemblage by Rachel Hurst.

Drawing (on) the Context
Scanning, Designing, Building
Bernadette Devilat and Felipe Lanuza

Figure 1–14
Bernadette Devilat and Felipe Lanuza.

Survey < > Creation
The Illustrative Scan and the Explorative Drawing
Maya Lahmy

Figure 1–8
Maya Lahmy.

Beyond Millions of Plans
A Geometry of Clouds
Natalie P. Koerner

Figure 1
Diller Scofidio + Renfro.

Figure 2
Christian Kerez Zurich AG.

Figure 3
© 2009 by Cornell University. Used by permission of the publisher, Cornell University Press.

Plans for a Plentiful Future
Fredrik Torisson

Figure 1–3
Public domain.

Figure 4
Photo by Anna Reuter Metelius © Museum of Gothenburg.

Figure 5–8
Courtesy of Stadsbyggnadskontoret, Gothenburg.

Real Berlin
Gentrification's Grip on Plans and Renderings
Anna Hougaard

Figure 1–3
Photos by Anna Hougaard.

Figure 4–10
Anna Hougaard.

Metropoliz Future Forest
Drawn Prospects
Olivia Valentine

Figure 1–8
Olivia Valentine.

Raw Plans
Robin Schaeverbeke

Figure 1–7
Robin Schaeverbeke.

Architecture without Plans
Design Strategies Based on Chance Operations
Sean Griffiths

Figure 1, 3
Sean Griffiths.

Figure 2, 4–10
Courtesy of the University of Westminster.

The Architectural Virtual
From Language to Experience
Sophia Banou

Figure 1–3
Drawing Matter Collections.

Artificial Landscapes
Guro Sollid

Figure 1–2
Guro Sollid.

Yeryüzü + Gökyüzü and Peregrine Projections
Fırat Erdim

Figure 1–8
Fırat Erdim.

The Veiled Matrix of Architectural Drawing
Penelope Haralambidou

Figure 1–3, 6–7, 12, 17
Penelope Haralambidou.

Figure 4
Bibliothèque Littéraire Jacques Doucet, Paris.

Figure 5
Photo by Andy Keate, 2007.

Figure 8
Libraries of Heidelberg University.

Figure 9–10, 14
Photo by Andy Keate, 2009.

Figure 11
Photo by Penelope Haralambidou, 2009.

Figure 13
Sylvette Baudrot.

Figure 15
Stiftsbibliothek, Saint Gall, Switzerland, MS 1092.

Figure 16
The J. Paul Getty Museum, Los Angeles.

You Wouldn't Have Known Her
Plans, Prose, and Photography
Maja Zander Fisker

Figure 1–4
Maja Zander Fisker.

Four Ways to Occupy a Hearth
On Conceiving the Invisible
Katica Pedisic

Figure 1–8
Katica Pedisic.

Creaturely Plans
Reorienting Ground and Subject
Julia Sedlock and Joseph Altshuler

Figure 1–2, 12–14
Courtesy of Design With Company.

Figure 3
Courtesy of Jimenez Lai.

Figure 4–7
Courtesy of Bureau Spectacular.

Figure 8–11
Courtesy of Pita & Bloom.

SANAA's Playtime
Communication and Interaction in Kazuyo Sejima's and Ryūe Nishizawa's Architectural Drawings
Kassandra Nakas

Figure 1–4
Courtesy of SANAA, Tokyo.

Name Index

Subject Index

Graphic design, layout, and typography:
Diethard Keppler, Marbach am Neckar and Philippa Walz, Stuttgart

Cover illustration by Maya Lahmy

Copyediting: Monica Buckland, North Shields
Proofreading: Elizabeth Kugler, Wayland, MA
Editor for the Publisher: Andreas Müller, Berlin
Production: Amelie Solbrig, Berlin

Paper: Arctic Volume White, 130 g/m²
Printing: optimal media GmbH, Röbel/Müritz

Bibliographic information published by the German National Library
The German National Library lists this publication in the Deutsche Nationalbibliografie.
Detailed bibliographic data are available on the Internet at http://dnb.dnb.de.

Library of Congress Control Number: 2020933026

All articles in this book have been subject to a blind peer review.

P.O. Box 44, 4009 Basel, Switzerland
Part of Walter de Gruyter GmbH, Berlin/Boston

Printed on acid-free paper produced from chlorine-free pulp. TCF ∞

Printed in Germany

ISBN 978-3-0356-1874-7

9 8 7 6 5 4 3 2 1 www.birkhauser.com

The Royal Danish Academy of Fine Arts,
Schools of Architecture, Design and Conservation

DANISH ARTS FOUNDATION

15. Juni Fonden